CONQUERORS AND SLAVES

SOCIOLOGICAL STUDIES IN ROMAN HISTORY
VOLUME 1

CONQUERORS
AND
SLAVES

SOCIOLOGICAL STUDIES IN ROMAN HISTORY
VOLUME 1

KEITH HOPKINS
Professor of Sociology, Brunel University

CAMBRIDGE UNIVERSITY PRESS
Cambridge
London   New York   Melbourne

Published by the Syndics of the Cambridge University Press
The Pitt Building, Trumpington Street, Cambridge CB2 1RP
Bentley House, 200 Euston Road, London NW1 2DB
32 East 57th Street, New York, NY 10022, USA
296 Beaconsfield Parade, Middle Park, Melbourne 3206, Australia

First published 1978

Printed in Great Britain
at the University Press, Cambridge

Library of Congress Cataloguing in Publication Data
Hopkins, Keith.
Conquerors and slaves.
(Sociological studies in Roman history; v. 1)
Bibliography: p.
Includes index.
1. Slavery in Rome. 2. Social structure.
3. Rome – Social conditions. 4. Rome – History.
I. Title. II. Series.
HT 863.H66   301.44'93'09376   78-90209
ISBN 0 521 21945 0

CONTENTS

v

Contents

PLATES

TABLES

FIGURES

PREFACE

This is a book about the Roman empire. It is not a narrative history, but an attempt to analyse a changing social structure and to evoke a lost world. It is also an attempt to apply some modern sociological concepts and techniques to Roman history. That may seem strange, but it would not have seemed strange to the founding fathers of sociology, Marx and Weber, nor to Pareto. Weber wrote two long works about the ancient world. Yet most students of sociology learn more about the Arapesh, the Nuer and the Trobrianders than they do about the Romans or the Chinese, who created and preserved mighty empires and highly influential cultures.

Social historians of the post-mediaeval world have long taken advantage of developments in the social sciences. Economic history, demographic history, quantitative history have become accepted, productive, even fashionable branches of history-writing. But classical historians, with some notable exceptions, have typically insulated themselves from these trends with the notion that the ancient evidence is too fragmentary and the ancient world too alien for these modern concepts to be easily applied.

All history is contemporary history and reflects not only the prejudices of the sources but current concerns and concepts. The achievements of the Roman world need to be interpreted with empathetic understanding of what the Romans themselves thought and with concepts which we ourselves use. Modern historians might well take this for granted, but many ancient historians have allowed themselves to be isolated from mainstream modern history. Several factors have contributed: the rigours of learning classical languages, the organization of universities, convention and tradition. Whatever the causes, the results are clear: a wide gulf between the ways in which modern and ancient historians write their history.

This book like its twin volume (*Succession and Descent*) attempts to bridge the gap between modern concepts and ancient sources; sometimes they are woven together in a single analysis; at other times more can be gained from maintaining a counterpoint between modern and Roman perspectives. One objective is to experiment with methods borrowed from sociology in order to gain new insights into changes in Roman society – not new facts, but a different way of understanding the relationship between various changes.

This is not the place to embark on a long discussion about methods. That requires an abstract language of its own. But let me mention one difficulty. Throughout this book I try to explore some of the long-term consequences of repeated actions, for example, the consequences of importing slaves into Italy during the period of Rome's imperial expansion, or of allocating colonial plots to emigrant Italian peasants. I want to explore the consequences of these actions independently of the intentions of individual actors. Actors often did not know the long-term consequences of their actions. Therefore, I cannot properly follow the conventional practice of citing quotations from an ancient source in order to authenticate each step in the argument. The ancient source, if we are lucky, tells us only what an ancient author thought was happening and how he felt about it, or how he thought that others felt about it. That is obviously important, but partial. In the face of this difficulty, we have to look out for other methods by which we can validate analyses. Of course neither effort nor awareness of the difficulties guarantees success.

History is a conversation with the dead. We have several advantages over our informants. We think we know what happened subsequently; we can take a longer view, clear of ephemeral detail; we can do all the talking; and with all our prejudices, we are alive. We should not throw away these advantages by pretending to be just collators or interpreters of our sources. We can do more than that. Almost inevitably, whatever our ambitions, we finish up by foisting simplifying fictions on the complexities of a past which is largely lost. At first sight, this may seem unflattering; but it helps account for some of the differences between successive generations of historians. Historical interpretations do not necessarily get better; many simply change. Even so, one of the persistent problems in each generation is how to choose between competing fictions. That is where sociological methods can be helpful. And that is why these two books make use of sociological concepts and arguments, set out explicit hypotheses, and seek to support those arguments with models, figures and coordinates, as well as with quotations from the sources. They are all attempts to reveal how Romans thought and to measure links between factors; they are attempts to limit the arena within which elusive and competing truths may probably be found.

Preface

Modern historians with their wealth of data sometimes seek to discover why actors behaved as they did; they seek to recover intention. Ancient historians for the most part know only about behaviour; they are therefore sometimes tempted to read back from behaviour to intention by imputing rationality. Two obvious problems arise: whose rationality? and should we assume that actors (emperors, generals or peasants) were rational? In the chapter called 'Divine emperors', I try to show how sociologists are concerned not only with statistics and models but also with understanding actors' thoughts and feelings and with symbolic action; in this chapter I examine what we in our culture would probably call the irrational and the untrue. I suggest that certain untrue stories about emperors (rumours, predictions, miracles) were the currency of the political system, just as money was the currency of the economic system. These untrue stories have been largely neglected, because proper historians, like detectives, are trained to scent out the truth. Yet if we want to enter the thought-world of the Romans, we must restrain our prejudices and treat 'lies' seriously.

I have been extremely fortunate in my advisers. Professors P. A. Brunt and M. I. Finley have read chapter after chapter with meticulous care and critical acumen; Dr J. A. North has read the final version of each chapter and saved me from numerous errors of fact and thought. Professor Sir Henry Phelps Brown has given me repeated tutorials in economics and I would like to thank Professor R. P. Dore for his friendly encouragement. In addition several scholars have given me their advice on individual chapters: Christian Habicht and Chester Starr read Chapter I; David Apter and Edward Shils made suggestions about Chapter II; Ernst Badian improved Chapter III considerably; Robert Bocock gave me thoughtful advice about Chapter IV as did Geoffrey Lloyd about Chapter V.

This book has been over ten years in the writing and over that time I have incurred debts of gratitude to colleagues in several universities and to institutions which have been generous in their grants of research funds. I am particularly grateful to King's College, Cambridge for the grant of a four-year research fellowship, to the Institute of Advanced Study, Princeton which for two years, 1969–70 and 1974–5, allowed me to sit quietly reading and thinking in ideal circumstances; I am also very grateful to Professors Frank Gilliam and Carl Kaysen for numerous conversations, as well as to my other colleagues at the Institute. The Nuffield Foundation, the Social Research Division of the London School of Economics, the Social Sciences Research Council and Brunel University have each provided me with funds with which I could employ research assistants to help with the enormous task of

Preface

coding ancient data. I want to thank Lynda Rees, Graham Burton, P. J. Roscoe and Oliver Nicholson for hard work and amused tolerance. Finally, I should like to thank my colleagues at the University of Leicester who first taught me sociology, and my colleagues at the LSE and Brunel who tolerated my strange interests in the Roman world.

K.H.

London
November 1977

LIST OF ABBREVIATIONS USED

AE   *Année Epigraphique.*

Ancient Roman Statutes   A. C. Johnson *et al., A Translation with Commentary,* Austin, Texas, 1961

BMCRE   *Coins of the Roman Empire in the British Museum,* ed. H. Mattingley *et al.,* London 1923– .

CAH   *The Cambridge Ancient History,* ed. J. B. Bury *et al.,* Cambridge, 1923–39.

CCAG   *Catalogus codicum astrologorum gracecorum,* vol, 6, ed. W. Kroll, Brussels, 1903; vol. 8, ed. F. Cumont *et al.,* Brussels, 1911–29.

CIG   *Corpus Inscriptionum Graecarum,* ed. A. Boeckh *et al.,* Berlin, 1828–77.

CIL   *Corpus Inscriptionum Latinarum,* ed. T. Mommsen *et al.,* Berlin, 1863– .

CJ   *Codex Justinianus,* ed. P. Krüger, Berlin, 1877.

Corp. Pap. Jud.   *Corpus Papyrorum Judaicorum,* ed. V. A. Tcherikover *et al.,* Cambridge, Mass., 1957–64.

CPR   *Corpus Papyrorum Raineri,* ed. C. Wessely, Vienna, 1895.

CSHB   *Corpus Scriptorum Historiae Byzantinae,* ed. B. G. Niebuhr *et al.,* Bonn, 1828–78.

C. Th.   *Codex Theodosianus,* ed. T. Mommsen, Berlin, 1905.
        The Theodosian Code, trans. C. Pharr, Princeton, 1952.

D.   The Digest of Justinian, ed. T. Mommsen, Berlin, 1870.

ESAR   T. Frank *et al., An Economic Survey of Ancient Rome,* Baltimore, Md., 1933–40.

FD   *Fouilles de Delphes,* ed. G. Daux *et al.,* Paris, 1922– .

FIRA   *Fontes Iuris Romani Anteiustiniani,* ed. S. Riccobono *et al.,* Florence[2], 1940–3.

GCS   *Die griechische christliche Schriftsteller,* Leipzig, 1897– .

GDI   H. Collitz, J. Baunack *et al., Sammlung der griechischen Dialekt-Inschriften,* Göttingen, 1899.

IG   *Inscriptiones Graecae,* Berlin, 1873– .

ILAlg   *Inscriptions Latines de l'Algérie,* ed. S. Gsell, Paris, 1922–57.

ILS   *Inscriptiones Latinae Selectae,* ed. H. Dessau, Berlin, 1892–1916.

JRS   *Journal of Roman Studies.*

MGH   *Monumenta Germaniae Historica, Auctores antiquissimi,* Berlin, 1877–91.

NJ   Justinian's *Novellae,* ed. R. Schöll and W. Kroll, Berlin, 1895.

OGIS   *Orientis Graeci Inscriptiones Selectae,* ed. W. Dittenberger, Leipzig, 1903–5.

ORF   *Oratorum Romanorum Fragmenta,* ed. H. Malcovati, Turin[3], 1967.

PBSR   *Papers of the British School at Rome.*

List of abbreviations

PG   *Patrologiae cursus completus, series Graeca*, ed. J.-P. Migne, Paris, 1857– .

P.O.   *Patrologia Orientalis*, vols. 18–19, ed. R. Graffin and F. Nau, Paris, 1924–6.

P.Giss. *Griechische Papyri im Museum . . . zu Giessen*, ed. O. Eger *et al.*, Leipzig, 1910–12.

P.Lond. *Greek Papyri in the British Museum*, ed. F. G. Kenyon *et al.*, London, 1893–1917.

P.Oxy. *The Oxyrhynchus Papyri*, ed. B. P. Grenfell *et al.*, London, 1898– .

PSI   *Papiri greci e latini*, ed. G. Vitelli *et al.*, Florence, 1912– .

R.A.C. *Reallexikon für Antike und Christentum*, ed. T. Klauser, Stuttgart, 1950– .

RE   *Real-Encyclopädie der classischen Altertumswissenschaft*, ed. A. F. von Pauly *et al.*, Stuttgart, 1894– .

RIB   *The Roman Inscriptions of Britain*, ed. R. G. Collingwood and R. P. Wright, Oxford, 1965.

SIG   *Sylloge Inscriptionum Graecarum*, ed. W. Dittenberger, Leipzig³, 1915–24.

TAM   *Tituli Asiae Minoris*, ed. E. Kalinka *et al.*, Vienna, 1901– .

ZSS   *Zeitschrift der Savigny Stiftung.*

To find standard editions of classical authors, see *The Oxford Classical Dictionary*, ed. N. G. L. Hammond, Oxford², 1970, or W. Buchwald *et al.*, *Tusculum Lexikon griechischer und lateinischer Autoren*, Munich, 1963. For translations and texts, see the Loeb Classical Library; many useful translations are also in The Penguin Classics. Selected sources are translated with a commentary in N. Lewis and M. Reinhold, *Roman Civilization*, Harper Torchbooks, New York, 1966, two volumes.

Measures and coins
   The following rough equivalences are used:
   1 *modius* = 8.62–8.67 litres = 6.5 kg wheat
   1 *medimnos* = 52 litres = 39 kg wheat
   1 *iugerum* = 0.25 hectare = 0.625 acre
   4 HS (*sesterces*) = 1 *denarius* (*dn*) = 1 *drachma* (*dr*)
   100 *drachmae* = 1 *mna* (*usually*)

ACKNOWLEDGEMENTS

The following translations are reprinted by permission of Penguin Books Ltd:
   Plutarch, *Makers of Rome*, translated by Ian Scott-Kilvert (Penguin Classics, 1965), pp. 145, 159–60, 160–2
Copyright © Ian Scott-Kilvert, 1965
   Tacitus, *The Annals of Imperial Rome*, translated by Michael Grant (Penguin Classics, 1971), pp. 112, 175–6
Copyright © Michael Grant Publications Ltd, 1956, 1959, 1971
   Tacitus, *The Histories*, translated by Kenneth Wellesley (Penguin Classics, 1972), pp. 263–4
Copyright © Kenneth Wellesley, 1964, 1972

To Juliet

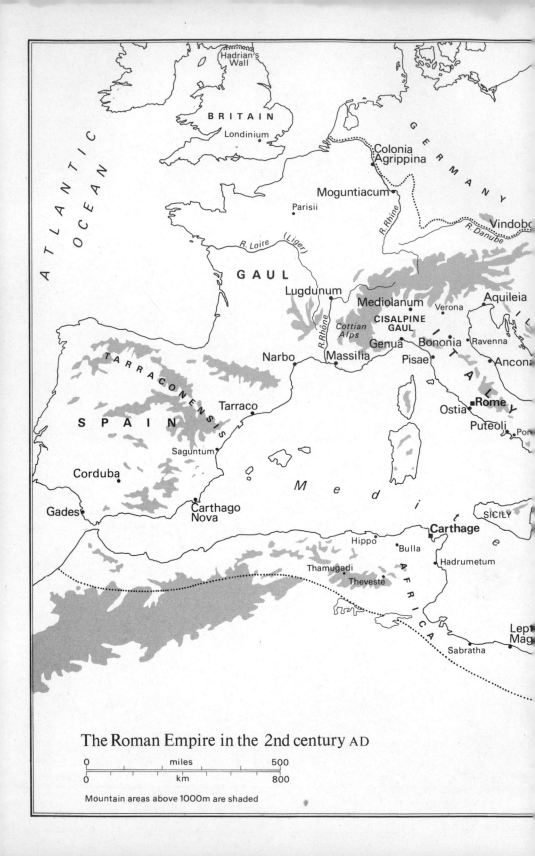

The Roman Empire in the 2nd century AD

Mountain areas above 1000m are shaded

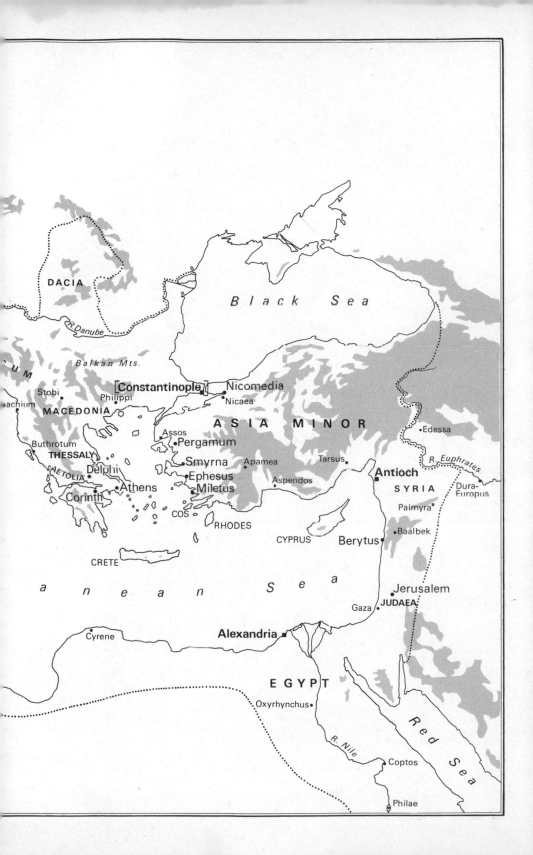

I

CONQUERORS AND SLAVES: THE IMPACT OF CONQUERING AN EMPIRE ON THE POLITICAL ECONOMY OF ITALY

THE ARGUMENT

At its height, the Roman empire stretched from the north of England to the banks of the river Euphrates, from the Black Sea to the Atlantic coast of Spain (see map). Its territory covered an area equal to more than half that of continental USA and it is now split among more than twenty nation states. The Mediterranean was the empire's own internal sea. Its population is conventionally estimated at about fifty to sixty million people in the first century AD, about one fifth or one sixth of the world population at the time.[1] Even today this would be considered a large national population, difficult to govern with the aid of modern technology. Yet the Roman empire persisted as a single political system for at least six centuries (200 BC–AD 400); its integration and preservation surely rank, with the Chinese empire, as one of the greatest political achievements of mankind.

The main subject of this chapter is the impact of acquiring an empire on the traditional political and economic institutions of the conquerors. Most of this story is well known. I shall not try to give yet another detailed chronological account. Instead I have selected certain repeatedly important elements in the process of conquest (such as the militaristic ethos of the conquerors, the economic consequences of importing two million slaves into Italy, the shortage of farming land among the free poor) and I have attempted to analyse their relationships to each other. This involves going over familiar territory, if sometimes by unfamiliar paths. Roman history can be profitably studied from several viewpoints which complement each other.

The acquisition of a huge empire in the last two centuries before Christ transformed a large sector of the traditional Italian economy. The influx of imperial profits in the form of booty and taxes changed

---

[1] For estimates of world population, based on backward extrapolation and on estimates of Chinese and Roman populations of this period, see D. M. Heer, *Society and Population* (Englewood Cliffs, N.J., 1968) 2.

the city of Rome from a large town to a resplendent city, capital of an empire. By the end of the last century BC, the population of the city of Rome was in the region of one million. Rome was one of the largest pre-industrial cities ever created by man.[2] It was here that aristocrats displayed their booty in triumphal processions, spent most of their income and competed with each other in ostentatious luxury. Their private expenditure, and public expenditure on building monuments, temples, roads and drains, directly and indirectly contributed to the livelihood of several hundred thousand new inhabitants. Immigration from the countryside was also encouraged by the grant of state subsidies on wheat distributed to citizens living in the city of Rome.

The growth in the population of the capital city and indeed in the population of Italy as a whole (see Table 1.2), implied a transformation of the countryside. The people living in the city of Rome constituted a huge market for the purchase of food produced on Italian farms: wheat, wine, olive oil, cloth and more specialised produce. To be sure, the city of Rome was fed partly from the provinces; a tenth of the Sicilian wheat crop, for example, was extracted as tax and was often sent to Rome. But a large part of the food consumed in the city of Rome and in other prosperous towns such as Capua and Puteoli also came from estates newly formed in Italy, owned by rich Romans and cultivated by slaves.[3]

The transformation of a subsistence economy which had previously produced only a small surplus into a market economy which produced and consumed a large surplus was achieved by increasing the productivity of agricultural labour on larger farms. Fewer men produced more food. Under-employed small-holders were expelled from their plots and replaced by a smaller number of slaves.[4] The rich bought

[2]   Rome was the largest city in the world and was perhaps not equalled in size before the rise of the great cities of China in the Sung dynasty. See G. Rozman, *Urban Networks in Ch'ing China and Tokugawa Japan* (Princeton, 1973) 35 and the compendious, useful but not obviously reliable T. Chandler and G. Fox, *3000 Years of Urban Growth* (New York, 1974). The population of London reached about one million in 1800 and it was then by far the largest city in Europe. In 1600, only two European cities had populations over 200,000 namely Paris and Naples.

[3]   There is no direct confirmation of this generalisation in the classical texts. But that does not matter. We must suppose either that large Italian landowners sold the produce of their estates to Italian townsmen, or that they got no return on the capital which they repeatedly invested both in land and in the slaves who worked it. The first generalisation seems more economical.

[4]   It is not possible to prove this assertion by the traditional method of selective quotation from classical sources. For example, Livy (6.12) suggested that the frequent wars in a district of central Italy in an earlier period might be explained by its high population. He noted that in his time the district produced few soldiers, and would have been deserted but for slaves. My assertion is compatible with such passages in the sources, but cannot be validated by them. Instead, I have tried to consider

up their land, or took possession of it by violence. They reorganised small-holdings into larger and more profitable farms in order to compete with other nobles, to increase the return on their investment in land and in slaves, and to exploit their slaves more effectively. Moreover, in many parts of Italy, large land-owners changed the pattern of land-use.[5] Considerable areas of arable land were turned into pasture, perhaps so that higher value produce such as wool or meat, instead of wheat, could be sold in the city of Rome, even after the heavy transport costs had ben paid. Other land was converted into olive plantations and vineyards, and the value of its produce increased. These improvements were important; they figured largely in Roman handbooks on agriculture. But their scope was limited by the size of the available market. Many peasant farms remained intact. After all, the urban poor constituted the only mass market, and they probably spent about as much on bread as on wine and olive oil together.[6] This

both the probability and the consequences of the assertion being wrong, and then to ask: What alternative assertion is more likely to be true? This procedure, based on a compatibility theory of historical truth, is used often in this book.

5   'I was the first to make shepherds give way to ploughmen on the public land', *Inscriptiones Latinae liberae rei publicae*, ed. A. Degrassi (Florence, 1957–63) n° 454. This was one of the proud boasts of a consul (? of 132 BC) who had a milestone, in the genre of a market cross, set up in a southern Italian town and inscribed with his achievements. The inscription is commonly understood to refer to the distribution of public land to small-holders in accordance with the Gracchan land laws (133 BC). Varro (*On Agriculture* 2, preface 4) also wrote that latterly Romans had 'turned arable into pasture out of greed and against the law'.

From such snippets, it is difficult to prove any general change in land use. But my general impression is that the rapid expansion of pasture and vineyards was based on the conversion of arable as well as on the extension of private property over hitherto unclaimed or common lands. On the growth in volume and prestige of Italian wines, dated to the second century BC, see Pliny, *Natural History* 14.87–8; on the growth of pasture, see A. J. Toynbee, *Hannibal's Legacy* (Oxford, 1965) vol. 2, 286ff.

6   The relative size of the markets for agricultural crops is obviously an important problem. The ancient data are clearly insufficient. As a sighting shot, without any implication that the prices in Rome were of the same order and for illustration only, I looked at the single case of Madrid in the mid-eighteenth century. Goods entering the city (which had a population of about 135,000 in 1757) were checked for customs; in 1757, imports totalled as followed: 96,000 *arrobas* of olive oil, 500,000 *arrobas* of wine, 520,000 *fanegas* of wheat. I took average prices for 1753–62 for New Castille from L. J. Hamilton, *War and Prices in Spain 1651–1800* (New York, 1957) 229 ff. and figures on consumption from D. R. Ringrose, 'Transportation and economic stagnation in 18th-century Castille', *Journal of Economic History* 28 (1968) 51–79. Of the three products, wheat consistuted 46% of the total costs; wine 45%; olive oil 9%. Wheat consumption works out at about 160 kg per person year, wine at 100 litres per adult year – which is rather low for wheat and high for wine. However, these figures can serve as only a very rough guide. For comparison, I posited the same consumption but with prices from Marseille, 1701–10; this produced somewhat different ratios of cost: wheat 64%, wine 19%, oil 17%; data from R. Baehrel, *Une Croissance* (Paris, 1961) 530ff. In Rome wheat was probably also the single most important product, in volume and value, particularly for the poor.

weakness in the aggregate purchasing power of the urban sector helped insulate a sizeable sector of the Italian peasantry from the agrarian revolution which transformed working practices on larger farms.

The conquest of an empire affected the Italian countryside in several other important respects. Military campaigns all around the Mediterranean basin forced prolonged military service on tens of thousands of peasants. Throughout the last two centuries BC, there were commonly over 100,000 Italians serving in the army, that is more than ten per cent of the estimated adult male population.[7] Global numbers disguise individual suffering; we have to think what prolonged military service meant to individual peasants, what its implications were for their families and for the farms off which they lived. Many single-family farms could bear the absence of a grown-up son, even for several years; military service may even have helped by giving them some alternative employment and pay. But in some families, the conscription of the only adult male or the absence of an only son in the army overseas when his father died meant increasing poverty and debt.[8]

Over time, mass military service must have contributed to the impoverishment of many free Roman small-holders. At least we know that thousands of Roman peasants lost their land. In addition invasions by Carthaginians and Celtic tribes, slave rebellions and civil wars which were repeatedly fought on Italian soil all contributed to the destruction of traditional agricultural holdings. Even so, more Italian peasants might have survived both the demands of military service and the destruction of war but for one other factor: the massive investment by the rich of the profits derived from empire in Italian land. The rich could establish large estates in Italy only by the wholesale eviction of Italian peasants from their farms. Typically these estates were

---

[7]   See Table 1.1 below, which deals with Roman citizen soldiers only. P. A. Brunt, *Italian Manpower 225 BC–AD 14* (Oxford, 1971) 425 lists the size of the Italian armed forces for the twenty-one years between 200 and 168 BC for which we have full information. The average size of the army and smallish fleet was about 140,000, drawn from an adult male population of about one million (*ibid.* 59).

[8]   In the traditional Roman histories, folk-heroes faced similar problems; it seems likely that their problems reflected anxieties which persisted. For example, Cincinnatus summoned to be dictator while working at the plough is said to have exclaimed: 'My land will not be sown this year, and so we shall run the risk of not having enough to eat' (Dionysius of Halicarnassus, *Roman Antiquities* 10.17). Another famous general, Atilius Regulus serving in Africa during the first war against Carthage wrote to the senate to say that the bailiff of his small farm had died, that a farm hand had taken the stock, and requested that a replacement be sent to see to its cultivation, so that his wife and children should not starve (Valerius Maximus 4.4.6). Poor soldiers had no such privilege.

4

cultivated by imported slaves. The displacement of large numbers of free peasants by slaves helped transform the agricultural economy of Italy, and fomented the political conflicts of the late Republic.

The mass eviction of the poor by the rich underlay the political conflicts and civil wars of the last century of the Roman Republic. For example, the possession of public land (*ager publicus*) and its redistribution to the poor became a major political issue, and exacerbated the tensions between the rich and the poor.[9] This public land in Italy had been kept apart out of land sequestrated by the Romans from conquered tribes or rebellious allies, ostensibly for the collective benefit. It constituted a significant but minor part of all Roman land, being by modern estimates well less than a fifth of all Roman land in the mid-third century BC, and hardly more than that in the second century BC (such estimates are inevitably crude); but its maldistribution became a political *cause célèbre*. The public land was concentrated in the hands of the rich; the laws which prohibited large holdings of public land were ignored (so Cato, frag. 167 *ORF*); and the rents which should have been paid to the state were by senatorial inertia left uncollected (Livy 42.19).[10]

A narrative history of the last century of the Republic would be punctuated by conflicts over this land, by land laws and by land distributions, which were more often proposed than effected. In 133 BC for example, a young aristocratic and revolutionary tribune of the people proposed the redistribution of the public land illegally held by the rich. He was assassinated by his opponents in the senate, but the land commission which he had founded succeeded in distributing

---

[9] Ancient commentators on the political struggles of the late Republic usually saw the main axis of conflict as between nobles and the people; see L. R. Taylor, *Party Politics in the Age of Caesar* (Berkeley, 1944). The direct opposition rich–poor is only rarely mentioned in historical sources of the period (see, for example Appian, *Civil Wars* 1.10). Nevertheless, it seems to have underlain much social and political conflict; see the interesting discussion by M. I. Finley, *The Ancient Economy* (London, 1973) 35ff.

[10] See Toynbee (1965): vol. 1, 166; vol. 2, 556–7). The traditional histories reflect this concern with the maldistribution of public land, sometimes anachronistically. Cf. Dionysius of Halicarnassus (*Roman Antiquities* 8.73–75; cf. 9.51) who lived in the reign of Augustus; he recorded a debate purportedly held in 486 BC, but it probably reflected typical attitudes of a much later period. A leading senator, Appius, said (73.4): 'As things now stand, the envy of the poor against the rich who have appropriated and continue to occupy the public lands is justified; it is not surprising that they demand that public property should be divided among all citizens instead of being held by the few...' But he went on to argue that splitting state-land into small lots would be troublesome to the poor, because they were poor; it would be better for the state to lease land in large lots: these would bring in large revenues, from which soldiers could be paid and fed. With some refinements, the suggestion was generally approved. For a long discussion of the evidence, see G. Tibiletti, 'Il Possesso dell' Ager Publicus', *Athenaeum* 26 (1948) 173–236.

some land to poor citizens. The trouble was that in spite of legal safeguards, the new settlers were as likely to be evicted as the old; the same forces were still at work. Again in the first century BC, citizen soldiers who had military power and the patronage of political generals such as Sulla, Pompey and Julius Caesar, occasionally secured small-holdings for themselves at the end of their service. But they usually took over land which was already being cultivated by other small-holders, and in addition, some of them failed to settle down on their lands, which were again bought up by the rich. Thus the successive redistribution of small-holdings probably did not significantly increase the total number of small-holders, even if it slowed down their demise.[11] The overall tendency was for poor Romans to be squeezed out of any significant share in the profits of conquest so long as they stayed in the Italian countryside.

The central place of land in Roman politics sprang from the overwhelming importance of land in the Roman economy. Land and agricultural labour remained the two most important constituents of wealth in all periods of Roman history. Manufacturing, trade and urban rents were of minor importance in comparison with agriculture. That does not mean they should be ignored; the deployment of ten to twenty per cent of the labour force in non-agricultural tasks is one of the factors which differentiates a few pre-industrial societies from the rest. In Italy at the end of the period of imperial expansion, the proportion of the population engaged in urban occupations may have risen towards thirty per cent (see Table 1.2; the figures are speculative), because the profits of empire and the economic changes, reflected in the change of occupation from country to town, from agriculture to handicrafts or to service trades, were concentrated in Italy. The city of Rome was the capital of the Mediterranean basin. In the rest of the Roman empire, the proportion of the labour force primarily engaged in agriculture was probably in the order of ninety per cent, as it had been in Italy before the period of expansion.[12] But even in Italy

---

[11] Soldiers were commonly given land which was already under cultivation; 'where the plough and reaping hook have been', as a law of Augustus on colonies stated (Hyginus, *On the Fixing of Boundaries*, ed. Lachmann (Berlin, 1848) 203). This led to repeated friction between colonists and the old inhabitants (see, for example, Granius Licinianus p. 34F). Some ex-soldiers settled by Sulla before 80 BC were involved in the rebellion of Catiline in 63 BC; according to Sallust (*Catiline* 16): 'they had squandered their resources and remembered their former victory and booty'. This seems an inadequate basis for thinking that all ex-soldiers were bad farmers. It was always assumed in the classical world that soldiers could turn into peasants and vice versa. On all this, see Brunt (1971: 294ff.).

[12] Some comparative evidence may help as a guide. Bulgaria (1910), Yugoslavia (1931) had 81% and 79% of their work-force engaged in agriculture. The figures for Turkey

6

at the peak of its prosperity, and at all levels of society, among nobles, bourgeois and peasants, power and wealth depended almost directly on the area and fertility of the land which each individual possessed. Land-holdings were the geographical expression of social stratification.

Among the rural population, even when slavery in Italy was at its height, free peasants probably constituted a majority of the Italian population outside the city of Rome.[13] By peasants, I mean ideally families engaged primarily in the cultivation of land, whether as free-holders or as tenants (often as both), tied to the wider society by the liens of tax and/or rent, labour dues and political obligation. The persistence of the peasantry is important; but so were the changes in the ownership and organisation of estates, and the mass emigration of free Italian peasants which made those changes in estate organisation possible.

Some indications of scale may be helpful; they are rough orders of magnitude only, though based on or derived from the careful analysis of the evidence by Brunt (1971). Rather speculatively I calculate that in two generations (80–8 BC), roughly half the peasant families of Roman Italy, over one and a half million people, were forced mostly by state intervention to move from their ancestral farms. They went either to new farms in Italy or overseas, or they migrated of their own accord to the city of Rome and other Italian towns. The main channel of their mobility was the army. In a complementary flow, many more than two million peasants from the conquered provinces became war captives

(1927) and China in the 1940s were 82% and over 80%. See O. S. Morgan ed., *Agricultural Systems of Middle Europe* (New York, 1933) 48 and 359; *Recensement général de la population 1927* (Ankara, 1929) 29; C. K. Yang, *A Chinese Village* (MIT, 1959) 23. The composition of these populations was already somewhat affected by their links with foreign, industrial markets. I think the comparable figures for the Roman empire would have been higher.

[13] It is impossible to calculate the ratio of free men to slaves outside the city of Rome accurately, but we can see whether our guesses are compatible with each other and with what else we know. For present purposes, I assume a total population in Italy of 6.0 million, which is between the best guesses of Beloch (5.5 million (*Die Bevölkerung der griechisch–römischen Welt* 436) and Brunt (7.5 million (1971: 124)). I follow Beloch in thinking that there were no more than two million slaves (see note 14 below). For crude estimates, which may be useful as illustrations of rural/urban distribution, see Table 1.2 below (p. 68).

If all the rural population worked on the land, and the agricultural land constituted 40% of Italy's surface (as against 55% in 1881), then at roughly 10 million hectares, it allowed over two hectares per person, which is feasible but not generous, given (a) low yields, (b) the high proportion of adults among slaves, and (c) their need to produce a surplus. For similar arguments, see Beloch (1886: 417) and Brunt (1971: 126). I agree with Beloch that the estimated slave population was extremely high for Roman conditions.

and then slaves in Italy.[14] Changes such as these affected even those peasants who stayed secure in their ancestral farms. Indeed, the growth of markets, the import of provincial slaves and taxes, the imposition of rents and a general increase in monetisation changed the whole structure of the Roman economy. But in spite of these changes and migrations, the solid core of Italian peasants remained peasants.

In this chapter, I shall concentrate on the impact of conquest on the two most important elements in the Roman economy, land and labour. We can see their changing relationship, for example, in the acquisition of large estates by the rich and the massive import of slaves to work them; both had deep social and political repercussions. The impact of victory on the conquering society presents us with a process of extraordinary sociological interest. Rome provides one of the few well-documented examples of a pre-industrial society undergoing rapid social change in a period of technical stagnation. Military conquest served the same function as widespread technical innovation. The resources of the Mediterranean basin were heaped into Italy and split the traditional institutions asunder. The Roman government tried to absorb the new wealth, values and administration within the existing framework. It failed, just as most modern developing countries fail, to establish institutions for the allocation of new resources without violent conflict.[15]

THE INTRUSION OF SLAVES

Two aspects of the transformation of the Italian economy in the period of imperial expansion stand out: the increase in the wealth of the

[14] There is no clear evidence on the number of slaves in Italy, and the best we can do is guess. Beloch (1886: 418) thought that there were less than two million slaves in Italy at the end of the first century BC; Brunt (1971: 124) thought that there were three million. The discrepancy serves as an index of the plausible margin of error.

One discrepancy should be mentioned here. Since male slaves predominated and mortality was high, the total of slaves ever imported was higher than the number of slaves at any one time. There is therefore little point in adding up the known figures of enslaved captives, even if they were accurate.

For a thorough discussion of the sources of slavery, see E. M. Schtaerman, *Die Blütezeit der Sklavenwirtschaft in der römischen Republik* (Wiesbaden, 1969) 36–70. She is quite right to point out how exceptional it was for Romans to enslave the conquered. But I still think that war was the most common source of slaves in the period of imperial expansion. Nor were war and trade mutually exclusive; enslaved prisoners of war were imported into Italy and distributed by traders.

[15] I have dealt with some of the problems of this process in 'Structural differentiation in Rome' in I. M. Lewis ed., *History and Social Anthropology* (London, 1968) 63–78 and also at the end of this chapter; more generally, see S. N. Eisenstadt, *The Political Systems of Empires* (New York, 1963), and N. J. Smelser in B. F. Hoselitz and W. E. Moore, *Industrialization and Social Change* (Paris, 1963).

Roman elite and the massive growth of slavery. Let us deal with slavery first (see also Chapter II). According to the best modern estimates, there were about two (or even three) million slaves in Italy by the end of the first century BC. That is about thirty-five to forty per cent of the total estimated population of Italy. Given our evidence, these figures are only guesses; they may well be too large; when slavery was at its height in the southern states of the USA, the proportion of slaves was only one third. However that may be, no one can reasonably doubt that huge numbers of slaves were imported into Italy during the last two centuries BC. Roman Italy belonged to that very small group of five societies in which slaves constituted a large proportion of the labour force.

When we compare Roman with American slavery, the growth of slavery in Roman Italy seems surprising. In the eighteenth century, slavery was used as a means of recruiting labour to cultivate newly discovered lands for which there was no adequate local labour force. Slaves by and large grew crops for sale in markets which were bolstered by the incipient industrial revolution. In Roman Italy (and to a much smaller extent in classical Athens), slaves were recruited to cultivate land which was already being cultivated by citizen peasants. We have to explain not only the import of slaves but the extrusion of citizens.

The massive import of agricultural slaves into central Italy implied a drastic reorganisation of land-holdings. Many small farms were taken over by the rich and amalgamated into larger farms so that slave-gangs could be efficiently supervised and profitably worked.[16] Even so, slavery was by no means an obvious solution to the elite's needs for agricultural labour. Many peasants had surplus labour, and free labourers worked part-time on the estates of the rich. The inter-dependence of rich men and of free peasants, many of whom owned some land and also worked as part tenants or as labourers on the land of the rich, is well illustrated in the following passage from the agricultural treatise of Varro (last century BC):

All agricultural work is carried out by slaves or free men, or by both; by free men, when they cultivate the ground themselves, as many poor people do with

[16] It is useful to distinguish between holdings and farms. Rich men had huge holdings of land, commonly divided into farms; many of these were much larger than peasant family farms, but they were not *latifundia*. This is deduced from the illustrations used by the agricultural writers Cato, Varro and Columella of farms varying from 25 ha (100 *iugera*) for a vineyard to 50 ha (arable) and 60 ha (olives), worked by 16, 8–11 and 13 slaves respectively. The recommended size of herds was 50–100 goats, 100–120 cattle, 100–150 pigs – large by peasant standards, but hardly ranching.

For testimony, see Cato, *On Agriculture* 10–11; Columella, *On Agriculture* 2.12; and on livestock, see Varro, *On Agriculture* 2.3–5 and P. A. Brunt, *JRS* 62 (1972) 154.

their families, or when they work as hired labourers contracted for the heavier work of the farm, such as the harvest or haying...In my opinion, it is more profitable to work unhealthy land with free wage labourers than with slaves; and even in healthy places, the heavy tasks such as the storage of the harvest can best be done by free labourers. (*On Agriculture* 1.17)[17]

The extrusion of peasants from their plots increased the pool of under-employed free labourers. Why did the rich not make use of free wage-labourers, instead of buying slaves out of capital? That is always one of the problems about mass chattel slavery. I argue below (p. 110) that slaves were normally quite expensive (though the evidence is sparse); to make a profit on their investment in slaves, slave-owners had to keep their slaves at work twice as long as Roman peasants normally needed to work in order to live at the level of minimum subsistence.[18] This implies that Roman agricultural slavery could work economically only if peasant small-holdings were amalgamated into larger units and if crops were mixed so as to provide slaves with full employment, and masters with a larger product from slaves' labour than was commonly achieved with free labour on small peasant farms. Masters also had to taken into account the risk that their slaves might die, and their investment might be lost; add to that the cost of supervision. The massive replacement of free citizen peasants with conquered slaves was a complex process, which is difficult to understand.

As with most sociological problems, each attempt at an explanation involves further explanations. An examination of the growth of slavery involves us in a whole network of changes which affected almost every aspect of Roman society. Why slaves? Was it the chance of greater profit which induced the rich to buy slaves, or was it rather the values of free men which inhibited them from working as the permanent dependants of other Romans? How far was the growth of slavery affected by the frequency of wars, the demand for citizens as soldiers, or the ease with which the conquered were enslaved? What was the fit between the increase in the size of farms, in the size of the surplus and of the urban markets which consumed the increased surplus? It is of course, much easier to asks questions than to provide answers. But for the moment I want to stress the complexity of the problem and the degree to which economic changes were connected with and

[17] See also: Cato, *On Agriculture* 5 and 144; Suetonius, *Julius Caesar* 42. The best discussion of Roman agricultural labour, although awkwardly arranged, is still W. E. Heitland, *Agricola* (Cambridge, 1921) and see also K. D. White, *Roman Farming* (London, 1970).

[18] See Chapter II, notes 15 and 23.

affected by political traditions and social values. Rather arbitrarily, I have decided to concentrate on seven processes, which in my view most affected the growth of slavery:

continuous war;
the influx of booty;
its investment in land;
the formation of large estates;
the impoverishment of peasants;
their emigration to towns and the provinces;
and the growth of urban markets.

I shall deal first with their interconnections, and then with each of the processes in turn in the later sections of this chapter (pp. 25ff.); but the processes were interwoven to such an extent that neatly segregated analysis of each factor has been impracticable.

A first look at the scheme

The diagram (Figure 1.1) provides an overview of the connections between these seven processes. I am not sure whether the scheme is more useful as an introduction or as a summary which should be put at the end of the chapter; it is meant, rather like a passport photo or a menu, only as a guide to a complex reality, not as a replacement for it. Its shape was gradually determined by a series of arguments which I shall set out briefly at first, and then elaborate.

The Romans conquered the whole of the Mediterranean basin in two centuries of almost continuous fighting. During these two centuries of conquest, a higher proportion of Roman citizens was under arms for longer than I have found in any other pre-industrial state.[19] Repeated successes in war enabled the Romans to bring back to Italy huge quantities of booty in the form of treasure, money and slaves. The accumulated treasure of the eastern Mediterranean was transferred to Rome. Booty delivered to the state treasury was soon supplemented by provincial taxes which then gradually became the chief

---

[19] In Prussia under Frederick William I and Frederick the Great for less than fifty years, and in France under Napoleon for less than twenty years, rates of recruitment perhaps equalled and may have surpassed average rates of recruitment in late Republican Rome. But these rates were not maintained for long compared with Rome. See *The New Cambridge Modern History* vol. 7, ed. J. O. Lindsay (Cambridge, 1957) 179 and 305; vol. 9, ed. C. W. Crawley (Cambridge, 1965) 32 and 64. I have not considered warlike tribes such as some Red Indians or the Zulu as comparable. On the general problem of military participation ratios see S. Andreski, *Military Organization and Society* (London, 1954).

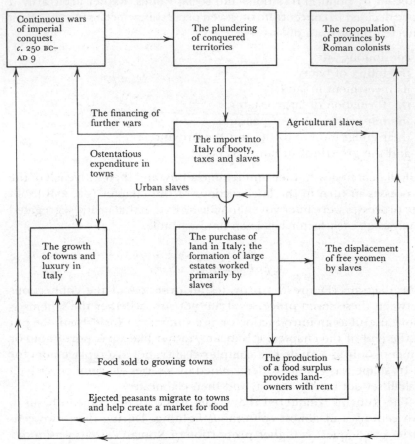

Figure I.I. The growth of slavery in Roman Italy – a scheme of inter-dependence

source of state revenue. The Roman elite enhanced its status by spending this new wealth on ostentatious display in the city of Rome and other Italian towns. Such expenditure provided new forms of employment for both free citizens and for slaves, and created a new demand for food in towns. This increased demand for food was met partly by imports of food raised as tax in the provinces, and partly out of a new surplus grown on Italian farms.

The same forces created new markets and a new surplus at roughly the same time. As members of the Roman elite grew richer, they invested a considerable part of their wealth in agricultural land in Italy. Land was the only safe and prestigious large-scale investment available. The rich concentrated their land-holdings and built up their estates near home on land previously occupied by citizens. Large numbers of the displaced citizens migrated to the city of Rome to take advantage of the increased expenditure there, or joined the army, or migrated to the newly opened northern Italian plain. It does not seem at all clear why the Roman land-owners so often preferred slaves to free workers. Several arguments have been advanced: the greater profitability of slaves, the cheapness of slaves (which I doubt), the liability of free small-holders to military service and their consequent unavailability as part-time labourers, and the reluctance of free citizens to work full-time as labourers on the farms of the rich. Whatever the reasons, several results seem clear. The economic situation of many free peasants deteriorated. Many of the 'conquerors of the world', as the Romans often called themselves, were ejected from their farms and displaced by peoples whom they had vanquished and enslaved.

Yet the massive import of *slaves* defined even poor *citizens* as belonging to a superior stratum (estate). The displacement of peasants had political repercussions which resulted in the reallocation of small-holdings to the landless and to ex-soldiers. These allocations temporarily alleviated but did not effectively improve the condition of poor citizens. State subsidies for food distribution to the urban poor increased the flow of migrants to the city of Rome, and, as I shall argue, further stimulated agricultural production on large estates, by underwriting the purchasing power of the urban poor. The final solution to the conflict of interests between citizen peasants and large land-owners was initiated by Julius Caesar and followed through under Augustus: the massive resettlement of Roman colonists in the provinces reduced the pressure from landless citizens and the urban poor on land in Italy; and it also allowed the further expansion of elite land-holdings in Italy.

These, in sum, are the arguments which I shall be putting forward in the rest of this chapter and which are summarised in the flow-chart (Figure 1.1). But I should like to add another perspective on the function of slavery in the political system. The exploitation of slaves permitted the Roman elite to expand its wealth to a level which was commensurate with its political control over the Mediterranean basin, without having to exploit the mass of free citizens overtly, except in their traditional role as soldiers. This statement may seem strange, if we consider the scale on which peasants were expelled from their lands. But it makes sense if we consider how much more obvious the exploitation would have been, if, for example, expelled peasant citizens had been reduced to working for rich Romans as domestic servants, as they were in England before and during the Industrial Revolution.

Slavery also made it possible to maintain agricultural production in Italy, in spite of the high levels of recruitment into the army and of emigration to the city of Rome. Unlike the Manchu conquerors of China in the seventeenth century, who latched on to the existing bureaucracy and became pensioners or sinecurists of the tax-system, the Roman conquering elite secured its wealth by the acquisition of land in the home country. As Max Weber saw, this process required changes in the laws governing the ownership of land so as to allow unlimited accumulation and secure tenure of public and private land.[20]

Once large urban markets had been established, land-ownership provided the elite with continuous income, whereas exploitation of the provinces did not. For under the Roman political system, aristocratic families had to seek election to political office from the plebs. The great majority of Roman aristocratic families ran the risk of not securing election to high office in each generation and the chance of provincial profit which went with it (on this see Chapter 1 in Volume Two of this work). When they did reach office, the pressure to make a profit, and to convert their booty into landed income was all the greater. Thus one of the main functions of slavery was that it allowed the elite to increase the discrepancy between rich and poor without alienating the free citizen peasantry from their willingness to fight in wars for the further expansion of the empire; slavery also allowed the rich to recruit labour to work their estates in a society which had no labour market; and it permitted ostentatious display, again without the direct exploitation of the free poor. Slavery made it unnecessary for the rich to employ the poor directly, except as soldiers.

This failure of the rich to employ the urban masses directly left the poor at the mercy of market forces. Agriculture was liable to sharp variations of production, and supplies to the city of Rome depended upon unreliable transport. Luckily for the urban poor, their power as citizen voters secured the use of state resources, through the agency

[20] M. Weber, *Die römische Agrargeschichte* (Stuttgart, 1891) 67ff. and 119ff. Roman law (in contrast, for example, to traditional Chinese law) was marked by the complete freedom of the head of the household to sell or testate land to whomever he wanted. Moreover, communal land was slowly transformed into privately held land (through the right of seizure, *ager occupatorius*), and the traditional limits on the amount which could be held were removed; by agrarian laws of *c.* 113–111 BC, private tenure of previously public land in Italy was confirmed. See E. G. Hardy, *Roman Laws and Charters* (Oxford, 1912) 35ff.

of politicians who wanted their favour. The state in turn secured supplies of wheat through taxation, and supplied a substantial sector of the market with wheat (34 kg per month per citizen) first at a fixed low price and later free. I argue below that this support by the state served to underwrite the capacity of the poor to buy more wheat and oil and wine produced on the estates of the rich. But the conversion of the capital's citizens into state pensioners, while it cushioned them against poverty, also heralded the demise of their political power.

A SKETCH OF THE ECONOMY

The Roman economy in Italy and the provinces, in all periods, rested upon the backs of peasants. Let us therefore begin by examining some factors which repeatedly constrained the relationship between peasants and the elite. Afterwards we can turn our attention to the economic conditions out of which the Roman state began its territorial expansion overseas. To simplify our task, we shall make two assumptions. These assumptions, like several which follow, are obviously speculative, but they do help us gain a clearer perspective of the Roman economy. One easy check on their plausibility is to think of the consequences of alternative asumptions. First, let us assume that four fifths of the Italian and provincial labour force were primarily engaged in producing food (I think the real figure was probably higher). And second, let us assume that the *average* consumption by townsmen, most of whom were poor, was near that of peasants. We can then draw two conclusions. First, agricultural productivity was low since it took four food-producing families to feed a fifth. It was only after the agricultural revolution in England in the eighteenth century that these average proportions began radically to be changed; in the USA now (1973 figures) for example, one farm worker produces enough food for over fifty people. Secondly, *on average*, Roman peasants consumed four fifths of their own produce and supported non-peasants with the remaining fifth.

As in any self-sufficient pre-industrial economy, the bulk of the empire's labour force was primarily engaged in producing food, most of which the producers also consumed. This was the most important element of the Roman economy. We may add to this picture by assuming also that peasants individually grew most of their own food and did not exchange much produce with each other. In addition, it seems likely that handicraft workers, because of the low level of capital investment, each produced little more than the average peasant. We can now see that an extremely large proportion of all that was produced both in Italy and in the provinces was never traded; it

15

stood outside the market, solid and inflexible, almost untouched by the forces of money. Analysis of the Roman economy has always to take that solid unmarketed core into account.

The methods by which the elite both created and extracted the peasants' surplus produce: taxes, rent and market exchange, constituted a second important element in the structure of the Roman economy. Of these three, in the empire as a whole, taxation gradually came to be the largest in volume, and the tax on land and crops comprised a very large proportion of all taxes; however, it should be stressed that the Romans made their way rather jerkily from a tradition of plunder to a stable system of taxation. And levying taxes did not preclude officials from private profiteering both at the moment of conquest and during the subsequent administration of conquered provinces.[21] To be comprehensive, therefore, we should add plunder, including slaves, and private profiteering to taxes, rents and market exchange as common methods of extracting a surplus from primary producers.

There were wide regional differences in the incidence of taxation. Roman citizens in Italy paid no tax at all on land after 167 BC. This privilege was preserved until the end of the third century AD. Who profited from it? Immunity from tax enabled landlords to charge higher rents and so helped push up the price of Italian land. In Egypt, by contrast, peasants living off irrigated Crown land paid no rent, but regularly gave up half their produce in tax. In other provinces, the most common rate of tax seems to have been a tithe of the crop (*decuma*).[22] If we take this tenth of the crop as an average tax for the

---

[21] Roman nobles thought themselves judged by their victories and by the value of their booty. For example, in 182 BC, a governor returned from Spain where he had one or two minor victories, 'He entered the city with an ovation [i.e. a minor triumph]. In his procession he carried 9,320 [Roman] pounds of silver, eighty-two [Roman] pounds of gold and sixty-seven golden crowns' (Livy 40.16). This passage implies both the public record of booty and competition. Even when Roman administrators took over previous systems of taxation, as in Sicily, they were still under pressure to make a profit for themselves. Laws to protect subjects were ineffective. One exceptionally rapacious governor (Cicero, *Verrines* 1.40) boasted that one third of the profits from the province would be used to pay off his patrons and protectors in case of trial for unjust extortion, one third for the jurors, and one third to secure a comfortable living. In the civil wars of the last century BC, rivals for power extorted as much as they could from the provinces, and it was only in the High Empire that extortion was firmly controlled; it was never suppressed. See P. A. Brunt, 'Charges of provincial maladministratlion under the early Principate', *Historia* 10 (1961) 189–227.

[22] A tithe was paid in Sicily and Sardinia. Tax was reckoned as a tithe in Asia, until the reform of Julius Caesar, but was probably often paid in money. A tax in kind was also collected in Africa (see for example *ESAR* 4.89ff). The evidence is collected by W. Schwahn in *RE sv Tributum* and A. H. M. Jones, *The Roman Economy*, ed. P. A. Brunt (Oxford, 1974) 151ff.

16

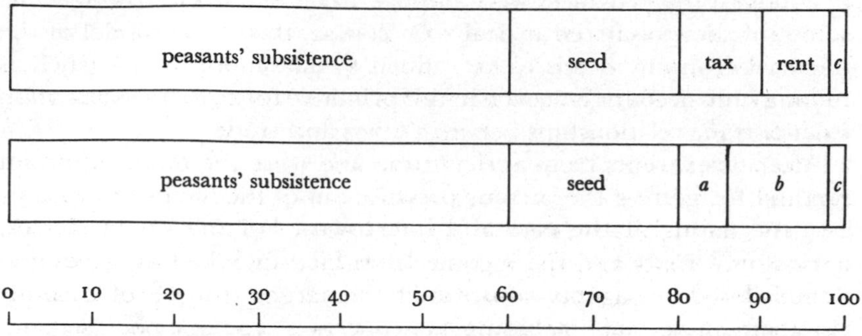

peasants' subsistence	seed	tax	rent	c

peasants' subsistence	seed	a	b	c

```
0    10    20    30    40    50    60    70    80    90    100
```

a = rent and tax paid in produce.

b = produce sold in the local market for cash to pay rent and tax in money.

c = produce sold in the market to buy goods for peasants' consumption.

* The scheme illustrates the large subsistence sector of the economy, the small non-agricultural sector, the equivalent functions of tax and rent, the low value of money exchange between peasant and town, the low average standard of living of peasants. It is, of course, crudely hypothetical and if roughly true, only true for the population as a whole.

Figure 1.2. Peasants ate most of their own produce:
a hypothetical scheme*

whole empire, which seems reasonable, then on our previous assumptions, land taxes brought in (or were equal in value to) about one half of the food consumed by non-peasants.

As the common use of the word tithe (*decuma*) for tax implies, a considerable volume of tax in the late Republic was extracted directly as food, not money. Wheat from Sicily and Africa, for example, was used to feed the army and the city of Rome. Even when taxes were raised in money, they were often spent by the state to buy food for Roman soldiers. The considerable reliance on taxes levied in food helped the Roman state support a large superstructure with fairly simple economic institutions and only a small market sector. The city of Rome, for example, depended for its prosperity on Roman political power and on the consequent inflow of taxes and rents; unlike pre-industrial London, it did not depend for its size on its capacity to export manufactures or on trade. It is worth noting that in so far as taxes were levied in money in the provinces and spent in Italy, they probably stimulated the import of an equal volume of goods by value into Italy, with which the provinces could, as it were, buy their money back, and pay their taxes in the next year. No doubt, it took quite a time to establish such a balance of trade and tax, so that in the early stages of conquest the provinces were impoverished and fell into debt, while some inflation occurred in Italy. Of course, this crude model of the imperial economy needs to be refined to take more factors (such as mining) into account, but even in this primitive form, it draws attention to important relationships between taxes and trade.

After taxes, rents from agricultural land were the most important method for getting the surplus produce out of the hands of peasants into the hands of the elite and into towns. For the upper classes, agricultural rents and the income from farms worked by slaves and administered by agents constituted the largest source of income. Government service (including tax-collection) came a poor second. Some rents too were collected in food not money; this practice restricted the market sector still further. In the empire as a whole, the total value of rents (including income from farms managed by agents) probably amounted to less than taxes. This was because many fewer people paid rent than paid tax, not because rent levels were lower. There was always a substantial body of independent, non-rent-paying peasants both in Italy and the provinces. Their numbers fluctuated but they never disappeared. Finally, from descriptions of peasant life in many other societies, it seems reasonable to suppose that although there was considerable variation, nevertheless most peasants in the Roman empire were poor; rent and tax took away most of their surplus; if there was anything left to spare, they were likely to eat most of it. Only a very small proportion of their gross product went on the purchase of goods manufactured (made by hand) in towns. But I do not want to exaggerate. The aggregate demands of fifty million peasants, even if most of them were poor, constitutes a significant market for urban produce.

The preponderance of tax plus rent over market exchange underlines the common view that in the Roman world the relationship between town and country was to a large extent one of exploitation.[23] The towns were 'centres of consumption', consuming the bulk of the townsmen's own produce as well as the bulk of the peasants' surplus. But it should not be forgotten that townsmen also provided services, for example of government and administration, which gave peasants a stable environment in which they could work. The price which the

[23] This was one of the basic perspectives in M. I. Rostovtzeff, *Social and Economic History of the Roman Empire* (Oxford[2], 1957). See also the evocative book by R. MacMullen, *Roman Social Relations* (New Haven, 1974), and the articles by M. I. Finley, 'The city from Fustel de Coulanges to Max Weber and beyond', *Comparative Studies in Society and History* 19 (1977) 305ff. and K. Hopkins, 'Economic growth in towns in classical antiquity', in P. Abrams and E. A. Wrigley eds., *Towns in Societies* (Cambridge, 1978) 35ff.

peasants paid for this peace was very high. As in other pre-industrial empires, it seems remarkable that they tolerated the impositions of government and landlords for so long.

Yeomen in early Rome

My main concern in this chapter is with the effects on the Italian economy of the imperial expansion which took place after Rome's long struggle against Carthage (264–202 BC). As background to this, I want briefly to describe some aspects of the early Roman economy which may be helpful in the discussion of later developments. There is one minor difficulty; we have no contemporary sources. We can talk of early Roman social history (that is, before the middle of the third century BC) only by working backwards from institutions which we know better in later periods, and by reconstructing a distant past from the images left us by later historians. Not much is certain and almost everything is disputed; the account given below is correspondingly dubious.[24]

For all its political power in central Italy, Rome in the early third century had a simple near-subsistence economy. There was little superstructure, no institutions such as a professional army or permanent bureaucracy which depended upon the regular delivery of a large surplus. There was little or no useful coinage made in Rome and probably little trade. Even the Roman elite was not particularly rich; witness the small area which it controlled (equal in 296 BC to about one quarter of Belgium) and the strong tradition of simple living which persisted into historical times. The chronic problems of the state centred on conquering hill-tribes, on rivalry between aristocrats, and among the poor on land shortage and impoverishment through debt.

Most of the labour force consisted of small farmers living on family farms, many of which, it seems reasonable to guess, were only just large enough to provide a minimum subsistence. Unfortunately there is hardly any sound evidence with which this generalisation can be validated; yet it seems more attractive than any alternative I can think of. There are several pieces of evidence, each insufficient or

[24] The structure of the economy in early Rome is rarely discussed in Roman history books which concentrate like the sources on political and military history. The view expressed here is compatible with and seemingly implied in the modern tradition, although many scholars might think it applies better to Rome say in the early fourth century BC. But see Toynbee (1965: vol. 1, 290ff.), and cf. K. J. Beloch, *Römische Geschichte* (Berlin, 1926) 333ff.; E. Paris and J. Bayet, *Histoire Romaine* (Paris, 1926) 77ff.; and see R. Besnier, 'L'état économique de Rome [500–264 BC]', *Revue historique de droit français et étranger* 33 (1955) 195ff.

untrustworthy in itself, which seem collectively to confirm it. I call this the wigwam argument: each pole would fall down by itself, but together the poles stand up, by leaning on each other; they point roughly in the same direction, and circumscribe 'truth'. I realise that it is dangerous to accept the general tenor of the evidence while doubting the truth of individual pieces. But this is what we are forced to do in reconstructing even the crude outlines of Rome's early social structure.

First, the traditional histories which present the Roman elite's picture of its own past imply a widespread ownership of land in early Rome. Although these histories are an almost inextricable mixture of fable and doubtful fact (e.g. heroes, battles, victories, temporary defeats, fictitious speeches on the battlefield and in the senate), the stories which they tell are unlikely to be completely false and on the mundane level are likely to reflect conditions at some early period. For example, Dionysius of Halicarnassus (*Roman Antiquities* 2.28) recorded that the second king of Rome, who reigned in the eighth century BC, appointed slaves and foreigners to sedentary and mechanical trades, and restricted Romans to agriculture and warfare. Secondly, the obligation of serving in the infantry, of providing one's own armour and of paying taxes depended upon the ownership of some, though apparently not very much land. It seems that the Roman army, unlike that of classical Athens, did not require heavy and expensive armour, and it was therefore recruited from a large proportion of the population.[25] Thirdly, the Roman census figures of adult male citizens (e.g. 262,321 citizens in 294/3 BC) suggest high population densities.[26]

[25] This is the conclusion of Beloch (1886: 26); it is based mainly on the mid-second-century account by Polybius (6.19ff.) of Roman soldiers' armour, which varied according to age and wealth. According to Polybius (6.19) the lowest property qualification for legionaries was only 400 *drachmae* = 400 *denarii*. This is difficult to interpret because of the lack of contemporary prices; at a cheap wheat price of 2½ HS per *modius*, it equals only 4 tons of wheat and so could not yield an income sufficient to support a family. Dionysius Halicarnassus (*Roman Antiquities* 4.18) and Livy (1.43) in their accounts of the reforms of Servius Tullius in the sixth century BC set the minimum property of soldiers at 1,250 and 1,100 *denarii*. The figures are probably anachronistic, and may instead refer to the third century BC. See the brilliant essay of E. Gabba, *Republican Rome, the Army and the Allies* (Berkeley, 1976) 1–69. Gabba takes the evidence to reflect a fall in the minimum property requirement for legionaries. Dionysius also averred that half the Roman population had less than this minimum; but he also tells us a lot which cannot be believed. I take the evidence to imply a low property requirement, a widespread ownership of land and a widespread obligation to fight.

[26] The transmitted figures for the early third century are unbelievable: they give an average density of 111 persons per km² in Roman territory, which is several times the figure for the agricultural population in Italy in 1936 (Brunt 1971: 54; Beloch 1886: 320). At the end of the third century BC, according to Brunt's estimate (*loc. cit.*), Roman territory had 36 persons per km² compared with 22 for the rest of Roman Italy. The traditional histories transmitted myths of overpopulation: for example,

Although these early figures are mutually inconsistent and probably inaccurate, the general inference of high population density seems corroborated by the high rate of emigration to colonies. Between 338 and 218 BC, the Roman government established forty colonies on conquered Italian land and filled them with a mixture of citizen and non-citizen settlers from around Rome. The sources give us figures on the number of adult males who went to several of these colonies (i.e. 300, 2,500, 4,000, 6,000); 4,000 adult male colonists would involve a total initial population of about 13,000 men, women and children, which seems too high.[27] Yet at a conservative estimate, the flow of emigrants to these forty Italian colonies must have exceeded one hundred thousand and may have reached a quarter of a million men, women and children.

Finally, stories featuring folk-heroes like Cincinnatus and Manius Curius Dentatus, noble but poor, implied that peasant land-holdings were usually small. The sources repeatedly cite land plots of two and seven *iugera* (0.5 and 1.75 ha) as traditional or sufficient. For example, 'There is a famous saying of Manius Curius [consul in 290 BC]...that a citizen not satisfied with seven *iugera* must be considered subversive (*perniciosum*); for that was the size of plots given to the people after the kings were driven out' (Pliny, *Natural History* 18.18). Like the early census figures, these figures of plot size seem distorted. At the most probable levels of productivity, a plot of seven *iugera* would barely provide half the minimum subsistence for an average family. Nor is it easy to see how much such a small income could regularly be supplemented; poor peasants were least likely to afford grazing animals; and it seems unlikely that *most* peasants in this early period were dependent for half their income on working the farms of the rich. The risk of being tendentious is obvious; even so, it is hard to avoid a general implication that peasant plots in early Rome were typically small.[28]

Dionysius of Halicarnassus (*Roman Antiquities* 1.16) wrote that in early times all the youths born in a certain year were sent out of Roman territory to look for land to conquer and settle. I assume that some truth lay behind these tales.

[27] The ancient evidence is conveniently but uncritically listed by E. T. Salmon, *Roman Colonization under the Republic* (London, 1969) 55–81. A colony of 6,000 adult males would involve a total population of about 20,000; if we assume a stationary population with an average expectation of life at birth of 25 years, then males aged 17+ constitute rather less than 30% of the population (see U.N. Model Life Tables in 'Methods for population projections by sex and age', *Population Studies* (New York, 1956)). The establishment of such large settlements seems out of proportion to Roman resources around 300 BC.

[28] It is obviously dangerous to take what the Romans believed about their past as evidence of their past, because of the difficulties later Romans had in knowing much about it. On the farmer heroes, see Heitland (1921: 134ff.). For a slightly different discussion of the implications of small colonial allotments in the second century BC see Brunt (1971: 194).

In sum, the absence of institutions dependent upon a large surplus, the absence of locally minted silver coins, the small scale of trade, the absence of groups of landless retainers living off rents, the widespread obligations of military service tied to the ownership of land, the probability that the population of central Italy was dense in spite of considerable emigration, and finally the evidence of smallish landplots, when all are taken together, seem to support the view that the Roman economy in the early third century BC was dominated by a wide central band of self-sufficient yeomen, that is by peasants who owned and cultivated their own farms) ²

Below the broad band of yeomen, there may have been a significant minority of dependent peasants who got *some* of their livelihood by working for those who were better off. Indeed many yeomen families living just above the margin of subsistence may have been recurrently dependent on wealthier neighbours. The varying demands of the family at different stages of its life cycle, the high annual variation in the size of crops which still bedevils Mediterranean agriculture, and the sudden imposition of taxes in order to meet an emergency, all reinforced a pattern of borrowing and dependence, which is common to most peasant societies. In some, this dependence was partly expressed through debt, high interest rates, debt-bondage and sale abroad into slavery. Debt bondage was made illegal in Rome in 326 BC, but it persisted in other parts of the empire and probably in Italy too until much later.[29]

Dependence was also expressed in the institution of clientship. In its idealised form, clientship was seen as a hereditary bond of interdependence similar to a blood relationship and sanctified by ritual penalties for its violation. Clients owed services, were meant to give their patron gifts whenever he had to pay ransom, dowry, fines or the expenses of public office. Ideally, the patron was expected to explain

[29] In early Rome, the laws provided for the savage treatment of debtors. According to the Twelve Tables (traditional date 451 BC), a debtor who could not pay his debt might be kept chained for sixty days by his creditor (fed at the creditor's expense), then be produced in public and either sold *abroad* as a slave, or executed (see *Ancient Roman Statutes* 8, Table 3). As a mitigation of this law, it was later possible 'for a free man to give his services as a slave, for money which he owed until he paid it' (Varro, *On the Latin Language* 7.105). Such men were called *nexi*, bondsmen, an indication in itself of their powerlessness. Cf. H. F. Jolowicz, *A Historical Introduction to Roman Law* (Cambridge³, 1972) 164ff. Eventually the maltreatment of debtors was seen to conflict with citizen rights. In 326 BC (the date is conventional) a law was passed which prohibited holding the body of a debtor as security (Livy 8.28; R. M. Ogilvie, *A Commentary on Livy* (Oxford, 1965) *ad loc.*). It was, said Livy, a new beginning of liberty for the plebs. It also reflected the power and will of citizens to defend their rights against the upper classes. But the practice of working off debts in slavelike conditions persisted.

laws to clients and to protect them against law suits. What seems important about this and seemed noteworthy to our sources was the idea of mutual service which distinguished Roman clientship from forms of dependence elsewhere, in which masters treated free dependants as though they were slaves. One difference lay in the assumption that Roman clients had something to give their patrons and were therefore not completely dependent upon them. This reciprocity in the client–patron relationship fits very well with my view that almost all citizens in early Rome owned some land. However, we should be cautious about accepting an idealised portrait of clientship; similar ideals in Japan, for example, have masked considerable exploitation. It seems likely that clientship significantly restricted the independence of some yeomen.[30]

The organisation of agricultural wage-labour in Rome seems to have assumed that most labourers owned some land. This can be deduced from the fact that the Romans apparently never developed a system of employing free labour for long periods similar to the English indenture, apprenticeship or annual hirings. Nor is there any evidence that Roman landlords regularly in the early period exacted labour from tenants as part of their rent; instead, the well-to-do employed free peasants usually for a day or for a specific job, such as harvesting or threshing.[31] Such intermittent work had several implications. First, labourers must have had land plots of their own to provide them with the bulk of their livelihood. Secondly, in the Roman world of the third century BC, there was no effective labour market of mobile, landless labourers. As a result, when the growth of empire induced a change in the patterns of agricultural production in Italy, new labour was

[30] This paragraph is in part a summary of the ideals set out by Dionysius of Halicarnassus, *Roman Antiquities* 2.9–11; see also A. Gellius, *Attic Nights* 5.13. The Roman lawyer Proculus (D. 49.15.7.1) held that clients were free, although inferior in authority and rank. R. P. Dore discussed a Japanese tract of 1934 (*Land Reform in Japan* (London, 1969) 55): 'These master-servant relationships, based...on the landlord's paternal care for his tenants and the tenants' implicit obedience of the landlord's authority may, of course, from one point of view be considered a fine and noble expression of the ideals of harmony and co-operation, of mutual regard and help.' But they often worked out differently in practice; cf. *ibid.* 39ff. See also on the recent exploitation of clients, S. F. Silverman, 'Exploitation in rural central Italy', *Comp. Stud. Soc. Hist.* 12 (1970) 327ff.

[31] This is the impression I get from Cato, *On Agriculture* (5 and 144f.); it is the earliest surviving such treatise from Rome, written in the second century BC. The small shares given to share-croppers, 1/6–1/8 of the crop depending on the quality of the land, would keep them alive only if they also had land of their own to work. In a subsequent publication, I shall discuss probable values of yield, labour input and household consumption in Roman agriculture. It is worth stressing that land-owners and tenants are in many peasant societies overlapping not separate categories. You can own some land and lease more.

New labour

recruited primarily by compulsion, through the institution of slavery.
Of course, even in the third century BC, there were some slaves in
Roman Italy, but not, I suspect, many. Most of the references to
slavery in early Rome imply small-scale slavery; others seem
anachronistic.[32] Thirdly, prosperous landowners who owned more
land than they could cultivate by their own labour used clientship
combined with tenancy and share-cropping as methods of ensuring
that their land was worked first at critical seasons, before peasants
looked after their own plots.

In sum, as I see it, the area governed directly by Rome in the early
third century BC was not large and rich enough to support sizeable
concentrations of wealth. The political system reflected the widespread
obligation to bear arms and the widespread ownership of land; although far from democratic, it effectively limited the extent to which
most citizens were exploited. The nobles collectively probably owned
much of the best land, but typically had only modest estates. Few of
the farms were large enough to require the employment of non-family
labour throughout the year. The bulk of agricultural land and of
common land was exploited by small-holders or yeomen peasants,
some of whom were partly dependent on the patronage of the
prosperous.

Most Romans were under-employed. Even independent yeomen
living just above the level of minimum subsistence had plenty of time
with nothing to do. An average peasant household producing its
minimum subsistence on quite good arable land used up very much
less than half of its own labour power. This chronic under-employment
is still common in many peasant economies using dry farming. It was
institutionalised in Rome in numerous public holidays and in popular
participation in politics. Above all, under-employment allowed the
state, when it could not extract a sufficient surplus of produce in the
form of taxes, to tax labour instead.

Surplus labour was taxed in the form of military service. Overall,
the poverty and underemployment of many Roman peasants permitted
a high rate of military mobilisation (regularly over ten per cent of adult
male citizens) throughout the last two centuries BC. In other words,
the lands of absent soldiers were cultivated by others. The disorgani-
sation and social costs involved were considerable. Soldiers' wives

[32] Such a method of argument is obviously dangerous: I have a picture of Rome in
the early third century BC; it had a simple, relatively undifferentiated economy. If
any evidence fits in with my view, I claim it as corroboration. Anything in the
traditional history which does not fit in with this picture, I call anachronistic. I see
the danger, but can think of no better method. For similar views and a discussion
of the evidence see Heitland (1921: 149–50); Tibiletti (1948: 173ff.).

and children, widows and orphans were left unprotected; their farms were more than usually liable to be encumbered with debt. They fell into the hands of the rich. Complementarily, in the traditional agricultural system, the rich depended for the cultivation of their farms on the surplus labour of the free poor, employed as tenants, share-croppers or as occasional labourers. But the conquest of an empire increased the incidence of military service, and either took free labour away or increased its unreliability. Besides, as the estates of the rich increased in size, so did their need for labour. Yet peasants, as we know from pre-modern studies, are typically reluctant to do more work than is sufficient to provide them with minimum subsistence. The Roman rich therefore looked elsewhere for full-time dependent labourers. They could not be drawn from the labour market, because to all intents and purposes it did not exist. Instead, slaves were captured in war and imported by force. The emigration of free labour into the army and the immigration of agricultural slaves were complementary.

CONTINUOUS WAR[33]

I want now to deal with the first of the seven factors which most affected the growth of slavery and the political economy of Italy. During the last two centuries of the Republic, the Roman state was almost continually at war. The Roman elite was permeated with pride in its military achievements; the histories of its past were filled with accounts of battles; its heroes and leaders were generals such as Fabius the Delayer, Scipio the Conqueror of Africa (Roman generals frequently took soubriquets from the lands which they had conquered), Pompey the Great and Julius Caesar. The centre of the city of Rome was packed with the trophies of war: altars and temples vowed in a moment of crisis in the battlefield and then built from the spoils; victory arches and triumphal statues; the columns of temples covered with shields and military insignia of every kind (Livy 40.51); and inscribed stones which both recorded achievements and inspired emulation in the young (for example, an inscription in the Temple of Mater Matuta, set up in 174 BC):

Under the Command and Auspices of Tiberius Sempronius Gracchus Consul, the Legion and Army of the Roman People conquered Sardinia. In this

[33] In this section, I am again especially indebted to Brunt (1971), although we disagree occasionally on interpretation. I have discovered that my arguments in this section and the next are similar to and complementary to those of W. V. Harris, *War and Imperialism in Republican Rome 327–70 BC* (Oxford, 1978).

province, more than 80,000 of the enemy were killed or captured. The State was well served; the allies freed; the revenues restored. He brought back the Army safe and sound, laden with booty. He returned to the City of Rome in Triumph, for the second time. In Commemoration of This Event, he gave this Tablet as a Gift to Jove. (Livy 41.28)[34]

When a Roman general had conducted a successful campaign, he wrote to the senate detailing his achievements. If his victories were over 'worthy enemies', and at least five thousand of them had been killed in a single battle, he might request a triumphal procession on his return to the city of Rome.[35] The scale of Roman slaughter is reflected in the award of over seventy triumphs in the two hundred years 252–53 BC.

The grant of a triumph was a prize reserved for senior Roman magistrates: praetors, consuls and dictators. Even for them it was an exceptional honour, a permanent emblazonment of the family line. It was the one occasion on which a general could legitimately parade his troops through the city of Rome. First came the magistrates and senators accompanied by trumpeters, then the spoils of war ceremonially displayed (and competitively enumerated in the public records): '...golden crowns weighing 112 [Roman] pounds; 83,000 pounds of silver; 243 pounds of gold; 118,000 Athenian *tetradrachmae*; 12,322 coins called Philippics; 785 bronze statues; 230 marble statues; a great amount of armour, weapons and other enemy spoils, besides catapaults, *ballistae* and engines of every kind...' (Livy 39.5; on 187 BC). Pictures and slogans, such as Julius Caesar's 'I came, I saw, I conquered', illustrated the general's achievements. After these, the prisoners of war: kings in chariots with ropes around their necks,

[34] The centres of modern cities in relatively non-militaristic countries also have their war memorials, statues of generals on horseback and May Day parades. I find it difficult to portray the intensity of Roman militarism – I use the word evocatively, not pejoratively. But a reading of Livy, or for that matter of any Roman historian, shows it clearly. Their concern with war was not merely a historiographical convention. Rather, historians put war at the centre of the stage because it deserved to be there. On Roman war statues see Pliny, *Natural History* 34.11ff.; on personal emulation see *ibid.* 35.2ff.

[35] See especially Valerius Maximus 2.8. There was a law forbidding generals to exaggerate the number of enemy killed; on entering the city triumphant generals had to swear the truth of their reports. Generals who had been refused public triumphs customarily (Livy 42.21) celebrated private triumphs just outside Rome. It was an indication of their competitive exhibitionism. See also Aulus Gellius, *Attic Nights* 5.6.21 on the difference between a triumph and a lesser 'ovation'.

Specific triumphs are described by Plutarch (*Aemilius Paullus* 32) and by Livy (34.52; 37.46; 45.35ff.). For an extremely detailed discussion, see H. S. Versnel, *Triumphus* (Leiden, 1970); otherwise usefully *sv Triumphus* in *RE* or DS. Lists of all triumphators in the history of Rome were, at least by the reign of Augustus, inscribed on large tablets on show on the Capitol; they survive incomplete (*Inscriptiones Italiae*, A. Degrassi (Rome, 1947) vol. 13.1, 534ff.).

princes in chains, the commanders of defeated armies – all fodder for philosophers intent on moralising about the wheel of fortune. Then came the victims to be sacrificed, bulls with gilded horns. And finally, the general himself; he was carried on a chariot, decorated with laurel and drawn by four white horses; beneath the chariot was slung a phallus. The general's cheeks were daubed with red; he was clothed, like Jupiter himself, in a purple cloak over a toga sown with golden stars. In one hand, he carried a sceptre crowned with an eagle, in the other a laurel branch. Above his head, a slave held a heavy gold crown. Each time the crowd cheered, the slave ritualistically murmured: 'Remember you are only a man.' The triumphal procession dramatised the splendour of Roman victories, reinforced public pride in the value of conquest, at once elevated the successful leader and yet fitted him into a well-worn slot, so that with luck his popularity would not subvert the power-sharing oligarchy.

Such public displays of prowess can serve as only one index of militarism in the Roman elite. There are many others: for example, the preoccupation of traditional histories with campaigns and battles. The modern reader may be inclined to skip these seemingly repetitious accounts. In so doing, he does less than justice to their consuming interest for Roman readers, and their prominence in the public records from which the histories were derived. The histories reveal a competition for glory among the Roman nobles which was itself in part the cause of war. For example, one consul (in 176 BC) was detained at Rome for an extraordinary election; 'he had long been anxious to get to his province, when luckily for his ambition letters arrived informing him that the Ligurians had rebelled' (Livy 41.17). In yet another case, when the enemy gave hostages and sued for peace, the consul (177 BC), who was still in Rome, was deeply concerned that he had lost his opportunity for victory (Livy 41.10). These should not be seen as the attitudes or acts of irresponsible madmen; rather, they should be seen as the recurrent products of a competitive elite culture which both provoked and effectively condoned belligerence. As one Roman general said: I do not negotiate for peace, except with people who have surrendered (Livy 40.25).

Roman political institutions reflected a similar concern with war. Every senior Roman office-holder was simply expected to be a competent general. The best index of this is the fact that even serious theatres of war were allocated to the elected magistrates *by lot*. This practice alone dictated the need for military experience early in a senator's career. During the second century BC, ten years' military service, usually from the age of seventeen, was the normal prerequisite for election to public office. Symptomatically, the first minor public office to which young nobles were elected was that of legionary officer (*tribunus militum*); this was not an essential step in the career of a successful leader, but it was both common and useful. It gave opportunity for personal glory in battle, as well as for military experience which might prove vital later. For once a man was elected to high office, as *praetor* or *consul*, he might well command a large army allocated by lot. During the first century BC, long military service was no longer required of young members of the elite. It became increasingly fashionable to concentrate instead on gaining experience in civilian politics and in advocacy in the courts in Rome. But some ambitious young men of rank still enlisted with the army, and served as aides (*contubernales*) to army commanders. Julius Caesar, for example, served in this capacity, although only for two or three years. And throughout the Republic, high office continued to involve the command of armies. Noble generals were still expected to defeat Rome's enemies, and to fight their way out of critical situations. Besides, military command always provided the main path to conquest, enhanced reputation, a triumph and booty.

The idealisation of military glory disguised the huge costs of war with rhetoric. Then as now, wars were fought in defence of territory, to protect allies, to secure liberty (Livy 35.16) and 'in the hope of peace' (Livy 40.52). 'The only reason for going to war', wrote Cicero, 'is that we may live in peace unharmed' (*On Duties* 1.35). There is in our sources no mention of the maimed or wounded. We hear only rarely of the devastation of crops, of livestock and of homes; such losses must have hit the poor much harder than the rich. Our sources do record the death in battle of just under 100,000 Roman and allied soldiers in the first half of the second century BC; significant losses, if they are to be believed, out of a total adult male population of probably less than one million at that time.[36] These figures take no account of the deaths through epidemics to which armies were prone nor of the imcompleteness of Roman records; in times of crisis, such as Hannibal's invasion of Italy and the civil wars of the late Republic, the impact of death and destruction was even greater. No doubt, the defeated 'barbarians' of northern Italy and the provincials fared even worse than the Romans. The death of numerous peasants in war both

[36] On Roman losses in war, see *ESAR* vol. 1, 110; for the Roman and Italian adult male population, see Brunt (1971: 54); on the impact of the second Punic war on Italian peasants see Livy (28.11 on 206 BC): 'It was not easy for the people [to go back to their farms] because free farmers had been wiped out by the war, there was a shortage of slaves, cattle had been stolen, farms ravaged or burnt.' See also Toynbee (1965: vol. 2, 10ff.); cf. Brunt's cautious qualifications (1971: 269ff.).

at home and abroad was one of the important factors making for vacancies on agricultural land in Italy.

Continuous war and the conquest of the whole Mediterranean basin precipitated radical changes in the pattern of military service. Traditionally, a high proportion of citizens were liable to serve in the army. The common style of fighting against nearby tribes had involved mostly summer campaigns by peasant soldiers. Even those who owned only small plots of land and who could afford to provide simple body armour and weapons were obliged to fight; they were often categorised persuasively as 'those with a stake in the community'.[37] The high level of military participation by citizens found its reflection in the shape of early political institutions (such as the *comitia centuriata*), in the political power of citizens, in citizens' legal rights, and in a perceived common interest (*res publica*), at least within the stratum of society which bore arms.[38] By the same token, slaves, resident aliens and women were excluded.

The repeated involvement of Roman armies in prolonged wars overseas in the last two centuries of the Republic brought the traditional system of recruitment to an end. The normal length of military service increased, and the burdens of military service gradually shifted from the broad band of citizen peasants who owned land and served occasionally as soldiers to a proportionately[39] smaller group of professional long-service soldiers, many of whom were poor and landless. It is difficult to attach definite figures to these trends, and perhaps even misleading. For one of the main characteristics of the Roman army

[37] Aulus Gellius, *Attic Nights* 16.10: 'But since property and family money were regarded as a hostage and pledge of loyalty to the Republic, and since there was in them a guarantee and assurance of love for one's fatherland, neither the proletariat, nor the *capite censi* [i.e. those with no property at all, or nearly none] were enrolled as soldiers, except in a state of emergency...' So similarly, Valerius Maximus 2.3.

[38] The *comitia centuriata* was the citizen assembly originally organised in fighting units, centuries (whence centurions), and divided between those liable for military service (*iuniores*), and those past the age of forty-six (*seniores*). Because they used to meet armed, they met outside the city walls in the Field of Mars. The cavalry (*equites*) and the first two classes (out of five classes categorised by the value of property owned) had a highly disproportionate weight in voting and if they were unanimous constituted a majority. But in elections, which were usually disputed, we cannot assume such unanimity. That said, the people (*populus*) as a whole, particularly in the tribal assembly, had considerable political power expressed, for example, in their election of nobles for office, and in their exclusive power to pass laws and to declare war. The protection of individual citizens against abuse of power by noble officials was vested in the Tribunes of the People. My discussion here needs some qualification; see Jolowicz (1972: 19ff.).

[39] The absolute size of the Roman army increased, but so by enfranchisement did the population of citizens from whom the soldiers were drawn. The proportion fell partly because of the increase in the length of service.

throughout the whole period of imperial expansion was the unpredictability of its size. Soldiers were enlisted not for a specific term of service, but for a campaign, which might last one or several years. The size of the army fluctuated according to the dangers facing the state. Nevertheless, the main outlines of a trend seem clear. I shall argue below that in the early second century BC, more than one half of all citizens served in the army probably for an average period of less than seven years. Roughly two centuries later, in the reign of Augustus, less than one sixth of all Italian-born citizens served in the army for a standard term of twenty years. A professional army had replaced armed peasants. (2 BC ½ served → AUGUSTUS ⅙ served.

These changes in the length of military service, in the social composition of the army and in its professionalism all reinforced the repercussions of the huge military effort on the political economy of Italy. The absence, on average, of 130,000 Italian peasants in the army was in effect a form of peasant emigration. Like death in war, it helped to create vacancies on Italian land, which the rich were only too anxious to occupy. But unlike death, it was temporary and unpredictable in duration. Some peasant soldiers returned after long service abroad only to find that during their absence their families had fallen into debt, or that their farms had been sequestrated by creditors. Moreover, the mere liability of peasants to be called away on service reduced their dependability as share-croppers or part-tenants. Military service aggravated the economic hardships of the poor, while it made possible an increase in land-ownership and prosperity for the elite. Roman victories overseas were creating an alternative source of labour, in slaves. Roman peasant soldiers were fighting for their own displacement.

Nor was this all. The changes in the pattern of recruitment stimulated the direct involvement of the Roman army in political conflicts in Rome. In the old days, at the end of a campaign, or between fighting seasons, peasant soldiers returned to their farms. The army was embedded in the peasantry. We can trace the process of its disengagement in the shortage of recruits with the traditional property qualification for military service, in the reduction and eventual formal abolition of the property requirement (107 BC), and in the allocation of farms to landless ex-soldiers, and finally, in the Principate in the location of long-service professional troops along the frontiers of the empire far from their birth place.[40] The new policy of recruiting

[40] The evidence on recruitment is conveniently gathered by W. Liebenam in *RE sv dilectus*, by Brunt (1971: 391–415, 625–44). I do not agree with Brunt (1971: 66) in his interpretation of Livy (24.18.7) that in 216 BC *only* 2,000 Romans had evaded

soldiers predominantly from among the poor or landless, even though conscription was sometimes unpopular and men were press-ganged into service, helped alleviate social conflict in Italy by offering them employment off the land. It helped solve the problems of recruitment, since the poor were more willing to serve for long periods than those who had farms to look after. The longer they served in the army, the more cut off they became from their original villages. But the policy created a new problem of what to do with a professional corps of landless soldiers who faced discharge without any prospects of a secure livelihood. The professional army relieved many peasants with land of the obligation to fight, but only at the cost of forging a new weapon of civil war.

Let us take a closer look at the Roman war effort. One obvious measure is the size of the army. Throughout the last two centuries of the Republic (see Table 1.1), the Roman army repeatedly totalled eight per cent or more of adult male citizens; the median size of the army (225–23 BC) amounted to thirteen per cent of adult male citizens. But in the years before the mass enfranchisement of the Italian allies (90/89 BC), the citizen army represented only a portion of the total Roman military effort. The Italian allies contributed on average about three fifths of the total Roman armed forces during thirty years (200–168 BC) after the war against Carthage, for which we have full information. In this period, the average size of the Roman/Italian armies was over 130,000 men. It was roughly the same for the period 80–50 BC, for which we also have good information (see Table 1.1); patchy evidence for the intervening period suggests that the allies

military service, or in his conclusion that the Roman soldiers, even in times of crisis were predominantly recruited from peasants owning land (*assidui*). On this see my review of Brunt (1971) in *JRS* 62 (1972) 192–3. I think Brunt overestimates the efficiency of Roman recruiting and the objective reliability of the sources.

The testimony for the minimum property requirements of soldiers is provided by Livy 1.43 (11,000 *asses*); Polybius 6.19 (4,000 *asses*); Cicero, *On the Republic* 2.40 or Aulus Gellius, *Attic Nights* 16.10.10 (1,500 *asses*). The changes seem difficult to date with any certainty, but see the interesting discussion by E. Gabba, 'The origins of the professional army at Rome' (Gabba, 1976: 1–19). The reduction in property qualifications supports the idea that there was a trend towards professionalisation and proletarianisation of the army during the last two centuries BC – so well analysed by Gabba (1976: 1–69) and by Brunt (1971: 405ff.).

In 107 BC according to Sallust, *Jugurtha* 86, Marius broke with tradition by enlisting volunteers mostly from the poorest classes. It was perhaps less of a revolution than the confirmation of a trend. It is important to stress that poor men had probably served before (how else could the Romans have kept such large armies in the field? – see below), that the landed peasantry were forcibly conscripted in the decades following, and that poor soldiers were probably recruited mainly from the countryside. See Brunt (1971: 403ff.), Gabba (1976) and J. Harmand, *L'armée et le soldat à Rome* (Paris, 1967) 11ff. On land allotments, see Brunt (1971:294–344).

repeatedly contributed more soldiers than Rome.[41] In both proportional and absolute terms, Roman military effort was immense. The size of the Roman army compares, for example, with that of the French army in the mid-seventeenth century, then the largest army in Europe, but that was drawn from a population of over twenty million – roughly three times as large as the population of Roman Italy.[42]

Right down to the end of the Republic, Rome is best seen as a warrior state. [The empire was won only through the massive involvement of the lower classes in war, an involvement which mirrored the militarism of the elite.] We can see this clearly enough if we consider the average length of military service. Unfortunately, as so often in Roman history, accurate information is missing. Moreover, it is important to stress that in the late Republic there was no fixed term of service. Annually elected generals were authorised by the senate to recruit legions, as the situation demanded, before they set out for the zone of war. Individual soldiers, when they enlisted, could have had very little idea how long their service would last. This instability was a significant factor in political instability, and should not be forgotten. Yet obviously such variation does not preclude an average. We know that citizens were liable to serve in the army for up to sixteen years (ten years for cavalry) between the ages of seventeen and forty-six. In the early second century BC, citizens who had served over six years continuously were thought overdue for return home (Livy 40.36.10); towards the end of the Republic, soldiers repeatedly served longer; the emperor Augustus instituted a professional army in which soldiers served for sixteen, then later twenty years.[43] It is tempting therefore to fill the gaps in our information by speculation; the probabilities are limited; the coefficients are clear; the shorter

[41] There is much scholarly argument about the trustworthiness of the figures transmitted by the sources for the size of legions, of armies and of the citizen population recorded in the Roman census. I am aiming here at rough orders of magnitude only; the figures would have to be widely awry to destroy the implications deduced here. The figures given here are based on Brunt (1971: 424–5 and 449). The average for 200–168 BC includes *c.* 10,000 marines and oarsmen; for 80–50 BC it is arrived at by multiplying the number of legions given by Brunt by their probable size (i.e. 5,500 men). Brunt (1971: 447) gives the average for 80–50 BC as 90,000, but this seems discordant with his own figures. On the ratio of allied and Roman soldiers, see Brunt (1971: appendix 26).

[42] Based on H. Delbrück, *Geschichte der Kriegskunst* (Berlin, 1920) vol. 4, 261; F. F. Helleiner in the *Cambridge Economic History* (Cambridge, 1967) vol. 4, 67.

[43] For six years service, see P. A. Brunt, 'The army and the land in the Roman revolution', *JRS* 52 (1962) 80; see also Appian, *Spanish Wars* 78 (*c.* 140 BC); A. Afzelius, *Die römische Kriegsmacht* (Copenhagen, 1944) 34ff., 47, 61; A. E. Astin, *Scipio Aemilianus* (Oxford, 1967) 167–72 (a very clear account). On longer service later, see R. E. Smith, *Service in the Post-Marian Roman Army* (Manchester 1958) 22ff.; Harmand (1967: 258–60).

Table I.I. *The Militarism of Rome: the numbers of citizens serving as soldiers in the Roman army, by decades, 225–23* BC

a	b	c	d
			Soldiers as a
Dates BC (mostly interval mid-points)	Estimated citizen population ('000)	Estimated size of citizen army ('000)	proportion of all male citizens (c/b) (%)
225	300	52	17
213	260	75	29 200 BC
203	235	60	26
193	266	53	20
183	315	48	15
173	314	44	14
163	383	33	9
153	374	30	8
143	400	44	11
133	381	37	10
123	476 or 366	32	7 or 9
113	476 or 366	34	7 or 9
103	(400)	50	13 100 BC
93	(400)	52	13
83	(1,030)	(143)	14
73	1,030	171	17
63	1,030	120	12
53	(1,030)	121	12
43	1,480	240	16
33	1,600	250	16
23	1,800	156	9 23 BC

Note to Table 1.1

All Pros's = Augustus.

The estimates of citizen population (col. *b*) are adapted from Brunt (1971: 13–14, 54–83 and 117–18). They are based on the nearest Roman census figure, plus the estimated number of citizen soldiers serving overseas; I have followed Brunt in adding an extra 10% to this total to allow for under-reporting in the census.

The sudden changes in the figures deserve explanation. The changes in 213 and 183 BC were largely due to the dis- and re-enfranchisement of 38,000 Campanians; in 83 and 43 BC, they reflect the enfranchisement of the Italian allies and Cisalpines. The figures from 123 BC onwards are less certain because of the difficulty of interpreting the census data. Up to 53 BC I have not included Italians living overseas, because they did not serve in the Roman army in sufficient numbers. Thereafter, I have included them, and have followed Brunt's figures for them; roughly 150,000 in 43 BC and 375,000 in 23 BC. The figures in brackets are even less certain than the others.

The estimates of army size (col. *c*) are also based on Brunt (1971: 44, 404, 418, 424, 432–49, 501–10). Between 198 and 59 BC, the figures given are averages for the decade (198–189, 188–179 BC etc), the others are for single years. I have gone further than Brunt in multiplying the number of legions in service by their nominal strength, that is 5,500 from 168–108 BC, and by 6,200 from 107 BC after the reforms of Marius to 91 BC. In the civil wars which followed, it seems that more legions were formed than could be fully manned, and to allow for this I have multiplied by 5,500 only, except where Brunt gives explicit figures. The margin of error may be quite large, but probably not so large that it would materially alter the percentage figures in column *d*.

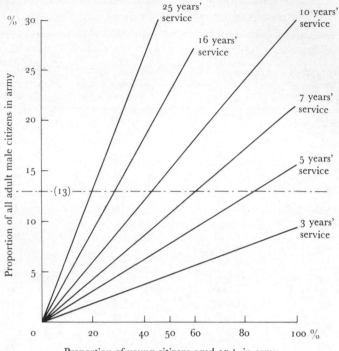

Figure 1.3. Young men's length of service in the Roman army – some co-ordinates. NB: the median size of the army 225–23 BC was 13% of all adult male citizens.

the average length of service, the larger the proportion of citizens involved.

In all probability, the burden of military service fell disproportionately on young men. Citizens became liable to military service on their seventeeth birthday. In preparing Figure 1.3, I have made four simplifying assumptions: (*a*) all men joined the army at age seventeen, (*b*) they all served the same length of time, (*c*) the rate of death among soldiers was the same as for civilians, (*d*) the average expectation of life was roughly mid-way between the high and the low found in pre-industrial populations ($e_0 = 25$).[44] None of the first three assumptions is likely to be accurate; but in so far as mortality among soldiers was higher than among civilians or if recruits joined the army significantly later than age seventeen, then the burden of service would

[44] The average expectation (e) of life at birth (o) among soldiers is estimated at twenty-five years ($e_0 = 25$).

34

have been even heavier than shown. On the other hand, if the citizen population (or if the sector of it which bore arms) was underenumerated and if the legions were systematically undermanned, then the burden was lighter than shown. Table 1.1 and Figure 1.3 should be used to illustrate limits of probability and rough orders of magnitude only.

That said, the conclusions seem staggering. An army which accounted for thirteen per cent of all citizens (the median of the last two centuries) could be raised by enlisting eighty-four per cent of seventeen-year-olds for five years, or *c.* sixty per cent for seven years, or forty-four per cent for ten years, or twenty-eight per cent for sixteen years. (The cohort of seventeen-year-olds (at $e_0 = 25$) equalled about three per cent of the adult male population; it diminished slowly each year after.) The qualitative and impressionistic evidence on enlistment in the early second century BC suggests that service was typically on the short side of this spectrum. By the end of the Republic service had become significantly longer. The implications are then inevitable; if the evidence on army size and citizen population is anywhere near right, then a very large proportion (say over half) of Roman citizens regularly served in the army for seven years in the early second century BC. By the reign of Augustus, the army was thoroughly professionalised, but an average of twenty years' service still required the enlistment of about one fifth of seventeen-year-old citizens. Among pre-industrial states, as far as I know, only Prussia under Frederick William I and Frederick the Great and Napoleonic France, and those only for short periods, achieved such consistent military effort.[45]

In sum, continuous wars were largely a consequence of the competitive ambitions of a militaristic elite, supported by a high rate of recruitment of peasants into the army. Wars affected Italian land and labour directly by destruction and death. Foreign invaders, rebellious slaves and insurgent Italians plundered farms, ravaged crops and slaughtered livestock. In addition, numerous Roman soldiers and Italians were killed or maimed in battle. The indirect economic and political consequences of warfare were even more serious. The military service of over 100,000 Romans/Italians at most times throughout the last two centuries of the Republic was equal to a significant emigration from the countryside.[46] Absent peasants were partly replaced by slaves; this 'emigration' of soldiers was one of the factors which permitted or even encouraged the formation of large estates. Or seen another

---

[45] See note 19 above.
[46] On the recruitment of soldiers predominantly from the countryside, rather than from the urban proletariat, see Brunt (1962: 69ff.). Some urban recruitment also occurred.

way, the pauperisation of many peasants on the one hand and the increases in labour productivity on the other hand, which were associated with agricultural innovation and economies of scale on large estates, were the two sides of one coin, just as they were in the agricultural revolution in England in the eighteenth century.

The transfer of the burden of prolonged military service from propertied peasants to the poor or landless had considerable political repercussions. In the medium term, it helped alleviate the unpopularity of conscription among peasant voters; since such large armies could not be filled exclusively with volunteers, the Romans had often relied also on persuasion and force. Our sources reveal the military levies as a repeated source of trouble. In one year (152 BC), for example, complaints of unfairness induced the consuls to select recruits by lot; on another occasion, similar complaints provoked the tribunes of the people to fine and imprison the consuls. Given that the executive arm of the Roman government was too weak to distribute the load equitably, it was obviously advantageous to shift the burden of military service on to fewer people drawn predominantly from those who were politically weakest, and who had least attachment to the land.[47] Poverty pushed them out, while army pay and the prospect of booty pulled.

The solution of the problem of recruitment had its price. At the end of their military service, landless soldiers needed means of support. In the undifferentiated Roman economy, that meant land. When the power of soldiers was wedded to the political ambition of a successful general, an army was in a position to get the land it wanted. Sulla, after his triumphant march on Rome in 82 BC, is said to have resettled twenty-three legions, depleted by war losses to perhaps 80–100,000 men, on Italian land made vacant by confiscation from towns which had opposed him.[48] Similar policies of resettlement were effected by other political generals; Pompey, Julius Caesar and Augustus. The numbers of soldiers resettled in Italy, perhaps a quarter of a million between 80 and 25 BC, were still fairly small as a proportion of the total labour force. But most of Italy was too densely populated to allow the easy assimilation of a sudden influx of large numbers of new settlers. The resettlement of ex-soldiers therefore usually led to the eviction of existing tenants or peasants. Like the small land grant scheme of the Gracchi, it went against the trend towards the formation of large estates. But there was nothing to stop the new small-holders from

[47] Astin (1967: 167–72); Livy 43.14 on 169 BC; Appian, *Spanish Wars* 49; Livy, *Summary of Book* 55.
[48] On land allotments to Sulla's soldiers, see Brunt (1971: 305).

becoming themselves the victims of similar economic or political pressures; they too might soon be evicted. The resettlement of ex-soldiers in Italy seems only to have replaced one group of small-holders with another; it did little to change the overall pattern of land-holding and it made a significant contribution to instability. Finally, the long-term political consequences of changing from a peasant to a professional army were serious. The gradual demilitarisation of the yeomanry undermined the traditional broad base of the Republican constitution. Landed peasants were relieved of the heavy burden of military service at the eventual cost, to put it somewhat dramatically, of their political liberty. Between Republic and Principate, the army changed from an expression of citizen power to an instrument of control. Citizens became the emperor's subjects.

THE PRODUCTS OF WAR

The main product of continuous war was empire. Its administration involved an increase in the professional skills of the Roman elite; for example, specialist lawyers became distinct from priests, soldiers from peasants, school-teachers from fathers, tax-contractors from plundering generals. These developments were paid for, initially out of booty and war indemnities, and eventually from the taxes imposed on the vanquished. Revenues from empire made possible the 'take-off' into political expansion and the financing of further wars. As the empire became more firmly established, the proportion of government income derived from booty diminished; indemnities were replaced by taxes; victorious generals were succeeded by Roman administrators. Indeed the transition from booty to taxes was an important part of the process of establishing the empire. The revenues of the state were secured. At the beginning of the second century BC, according to Frank's tentative estimates, about three quarters of the revenues of the Roman state came from abroad. By the middle of the first century BC, state revenues had increased to roughly six times their previous level; and almost all came from abroad.[49] As in other successful

---

[49] I follow here T. Frank's speculative estimate of gross revenues in the early second century BC: about 50–60 million HS per year (*ESAR* vol. 1, 141).

As a result of Pompey's conquests 63–60 BC, state revenues rose from 200 to 340 million HS (Plutarch, *Pompey* 45). Plutarch's comment is ambiguous; but I prefer this interpretation to a rise from 200 to 540 million HS, argued by E. Badian, *Roman Imperialism in the Late Republic* (Oxford[2], 1968) 78 and accepted by P. A. Brunt, *Social Conflicts in the Roman Republic* (London, 1971) 39. The importance of booty and indemnities is reflected in the detailed accounts of them preserved in traditional histories (e.g. Livy 34.46). For what it is worth, Frank estimates that booty and indemnities accounted for about two fifths of Roman state revenues in the first part

pre-industrial empires, the proceeds of victory were distributed, albeit somewhat unequally, among the conquerors.

Soldiers were among the first to benefit. At the end of a war, the commanding general regularly gave soldiers a share of the booty in cash. In the early second century BC, these grants were quite modest; on average barely enough to feed a family for three months. In the mid-first century BC, in the two particularly lavish cases we know of, the common soldier's share of the booty was enough to buy several years' food for a household or a modest plot of land.[50] We do not know how much booty soldiers succeeded in carrying off for themselves; but Roman commanders were often induced to allow their soldiers to plunder; sometimes the soldiers plundered a captured city without orders.[51]

Not only soldiers benefited. In 167 BC, as a result of one particularly large haul of booty from Greece, taxes levied on Italian land owned by Roman citizens were abolished; the land tax was not reimposed in Italy, except during crises at the end of the Republic. This is one of the factors which accounts for the high price of Italian land, since, other things being equal, rent could equal rent plus tax on provincial land.

As the profits of empire increased, distributions to the citizen body became more lavish. In part, the pay-off was vicarious and symbolic: public games were given to celebrate victories; one of their functions was that they reinforced popular pride in the army's achievements. In 123 BC, a popular tribune of the people had a law passed by which citizens living in the city of Rome received wheat at a subsidised price. From 58 BC onwards, the wheat was distributed free; the number of recipients fluctuated apparently between 150,000 and 320,000. In this way, a sizeable minority of all Roman citizens, at times over one

of the second century BC, when less than a third of revenues came from provincial taxes and mines. At the end of the Republic (see *ESAR* vol. 1, 322ff.) provincial taxes constituted the bulk of state revenues. The great hauls of booty taken by Pompey and Caesar were exceptional.

[50] From the early second century BC, we know of 17 gifts of money by generals to soldiers from booty (tabulated by Brunt (1971: 394). The median was 100 HS, the average 122 HS. At the conventional price of wheat (3 HS per *modius*), the average would have provided *c.* 40 *modii* = 260 kg wheat = about one quarter of a family's minimum annual needs. By contrast, Pompey gave his soldiers 6,000 HS (Plutarch, *Pompey* 45), Julius Caesar 20,000 HS (Appian, *Civil Wars* 3.44) and 24,000 HS (Suetonius, *Julius Caesar* 38). Augustus gave soldiers 12,000 HS after sixteen, later twenty years' service. See P. A. Brunt, *JRS* 52 (1962) 78ff.

[51] Ideally, Roman soldiers shared all the booty; according to Polybius 10.15ff. a specific body of soldiers, never more than half the army, was detailed to collect booty, while the rest stood guard. Ancient ideals of discipline sometimes broke down (e.g. Livy 37.32; Plutarch, *Lucullus* 14 and 19) Harmand (1967: 410–16).

quarter, received a direct share of the profits of empire. At most after 58 BC, the cost of the wheat-dole equalled a sixth of state revenues, while each recipient got about two fifths of the minimum subsistence requirements of a family; the wheat-dole helped the poor out, but it did not make work unnecessary.[52] The use of state resources to subsidise poor voters had several unintended and perhaps unperceived consequences. It encouraged the further migration of peasants to Rome; it was one of the factors which made possible the city of Rome's huge growth; and it held down the cost to the rich of employing free labour in the city of Rome. In addition, as I argue below, it helped support the market for the food grown on the farms of the rich. One final point. Most of the official revenues from empire went to finance more wars. Italian troops were paid and supported. In effect, the Roman government was providing alternative employment for Italian peasants; they were paid to keep off the land, which the rich wanted to occupy. One can understand the fury of conservative leaders when occasionally soldiers returned *en masse*, and through the patronage of their generals demanded land in Italy to settle on.

Above all, the income from empire flowed into the purses of the privileged. That was one of the chief advantages of being privileged, at once a token of high status and a means of reinforcing it. Throughout the second century BC, the rich became steadily richer, and in the first century BC, the process accelerated. Rich men boasted publicly of their wealth; the size of one's possessions or debts became matters of common knowledge. The richest nobles acquired private fortunes which equalled the revenues of small states, and could by themselves sustain private armies and dispense massive charity. One man, M. Licinius Crassus, reputedly the richest of his day, gave Roman citizens living in the city of Rome enough wheat to live on for three months in the hope of sustaining his political popularity while he was away seeking military glory. His fortune amounted to about 192 million HS, roughly enough to feed 400,000 families for one year. A contemporary notable reckoned that one needed 100,000 HS to live comfortably and 600,000 HS a year to live well, incomes roughly equal to two hundred

---

[52] On the wheat-dole in Rome, see Brunt (1971: 376–82). I calculate its cost very roughly as 5 (*modii* per month)×12 (months per year)×320,000 (maximum number of recipients)×3 HS (conventional wheat price) = 58 million HS from a revenue in 60 BC of more than 340 million HS. Cicero's polemical implication (*pro Sestio* 55) that free wheat for citizens cost the state a fifth of its budget was probably an exaggeration. I reckon the minimum living requirements of an average sized family at 1,000 kg wheat equivalent per year (*c.* 150 *modii*).

and one thousand two hundred times the minimum subsistence level of a family.[53]

As a result of this growth in wealth, the differences between the rich and poor in wealth and style of life widened. The position of the poorest, the urban proletariat and landless labourers, deteriorated sharply both absolutely and relatively to the rich. At the same time, sections of the population outside the traditional elite were also profiting from empire. This is my understanding of what happened, but it is difficult to document; elitist litterateurs did not discuss increasing differentiation outside the elite. One symptom of this development may be found in the booty distributed to soldiers. We have already seen that early in the period of imperial expansion the amounts given to soldiers by generals were very small; at the end of the period, they were, on the two known occasions, very large. In the earlier period (*c.* 200 BC), centurions regularly got only twice as much bounty as ordinary soldiers; in the last century BC, on one occasion, centurions received twenty times as much as ordinary soldiers (Plutarch, *Pompey* 33), and by the end of the Republic, the regular pay of centurions was five times higher than that of ordinary soldiers (Appian, *Civil Wars* 4.100); at the end of Augustus' reign, it may have been sixteen to sixty times higher.[54] Some soldiers still got double pay (*duplicarii*), but their position in the rank order was far below that of a centurion. At the other end of the scale it is worth noting that Pompey's senior officers (legates, *quaestors*) apparently got five hundred times as much as ordinary soldiers (*ESAR*, vol. 1, 325). The picture we get from all these examples is one of increasing differentiation within the army. It partly reflected the army's own increased professionalisation and bureau-

---

[53] The fact that the size of his fortune was public knowledge reflects the competition among nobles for wealth. In fact Pompey's fortune was significantly larger than that of Crassus. See Badian (1968: 81ff.); Plutarch, *Crassus* 2; Pliny, *Natural History* 33.134; Cicero, *Paradoxa Stoicorum* 49. It is noteworthy that Pompey's assets roughly equalled the state's annual revenues – an index of the weakness of the state machine relative to the nobility in the late Republic.

[54] On this, see P. A. Brunt, 'Pay and superannuation in the Roman army', *Papers of the British School at Rome* 18 (1950) 71 and the slightly different calculations in A. von Domeszewski, *Die Rangordnung des römischen Heeres* (Cologne², 1967) 111 extrapolating backwards from an early third-century inscription (*CIL* 3.14416). In 46 BC Caesar gave centurions the old traditional ratio, i.e. twice as much bounty as ordinary soldiers (Appian, *Civil Wars* 2.102); this was a clear exception to the trend I describe. However, it is worth noting that in this distribution centurions got 40,000 HS, which was enough to set them up as substantial peasants. The high ratio (20:1) of bounty given to centurions in 66 BC (see also Appian, *Mith.* 104) may also have been due to exceptional political circumstances. That said, the evidence of a trend, although scant and patchy, seems cumulatively convincing. See also Brunt (1971: 459) for a sensible discussion of the evidence.

cratisation; it also reflected, I think, the increased stratification of civilian society.

The main source of new wealth for nobles was provincial government.[55] The origins of provincial administration in conquest affected its style. Like the Roman army, provincial administration was controlled by high-status amateurs, who held office for short periods only and saw in it an opportunity to enhance their status and make a profit. The importance of war booty declined, though the plunder collected by the armies and officers of Sulla, Pompey and Julius Caesar provides notable exceptions. Instead Roman aristocrats made money from the supervision of taxation and the dispensation of justice. In the first century BC, a cautious and unexploitative governor of a province could make enough profit from a single year in office to set up his family in style for generations. Many governors and their aides saw a tour in the provinces as an opportunity for making their fortunes, or for restoring them after they had been debilitated by the cost of securing election. The scale of Roman exploitation of the provinces is reflected in the fact that the first permanent judicial tribunal established in Rome was set up (in 149 BC) to deal with complaints by provincials of illegal extortion. At best, the tribunal provided provincials with an opportunity to recuperate some small part of the losses they had incurred and, for what it was worth, to punish governors who had oppressed them. At worst, the tribunal was plagued by domestic Roman political intrigues and collusions. But perhaps its most important function, its unintended consequence, was merely to establish a convention as to the level of extortion which would be condoned.

Even a well-intentioned governor, like Cicero, was restricted by his obligations to other senators and tax-farmers, and by their expectations based on what previous governors had allowed. Cicero, who governed Cilicia (at that time the southern and eastern part of Turkey plus Cyprus) in 51–50 BC, set himself up as a model of propriety. He restrained his own aides; but he needed the political support of his friends at Rome too much to be able to withstand their demands successfully. For example, he found that the towns of Cyprus had paid the previous governor 4.8 million HS (roughly enough to feed 10,000 families for one year) in order to avoid having soldiers garrisoned there. This was only one item in the governor's profits. Cicero osten-

---

[55] The scale of Roman plunder is illustrated by Badian (1968: 82ff.), and discussed in more detail by R. O. Jolliffe, *Phases of Corruption in Roman Administration* (Diss. Menasha, Wisc., 1919), mostly excerpts from Cicero interestingly discussed.

tatiously abstained from squeezes like this. Indeed, he returned one million HS from his allowance to the treasury to the chagrin of his aides who expected it to be distributed to them. Even so, Cicero tells us that he made 2.2 million HS for himself, probably out of the money allocated to him for the upkeep of the soldiers assigned to his province. Throughout his governship, Cicero was engaged in regulating the collection of debts already incurred by provincials (and by the king of a neighbouring principality) and already swollen by interest. Colleagues in Rome pressed him to appoint their business agents as officials (*prefects*) or to send in troops to enforce their requests for payment. Apparently other governors often did this. Only recently, the agent of one noble senator had shut up some town councillors in their council house in an attempt to enforce payment of a debt swollen by a high rate of interest, and had not released them until five had died of starvation.[56] Exaction of such debts extended the scope of profiteering from provinces well beyond the short tenure built into the Roman system of governorships.

Most Roman administrators were probably less callous. Yet there are sufficient stories from the late Republic to indicate the scale on which the accumulated treasures of the conquered provinces were transferred to Rome, and hints of the methods used to extract them. In effect, most Roman governors and their aides could exercise their power, in pursuit of profit or pleasure, arbitrarily and without fear of reprisal. Let me give an example, taken, I am afraid, from a somewhat biased source: a prosecutor's speech (Cicero, *Against Verres* 2.1.64ff.) against a governor on trial for extortion in 70 BC. It describes an episode earlier in his career for which he was never tried; the prosecutor probably cast it in the worst possible light. Nevertheless, it seems revealing. As the governor's aide (*legatus*), Verres was quartered in a small town in what is now western Turkey; he lusted after the daughter of a leading citizen; this citizen gave a feast in Verres' honour; during the feast Verres ordered the doors locked and demanded that the girl be brought to him. There ensued a battle between the house slaves and those of Verres, in which one of Verres' official guards was killed. Next morning, the townspeople, who sided with

<hr/>

[56] On Cicero's governorship, see best his *Letters to Atticus*, ed. D. R. Shackleton Bailey (Cambridge, 1968) vol. 3. Specific references used here are (in the old enumeration) 5.21; 6.1; 7.1; and *ad Fam.* 5.20.9. It is difficult to know what was normal; exploitation may have worsened considerably during the last decades of the Republic. The ravages committed were public knowledge, regretted and condoned: 'Words cannot express, citizens, how hated we are among foreign nations because of the lust of those we have sent to govern them during the past years and the damage they have done' (Cicero, *On the Manilian Law* 65; cf. *ad Fam.* 15.1.5).

their own citizen, gathered to batter down the door of the house in which Verres was lodged, but were eventually dissuaded from harming him by a group of Roman citizens living in the town. Verres escaped, but quickly brought the father of the girl to trial for the murder of his guard. He fixed this by getting the jury packed with Roman citizens to whom provincials owed money and who would welcome his help in getting their debts paid. The prosecutor was a money-lender too; the father could find no one who was willing to defend him and risk offending the governor. He was found guilty and executed. So much for Roman justice.

It seems worth stressing that taking private profit from public office was built into the Roman system of provincial administration. To some extent, of course, corruption, overtly recognised as wrong but condoned, has been and still is the hall-mark of bureaucratic administration.[57] The exceptions are few and notable. But I am not thinking here of the routine inability of a central administration completely to control the income of its officials. Rather I am thinking of the methods first adopted by the Romans to secure revenues from the rapidly expanded empire. As in many other pre-industrial empires, the Roman government commonly sold the right to collect taxes to private individuals (tax-farmers, *publicani*). This had long been the practice in Italy for the collection of fees from state lands and buildings, as well as in the letting of state contracts, and had been common in the Greek kingdoms of the eastern Mediterranean which the Romans absorbed. Since there was at Rome no tradition of employing men of high status on a salary for a long term, either in the public or the private sphere, there was no effective alternative to tax-farming easily available. How else could the Romans have taxed their provinces regularly? To be sure, several variants of tax-farming were known and used in different parts of the empire (for example, in Sicily and Asia). Yet the variations did not matter either to the Roman state or to the provincial tax-payers as much as the degree of control exercised by Roman magistrates over the tax-farmers.

For the Roman government, tax-farming had several advantages. Once the tax contracts had been auctioned, the government received cash in advance, probably with Italian land pledged as security for

---

[57] The article by C. K. Yang in D. S. Nivison and A. F. Wright, *Confucianism in Action* (Stanford, 1959) is very suggestive.

See now, E. Badian, *Publicans and Sinners* (Oxford, 1972), the best even if a sometimes polemical discussion of Roman Republican tax-farming; on the Principate also, see M. I. Rostovtzeff, *Geschichte der Stattspacht* (Leipzig, 1901) 39ff.; cf. G. Urögdi, *sv Publicani* in *RE* Supplement-Band XI, col. 1184–1208.

further payment and orderly conduct.[58] Since contracts regularly lasted for five years, the government secured its revenue and could commit itself to expenditure, such as a foreign war, which might last several years. By selling the right to tax, the government transferred its risk to the tax-farmers and their guarantors. One of the main risks was a bad harvest; and harvests often were bad; provincials might not be able to pay their taxes in full, or if the tax was a fixed proportion of the crop it might not yield as much as the tax farmers had paid for the contract and its administration. Such shortfalls did happen, and on two occasions we know that the tax-farmers asked the Roman senate to remit part of the price agreed at the auction.[59]

Tax-farming also had disadvantages for the state. Collusion between bidders at auctions prevented the state from getting the best price. Even when tax-farmers bid high, they were more likely to screw extra taxes out of provincials than to suffer losses themselves. The main problem, as has already been suggested, was that the efficiency of tax-farming as an instrument of good government depended upon the effectiveness of the supervision of the tax-farmers. In a small society, tax-payers could soon have made their dissatisfaction with abuses felt; in a monarchy, the king or emperor has an interest in preserving the tax-paying capacities of his subjects and no special interest in the enrichment of tax-farmers. However, in the oligarchic early Roman empire (200–31 BC), the provincials had almost no power and were hundreds of miles, even months away, from the centre of power. The governors, whose task it was to supervise the tax-farmers, ruled usually for only one year and had little knowledge of the special problems of the province to which they had been assigned and had no permanent skilled staff on whose experience they could draw. Both governor and tax-farmer were usually interested in making a private profit; there were often disputes over the division of the spoils; my impression is that collusion was the most frequent solution to the conflict, to the detriment of the provincials.[60]

[58] An inscription from Puteoli, set up in 105 BC, records that a municipal building contractor had to pledge land against proper fulfilment of his contract (*CIL* 10.1781 = *FIRA* 153). This is thought to have been typical and traditional; see similarly, Polybius 6.17 and Cicero, *Verrines* 2.1.142–3; Ps. Asconius 252 St; Schol. Bobb. 106 St.

[59] Plutarch, *Cato the Elder* 19; Cicero, *ad Att.* 1.17.9; *On the Manilian Law* 16; other references in *ESAR* vol. 1, 345. Collusion was the complement of risk.

[60] Cicero, *Letters to Atticus* 6.1.16: 'You seem to want to know how I manage about the tax-farmers. I dote upon them, defer to them, butter them up with compliments – and arrange that they harm nobody...My system is this: I fix a date...and say that if (the provincials) pay before that date I shall apply a rate of 1 % (interest per month): if not, then the rate in the agreement. So the natives pay a tolerable interest

Dependence on tax-farming was a symptom of the central government's weakness throughout the Republic. Firstly, the Roman senate had no cadre of middle and lower level provincial administrators under its control; it could therefore provide only an extremely limited service, if any, to its newly conquered subjects. During the Principate a salaried officialdom did evolve out of the emperor's own household; it was staffed predominantly by slaves, and headed by ex-slaves and a few knights.[61] Its establishment spelt a slow death for tax-farming, while its small size highlights the meagreness of provincial administration during the Republic. Secondly, the Republican government had a small budget; reliance on tax-farming implied that groups of wealthy men could raise huge sums of cash more easily and could better afford to spread their risks over a few years than the government. This is an index of the generally low proportion of gross product siphoned off from the provinces in taxation in the early stages of imperial conquest overseas and suggests that during this early period of empire the share of provincial profits which found its way into private hands was greater.

One of the most important functions of tax-farming was to give prosperous non-senators and especially knights a share in the profits of empire; there was no other established channel by which this could be done. Polybius (6.17) writing in the middle of the second century BC, with some exaggeration, stated that 'almost everyone' in Italy seemed to be involved in some way with public contracts. Moreover, tax-farming provided the financial framework which underpinned the development of the political 'third force' (Pliny, *Natural History* 33.34), the knights, about whom more in a moment. Finally, the system of tax-farming helped preserve the traditional amateurishness of the nobles. Throughout the century of expansion which followed the defeat of Carthage, the provinces were governed by a handful of aristocrats and their followers sent out each year by the senate. Their very short tenure of office, the small scale of the administration which they controlled, and their exclusion from tax-collecting all helped preserve the oligarchy, which depended upon limiting each aristocrat's power.

Ideally, good provincial administration depended upon a balance

and the tax-farmers are delighted with the arrangement...' trans. D. R. Shackleton Bailey (Cambridge, 1968) vol. 3, 95. Cicero thought himself a model governor, as he was, compared with Verres (Cicero, *Verrines* 2.2.170). Badian (1972: 76) points out cases of the long-tenure of tax-contracts in particular towns and regions and the large size of companies. Oligopoly suggests collusion, then as now.

61 On patrimonial bureaucracy, see particularly Max Weber, *Economy and Society* (New York, 1968) vol. 3, 1006ff.

being kept between the competing interests of nobles, tax-farmers, citizen soldiers, citizen voters, and provincials. The increase in the profits attainable upset the balance, sharpened the conflict and turned the exercise of control over profit-making into a political football. At the beginning of the second century BC, the collective power of the oligarchy was strong enough to restrain both individual governors and tax-farmers, at least within very broad bounds. Even then, however, there was a reluctance on the part of senatorial judges to punish fellow senators for faults committed against mere provincials; convicted governors were allowed simply to go into exile to allied towns less than 40 km (25 miles) from Rome.[62] Condonation at home led to licence abroad; the senate perceived the problem but was either unwilling or unable to do anything to control it effectively. On one occasion in 167 BC, it ordered some very profitable mines in Greece to be closed, on the grounds that working them gave Roman tax-farmers too much opportunity for oppression, while handing them over to local contractors would not have produced any better results. Tax-farmers, the historian Livy commented (45.18), deprived either the state of its right or provincials of their liberty. But the whole empire could hardly be run with such ostrich-like tactics.

In 123 BC, service on the jury in the court which tried provincial governors for extortion was restricted to knights, to whose ranks the wealthiest tax-farmers belonged. This restriction has been taken by both Roman and modern writers as an important symptom of a conflict of interest between senators and knights, which is a major theme in political thinking throughout the last century of the Republic.[63] Certainly the restriction of jury service to knights was consciously intended as a flamboyant political act (Gaius Gracchus said that he had thrown daggers into the forum; Cicero, *On Laws* 3.20), at once an attack on the senate and an identifying focus for the stratum of knights. Gracchus had given the state two heads (Varro, frag. 114R)

Yet too much can easily be made of this conflict; in all the serious political conflicts which followed, both senators and knights were on each side; more knights were simply Italian land-owners than tax-farmers; in no reasonable sense of the term was the conflict a class conflict. Perhaps the control of juries by knights can more profitably be seen as a method of recognising the enlargement of the elite

---

[62] On this see Badian (1972: 11–47); Livy 43.2.

[63] See the incisive review of E. Badian, 'From the Gracchi to Sulla', *Historia* 11 (1962) 203–9; the detailed, evocative, though heavily prosopographical history of E. Gruen, *Roman Politics and the Criminal Courts 149–78 BC* (Harvard, 1968); and the brief suggestive chapter on knights by C. Meier, *Res Publica Amissa* (Wiesbaden, 1966) 64–95. See also note 70 below.

involved in profiting from the provinces, and the accommodation of that enlarged elite within the political system while preserving executive monopoly by a senate of only three hundred members. This view seems corroborated by the promotion of more than three hundred knights to the senate in 81 BC; this was another attempt to solve the same problem, which avoided an institutionalised clash between elite social groups.

That said, there was an identifiable tax-farming interest, centred among wealthy, politically active knights in Rome. Their access to and temporary monopoly of juries which tried senatorial governors for corruption weakened the governors' capacity to supervise the corrupt activities of tax-farmers. The notorious conviction in 92 BC of Rutilius, an innocent, indeed reputedly incorruptible acting-governor was merely one extreme case; its importance was symbolic, a warning to other governors to trim their sails. In Cicero's correspondence from his province and in his [?] brother's pamphlet on electioneering, we can see that tax-farmers were a force to be reckoned with.[64] 'You seem to want to know how I manage about the tax farmers. I dote upon them, defer to them, butter them up with compliments...' (Cicero, *Letters to Atticus* 6.1.6 – see note 60).

The knights' domination of the jury courts for more than a generation confirmed the power and wealth of the tax-farming companies. The increased competition between aristocrats for office (after 81 BC) ensured the continuance of what had become a tradition; senatorial administrators and tax-farmers colluded in getting rich at the expense of the weakest party, the conquered provincials.

In sum, while senatorial generals and governors won battles, captured towns, imposed taxes, drew expenses and dispensed 'justice', Roman knights collected taxes and administrative charges, amenably lent provincials money with which to pay their taxes, at a suitable rate of interest (cf. Plutarch, *Lucullus* 7ff.), and in case of non-payment foreclosed on the mortgages. In this way, among others, Roman citizens became the owners of large estates in the provinces, and the conquering elite of the Romans gradually acquired wealth commensurate with their conquest of the Mediterranean basin.[65]

[64] [?Q.] Cicero, *Guide to Electioneering* (*Comm. Pet.*) 3; Gruen (1968: Appendix E) listed 22 known cases brought before the extortion court between 119 and 91 BC; eleven cases resulted in acquittal; two of the convicted committed suicide. The evidence is probably very incomplete; yet what we know reveals neither outright persecution of senators by equestrian jurors nor condonation. After 70 BC juries were drawn from senators, knights, and the stratum just below the knights.

[65] There is little evidence of senatorial land-holdings overseas before the Principate. Senators were restricted from travelling abroad privately, and may have been forbidden explicitly from owning land outside Italy (Cicero, 2 *Verrines* 5.45); in any case, it would have been difficult to be sure of getting stable revenues from estates

THE FORMATION OF LARGE ESTATES

The profits of empire, were the single most important factor in gradually building up the wealth of the Roman elite. A large portion of the profits taken out of the provinces was invested in land, especially in Italian land. Since the Roman upper classes got most of their regular income from land, a general increase in their wealth was necessarily accompanied by the formation of larger estates. This strong link between (1) imperial profits, (2) the increased wealth of the elite and (3) the formation of large landholdings often seems overshadowed by the more dramatic processes, which we discussed in the last section: the violent acquisition of fortunes in the provinces, their ostentatious display in the city of Rome, and the manipulation of free floating cash by financiers, like Crassus and rich tax-farmers. Of course, the transfer of money from the provinces and its investment in Italian land was a gradual process; its gradualness may have contributed to its neglect. In any one year or even generation, the volume of profits brought back from the provinces was smaller than the inherited stock of capital; and once the year's profits were invested, they too became part of the common capital. Thereafter, they were redistributed through the normal channels: dowry and inheritance, supplemented by bankruptcy and confiscation. Thus at any one time, these normal channels for the transfer of property seemed of more importance to contemporaries than provincial profits.

To be sure, a significant proportion of booty was spent rather than invested. Whether invested or spent, the money was passed on to someone else. The same money could be used to pay creditors, who might buy luxuries with it; they, in turn, might buy land from peasants, who then used the same money to buy clothes and food... The concept 'the multiplier effect of money' refers to such sequences.

The high cost of maintaining status by ostentatious expenditure and of securing election to public office were important factors underlying profiteering in the provinces. Nobles, particularly in the first century BC, commonly incurred debts in the hope of paying them off afterwards with what they made out of provincial office.[66] Retainers as well as

abroad which could not be personally supervised. This may partly explain the concentration of senatorial estates in central Italy. Knights did own estates abroad during the Republic and clearly spent some time in residence there. See E. Rawson, 'The Ciceronian aristocracy and its properties', in M. I. Finley ed. *Studies in Roman Property* (Cambridge, 1976) 85ff.

[66] For a discussion of debt, see M. W. Frederiksen, 'Caesar, Cicero and the problem of debt', *JRS* 56 (1966) especially 128–30; Cicero (*Catiline* 2.18; *Offices* 2.78ff.) mentioned a category of rich men, heavily in debt. For Pompey, see Pliny, *Natural History* 37.16 and *ESAR* vol. 1, 325.

creditors had to be paid. Pompey, in 61 BC, for example, probably gave each of his lieutenants one million HS (*c.* 2,000 tons wheat equivalent). Huge sums were lavished on prestigious displays, silver plate, marble statues and other *objets d'art.* One indication of increasing wealth is that the finest town house in the city of Rome in 78 BC was said not to have been even in the top hundred a generation later (Pliny, *Natural History* 36.109). The senate tried to preserve traditional simplicity (and so to restrict competition from rich *arrivistes*) by a whole succession of laws restricting consumption, for example, at feasts and funerals;[67] but in vain. Senators and leading knights maintained elaborate households staffed with hundreds of slaves, including cooks, scribes, librarians, doctors, name-callers, at once a mark of their culture, and of an extravagance which enhanced their status.

This expenditure of provincial profits in the city of Rome particularly concerns us here because it considerably expanded the market for agricultural produce. Nobles kept and fed slaves, built palaces, commanded services and spent money which by its multiplier effects gave lots of people enough money to buy food. Without this expansion of the city population and market, and a similar expansion in other Italian towns, investment by nobles in Italian agricultural land would have been useless.

As in most other pre-industrial societies, land-ownership was the bedrock of wealth. Generally speaking, both senators and knights derived the bulk of their incomes from land. The richer they became, therefore, the larger their land-holdings. But good agricultural land in central and southern Italy was already cultivated, much of it by free peasants. The formation of large land-holdings inevitably involved their expropriation and expulsion. The process was gradual, and estates were enlarged piecemeal, as and when opportunity offered. This partly explains why large land-holdings in Italy during the late Republic typically comprised several scattered estates. This fragmentation of land-holdings was politically important in that it by and large precluded Roman aristocrats, unlike European feudal lords, from basing their power on the control of a particular territory.[68]

---

[67] Levels of ostentatious expenditure rose considerably after Rome's conquest of the eastern Mediterranean (see Pliny, *Natural History* 33 passim, but especially 138ff.). On sumptuary laws, see for example, Aulus Gellius, *Attic Nights* 2.24 and I. Sauerwein, *Die Leges Sumptuariae* (Diss. Hamburg, 1970).

[68] Of course, Roman aristocrats had local political connections and clients. In 83 BC, Pompey recruited troops in Picenum 'because of his father's reputation there' (Appian, *Civil Wars* 1.80), but his support there melted away in the civil war against Julius Caesar in 49 BC. See also Caesar, *Civil Wars* 1.34 and 56, and M. Gelzer, *The Roman Nobility* (Oxford, 1969) 93f. Other political connections were much more important.

Land was the main source of wealth, and wealth was a mainspring of political power. (The trouble was that the rich and poor were competing among themselves and with each other for a strictly limited resource) Conflict over the ownership of land in Italy constituted a major axis of political activity throughout the last two centuries of the Republic. The conflict was expressed, for example, in laws limiting the extent of public land which a citizen could hold, in mass confiscations of property and its redistribution to soldiers and other citizens, and in the induced migration of citizens away from their homes to distant and less populated parts of Italy. As we have seen, the changing pattern of land-ownership led to the mass importation of slaves and to the emigration of the free poor from the land to the army and to the city of Rome. The resulting evolution of a professional army (or perhaps more accurately, a core of long-service soldiers) and of an urban proletariat upset the traditional balance of power and contributed to the chaos of the last decades of the Republic. The solution to the conflict over land is interesting: the emigration of several hundred thousand citizens to the provinces, organised by Julius Caesar and Augustus, relieved the pressure of the poor on Italian land; complementarily, the advent of peace and the integration of the empire under the stable administration of the emperors enabled the Italian rich increasingly to own land in, and transfer rents from the provinces (see note 65).

As usual, the evidence for many of these assertions is both fragmentary and disputed. But the main outlines seem clear enough. For example, we have no detailed information on senators' or knights' incomes, on the relative importance of agricultural and urban rents, of income from loans or tax-farming, commerce and manufacture. But it is revealing that ancient authors simply assumed that rich men were land-owners, that land was their prime source of wealth. Cicero for example, in a philosophical discussion of the very rich and the comfortably rich man noted that 'he takes 600,000 HS from his farms, I take 100,000 HS from mine' (*Paradoxes of the Stoics* 49). The minimum census qualification for senators and knights (1 million and 400,000 HS respectively) was expressed in value of property, mostly landed property, and not in terms of income. Julius Caesar's and the emperor Tiberius' laws on debt presupposed that large-scale debtors had given land as security, and seem to have required creditors to invest two thirds of rapid loans in Italian land. Two common words for wealthy (*locuples, possessor*) both imply the ownership of land.[69] Even the poli-

---

[69] On laws of debt, see Tacitus, *Annals* 6.17; Suetonius, *Tiberius* 48; and Frederiksen (1966) 134ff. The word *possessor* originally, and apparently still in the time of Cicero, referred to someone who held public land without full title (on this see C. Nicolet,

tically powerful minority of knights who specialised in tax-farming probably operated from a basis of land-owning. This is implied by the fact that they were required to give land as security for the performance of their contracts (see note 58). It follows *a fortiori* that lesser knights, locally powerful in their Italian home towns, were primarily land-owners; indeed Cicero referred to them several times collectively as farmers, countrymen (*agricolae, rusticani*).[70] Besides, it seems obvious that in a predominantly agrarian society, without a sophisticated administrative superstructure, land would be the major source of wealth. Even if a man made a lot of money in some other way, he would achieve both high status and security by investing it in land (Cicero, *On Duties* 1.151).

The prevalence of land-owning among the Roman rich did not mean that senators and knights got their income only from land. Land-ownership was compatible with the pursuit of other financial interests. In the modern world, the specialisation of occupations tempts us to think of land-owners, bankers, financiers, tax-officials and businessmen as different people. In Rome, they were often the same people. It was common for large land-owners, for example, not to rent out all their land to free tenants, but to exploit some of it directly. Typically, a slave manager (*vilicus*) was put in charge of the day-to-day running of a rich man's farm. But it seems probable that many rich men, even nobles, took a direct and lively interest in the sale of surplus produce from their estates, though explicit evidence on this is scarce.[71] Similarly it seems probable that many rich men, even nobles, set up their slaves and ex-slaves in business, providing them with

L'ordre équestre à l'époque républicaine (Paris, 1966) 301). On *locuples*, see Cicero, *de republica* 2.16; Aulus Gellius, *Attic Nights* 10.5. The prevalence of land in the estates of the rich persisted. The emperor Trajan ordered senators to have one third of their fortunes in Italian land; Olympiodorus (frag. 44) tells us that in the fourth century wealthy senators got one quarter of their incomes in the form of farm produce, the rest from rents.

[70] By a swing in intellectual fashion this view of the knights has become widely accepted: the pioneering essays were: P. A. Brunt, 'The Equites in the Late Republic', *Second International Conference of Economic History 1962* (Paris, 1965) vol. 1, especially 122ff. and Nicolet (1966: 285ff.); see also Meier (1966: 64ff.). The previous view that knights were primarily a class of businessmen was over-modernising.

[71] Nobility does not preclude concern with money; see the very interesting study of the fortunes of English aristocrats by L. Stone, *Family and Fortune* (Oxford, 1973). We have no such information about Roman nobles; some like Cato, Varro and Pliny obviously cared about their estates. Epictetus (*Discourses* 1.10) says that the conversation of non-philosophers presumably in court circles turned on accounts, land prices and wheat prices. Senators' names survive on wine-jars and bricks, presumably made on their estates (*ESAR* vol. 1, 355 and 5, 208–9); such labels are indices of involvement but not of close care. In brief, we don't know how much the predominant culture induced aristocrats typically to care for or ignore their sources of income.

capital and in one way or another taking a share of their profits. This is one factor which would help to account for the dominance of ex-slaves in the commercial life of Rome and other Italian cities (see Chapter 11). But it is only a conjecture; we have no testimony on how closely, or whether slave-owners supervised such business activities.

The involvement of senators in trade or commerce of any sort has often been denied, and in support of this view much is usually made of a law passed in 218 BC forbidding senators the right to own large ships. They were allowed to own small ships, of under seven tonnes burden 'enough to carry crops from the farms. All profitmaking was thought demeaning for senators' (Livy 21.63). But we know that by 70 BC this law was a dead letter, and that by then senators were deeply involved in loan finance, either directly or through agents. The young noble Brutus, for example, lent money to a town in Cyprus at four per cent monthly compound interest and got the senate to pass a special decree exempting his loan from normal regulations limiting interest rates. M. Crassus had quite openly built up his fortune partly by speculation in metropolitan property.[72]

Ideally, nobles were not expected to be interested in profit-making; we find similar ideals in other pre-industrial 'high cultures'. But the ideal was both honoured and violated; indeed many ideals exist because they are generally not achieved. Ironically, Cicero approved of trade, provided it was on a large scale; only small scale trade seemed demeaning to him (*On Duties* 1.151). Probably attitudes had changed in the course of Rome's expansion. Senators could be barred from profit-making by law in 218 BC because it was relatively unimportant. When banking, loan-financing and commerce grew in importance, I suspect that senators participated, even in violation of traditional values.

But commerce and finance were only the cream on the cake, not the cake itself. We have no Roman figures, but estimates from England in 1801 are suggestive. The average income of the top two thousand merchants and bankers was only 2,600 pounds sterling per year, compared with 8,000 pounds sterling per year for the top group of landowners, and 3,000 pounds sterling per year for the upper gentry.[73] By that time England was much more industrialised and commercially

---

[72] Plutarch, *Crassus* 2; on Brutus, see nn. 55 and 56 above; Cicero (*Verrines* 5.45) said that the law on ship-owning by senators was ineffectual, but it survived in a law of Julius Caesar – see the Leiden fragment of Paul's *Sententiae* (edd. G. G. Archi et al. Leiden, 1956).

[73] G. Mingay, *English Landed Society in the Eighteenth Century* (London, 1963) 21 (cf. 26). The number of land-owners discussed was smaller (400+750), but their aggregate wealth was greater than the merchants' and bankers'.

sophisticated than Rome ever became. The ratio of agrarian to non-agrarian incomes in Rome, even in the exceptional conditions of the Republic, was almost certainly higher. The high status of large land-owners was enhanced by their huge wealth (*nihil dulcius agricultura*).

Even if Roman land-owners had wanted to invest in business, they faced one difficulty which constituted a serious obstacle to economic growth. The Romans never evolved a legal form for commercial or manufacturing enterprises similar to our joint stock company, which had the advantage of limiting investors' liability, and of preserving the business as a unit beyond the death of its owner. It was only in the spheres of tax-farming and mining that the Romans devised a corporation (*societas*). The right to collect taxes in each province was auctioned every five years; the sums and the risk involved went beyond the scope of individual fortunes. To solve this, tax-farming corporations were set up which took in investments and guarantees from numerous individuals. Each corporation existed as a juridical entity, but was much more liable to dissolution than modern corporations. Indeed the death or withdrawal of the president (*manceps*) was apparently sufficient in some circumstances to necessitate dissolution.[74] Investment in tax-farming thus depended on success in periodic auctions, and might be intermittent as well as short-term. Perhaps the system worked, only because Roman tax-farmers, as we have seen, worked from the more stable base of land-owning.

The organisation and aggregated capital of tax-farmers were never applied to trade and manufacture; they remained very fragmented, dominated by small, single-family businesses. The largest had slave-workers, but typically employed far fewer men than large agricultural estates (*latifundia*);[75] besides, there was in trade and industry no equivalent overlord institution such as tenancy, which allowed the large-scale, coordinated exploitation of the poor by a single rich man. Perhaps a few fortunes may have been made in trade, but not many and not large fortunes. Traders, unlike tax-farmers, did not constitute a group which [?] Q. Cicero thought worth courting in elections; while in much later times, the fortunes of prosperous merchants in the

---

[74] Cf. Badian (1972: 67–81); G. Urögdi, *sv Publicani* in *RE*, Suppl. XI, col. 1184ff.
[75] I think the largest factory we know of in the ancient world was in Athens in the fourth century BC – a shield-factory with nearly 120 men (Lysias 12.19). By contrast, Pliny's estate in Umbria, would have employed several hundred men, in different tenancies. The important texts are Pliny, *Letters* 10.8; 3.19; Columella, *On Agriculture* 2.12. For a detailed discussion, see R. P. Duncan-Jones, *The Economy of the Roman Empire* (Cambridge, 1974) 19–20, 48–9; I agree broadly with his conclusions, but his calculations depend too much on fixed assumptions.

empire's chief trading city, Alexandria, were perhaps only a fraction of those of large land-owners.[76]

It was the shortage of alternative investments and the high status of land-owning which above all induced men to invest capital in land. Among senators there was an additional pressure. The opportunity to profit hugely from empire occurred infrequently. Many senators had only one or two chances in a life-time to hold government posts in the provinces, and that in a junior capacity (as *quaestor* or as governor's aide – *legatus*). A more favoured group, which varied from two to three fifths of those who entered the senate, were elected to the office of *praetor* and so became eligible for appointment as provincial governor. In theory, each official had the opportunity to govern a province for one year, since the Romans for long periods kept a balance between the number of provinces and the number of senior elected officials (praetors and consuls).[77] In fact, there were often lags and shortages, especially at the very end of the Republic, so that some officials like Verres or Cicero's brother, for example, governed a province for three years, while others, although eligible, never governed a province at all. We show in Chapter 1 of Volume Two of this work that only an extremely small number of leading families secured access to high office for one of their sons in each generation; for example, only four per cent of consuls 249–50 BC (N = 364) came from families with consuls in six successive generations; complementarily, over a quarter of the consuls came from families with only one consul in two centuries. The bulk of senators, therefore, could not be sure that either they or their sons would have another opportunity to make money out of high office. The senators who were successful therefore felt constrained to make their pile and invest it in land. It might have to support the family for generations.

We have no exact evidence on the increased size of rich men's land-holdings. Pliny's famous remark that 'large estates ruined Italy' (*Natural History* 18.35) is as much moral judgement as fact, dates from the mid-first century AD, and may mark the culmination of a long process. Acquisition and aggregation of estates had probably been going on for centuries, as the central Roman elite strengthened its hold over the territories of Italian towns and tribes, when they became politically assimilated to Rome. We have only very general indications

---

[76] [?Q.] Cicero, *Guide to Electioneering* (*Comm. Pet.*). On Alexandrian trade, see Jones (1964: 870–1); the evidence which Jones cites comes mostly from the sixth century AD; it is the only such evidence we have, and his conclusions are often referred to. Unfortunately, the testimony cited hardly authenticates Jones' conclusion. Nevertheless he may well be right. See also Jones (1974: 35ff.).

[77] F. B. Marsh, *The Founding of the Roman Empire* (Oxford, 1927), 2ff.

from the late Republic; but we can risk some estimates. First, if the modern conventional estimates of the number of slaves in Italy are anywhere near right, then by the mid-first century BC there must have ben over a million agricultural slaves in Italy. The slave rebellions in Sicily and Italy (135, 104 and 73 BC), each of which attracted tens of thousands of rebel slaves, corroborate this view. Secondly, the writers on agriculture whose works survive: Cato, Varro and Columella, all assumed that slaves would form the main work force on their own and their readers' estates. Cato described two farms as examples, one with thirteen, the other with fifteen slaves (Varro, *On Agriculture* 1.18). Either figure implies slave-farms several times larger than a single-family peasant farm.

Thirdly, the development of a specialist literature on agriculture is itself an indication of an increase in entrepreneurial, or even 'capitalistic' agriculture. Its beginnings apparently date back to the official translation of a Carthaginian treatise, commissioned by the senate shortly after Rome's victory over Carthage (202 BC). Cato, Varro and Columella are only the surviving tip of a vanished iceberg; we know only isolated facts about other writers on agriculture; Cicero, for example, translated Xenophon's treatise *Economicus, A Discussion on Estate Management* into Latin. There is a marked development in sophistication from Cato through Varro to Columella, and it is tempting to think that this was a reflection of a general advance in knowledge. That said, a brief reading of early nineteenth-century English agriculture handbooks shows how backward Roman agricultural writers were, especially in their capacity to determine the relative profitability of crops.[78]

Finally, if Roman nobles' and knights' incomes came in large measure from rents, or from the direct exploitation of land, then the areas of good land which a rich man controlled must have been large. Figures are difficult to arrive at, and depend on several debatable assumptions; besides, there must have been very considerable differences according to the fertility and location of the farm, the type of crop, to say nothing of annual fluctuations in the size of the harvest and in price. In spite of all these difficulties, a single example may be suggestive. If, on average, Roman senators got only 60,000 HS a year from agricultural rents (this is low; it was only ten per cent of Cicero's very rich man's income), and if rents equalled thirty per cent of the

[78] For ancient agricultural writers, the most recent and very full discussion is by White (1970). It is in my view often apologistic and so should be read with some scepticism. Examples of eighteenth- and nineteenth-century English agricultural writings can be found in A. Young's periodical, *Annals of Agriculture* 1784–1815.

gross crop (which is high), then at a conventional price for wheat, it works out that 600 senators together owned land sufficient to maintain 200,000 peasant families (i.e. 800,000 men, women and children) at the level of minimum subsistence. This was a fifth, at least, of Italy's free peasant population.[79] One can play around with such figures, but they serve to give rough orders of magnitude. Whether doubled or halved, they show beyond reasonable doubt that the increased landed wealth of the senate (to say nothing to the *equites*) was bought at the cost of a huge displacement of peasants.

LAND IN POLITICS

The creation of large estates in Italy commensurate with the wealth, power and ostentation of the Roman elite, 'conquerors of the world', required the mass extrusion of Italian peasants from their land. We need to examine the process of their dispossession and its political consequences. For a long time the evacuation was kept within orderly channels: the poor sold out and emigrated to colonies established by the state in Italy or went by themselves to the city of Rome. Wars were one of the prime agents of change; as we have seen, they kept on average 130,000 Italian soldiers off the land. But that was not all. Hannibal's invasion of Italy had sent thousands of peasants scurrying for the protective walls of Rome. Their farms and cattle were destroyed. When Hannibal had retreated, the consuls were instructed by the senate to help reluctant peasants back to their deserted farms (Livy 28.11). Two years after the war was over, in 200 BC, a lot of Italian land was up for sale (Livy 31.13, cf. 25.36); men of high social standing, who in time of crisis had lent money to the state, demanded that their loans be repaid so that they could take advantage of the market. The government was unable to pay in cash because it was financing other wars; instead it gave its creditors large tracts of state land at peppercorn rents. The civil wars and judicial confiscations of the first century BC gave similar opportunities for the surviving rich to accumulate large estates.[80]

[79] The values used here are: prices of wheat 3 HS per *modius* of 6.5 kg; yield 5 times seed; a minimum subsistence for an average family of four persons of 1,000 kg wheat equivalent per year. So [600 (senators)×60,000 HS (income)/3 (HS price per modius wheat)]×[100/30 (gross product as a proportion of rent)×6.5/1,250 (kg per *modius*/ gross family consumption in kg wheat equivalent = 1,000 kg net of seed)] = 208,000 families who could live off aristocrats' land as discussed. If you do not agree with these values, please consider the implication of changing each of them up or down; for example, if the normal price of wheat was less than 3 HS per *modius*, then the area of land occupied by the rich was larger.

[80] See conveniently Brunt (1971: 300–4, 327–8) for discussion and references.

Land in politics

The upsets of war can also be traced to the programme of colonisation organised by the Roman senate between 194 and 177 BC. In this period, the population of central Italy was diminished by about 100,000 men, women and children. They were resettled in over twenty colonies, predominantly in the extreme south and in northern Italy. The large numbers and the very small plots of land which most of them apparently received are evidence in themselves of considerable impoverishment.[81] Peasants were unlikely to walk three hundred or more kilometres from their ancestral homes in central Italy, carrying with them all that they possessed, into new and often hostile territory, unless they were pushed hard – especially when for many of them the prize was less than four hectares (ten acres) of land; to add insult to injury the settlers sometimes forfeited their full Roman citizenship – though they received extra land in compensation.

Other peasants migrated to the towns, above all to the city of Rome. Once again we have only fragments of information to be pieced together. (In 187 BC, and again in 177 BC, the Latin allies together 'complained to the senate that a large number of their citizens had migrated to Rome and had been assessed there' (Livy 39.3). If this went on, they said, their towns and farms would be deserted. Already they found it difficult to meet their obligations to provide soldiers (Livy 41.8). On each occasion the senate directed an official to flush out recent immigrants of Latin origin; we are told that on the first occasion twelve thousand Latin men were instructed to go back home; with their

---

[81] This calculation is based on the assumption that colonies of known size were typical of those of unknown size.

	Total adult males
13 maritime colonies (size of 5 known; 300 settlers each)	3,900
4 citizen colonies (size of 3 known; 2,000 settlers each)	8,000
5 Latin colonies (size of 5 known)	19,600
	31,500

I assume that adult males contributed $c.$ 30% to the total population. There were probably no more colonies founded until 128 BC (Auximum), though there was an allotment of public land to individuals in 173 BC. We do not know why this fifty-year gap occurred.

The size of land allotments is known in 11/22 colonies. In the maritime colonies, citizens apparently received 5–6 iugera (1.25–1.5 ha; n = 3/13); more in other citizen colonies (5, 8, 10, 51½ iugera); and much more in Latin colonies (15, 20, 50, 50 iugera; n = 4/5) as though in compensation for loss of citizenship. Citizens got 10 iugera in individual allotments in 173 BC. Cavalrymen and centurions received more. It seems likely that colonists supplemented their living on small allotments by working the land of rich settlers who occupied public land; how else would they have got the working capital to move, why else would rich Romans have helped move them? Colonies thus recreated the social situation in central Italy – this idea is also put forward by Brunt (1971: 194). For details of colonies, see *ESAR* vol. 1, 122–3.

57

dependants they constituted a sizeable body. New regulations restricting immigration were passed, but were evaded by a legal fiddle, and it is doubtful if migration to the city of Rome was ever stopped by simple administrative decree. Another indication of the growth in the city's population can be found in the attempts made to increase the water-supply. Money was allocated for a large new aqueduct in 179 BC, but the plans were blocked by an aristocrat through whose lands it had to pass (Livy 39.41); it was completed eventually in 143 BC; yet another aqueduct, Rome's fourth, was built in 125 BC. Some of the city's extra population were slaves and their offspring. Many of the rest were Italian peasants pushed out by the large land-owners and by the demands of military service and pulled in by the huge sums of money being spent in the city. As a result some areas of the Italian countryside were denuded of free peasants. In 180 BC, for example, 40,000 defeated northern tribesmen (Ligurians; the figure includes wives and children) were resettled in the central Italian highlands (Livy 30.38). It was a good idea; the settlement survived for at least three centuries.[82] But it was a palliative not a cure for peasant emigration.

To a contemporary Roman noble, the changes must have seemed so fragmented and varied in their contexts that they hardly constituted a single process at all: he had more money and acquired more land; a few poor farmers were bought out or evicted; more shacks could be seen along the road into Rome, perhaps more beggars were at his door; some more slaves entered his household; too many Greek philosphers and new morals in Rome – a bewildering variety of events, the concern of no one in particular to cope with or to prevent. When migration caused difficulties by upsetting existing arrangements (as it did by reducing the allies' capacity to produce troops), then the authorities did what they could. They forbad immigration. There was little more that they could do.

With the wisdom of hindsight, Roman historians later saw the cumulative impact of evicting small-holders.

Whenever the Romans annexed land from their neighbours as a result of their wars, it was their custom to put a part up for sale by auction: the rest was made common land and was distributed among the poorest and most needy citizens, who were allowed to cultivate it on payment of a small rent to the public treasury. When the rich began to outbid and drive out the poor by offering higher rentals, a law was passed which forbade any one individual to hold more than 500 *iugera* [125 ha] of [state] land. For a while this law restrained the greed of the rich and helped the poor, who were enabled to

[82] See the Ligures Baebiani (*CIL* 9.1455 of AD 101), named after Baebius one of the consuls who settled them there. On the aqueducts, see T. Ashby, *The Aqueducts of Ancient Rome* (repr. Washington, DC, 1973).

remain on the land which they had rented, so that each of them could occupy the allotment which he had originally been granted. But after a time the rich men in each neighbourhood by using the names of fictitious tenants, contrived to transfer many of these holdings to themselves, and finally they openly took possession of the greater part of the land under their own names. The poor, when they found themselves forced off the land, became more and more unwilling to volunteer for military service or even to raise a family. The result was a rapid decline of the class of free small-holders all over Italy, their place being taken by gangs of foreign slaves, whom the rich employed to cultivate the estates from which they had driven off the free citizens. (Plutarch, *Life of Tiberius Gracchus* 8; translated by I. Scott-Kilvert, Penguin Books).

In 133 BC, the concentration of land in the hands of the rich erupted as a major political issue. Almost inevitably it has ben presented as a conflict between rich and poor, between great land-owners and the landless. Like important political issues in other societies, it was inter-shot with private ambitions, ideologies and other political problems; nevertheless, it seems reasonable to think that the redistribution of land was the crucial issue. The events of that year are especially important because they epitomise and herald the next century of internal strife. In particular, Gracchus' land law was one of twenty attempts made in the course of the next hundred years to solve the agrarian problem by law and by the redistribution of land to the poor.[83] But before we discuss the attempted reforms of Tiberius Gracchus, I want to outline three structural features which determined the shape of the conflict.

First, even though the aristocrats in the senate dominated Roman political decision-making, large sections of the plebs retained considerable power: the popular assemblies were courted by and chose between aristocrats in the election of the highest officials, and they had the formal power to pass laws. The idea that the senate and the Roman people (SPQR is still stamped on drains in Rome) were partners in government was to a large extent myth, but a myth with life still in it.

Secondly, the tribunes of the people, as the name of their office implies, were ostensibly obliged to protect the specific interests of the people. To be sure, they did not always fulfil this obligation; most must have been content to abide by the *status quo*. Indeed, the tribunes were usually aristocrats intent on making their way in a senatorial career. Yet in spite of the demands of their careers, tribunes of the people repeatedly cast themselves as thorns in the flesh of senatorial con-

[83] 19 agrarian laws are listed in *RE sv Leges agrariae*, dated 133–44 BC; the list is not necessarily complete. There were three such laws in the previous century. The discussion of these laws by Brunt (1971) is excellent.

servatism. The events of 133 BC merely confirmed a long tradition. In history, it had been tribunes of the people who had proposed agrarian reform or the restriction of senatorial privilege. And in the recent past, in 151 and 138 BC, tribunes had even imprisoned the consuls in protest against the injustices of the military levy.[84]

The popular assemblies and the tribunate provided legitimate and established channels for the expression of conflict. Some Roman leaders thought that their suppression would eradicate the conflict; the tribunate was curbed temporarily by Sulla, and popular assemblies were in effect controlled subsequently by the triumvirs. As a result, the lines of conflict became more explicitly drawn elsewhere; political issues were decided instead by generals and their armies.

Thirdly, we must consider public or state land (*ager publicus populi Romani*). This legal category of land had been very important as a cover under which large private estates were formed. State land consisted of land which the Roman state had taken over from Italian communities (usually one third of their territory) when they were first conquered, plus other lands confiscated by the Roman state; for example, Roman allies who sided with Hannibal during his invasion of Italy were punished by having their land confiscated. Some of the land was given to colonists, or sold, or leased; but the greater part, according to the second-century historian Appian, was not allocated. Anyone could occupy it (it was called *ager occupatorius*) on payment of a rent to the state, although this occupation gave no legal security of tenure.

It was the rich who took most of this unallocated land. In time, they became confident that they would not be dispossessed. They acquired the lands nearby, including the plots of the poor, sometimes by purchase with persuasion, sometimes by force so that in the end they cultivated large estates not farms ...(Appian, *Civil Wars* 1.7)

There is evidence that obligingly the rents, normally a tenth of the crop on arable land, were often not collected, and the laws which restricted how much state land a man could hold were evaded with impunity.[85] Land which had been conquered by the Roman people and which was nominally exploited for its collective benefit cast a thin veneer, as often before and since, over the disproportionate profit of the rich.

[84] Livy, *Summaries of Books* 48 and 55, and see J. Bleicken, *Das Volkstribunat der Klassischen Republik* (Munich², 1968).

[85] See the commentary on Appian, *Civil Wars* 1.7 by E. Gabba (Florence, 1958); Livy 42.1 and 19; Cato's speech in 167 BC (*ORF*³ 167), which implies that men held more than 500 *iugera* of state land with impunity.

The political power and privileges of land-owners were so deep-rooted that no one at this stage suggested a general redistribution of land which belonged in full title by 'right of perpetual possession' (Cicero, *On Behalf of Milo* 78) to private Roman citizens. Such a suggestion would have united the opposition. But the status of state land, with its connotation of being a collective good (*ager publicus populi Romani*), in technical terms held 'precariously', occupied not owned, was ambiguous, and provided sufficient leverage to make its redistribution legitimate.

With these factors in mind let us turn to the events of 133 BC. Tiberius Gracchus was born into a noble family, the son of a man who had twice been consul and censor. As a young official, he served with the army in Spain and helped negotiate peace terms after a Roman army had been defeated there, terms which the senate subsequently repudiated. In his travels through Italy, Gracchus had been struck by the extent of estates cultivated by slaves and by the decline of the free peasantry. The slave rebellion which broke out in Sicily in 135 BC must have reinforced his views. On his return to Rome, he was elected tribune of the people and proposed that state land be redistributed to the poor. One effect of this would have been to increase the number of property-holders liable to serve in the army. A similar proposal had been put forward a few years earlier by Laelius, but had been dropped because of the opposition which it aroused. Needless to say, the rich were opposed to Gracchus' proposals also. To describe Gracchus' campaign for his law, I cannot do better than quote the account by Plutarch, written in the second century AD, but drawn from much earlier sources.[86]

Tiberius [Gracchus]...went straight to the root of the matter as soon as he had been elected tribune. He was encouraged in his plans, as most writers report, by Diophanes the orator and Blossius the philosopher...Some writers consider that Cornelia was at least partly to blame for Tiberius' death, since she often reproached her sons with the fact that the Romans still referred to her as the mother-in-law of Scipio, but not yet as the mother of the Gracchi. Others maintain that Tiberius was also influenced by his jealousy of a certain Spurius Postumius. This man was of the same age as Tiberius and a close rival as a public speaker. So when Tiberius returned from the campaign against Numantia and found that his adversary had far outdistanced him in fame and influence and had attracted general admiration, it seems likely that he resolved

---

[86] The literature on the Gracchi is mammoth. I have followed Astin (1967: 161ff.); and see D. C. Earl, *Tiberius Gracchus* (Brussels, 1963), J. Carcopino, *Autour des Gracques* (Paris², 1967), and especially E. Badian, 'Tiberius Gracchus and the beginning of the Roman Revolution', in H. Temporini ed., *Aufstieg und Niedergang der römischen Welt* (Berlin, 1972) vol. 1.1, 668–731.

to outdo him by introducing a challenging political programme, which would arouse great expectations among the people. However, his brother Gaius has written in a political pamphlet that while Tiberius was travelling through Etruria on his way to Numantia, he saw for himself how the country had been deserted by its native inhabitants, and how those who tilled the soil or tended the flocks were barbarian slaves introduced from abroad; and that it was this experience which inspired the policy that later brought so many misfortunes upon the two brothers. But it was above all the people themselves who did most to arouse Tiberius' energy and ambitions by inscribing slogans and appeals on porticoes, monuments and the walls of houses, calling upon him to recover the public land for the poor.

He did not, however, draft his law by himself, but consulted a number of the most eminent and respected citizens . . . And certainly many will agree that no law directed against injustice and avarice was ever framed in milder or more conciliatory terms. For the men who deserved to be punished for breaking the law, and who should have been fined as well as obliged to surrender the land which they had been illegally enjoying, were merely required to give up their unjust acquisitions – for which they were compensated – and to allow the ownership to pass to those citizens who most needed the land. But even though this act of restitution showed such tenderness for the wrongdoers, the people were content to forget the past so long as they could be assured of protection against injustice in the future. The wealthy classes and landowners on the other hand, were bitterly opposed to these proceedings: they hated the law out of sheer greed, and its originator out of personal resentment and party prejudice, and they did their utmost to turn the people against the reform by alleging that Tiberius' object in introducing a redistribution of land was really to undermine the foundations of the state and stir up a general revolution.

However, these tactics achieved nothing. Tiberius was fighting for a measure which was honourable and just in itself, and he was able to summon up an eloquence which would have done credit to a far less worthy cause. The result was that whenever he mounted the rostra to plead the case of the poor with the people crowding around him to listen, the effect of his words was overwhelming and no other orator could stand against him.

'The wild beasts that roam over Italy', he would tell his listeners, 'have their dens and holes to lurk in, but the men who fight and die for our country enjoy the common air and light and nothing else. It is their lot to wander with their wives and children, houseless and homeless, over the face of the earth. And when our generals appeal to their soldiers before a battle to defend their ancestors' tombs and their temples against the enemy, their words are a mockery and a lie, for not a man in the audience possesses a family altar; not one out of all those Romans owns an ancestral tomb. The truth is that they fight and die to protect the wealth and luxury of others. They are called the masters of the world, but they do not possess a single clod of earth which is truly their own.'

To such oratory as this, the utterance of a noble spirit, delivered with a genuine passion to a people profoundly moved and fully aroused to the speaker's support, none of Tiberius' adversaries could make an effective reply. (Plutarch, *Life of Tiberius Gracchus*, 8–10; trans. I. Scott-Kilvert, Penguin)

Land in politics

The conflict gradually escalated. In defiance of convention, without consulting the senate, Gracchus put his proposals directly to a vote of the people; a fellow tribune used his veto to block the proceedings. Then Gracchus, again by popular vote, had him set aside – an action which was unprecedented and possibly unconstitutional. But the new urban proletariat and the peasants living near Rome and a minority of nobles supported him. The land law was passed; the ancient law limiting holdings of state land to 500 *iugera* (125 ha) was reaffirmed. A land commission was set up to survey the state land and allocate the surplus to the poor. A few of their land-markers (*cippi*) still survive. The new small-holders then needed money to stock their farms, but traditionally only the senate authorised expenditure; Gracchus invaded the senate's preserve by proposing a law to the people by which extra revenues from Asia Minor would be diverted for distribution to the new farmers and more generally to the poor remaining in the city (Livy, *Summary of Book* 58).[87] One can imagine the outrage of conservative senators; the use of public money for a hand-out to the plebs was revolutionary: all the more so because the political prestige of being the benefactor of the people would accrue to Tiberius Gracchus. But the final straw was Gracchus' attempt to stay in office by seeking re-election, once again in violation of tradition. On the day of the elections, a posse of vigilante senators led by the chief priest (*pontifex maximus*), himself the occupant of large tracts of state land, openly assassinated Tiberius Gracchus and four hundred of his immediate followers.

The whirlwind political career of Tiberius Gracchus lasted less than a year. Yet it is important, partly because it was the precursor of further civil conflicts and partly because it illustrates the intersection of political conflict with nearly all the factors of social and economic change which we have been discussing: the increasing wealth of land-owners, the emigration of poor peasants, the growth of slavery, the shortage of recruits for the army, the power of the senate, the rise of the urban plebs, the competition between nobles and the use of imperial revenues as a weapon of political conflict.

In the short run, paradoxically, both Gracchus and his assassins were successful. The assassins restored the supremacy of the senate and secured peace by further judicial executions. On the other hand, in spite of Gracchus' death, the land commission persisted in its work and apparently succeeded in distributing land to several thousand citizens. Gracchus was more effective dead than alive. However, in 129 BC, representatives of the Italian allies objected strongly to the distribution

---

[87] Some of what is recorded in ancient histories may not have happened; but in politics, rumours and beliefs about what is happening are often very important.

of state land located within their territory, and their opposition was enough when combined with powerful patronage at Rome to hamstring the commission's activities.[88] In 128 BC, as though by compensation, a new colony was established in Italy, the first for fifty years; three or four more followed soon afterwards, two of them at the instigation of Tiberius Gracchus' brother Gaius, who was tribune of the people in 123 BC.[89] After all, colonies in distant territories served the same function for the poor as land-allotments, only the land was not taken from the rich. Gaius Gracchus also had the restrictions previously placed on the land commission removed, but even so it seems not have achieved much; it was abolished probably in 119 BC, as part of the backlash which followed Gaius' assassination.

Throughout, one basic problem remained untouched. The new small-holders who had received land from the state either individually or as colonists, were liable to suffer from the very same pressures which had previously driven them or their fathers off the land. Tiberius Gracchus had foreseen this problem and tried to legislate against it; under his law, the new land-holders were forbidden to sell their land; I doubt that the law was effectively enforced; in any case its provisions were formally abandoned, probably in 121 BC. After all the fuss, what had the Gracchi achieved?

In the long run, seen, that is, in the context of the events of the next century, both land laws and violent repression failed to deal adequately with the social consequences of empire. They can best be understood as vain attempts to battle against the general trend. It is only long afterwards when we have seen the same or similar violent conflicts recurring that we feel encouraged to think of broad socio-economic changes. Such overviews are the privilege of historians. Contemporary actors have more on their minds, both to enrich and to cloud their views. Our sources record some, but only some of their perceptions and actions.

THE SOLUTION – MASS MIGRATION

Conventionally, modern historians of the ancient world have tried to reconstruct from their partial record each successive crisis, looked at

[88] The census return for 125/4 BC perhaps recorded 76,000 more citizens than that of 131/0 BC. Interpretations vary, but it seems likely that the distributions of land by the Gracchan commissioners was partly responsible for the rise; see Brunt (1971: 77ff.).

[89] I follow Salmon (1970: 110) in dating Auximum to 128; there might have been more colonies founded but for the fact that they became a central political issue. A rival tribune to Gaius Gracchus upstaged him by proposing the foundation of twelve colonies for the poorest citizens, apparently without having the slightest intention of executing his proposals once they were confirmed.

in its own context. The heroes and villains of this reconstructed world are the society's leaders, 'men who shaped history': the Gracchi, Marius, Sulla, Pompey, Julius Caesar, Augustus; the main subject matter of such history is the factional rivalries of aristocratic cliques; in other words, the world as Roman notables and historians saw it. Modern historians have made it their job largely to understand these leaders' motives and intentions, their behaviour and its consequences and to describe each of them, one after the other. I do not mean by this that ancient history has consisted mostly of biography or annalistic history, but rather that elite individuals loom large in ancient and modern history books of Rome, and that these history books are organised primarily by time, not by topic or problem. Conventional ancient history is thus very different in flavour from contemporary post-mediaeval history. At best, it recaptures the authentic feeling of what it was like to have lived in the ancient world. At worst, it is only descriptive and scholastic; minor persons are given a spurious importance, either by the elitist prejudice of the sources or by the mere accident that a mention of them has survived. The evidence is often so thin that motives, the stuff of biography, can be deduced only from behaviour – a speculative process to say the least. Above all, modern historians of the ancient world tied to testimony, systematically neglect those factors or processes of which the ancient actors and the sources were unaware.

Instead of embarking on yet another detailed account of the recurrent disputes over land during the late Republic, I want to concentrate on one aspect which seems especially important. I want to generalise about what I shall rather clumsily call the structure of the situation. This implies that we can plausibly subsume a whole series of events, such as the twenty land laws spread over a century, as symptoms of a single problem. This act of generalisation has further serious implications. It implies that the actions of individual legislators were moulded not only by immediate considerations but also by long-run factors of which they were not necessarily aware; it follows that the validity of the generalisation cannot depend on whether contemporaries perceived it; it cannot be validated, though it may be corroborated by citing a passage from Cicero. Its acceptability must depend instead on its internal coherence, its economy, its fit with the known facts and with some implicit, covering laws. But enough of theory.

In the Roman economy, because it was relatively simple, land was the chief source of livelihood and the predominant form of distributable wealth. Peasants, soldiers, tax-farmers and aristocrats wanted land and more land. Preferably they wanted land in Italy. The conquest of an empire gave important groups within the society control over unprecedentedly large resources. Competition for a finite quantity of land increased, and decisions about the control over land repeatedly became an important political issue; the settlement of Sulla's veterans, for example, the abortive land bill of Rullus in 63 BC, and the difficulty of securing land for Pompey's veterans come readily to mind. The twenty land laws, proposed or passed; the confiscations of land from rich and poor; its redistribution to the landless, to ex-soldiers and to the noble followers of successful war chiefs or to wealthy opportunists, as well as the private acquisition of land by the rich can all be seen as variations on the theme: who was to get what out of the profits of empire? The bitter competition for a limited good fuelled the political conflicts of the late Republic; I do not mean by this that competition for land was the sole cause of conflict.

The solvent was civil war, which involved the recruitment of huge armies, separated half a million Italian peasants between 49 and 28 BC from the soil and made them, as it were, available for emigration.[90] The solution was the acceptance by substantial numbers of rich and poor of alternative goods; a mass of peasants, in my view, migrated to the city of Rome where they were subsidised by the state with gifts of free wheat; much larger groups were resited either on new farms in Italy or in the provinces. The rich too, first knights then senators, acquired estates outside Italy. Thus both social strata gradually accommodated their traditional ambitions to the opportunities offered in an enlarged empire.

The scale of migration by the Italian poor is amazing. Between 80 and 8 BC, in two generations, it seems that roughly half the free adult males in Italy left their farms and went to Italian towns or were settled by the state on new farms in Italy or the provinces (see Table 1.2). This statement is derived from the surviving official figures: the census under Augustus of 28 and 8 BC, the number of soldiers under arms or discharged, and the number of new colonies founded or refounded. Before I go further, I should stress four elements in my discussion: first, the numbers given provide rough orders of magnitude only; secondly, they are largely based on or derived from the careful analysis of the evidence by Brunt (1971); thirdly, they describe net migration only, that is they take no account of the several moves individuals may have made from before their final settlement (for example, from farmer to landless labourer, perhaps to town, then soldier and eventually colonist); fourth, they concentrate on state-organised migration, for which evidence survives in official records; they take almost no account of private movements, either of the men,

90 Brunt, (1971: 511).

women and children uprooted to make room for official settlements or of individual migrants, who may have become progressively more numerous, as nuclei of Italians provided a base for further migration in northern Italy and throughout the Mediterranean basin.[91] I realise that the figures are speculative, but if Brunt's basic framework is accepted, I do not see how they can be wildly wrong. They show the sheer size of the cumulative changes in the late Republic, of which our sources give us only successive glimpses.

In Table 1.2, I have summarised my derivations from the evidence and in the notes to the table I have given some reasons for the figures. The most striking change is the decline in the free rural population by 1.2 million (from 4.1 to 2.9 million; a drop of 29%). It is an enormous figure; it must hide colossal human misery; it may not be accurate, but it gives a sense of scale which is missing from our sources. Moreover, it seems likely that most of the change was concentrated in the last century BC.

Where did the rural population go? We know that wheat was distributed free of charge to 320,000 citizens in 46 BC and to 250,000 citizens in 29 BC. This evidence indicates that the city of Rome attracted large numbers of immigrants (both free and slave, since we can call slaves forced immigrants); it seems plausible that a significant part of the overall urban growth (arbitrarily I guess about half) was due to peasant immigration. The city also served as a channel for further migration; in an effort to reduce the burden of feeding the city, Julius Caesar resettled 70,000 adult male proletarians in colonies overseas (Brunt 1971: 257); it was only part of his programme of colonisation. Between 45 and 8 BC, it seems that about one hundred colonies were established overseas, with an estimated average of 2–3,000 adult male settlers each, most of them ex-soldiers. To be sure, not all the colonies received settlers from Italy, and in others, groups of Italians already settled there provided the core of the new colony. But in spite of these qualifications, over 250,000 adult males from Italy, about one fifth of all that lived there (N = c. 1.2 million), were decanted from Italy by the Roman government in a single generation.[92]

The main channel for this type of mobility as we have seen, was the army. Between 49 and 28 BC, 500,000 Italian males served in the armies

---

[91] The cautionary remarks of Brunt (1971: 159–65) are worth noting; private migration by poor peasants was difficult and hazardous and has often been thoughtlessly exaggerated. But large-scale private migration in agrarian states has sometimes occurred.

[92] Brunt (1971: Appendix 15) ascribes less than 100 provincial colonies to Caesar, the triumvirs and Augustus. F. Vittinghoff, *Römische Kolonisation und Bürgerrechtspolitik* (Wiesbaden, 1951) 148–50 gives 104 colonies.

Table 1.2. *Population changes and migration in Italy[a] 225–8 BC: some speculative figures ('000)*

	A – Population changes				
	Men, women and children		Adult males (aged 17+ years)[b]		
	225 BC	28 BC	225 BC	28 BC	gain (loss)
Free	4,500[c]	4,000	1,350	1,220	(130)
Slave	500	2,000[d]	150	600	450
Total	5,000	6,000[d]	1,500	1,820	320

	B – Rural/Urban[e] split				
Rural free	4,100	2,900[g]	1,230	870	(360)
Rural slaves	} ?500	1,200[g]	} ?150	360	} 450
Urban slaves		800		240	
Italian towns free	250[f]	500[h]	75	150	75
City of Rome free	150	600[j]	45	200[g]	155
Total	5,000	6,000	1,500	1,820	320

C – Migration from Italy overseas[k] – Adult males (aged 17+ years)			D – Decline of free rural population – Adult males (aged 17+ years)	
Before 69 BC	125		Emigrants overseas, 225–28 BC	265
69–49 BC	25			
49–28 BC	165		To Italian towns	100[n]
Sub-total	(net) 265[l] 315 (gross)		Total loss	365
28–8 BC	100[m]			

E – Growth of Italian towns and City of Rome – Adult males (aged 17+ years)

225–28 BC
Rural free to urban	100[n]
Ex-slaves to urban free	130[p]
Total gain	230

F – Rural migration within Italy[q] – Adult males (aged 17+ years)

Gracchan reforms 133–120 BC	10
Sullan veterans c. 80 BC	80
Pompey's veterans 59 BC	50
Civil wars 41–36 BC	60
Augustan settlement (1) 30–28 BC	57
Augustan settlement (2) 28–8 BC	3
Total	260

The solution – mass migration

a   This includes northern Italy (Cisalpine Gaul).

b   Adult males aged 17+ years are reckoned here as 30% of the total population. In a stationary, i.e. self-reproducing, population this implies an average life expectancy at birth of 27 years. This is probably too high. It could also be justified, but only in the short term, by a fall in the birth rate (Brunt 1971: 117); the exclusion of infants aged less than one year from the Roman census-returns would raise the proportion of adult males in the remaining population by less than one per cent. If the average expectation of life at birth was 25 years in a stationary population, adult males aged 17+ years would be roughly 26% of the total population. These calculations are based on U.N. Model Life Tables (see note 27). The number of adult males available in Rome was therefore probably less than the 35% proposed by Brunt (1971: 117).

c   I accept Brunt's (1971: 59,121) estimate of the Italian free population of Italy at 3.1 million in 225 BC, plus 1.4 million for Cisalpine Gaul.

d   See notes 13 and 14 above; the slave population here includes a full quota of men, women and children, a situation probably not achieved until later. In the first century BC, at the height of imperial expansion, the ratio of adult males among war captives and in the slave population as a whole must have been abnormally high. I suspect therefore that the figure given here is too high. The figure for adult male slaves is better.

e   Urban/rural here indicate the type of job-non-agricultural/agricultural, rather than the place of residence. Thus a peasant living in a town but working in his fields counts as rural. There were 434 towns in Italy (Beloch 1886: 442).

f   The free urban population is reckoned at 9% of the total free population. In the modern era, the city of Rome achieved a population of 150,000 again only in the seventeenth century, and was then fed primarily from local Italian sources. On size, see K. J. Beloch, *Bevölkerungsgeschichte Italiens* (Berlin, 1937) 13; on feeding Rome, see J. Delumeau, *La vie économique et sociale de Rome* (Paris, 1959) vol. 2, 521ff.

g   The rural population in 28 BC is put at 4,100,000 free and slave as against 4,100,000 plus slaves in 225 BC. But note that the cultivated area was appreciably larger in 28 BC thanks to the drainage and clearance of parts of northern Italy.

h   The total urban population in 28 BC is here arbitrarily estimated at 1.9 million including slaves, that is 32% of the population of Italy; that is very high for a pre-industrial state, though of course Rome was the capital of the empire, not just of Italy. I assume that the high consumption in Rome produced ancillary urbanisation in Italy; even so the figures here at 0.5 million free urban and 0.5 million slaves (nearly 20% of the population outside Rome) are high.

j   The number of citizens receiving free wheat under Augustus in 29 BC was 250,000 (Suetonius, *Augustus* 41) though that may include some boys aged 10+ years, and some men rurally occupied, living near Rome. That said, 200,000 is a low estimate for adult male recipients, which at 30% would imply a total free population of 670,000. To be on the safe side, I have taken a total free population for the city of Rome as 600,000, which presumably limits the probable number of slaves in Rome to about 300,000–350,000.

k   Derived from Brunt (1971: 262–4); the figure for Italian emigrants overseas before 49 BC includes Italians settled in more than a dozen colonies and other less formal settlements (such as that of the colonists at Carthage sent out in 122 BC, and of veterans in Spain); cf. Brunt (1971: 204ff.). Brunt almost completely discounts the 'mythical' record that Mithridates in 88 BC had 80,000 Italians massacred in Asia Minor; I am convinced that this number is an exaggeration; but Brunt may also have overstated his case, in his attempt to fit scattered data to the surviving census figures. At least his figures for overseas migration are cautiously low.

l   Some of the Italians abroad in 49 BC were caught up in the ensuing civil wars, and were killed or re-entered the settlements made after 49 BC. Brunt constructed the figure of 265,000 to take this into account; it refers to the number of adult male citizens of Italian origin living overseas in 28 BC. However, the total loss of Italian adult males through emigration by 28 BC is estimated at 315,000.

m   Brunt (1971: 264) reckons that the number of legionaries discharged between 28 and 8 BC was 127,000 or more, but thinks that only about 100,000 of these were settled in 42 colonies overseas. This reduction is perhaps large enough to make unnecessary a further reduction to take account of legionaries of non-Italian origin.

n   The figure for rural–urban migration appears arbitrary at first sight, and of course it is. It is derived from Brunt's figures, though he may not agree with my conclusion. In my view, the reduction in rural population was made possible primarily by the transfer of people elsewhere; thus, in this scheme, rural–urban migration (sub-tables D and E: 100,000) plus net rural overseas migration (sub-table C: 265,000) roughly equalled the loss in rural free population (sub-table D: 365,000). Of course, this is much too neat. The free rural poor may not have reproduced themselves, though I think that Brunt exaggerates this risk; after all, poverty does not by itself prevent reproduction. It seems plausible that substantial numbers of peasants migrated to Rome and other Italian towns. The number given here (100,000) is a crude guess.

p   This is also a crude guess. The evidence of tombstones suggests that the number of freed slaves was high both in Rome and other Italian towns.

q   These figures for rural migration within Italy relate to state allotments only. I have no idea how many people received Gracchan allotments, but five colonies were established in Italy 128–122 BC, so that the figure given here is minimal. The figures for 80–28 BC are taken from Brunt (1971: 342); the figure for 28–8 BC refers to the year 25 BC only; but there were other settlements of soldiers sent to colonies and towns (cf. Augustus, *My Achievements* 3).

of competing generals in a series of civil wars (Brunt 1971: 511). Victorious generals, Sulla, Julius Caesar and his political heirs, Antony and Augustus, all raised large armies to support their cause. When victory came, they sought peace by disarmament and gifts of land. They hoped that if an emergency arose, colonies of their ex-soldiers would be a source of support (Appian, *Civil Wars* 1.96; 2.140). For this purpose, only colonies in Italy would be useful. Between 80 and 28 BC, over a quarter of a million soldiers (and that is a conservative estimate) were given new farms in Italy (Brunt 1971: 34).

At first sight, it may seem clear that the resettlement of so many men on the land either increased the number of peasants or at least helped stem their decline; to some extent, of course, it did, just as it helped populate what were then the less favoured parts of Italy. But in many parts of Italy, arable land could be given to poor citizens only if it was taken from others. Our evidence also suggests that many of the new settlements were created only at the cost of evicting other small-holders.[93] The numbers involved were simply too large to be accommodated on vacant land. Even the estates of the rich were too small or scattered for a regular colony. So large tracts of land were taken away from towns which had supported or even sympathised with the losing side. Evidence from over a century later shows that, in some places, successive waves of colonists retained their separate identity even within a single community; for example, in Arezzo there were three groups, the old inhabitants, the 'faithful' that is Sulla's veterans, and the Caesarians (Pliny, *Natural History* 3.52). It was also said that some ex-soldiers made bad farmers, or simply got bad land (Sallust, *Speech of Lepidus* 23), or were drafted back into the army; in other cases, a new wave of victorious soldiers in their turn evicted the old soldiers, or their widows and sons (Dio 48.9). Each fresh expulsion severed more peasants from the land, created fresh reserves for the armies of conquest and new migrants to Italian towns. The painful cycle of expulsion, military recruitment, civil war and the reallocation of land achieved little except to make a different set of poor peasants landless.

Among the elite, an equally vicious circle operated. As we have seen, the Roman rich wanted to invest a large part of their provincial profits in Italian land; the estates of other rich men were obvious targets for their greed. Previously, the Romans had achieved a political culture in which men in the city went unarmed; the toga was a symbol of that

[93] My discussion here is the briefest synopsis of Brunt (1971: 300ff.). Some of those resettled in Italy might have been evicted later, then re-enlisted in the army and then settled in colonies overseas. I think the element of double-counting is small and covered by Brunt's scaling down of ancient estimates.

achievement.[94] In the last decades of the Republic, social control of private violence broke down, so that in both town and country, rich men kept bands of armed slaves to protect their property; some, if occasion offered, used them to seize the property of others. Three cases of violent seizure of estates survive in the speeches of Cicero; the frequency of violence is also reflected in the formulas of legal injunction (*interdicta*) which ordered the restitution of property; two of the four commonly-used formulas envisaged violence or armed violence as the method which had been used to gain possession of land unjustly.[95]

This private violence pales into insignificance when compared to the violence which pervaded the two main periods of civil war (90–80 BC; 49–31 BC). Murder ·by decree (proscriptions) and confiscation of property hit the rich in particular, partly because they had been politically prominent, and partly because they were rich. The victors needed to raise money from the sale of their estates or wanted to reward their followers by letting them buy estates at knockdown prices. One of Sulla' ex-slaves, for example, is said to have bought estates valued at six million HS for only two thousand HS (Cicero, *In Defence of Roscius of Ameria* 6); Crassus built his fortune on the misfortunes of the proscribed. Sulla in the end is said to have killed or banished 105 senators and 2,600 knights (Appian, *Civil Wars* 1.103). Their property was up for grabs. Altogether it must have amounted to a sizeable proportion of the total wealth owned by the elite. Very little of it was used to provide lands for the poor. Part of it merely qualified a new set of men for membership in the elite – a change of personnel but not of structure. But part of it made possible a significant change in the distribution of wealth: the surviving rich became immensely richer. They in their turn raised the level of competitive expenditure at Rome and of exploitation in the provinces, and so kept the vicious circle turning. The junta formed in 43 BC after the assassination of Caesar had 300 senators, about a third of the senate at that time, and 2,000 knights proscribed and probably executed; their property was confiscated. In the civil wars which followed yet more

[94] The Roman general going out to war ceremoniously put on military clothes (*paludamentum*) and could re-enter the city as a soldier accompanied by his armed troops only if he was awarded a triumph by the senate. Romanists who take this level of political culture for granted will see from B. Cellini's *Autobiography*, for example, how difficult it was to re-establish after the Middle Ages. At least, in Rome, Cicero tried to get redress for his clients in court.

[95] Cicero, *Pro Quinctio, Tullio and Caecina*, and cf. also *Pro Cluentio* 161; *Pro Vareno* frag. 5; on restitutory injunctions (e.g. *si quis...ex possessione vi eiectus sit*) see A. H. J. Greenidge, *The Legal Procedure of Cicero's Time* (Oxford, 1901) 210ff.; and Jolowicz (1972: 259ff.).

senators and knights were killed; their deaths made a novel political solution easier.

The imposition of a monarchy by the victorious general Octavian (Augustus) radically changed the terms of competition between aristocrats. Private violence, exploitation in the provinces and recourse to the army as the decisive weapon in political struggles were severely restricted. There were no more civil wars for a century.

For the moment I want to concentrate on what can be seen as the economic underpinning of the Augustan settlement, a factor which is usually ignored. Augustus' political solution was rendered viable, as I see it, by the cumulative effects of reducing the pressure on Italian land. Of course, this was a necessary not a sufficient condition. It was achieved partly by large-scale, state-assisted migration overseas (Table 1.2C); partly by rural–urban migration (Table 1.2E); and partly through the integration of an empire-wide economy which encouraged the richest Romans to own estates outside Italy.

The mass movement of men overseas was started by Julius Caesar, but as in so many other things it was Augustus who followed his plans through effectively. Both policies seem to have been determined by immediate factors: for example, by the pressing need to ease tension after a civil war by disbanding troops, and to provide them with alternative means of support. Traditionally support for veterans involved the acquisition of Italian land, but that was expensive, politically and financially. Seizing the land, as the triumvirs (including Octavian) did in 41 BC, created unrest; buying it, as Augustus did after 31 BC (*My Achievements* 16), cost 600 million HS, roughly equal to twice the annual cost of maintaining the imperial army.

Provincial land was cheaper; moreover, it belonged to subjects; and there was the added advantage to the central government of having Roman veterans settled among the conquered. But there was no tradition of overseas colonisation. It must have seemed a revolutionary innovation. The first proposal had been made by Gaius Gracchus in 123 BC; unfortunately for his experiment, he chose the old site of Carthage for his new colony, which added superstitious fears about the rebirth of an enemy to the existing political opposition; wolves were said to have torn up the new boundary stones overnight, and the plans were left uncompleted (Plutarch, *Gaius Gracchus* 9). In the next seventy years, only five colonies were founded overseas; we know little about them. When he was dictator in 45 BC, Julius Caesar was the first to organise colonies overseas on a grand scale; his declared policy at home of no-victimisation against his enemies (*clementia*) and his slogans: 'Security' and 'Peace' (*quies, pax, salus*) were incompatible with large-scale resettlement within Italy – although his other slogans 'Peace in the Provinces' and 'Safety in the Empire' (Caesar, *Civil Wars* 3.57) might have limited his actions in the provinces as well. Besides, the main objects of his migration policy were citizens living in Rome; they were expensive to feed, a noticeable burden on the state budget, and they had less power than veterans to resist transportation.

Whatever the intentions or determinants of the policy, one of the functions of overseas settlements was that it significantly reduced the number of free Italians (by 165,000 = 13% in 17 years, 45–28 BC), who might legitimately claim a right to earn their living from Italian land. The further recruitment of Italian soldiers for imperial armies and the settlement of 100,000 of them in the provinces during the next twenty years (28–8 BC; *c.* 9% of Italian adult males) served the same function. Indeed, military service by Italians was maintained at such a high level that it *inevitably* led to a shortage of young Italian males, and induced the Roman government to recruit provincials instead. The emigration of poor peasants from Italy not only reduced the likelihood of unwelcome political pressure from below, but also made more Italian land available for occupation by the rich.

The migration of peasants to the city of Rome served a similar function, and brought even more benefit to the Roman rich. I am not referring here to the fact that the Roman rich depended for their increased wealth upon the increased purchasing capacity of Italian townsmen in order to derive profits from their farms. My argument here is different and deserves some elaboration. In an effort to secure the electoral and legislative support of the plebs, Gaius Gracchus in 123 BC had passed a law providing citizens living in the city of Rome with a monthly allowance of wheat at a stable, state-subsidised price. The allowance remained fixed at more than enough for a man, not enough for a family (five *modii* = 33 kg). The growth in the city's population must have increased the average price of wheat, to say nothing of the fluctuations caused by the political crises which affected supplies. So Gracchus' scheme was probably very helpful as well as popular, though it must have encouraged more peasants to migrate to the city. But its partisan origins gave it a bumpy ride in the post-Gracchan period; it became a political shuttlecock, rejected by conservatives, promoted by demagogues; the scale and cost of the scheme varied. But from 58 BC onwards, wheat was apparently given free of charge to all citizens living in the city of Rome. The number of recipients rose to 320,000 by 46 BC; Julius Caesar cut the figure drastically to 150,000, but it rose again to 250,000 by 29 BC.

One of the functions of wheat distributions was to underwrite the purchasing power of Italy's largest market for food. The rich were rich largely by virtue of selling the surplus produce of their farms.

73

The purchasing power of the proletariat must often have been in doubt. What better way of guaranteeing sales than to arrange purchase by the state instead of by the consumers? Contemporary leaders may not have seen the economic advantages of wheat doles for their own stratum; they may not have seen the long-term economic advantages of emigration overseas. We do not know. Even if they did, other considerations, for example the heavy cost to the treasury of gifts of wheat, or the power of the soldiers on occasion outweighed them. But it is more likely that they saw the wheat-dole as a political or moral issue; a way of keeping the plebs quiet, which had its origin in a partisan attempt to bribe the plebs with state resources, but which had unfortunately become a traditional right. The senatorial historian Tacitus later dubbed it a symptom of the moral degradation of the Roman plebs, marking their decline from independence and vigour; all they wanted was 'bread and circuses'. This too has been the keynote of its interpretation by modern historians. But the moral decadence of the poor was compatible with profit by the rich; the moral and the functional interpretation are complementary, not competing.

It could be argued that most wheat given to the poor came from abroad in the form of taxes; even so, the supply of free wheat enabled poor citizens to spend the money which they would have spent on wheat on extra food instead. We know that the urban poor in under-developed economies today have a high propensity to spend extra money on food. I suggest that the Roman poor spent the money released by gifts of wheat on wine and olive oil produced on the estates of the rich. The function, the unintended consequence, of giving wheat free to the plebs was an increase in prosperity for rich landowners.

STRUCTURAL DIFFERENTIATION AND THE WIDER IMPLICATIONS OF CHANGE: THE ARMY, EDUCATION AND THE LAW

Up to now we have dealt with changes in the Roman political economy in terms of the interaction of seven factors, set out in the schema of interdependence. This provided us with one perspective on a nexus of events. It may be useful to finish this chapter by looking once more at the same events and their implications but from a different perspective, by using the concept structural differentiation.[96] This

---

[96] In using the concept 'structural differentiation' I do not imply a necessary evolution in one direction. The concept is used retrospectively and analytically: this is how I perceive what happened, rather than as a total explanation: this is how it had to happen. For sophisticated elaboration, see T. Parsons, *Societies: Evolutionary and Comparative Perspectives* (Englewood Cliffs, N.J., 1966) 21ff. and Eisenstadt (1971). Cf. note 15 above.

concept implies that as societies become more complex, some institutions separate out and become more functionally specific; these newly emergent institutions (for example, a professional army) then establish their identity by developing norms and values specific to the institution (such as rules of conduct specific to soldiers, even a 'military' law); their members compete with other social groups for resources (for example, by claiming resettlement farms for veterans), and they even challenge the central government for higher rewards (as in civil war).

At this point we come up against a problem. Ideally, the argument should advance on two fronts at the same time, the conceptual and the empirical; but that is difficult. Therefore, I shall begin by examining three important Roman institutions, the army, education and the law, in order to illustrate similarities in their development. This involves making forays into new territory at the end of a long chapter, but we can deal with the army briefly since several changes in military organisation have already been discussed, and we can make some economies in our discussion of education and law by comparing their state at the beginning and end of the period of imperial expansion. This crude juxtaposition of extremes hardly does justice to their history, but it serves to highlight some of the changes which occurred. Then finally, we can return to the concept structural differentiation, looking back to the descriptions for empirical illustrations.

The Roman army was originally embedded in the peasantry; land-owning citizen peasants who provided their own armour served as soldiers and at the end of a season's fighting returned to their farms; daily pay provided sustenance and compensation for absence from their land.[97] By the end of the last century BC, citizenship but not land-ownership was prerequisite for service in the legions; soldiers served for a standard period of twenty years, usually outside Italy. As a reflection of the soldiers' long service, they were paid only three times a year, and at a rate which roughly equalled twice the level of minimum substistence for a peasant family. And on retirement, legionaries received a resettlement bounty which equalled more than thirteen years' pay. Soldiering had thus become a privileged occupation, paid for in taxes by conquered provincials. The army had become fully professional. It had been transformed from a self-armed citizen militia into an instrument of imperial control and defence, isolated by distance from the central political institutions in the city of Rome and dependent upon the regular delivery of money taxes. Its existence thus depended upon other changes in the political economy of the empire.

[97] See Gabba (1976) and Smith (1958).

75

Secondly, education.[98] The importance of education for our present argument lies not only in the similarities between its development and the changes in the army, but also in the contribution which education made to the coherence of the elite in a rapidly growing social system. Originally and ideally, Roman boys learnt what they needed to know at home and in military service. The elder Cato (consul 195 BC), for example, who was a devoted traditionalist taught his son himself; he taught him to read and to write; he taught him law and physical prowess: throwing the spear, fighting, riding, boxing and swimming. He said that he did not want a slave pulling his son by the ear for errors, nor would he have his child owe gratitude to a slave for a gift so valuable as learning (Plutarch, *Cato the Elder* 20). But even in that period, he was apparently an exception; leading Romans usually had their young children, both boys and girls, tutored at home by Greek slaves or sent to school. According to Plutarch (*Roman Questions* 278E), the first fee-paying primary school was set up in the city of Rome in the second half of the third century BC by a Greek ex-slave; but modern scholars have mostly doubted that formal group teaching in basic writing could have started in Rome so late.

The beginning of secondary education at Rome, that is education in Greek and Latin language and literature (*grammatikē*), dated from the middle of the second century BC, when a Greek on an embassy to the Roman senate fell down and broke his leg, and during his convalescence gave numerous and startlingly popular lectures (Suetonius, *On Grammarians* 2). Before then, again according to Suetonius (*ibid.* 1), the Romans were too uncivilised and belligerent to spare time for scholarship. But it is also possible to date these beginnings earlier to the work of Livius Andronicus, who was brought to the city of Rome as a prisoner of war from a Greek town in southern Italy towards the middle of the third century BC. He taught Greek literature and also wrote Latin plays and poems; his translation of Homer's *Odyssey* marked the beginning of Latin literature as we know it, and it was for centuries used as a school text-book.

Exact dates for the start of complex changes have an element of fiction in them. What matters for our present purposes is that in the period of imperial expansion, Latin high culture was created in the image of Greek models. As Horace wrote: 'Captive Greece overcame her barbarous conqueror and brought civilisation to wild Latins'

[98] I follow here the excellent book by H. I. Marrou, *A History of Education in Antiquity* (London, 1956) 229ff. (there is a sixth French edition published in Paris, 1964); see also, A. Gwynn, *Roman Education from Cicero to Quintilian* (Oxford, 1926); M. L. Clarke, *Rhetoric at Rome* (London, 1953) and *Higher Education in the Ancient World* (London, 1971).

(*Epistles* 2.1.156). As part of this process of cultural change, the Roman elite learnt the Greek language and Greek literature, as well as what there was of Latin literature. Their children attended secondary school from the age of about twelve to fifteen. Educated Romans were expected to be proficient in Greek as well as Latin. Some Roman magistrates delivered elegant speeches in Greek to conquered provincials; some even wrote Roman histories in Greek. The cult of Hellenism had its fatuities, but it also in due course fostered the growth of Latin drama, poetry, history, philosophy and rhetoric.[99] An idea of scale may be helpful; according to Suetonius, there were more than twenty flourishing grammar schools in the city of Rome towards the end of the Republic (*On Grammarians* 3). We can speculate: if each of the twenty schools graduated only ten students aged fifteen each year, and that is a modest assumption for a flourishing school, then at any one time there were about seven thousand adult Romans, who had been educated in the city of Rome. Double or quadruple the number (it can only be a very rough figure, since the base number given by Suetonius may not be trustworthy), and the number of educated adults remains a small proportion of the total living in the city of Rome.

Roman education also had a third stage, which these few Roman boys entered when they were about sixteen years of age and had assumed adult dress (the *toga virilis*). The main subject was rhetoric, which was also Greek in origin. The introduction of formal teaching in rhetoric, first in Greek and then in Latin, aroused considerable opposition. Conventional Romans apparently thought that formal rhetorical skill was a waste of time, a tricky way of making shallow arguments sound plausible. 'Keep to the subject', said Cato, 'and the words will follow' (Cato, ed. H. Jordan (Leipzig, 1860) 80). That was the tradition of real Romans; and Cato was not alone in his opinion. In 161 BC, the Roman senate passed a decree ordering that philosophers and teachers of rhetoric should be expelled from the city of Rome.

Fashion prevailed over law. Six years later, the distinguished philosopher Carneades, founder of the new Academy at Athens, came with

---

[99] Polybius (39.1) recounts with scorn the activities of A. Postumius Albinus, consul of 151 BC, who was a fervent admirer of Greek culture, and by his extravagances brought admiration for Greek culture into disrepute 'among the older and most distinguished of the Romans'. He even wrote a poem and a history in Greek, and in the preface asked his readers to excuse his mistakes, since he did not have a complete mastery of the language. Cato ridiculed him for this and said it was like a man who put his name down for a boxing contest, and then when the time came for the fight, excused himself to the spectators because he could not bear being hit.

other philosophers on an embassy to Rome. Plutarch has left a lively picture of the impact which the learned Greek delegates made:

...all the young Romans who had any taste for literature hurried to frequent their company and listened to them with delight and wonder. Above all they were spellbound by the grace and charm with which Carneades expressed himself...His discourses attracted large and admiring audiences...The report spread that a Greek of extraordinary talents had arrived, who could subdue all opposition beneath the spell of his eloquence, and who had so bewitched all the youth of the city that they seemed to have abandoned all their other pleasures and pursuits and to have run mad after philosophy. Most of the Romans were gratified by this, and were well content to see their sons embrace Greek culture...But Cato...was deeply disturbed. He was afraid that the younger generation might allow their ambitions to be diverted in this direction, and might come to value most highly a reputation that was based on feats of oratory rather than upon feats of arms. (Plutarch, *Cato the Elder* 22 translated by I. Scott-Kilvert, Penguin Books)

Rhetoric was banned again in 92 BC, that is just after it was first taught publicly in Latin in the city of Rome (Suetonius, *On Rhetoricians* 2). The censors' edict was adamantly conservative:

It has been reported to us that there are men who have introduced a new form of teaching, and that our youth is frequenting their schools; that these men have assumed the title of Latin rhetoricians, and that our young men idle whole days there.

Our forefathers instituted what they wished their children to learn and the schools to which they should go. These innovations, which run counter to the customs and traditions of our ancestors, neither please us, nor do they seem proper.

Therefore it seems to be our duty to make our opinion known both to those who have the schools and those who have become accustomed to attending them. We do not approve. (Suetonius, *On Rhetoricians* 1)

Repression failed; rhetoric flourished. Rhetoricians developed complicated rules on rhythm, on style, on the organisation of arguments; they taught advocates how to plead in court, and would-be politicians how to sway the electorate; all were taught how to expatiate on moral problems, and how to eulogise the dead. Each branch of oratory had its proper name: 'judicial, deliberative, demonstrative'; further complexities followed: 'A legal issue is divided into six sub-types: Letter and Spirit, Conflicting Laws, Ambiguity, Definition, Transference and Syllogism' (?Cicero, *Ad Herennium* 19, cf. 2). All these categories were borrowed from the Greek and solemnly translated into Latin. Thus differentiation in education bred a special language (the phenomenon is not peculiar to sociology), by which *cognoscenti* distinguished themselves from, and in their own opinion elevated themselves above outsiders.

Structural differentiation

The assimilation of a new profession brought with it problems of relativities in status and pay. In the late Empire, according to the Edict on Maximum Prices (AD 301), rhetoricians were paid five times, grammarians four times as much as primary school teachers. Unfortunately, the evidence from earlier periods is patchy. But clearly some grammarians fetched fancy prices; one was bought as a slave for 700,000 HS; another was said to have made 400,000 HS per year from his school; and another was chosen by the emperor Augustus to be the tutor of his grandson; he was moved with his whole school to the imperial palace and was paid an annual salary of 100,000 HS, which was roughly equal to 200 times the level of minimum subsistence of a peasant family (Suetonius, *On Grammarians* 3, 17 and 23). That too was the regular salary paid to professors of rhetoric who held state chairs in the city of Rome – they were founded in the middle of the first century AD, but there were none for language and literature. In any case, all such men were exceptional; that is why we know about them. Even so, they reflect the high value put upon learning by influential members of the elite.

Many teachers of rhetoric and literature were Greeks, even slaves by origin. Their social acceptability is therefore surprising. According to Suetonius, some rhetorians were so well received in Rome that some advanced to senatorial dignity and to the highest magistracies (*On Rhetoricians* 1), but he cited no examples. However, it seems probable that teaching was a channel of social mobility; it was also an instrument for the socialisation of aristocrats. Roman aristocrats wanted to be litterateurs; therefore expert litterateurs had a credit with aristocrats by which they could advance their own status. This movement affected both teachers and pupils. Among the upper classes in Rome, as in traditional China and Japan, informal competition for status often took the form of peppering conversation or correspondence with literary allusions, philological niceties and rhetorical flourishes.[100] Education was to the cultural economy what money was to the monetary economy, a *lingua franca* by which elites of various sub-cultures could be assimilated and fused.

This functional 'explanation' of cultural change is not sufficient by itself; but it supplements the conventional diffusionist view that the Roman elite simply imitated and assimilated Greek culture. In short, neither view is completely satisfactory; yet whatever its cause, the result

---

[100] This is as evident in the Greek allusions in Cicero as in the scholastic discussions of Aulus Gellius (*Attic Nights*) and of Fronto, the tutor of the emperor Marcus Aurelius. For similar conventions, see *The Tales of Genji* by the Lady Murasaki (London, 1965) and *The Pillow Book of* Sei Shonagon (London, 1967) together with the brilliant evocation by I. Morris, *The World of the Shining Prince* (London, 1964).

of imitation was that most upper-class Italians, Romans, Greeks, conquerors and conquered alike, shared an identical high culture which was by origin alien to all except the Greeks. Educated Greeks therefore acted as the high priests of this culture. But Romans also won membership by acquiring a borrowed education.

We have come a long way from the old Roman system of education in the home. As in modern industrialising states, education was taken out of the family and was located instead in functionally specific institutions, namely schools. The old-fashioned role-model of the father was too simple for training the leaders of a complex society. As we have seen, young Romans did learn Greek and Latin literature, rhetoric and law, in addition to and often, as Cato feared, instead of military service. Children were now taught by specialised qualified personnel with new names for new roles (*grammatistēs, litterator, calculator, paidagogus, hypodidaskalus, grammaticus, rhetor*); the new personnel spoke a new-fangled professional language, and acted out their roles in newly founded institutions (*ludi, scholae*) which were distinguished by specific norms and values, ranging from sophistry through philological correctness to scholasticism.

Similar developments occurred in the administration of justice.[101] New institutions were created, and they were staffed by new personnel, specialised lawyers (*iuris consulti*) and advocates (*advocati, causidici, patroni*), who not only filled new roles but also talked and wrote in a specialised language, the language of Roman law. The traditional source of Roman law was the Twelve Tables of 451 BC, a primitive codification, closer in style to Moses than to Hammurabi. The Twelve Tables set out some ground rules for legal procedure and punishment in archaic and often arcane language. It is noteworthy that several provisions left the exaction of vengeance for wrongs to the injured party, even if the state magistrate had intervened earlier to judge the wrongdoer guilty. The Twelve Tables survive only in fragmentary quotations, but the following clauses give their clipped flavour:

If one summons him to justice, he shall go. If he does not go, summon a witness. Then shall one seize him. (1.1)
If one has broken his limb, there shall be strict retaliation, unless one has made a pact with him. (8.2)
If theft has been done by night, if one has killed him, he shall have been killed lawfully. (8.12)

[101] Roman law is a jungle into which visitors stray at the risk of getting lost or in fear of being mauled by the resident scholarly tigers. I have been guided by W. Kunkel, *An Introduction to Roman Legal and Constitutional History* (Oxford, 1973); Jolowicz (1972); F. Schulz, *History of Roman Legal Science* (Oxford, 1946); Greenidge (1901). I am very grateful to Mr J. A. Crook for advising me how to correct several errors in this section.

Structural differentiation

At the end of our period by contrast, that is at the end of the last century BC, the Romans had several different specialised criminal jury courts, a large body of statute law, criminal, private, public and procedural (such as the Cornelian law on murder, or the Falcidian law which restricted the proportion of an estate which could be left in legacies, or the Caecilian law which forbad composite laws and prescribed a delay between the publication and the passage of a bill); there were published commentaries on traditional law and procedures, books of legal opinions and the edicts of the praetors, who were the chief judicial magistrates of Rome; these edicts were in effect supplementary procedural rule-books. All these together formed the basis of a sophisticated legal system, quite different in its tenor from the archaic law, and strikingly similar (*mutatis mutandis*) in its careful phrasing to modern legal language. The following quotation is taken from a set of municipal regulations (the so-called *Lex Iulia Municipalis*):

(10) If anyone, who in accordance with this law should properly maintain the public street in front of his property, does not maintain it as he properly should, in the judgement of the aedile concerned, the latter at his discretion shall lease a contract for its maintenance. For at least ten days before he awards the contract, he shall post in front of his tribunal in the Forum the name of the street to be maintained, the day on which the contract shall be given and the names of the property owners on that part of the street. To the aforesaid owners or their agents at their houses he shall give notice of his intention to lease the contract for the aforesaid street and of the day on which the contract shall be given...(*Ancient Roman Statutes* 113)

The law was obviously drafted by professionals (cf. Cicero, *On His Own House* 48), and in its sophistication reflected the conflicts of interests which had to be catered for and the loopholes in previous drafts which were now closed. Such formal laws seek to avoid open conflict by outlining predictable consequences for misbehaviour.

The significance of this sophistication should not be exaggerated. Just as the justice of the Twelve Tables unrealistically presupposed all claimants' capacity to haul the defendant to court together with the disputed object, so throughout Roman history the execution of judgement was the weakest link in the Roman legal system.[102] There were few courts; they were available preponderantly to the rich and powerful; bribery was rampant. We know very little about poor criminals; we suspect that sophisticated justice was rarely available to them. That is an obvious limitation of justice in all pre-industrial states, and in industrial states as well. That said, appeals from modest litigants

[102] J. M. Kelly, *Roman Litigation* (Oxford, 1966) somewhat idealises modern judicial systems, but points up the inadequacies and distortions in Roman legal practice, as apparently few scholars had done before him.

do survive in the later Roman law codes; and it seems probable that some poor people got access to the courts in all periods. Yet inevitably most cases about which we know concerned the privileged.

With these qualifications in mind, let us very briefly review some developments in the Roman legal system. Once again I should enter the caveat that much is uncertain and nearly everything is disputed, and in a brief account I shall inevitably simplify complex issues. However, at the beginning of the period of imperial expansion overseas, procedures in Roman law were still highly ritualistic. Litigants had to appear in court before the magistrate together with the object whose possession was disputed. If the disputed object was immovable, then originally the magistrate had visited the site, 'but when the boundaries of the Roman state were extended and the magistrates were fairly busy with legal business, they found it difficult to go to distant sites to settle claims' (Aulus Gellius, *Attic Nights* 20.10). And so by an agreed fiction, a clod of earth or a roof tile was used as the visible symbol of a disputed farm or house: the change was both an index of the pedestrian concreteness of old Roman legal practices and of its transcendance by legal fictions.

The case was opened before the magistrate by the claimant, who with a rod in his hand pronounced a series of formulae;[103] for example:

'I affirm that this man [a slave] is mine by Quiritary right according to his proper title. As I have spoken, so you behold: I have laid my rod on him.' And at that moment he laid his rod on the man. His opponent said the same words and performed the same act...and then the magistrate said: 'Unhand the man, both of you.' (Gaius, *Institutes* 4.16)

Recitation of further formulae followed, and to quote Gaius again:'the excessive technicality of the old law-makers was carried so far that if either party made the slightest error, he lost the suit' (*Institutes* 4.30). So too in Roman religious rites, any error in procedure made the rite void. The rest of this preliminary action before the magistrate took the form of a sacred wager (*sacramentum*) for a fixed sum; according to the value of the disputed object, the wager was for 50 or 500 *asses*, apparently equivalent to five or fifty sheep (Aulus Gelius, *Attic Nights* 11.1), a substantial sum, which was forfeited by the loser together with the disputed object.

This antique procedure, which was only one of several which evolved, shows up some important aspects of early Roman law. First, it was ritualistic, but then so is much modern legal procedure. Secondly

[103] The rod signified a spear, which in turn symbolised rightful possession, see Gaius, *Institutes* 4.16.

it was formalistic, in that recited words were invested with symbolic or ritual meaning. Thirdly, it was rigid, in that the form of action was fixed and precluded the possibility of a compromise judgement between competing claims, both of which might have had some right on their side. The court took the form of a tournament without weapons, in which there had to be a victor and vanquished. Finally, it was restrictive, in that the wager was for a significant sum, so that poor litigants were effectively excluded. But once the formal process before the magistrate was over, the case was then argued in a second action before a lay judge appointed by the magistrate, and this second action may well have been conducted informally and in a manner which changed with changing conditions.

As the sphere of Roman influence widened, Romans had extensive legal dealings with foreign nationals; they also faced the new problems of governing a complex state. These changes must have encouraged corresponding developments in Roman law; but obviously, there was no neat fit between imperial expansion and increasing legal sophis tication, only an observable trend in substantive law and in legal procedures. For example, the scope of law widened to cover consensual contracts and there was considerable elaboration of the law relating to unjustifiable damage to property; such changes in substantive law may have been an important factor in inducing increased flexibility in procedure. Moreover, as in education, law was considerably affected by Greek scholars, who introduced Greek dialectical distinctions into Roman jurisprudence. Cicero, for example, in a lost work, proposed and may even have executed a systematisation of Roman law (*De iure civili in artem redigendo*).

The old forms of litigation by strict formula were gradually circumvented and then supplanted, probably from the second century BC onwards, by a new legal procedure. The presiding magistrate, normally the praetor, after hearing both parties settled on a rubric or terms of reference (confusingly the Latin for this is *formula*), suited to the facts of the particular case and to the claims and counterclaims of the litigants; these were the terms of reference by which the judge (*iudex*) decided the case in a subsequent hearing. This system allowed successive magistrates (especially the praetors) considerable discretion both in adapting existing statute law to changing conditions, and in effectively creating new substantive law by supplementing statute law, often through the imaginative use of legal fictions. For example, some private legal actions were formally available only between Roman citizens; the magistrate in his rubric could authorise the judge to assume that the alien, if liable, should pay damages as though he were a Roman citizen. Or to cite another example, in traditional law, cases had been decided by legal rights of possession; under the new-style rubrics, the magistrate might instruct the judge to decide the case on the basis of what should be done as a matter of good faith (*bona fides*). Thus equity and sometimes even intention supplemented strict law.[104]

There were also changes in the practice of criminal law; in the old days, important criminal cases had regularly been heard on appeal before the so-called courts of the people (*iudicia populi*), with a potential cast of hundreds, even thousands; these courts had the same composition as the popular assemblies, the *comitia centuriata* and *tributa*, which also voted on legislation and elected officers of state. But from the middle of the second century BC onwards several separate and much smaller jury courts (*quaestiones*) each specialising in a specific type of crime, such as extortion, bribery, treason and murder, were established. The change was not an unqualified success. The reduction in the size of the juries made them more accessible to corruption.

The range of cases tried in these criminal courts was both narrower and wider than in modern criminal courts. It was narrower because most petty crimes were dealt with summarily on the street or by minor magistrates from whom there was little effective chance of appeal. Besides, some crimes against property, such as theft, were regarded as matters of private law.[105] The sphere of Roman criminal courts was also wider than it is now, because in the late Republic political conflicts

---

[104] 'The praetorian law is what the praetors have introduced to help, supplement or correct the civil law, in the public interest' (D. 1.1.7.1: Papinian). The following rubric is typical; please note its emphasis on reparation and good faith. 'X shall be judge (*iudex*). Whereas Aulus Agerius [the plaintiff] deposited with Numerius Negidius [the defendant] the silver table which is the subject of this action, for whatever on that account Numerius Negidius ought to give or do to Aulus Agerius in good faith, you, judge, shall make Numerius Negidius liable to Aulus Agerius' (Gaius, *Institutes* 4.47). And on the importance of intention, of the spirit as against the letter of the law, see for example Cicero, *On Behalf of Caecina* 53 and 67.

But I should not exaggerate the flexibility of Roman lawyers in the late Republic. For example, in the edict, it was held that when a man left as a legacy 'all his female slaves together with all their children', and one of the female slaves died, the child of the dead female slave should not be part of the legacy, because the testator had legated the child only as an appurtenance of the mother. Later imperial jurists objected to this literal interpretation, because it defeated the wishes of the dead man (D. 30.63: Celsus). Cf. Schulz (1946: 79) for other examples.

[105] Cf. Aulus Gellius, *Attic Nights* 20.1 and Gaius, *Institutes* 3, 189: 'By the law of the Twelve Tables, the punishment for thieves caught in the act was capital. A free man was whipped and then solemnly 'assigned' by the magistrate to the man from whom he had been stolen. Lawyers of old debated whether this 'assignment' (*addictio*) made the thief a slave or a debt bondsman. A slave caught in theft was similarly whipped and executed. But in later times, the cruelty of the punishment was frowned on, and the praetor's edict established, for both slave and free person, a suit for four times the value.' Such civil suits must have had limited applicability except against rich thieves.

within the elite took the form of charges in the criminal courts. Faction leaders, or their close supporters were accused of treason, of corruption, of violence, sometimes with good cause, sometimes without, by members of rival political factions and by orators who hoped that success in the courts would serve as a spring-board for their political ambitions. The judicial process was a weapon in factional politics; for example, we know of over one hundred criminal cases involving the political elite in the twenty years 70 to 50 BC.[106]

Roman law was not merely a means of expressing and therefore of controlling political conflict within the ruling class, it was also a mechanism for protecting upper class property. Cicero made this point powerfully:

If the civil law is...neglected or not carefully defended, there is nothing which anyone will be sure about possessing, either to be inherited from his father, or to be left to his children. What is the advantage of having a house or a farm left you by your father...if you cannot be certain of keeping what is yours by the law of ownership? Believe me, what each of us has inherited is more a legacy of our laws and constitution, than of those who left it to us. A father can bequeath a farm; but the enjoyment of the farm, without anxiety or danger of litigation is bequeathed not by the father, but by the law. (*On Behalf of Caecina* 73–4)

Of course, this is rhetoric, But there was some truth in it. Roman law helped protect property, not just in Rome, but also in the Italian towns which came under Roman domination, and in the provinces.[107]

All these changes in civil procedure and in the form of the criminal courts induced corresponding changes in legal personnel. In the old days, patrician priests had monopolised the knowledge of legal formulae. Legal knowledge was a branch of religious knowledge and was therefore zealously guarded (Cicero, *On Behalf of Murena* 25). According to tradition, the monopoly was first breached in about 300 BC, when the secretary of a noble censor was said to have stolen from his master the procedural formulae, the ritual recitation of which

---

[106] See E. S. Gruen, *The Last Generation of the Roman Republic* (Berkeley, Calif., 1974) 260ff. for a long and lively account of the charges and counter-charges brought, especially in the period preceding Caesar's rise to supreme power.

[107] The need to apply Roman law in Italian towns and in the provinces was probably a major factor in inducing flexibility. Roman law increasingly had to cover cases between parties with different legal systems. We hear a lot of Roman corruption and mismanagement in the provinces, and rightly so. But there is also impressive evidence of sophisticated thought about how best to manage relations between city-states, which when they were independent had often settled their conflicts by war not law. The following clause cited by Cicero seems typical of several: 'If a private citizen sues a municipality, or if a municipality sues a private citizen, then the senate of another city shall be appointed judge, and each party shall have the right to challenge one of the cities proposed' (*Against Verres* 2.2.32).

opened civil actions. He published them in the first Roman law book (Livy 9.46). A century later, a consul, Sextus Aelius Paetus, brought credit on himself by publishing new and modified formulae, which had come into use with the growth of the state, together with a commentary on the Twelve Tables (D 1.2.2.7: Pomponius). But in spite of this publication, nobles and priests of the state cults, or at least successful senators still had a virtual monopoly of legal knowledge and skill (Cicero, *On Duties*, 2.65).

The introduction in the second century BC of flexible rubrics, or terms of reference adapted to the facts of each case, changed legal procedures from ritualistic rigmarole to an exercise of legal skill. The presiding magistrate had to adjudge and amend complicated terms of reference put up by the litigants and pass them on to the judge (*index*) who actually tried the case. These terms of reference or rubrics (*formulae*) were partly a matter of precedent; they were codified in the praetor's *Edict*, the set of rules and procedures which were handed down from one praetor to the next; but the terms of reference also had to fit the matter in dispute; they might vary according to facts of the case or the point of law involved. Yet praetors were elected for only one year in office, and they were assigned to military or legal duties by lot.

In short, they were not necessarily experts. They depended upon advice. Magistrates, judges, and litigants all sought advice from the same quarters, from legal consultants (*iuris prudentes*). These men formed a new and growing profession divorced from the old religious law, which from the end of the Republic no one studied anymore (Cicero, *On Oratory* 3.136). The break between priests and lawyers opened the profession to outsiders; and in the last century BC several distinguished legal consultants are known to have been of equestrian, not senatorial status.[108] Knowledge of the law served as a platform for a political career, probably as a less prestigious alternative to military service. Cicero gives us a picture of the budding lawyer:

Servius [later consul in 51 BC] did his service in the city here with me, giving legal opinions, engrossing documents, and giving advice, a life full of worry and anxiety. He learned the civil law, worked long hours, helped many clients, put up with their stupidity, suffered their arrogance...He was at the beck and call of others, not his own master. A man wins widespread praise and credit with others when he works hard at a discipline which will benefit so many.

[108] This is documented by W. Kunkel, *Herkunft und soziale Stellung der römischen Juristen* (Graz², 1967) 48ff.

But for all that, Cicero preferred the claims of his own client, who had been in effective command of an army. 'Who can doubt that military glory confers more distinction in pursuit of a consulship than achievements in civil law?' (*On Behalf of Murena* 19 and 22). Orators also, in Cicero's opinion, ranked above lawyers, But relative ranking concerns us less for the moment than the differentiation of the professions. Pleaders (*advocati, causidici, patroni*) were distinct from legal consultants (*iuris prudentes*); and members of each group bolstered the differences with hostile stereotypes.[109]

Finally, I should stress that the changes in the law which I have described were gradual not thoroughgoing. Civil actions by ritual formula (*legis actio*) and criminal charges before large popular juries (*iudicia populi*) persisted to the end of the Republic. Old and new co-existed, not always comfortably, as the ruling groups attempted to keep the new within the mould of tradition. For example, by the Cincian law of 204 BC, the payment of fees or gifts to lawyers was strictly limited. Ideally, the advocate was expected to defend his client as a favour, to increase his prestige but not his wealth (Cicero, *On Duties* 2. 65–6). The obligation which the client then owed his patron was unspecified and unactionable. In this way, advocacy would have remained an avocation for propertied gentlemen. But the Cincian law, like many Roman laws, was a *lex imperfecta*, that is a law which forbade an act, but which neither penalised nor annulled a contravention. Not surprisingly, therefore, the law was evaded, in spite of its reinforcement under Augustus (Dio 54.18; cf. Tacitus, *Annals* 11.5–7).

But to a surprising extent, the system of not paying lawyers did work. Cicero, for example, received substantial sums from his clients, but only in their last testament or will; he claimed to have received the huge sum of twenty million sesterces by bequests (Cicero, *Philippics* 2.40). Even in the changing conditions of the late Republic, members of the elite shared values and honoured obligations after a lapse of time, sometimes of a generation, and in matters for which we should want an immediate and specified recompense. To be sure, a system of unspecified mutual obligation does exist in our society, in contemporary upper middle class culture in Britain and the USA. But it is reserved for relatively unimportant sectors of behaviour. For example, I invite you to dinner without exacting from you the specific obligation to invite me back. But for most exchanges, we translate important obligations into money terms and often reinforce our expec-

[109] For lawyers derogatory of orators, see the views cited by Cicero, *On Oratory* 1.165; *Topica* 51; and vice versa: *On Behalf of Murena* 25.

tations of repayment by contracts. Indeed, money so dominates our system of social exchange that we commonly express other social matters, such as job satisfaction or even social rejection in money terms: 'it pays well'; 'sorry, I can't afford to go to the pub, or to the movies, or on holiday with you'.

In Roman society, the sphere of diffuse unspecified obligation was traditionally very wide. Originally, it centred in the nexus of kinship and then radiated out along lines of patronage. One symptom was the practice of marrying a daughter off in order to cement an alliance between political factions. Another was the appeal to the ties of kinship or of friendship to win private advantage, even in contravention of the law. Any governor, any magistrate, any judge or juryman was pressured to show favour, to give benefits to relatives, to friends, to the friends of relatives and to the relatives of friends. Kinsmen were expected to stick together, but the extension of kin ties through marriage necessarily brought conflicts of interest. Cicero complained:

You compassionate. I was your connexion by marriage; at your election [to consul] you had appointed me to be the first overseer of the tribe which opened the voting...you called upon me to speak third in the senate; and yet you handed me over bound to the enemies of the republic; with arrogant and heartless words you drove from your feet my son-in-law, your own flesh and blood (*propinquum*) and my daughter who was bound to you by ties of marriage (*adfinem*). (Cicero, *To the Senate after his Return* 17, trans. Loeb Classical Library)

Elite politics were too complicated to run exactly along kin lines, but not complex enough to develop rival ideological groupings. Attempts to extend factions through marriages were sometimes thwarted because women, from being pawns in the power game of men, arrogated some power to themselves; they benefited considerably from the rule of law which protected their property, as distinct from their husbands'; and they were able to initiate divorce and subsequent remarriages for themselves. The conservative institution of marriage in this way served as a vector of social change and induced a level of female emancipation in the Roman elite which has rarely been matched in human history.

Personal obligations to and claims from wives and kin, friends and patrons were incompatible with the formal rule of law, incompatible too with the impersonal 'rationality and diligence' which administration of the provinces ideally required. Some Romans were conscious of the conflict between impersonal ideals and personal profit. But to be a full member of the elite club, one had to win favours for one's own friends and to bestow favours on the friends of others. Letters of recommendation, of which there are so many in the published correspondence of Cicero, Pliny and Symmachus, were the personal cheques of the system: the member's credit depended upon his power to place friends in positions of profit.[110] Patronage and corruption (which is the appropriation of a public office as private property) were just two sides of the same coin. Their persistence and prevalence undercut any thoroughgoing changes towards the formal legal or bureaucratic administration of the empire.

We have gone far enough. It is time to reconsider the concept structural differentiation. This can now be done in rather abstract terms, with only brief references back to the developments in the army, education and the law, which we have just discussed. I should stress that these three areas were selected only as illustrations of the ramified changes which occurred in the wake of empire. A full social history would deal as well with similar changes in other areas of social organisation, such as agriculture, trade, architecture, and administration.

I do not like formal definitions, but in this case perhaps one may help. Structural differentiation refers to the process by which an undifferentiated institution (for example, a family group charged with multiple functions) becomes divided into separate institutions (such as schools for education, factories for production), each charged with a single main function. I shall treat the implications of structural differentiation under five headings: separation, competition, old against new, periphery against centre and the growth of state power.

First, the newly differentiated institutions, such as, for example, the Roman army, schools and the law-courts, developed norms and values which legitimated their identity as separate and autonomous parts of the society. Military tactics and military law, or complicated rules of grammar and rhetoric, of legal language and procedures all serve as convenient examples of new norms, which differentiated each institution from the others. But above all, the development of specific professional and often full-time social roles (soldier as distinct from peasant, orator and advocate as distinct from noble or priest), indicated the development of personnel, specific to the new autonomous institutions.[111]

---

[110] For example, Cicero congratulated his brother on his three-year governorship of a province in which he had not been moved from the 'highest integrity and self-control' by the gift of a picture, a slave, a woman, or by money (Cicero, *Letters to his Brother Quintus* 1.1.8). Cicero also told his brother (*ibid.* 1.2) that lots of people had asked him (Cicero) to recommend them to his brother's secretary, who was an ex-slave. What worried Cicero was the low status of the intermediary, not the request for favours.

[111] The concept autonomy is problematic, easier to think about than to operationalise, but then that is true of several useful concepts, such as cowardice or envy. Perhaps two points are worth making: the autonomy of institutions was relative not absolute; secondly, I should stress that my concentration here on autonomy is a tactic not a commitment; integration (how the differentiated institutions operated with each other) and conflict should also be considered.

Secondly, the new differentiated institutions necessarily competed with each other for society's resources, whether these resources were expressed in terms of pay, prestige or personnel. The circumstances of this competition were quite exceptional for a pre-industrial society. A pre-industrial society can be defined, not merely as a society whose major source of energy is the muscle power of men and animals, but also as a society whose very small surplus production is bespoken, embedded, routinely used for the same purpose, year after year. But Roman society, because the fruits of conquest were being heaped into Italy, temporarily escaped from some of these limitations. It had massive resources available, for which there was no traditional allocation in the society. The resources were 'free-floating'. Romans therefore faced the new and bewildering problem of how these resources were to be used, and for whose benefit.

We know one general answer: the rich grew richer. But that is too simple a rubric to cover the complicated expansion of Roman society, as it moved from large city-state to imperial power. There was competition among the rich, for example, between equestrian tax-farmers and senatorial governors over the division of provincial spoils. There was competition within the elite for prestige; witness the strenuous attempts by some members of the elite to master Greek, the language of a conquered culture. There were also experiments in competition, reflecting the elite's uncertainty about the criteria for achieving high status; hence exaggerated payments and high fees to rhetoricians, doctors, actors, artists and architects. Such payments elevated these new professions to the status of sub-elites, sharing in Rome's new-found wealth. And there were also attempts by members of the non-elite to win a greater share of the society's wealth: claims for higher pay, more plunder and larger farms from soldiers, for free wheat and more entertainment from poor metropolitan voters. All these claims were made feasible by the huge influx of free-floating resources, and were encouraged by the instability of social relations fostered by unaccustomed wealth.

Thirdly, as society changed, there were conflicts between the old elite whose power was based on the control of traditional resources (such as land, prestige, or the memory of ancestors' status) and a new elite which partly drew its power from new institutions (control of the army, oratorical skill, legal knowledge). In part, this distinction is conceptual rather than real, in so far as new members of the Roman elite, often from allied Italian city-states, already had land and thanks to grants of Roman citizenship could acquire political office in Rome. Land and political office were the two hall-marks of the traditional elite.

Complementarily, members of the old elite could and did acquire new skills. Old and new elites do not therefore refer to fixed groups. But in any society, social change involving new ideas, new values, spreads at an uneven pace; different sectors of the population, young and old, peasants and metropolitans, assimilate change at different rates and often justify their behaviour with hostile stereotypes of those who are different. Change was subjective as well as objective. For example, when Cicero became consul, the first of his family to be so successful in politics, he still felt at a disadvantage compared with those whom he thought had inherited 'nobility'.

In our previous discussion of the army, education and the law, we have considered several instances of conflict between the old-fashioned and the new-fangled. And we have seen the problems which arose from innovations, such as the recruitment of the landless to the army, the introduction of Latin rhetoric and the creation of jury-courts. Another brief example may be helpful. In the last century of the Republic, the equestrian order emerged as a separate legally-defined social stratum, whose richest members were both tax-farmers in the provinces and Italian land-owners. Modern research has shown that in many economic and social respects, these knights were similar to senators, and that in all social conflicts, both senators and knights fought on each side. Objectively, therefore, the distinction between senators and knights is not important; but contemporary Romans apparently perceived knights as a social group which was to a significant extent engaged in a struggle with the senate. Cicero, for example, thought that concord between senators and knights (*concordia ordinum*) would form a satisfactory basis for stable government and would end civil strife. The dichotomy senate–knights was important, even if it was misconceived. It illustrates how differentiated institutions became points of reference by which members of a society organised their social maps; distinctions between differentiated parts of the society became items in the political vocabulary and were turned, sometimes unrealistically, into axes of political conflict.

Fourth, the distribution of resources between conflicting institutions is often or ultimately the responsibility of the central government. The newly emergent institutions were therefore likely (*a*) to test the limits of the central authority's power and (*b*) to challenge the political authority of the government at the centre; the purpose might be to win extra resources (for example, control of the jury-courts by knights, or resettlement-farms for veterans) or simply to confirm the place of a group within the social order. Let us illustrate these processes. By tradition, state priests had the right to declare certain political or legislative activities illicit, if they ascertained that something had gone awry in the appropriate rites. But in several critical instances, priestly strictures were disregarded; political leaders proceeded with law-making in spite of religious bans, just as generals fought battles after blindly ignoring unpropitious signs. The political triumphed over the religious; the status and power of priests were correspondingly lowered.

Attacks on the central government by political generals with armies at their backs were more difficult to survive and deserve more detailed attention. Indeed, the escalation of civil wars between rival generals (Marius and Sulla, Pompey and Caesar, Antony and Octavian) eventually led to the dissolution of the Republic and to the concentration of political power in the hands of a single successful political general, Octavian (later called Augustus). But this successful concentration of power need not have happened; the huge empire, like the Persian empire or the empire of Alexander the Great, could have split into separate territorial satrapies, and almost did when Antony allied with Cleopatra in Egypt. There is no universal law that military conflict leads to a concentration of political power, although it is a phenomenon which has been frequently observed. In short, we cannot explain Augustus' success by invoking or implying some non-existent law of the centripetal tendency of military power.

One major problem which the Roman state faced was the subordination of the military to the political. It is still a recurrent problem in many economically under-developed states today.[112] In the Roman Principate (31 BC–AD 235), the problem was solved for long periods; the famous Roman peace, the *pax Romana*, afforded Roman subjects protection from civil wars as well as from external attack. But in the late Republic, the delicate balance between the political and the military was upset by two factors: the concentration of power in the hands of super-generals and the exacerbation of political conflict. Let us deal with each briefly.

The conquest of a huge empire repeatedly confronted the Roman state with military problems which required more comprehensive and longer lasting military commands than could be comfortably tolerated by a power-sharing and egalitarian (among peers) oligarchy. For example, in 67 BC, in order to clear pirates from the eastern Medi-

---

[112] Mass poverty, rapidly rising expectations, expanding central government expenditure which threatens traditional elites, and the insecurity of army officers are some of the important factors in the *coups d'état* in underdeveloped states. See S. E. Finer, *The Man on Horseback* (London, 1962), K. Hopkins, 'Civil-military relations in developing countries', *British Journal of Sociology* 17 (1966) 165ff.; I. Horowitz, *Three Worlds of Development* (New York, 1966) 254ff.

terranean, Pompey the Great was, in the interests of military efficiency, given a command which covered several ordinary provinces; this inevitably raised Pompey above other senatorial generals. Similarly, Julius Caesar secured the command of a large army, in effect for ten years; and it was this extra long command which allowed him to conquer Gaul. Thus Romans repeatedly created super-generals in the interests of imperial expansion, and then waited in fear and anxiety, wondering whether the super-generals, like the generals of old, would subordinate themselves, when their victories were won, to the state.

Sometimes they did; at other times, they unleashed their forces against the city of Rome, or against the senate's hastily appointed defenders. The mere fact that Roman generals and soldiers were willing to attack the city of Rome was index enough of deep-seated political instability. What had changed? Part of the explanation of the changed behaviour of the elite lay in the exacerbation of political conflict, and in the breakdown of the traditional system of the serial exchange of political offices within the elite, based on reciprocity and on trust as to the limited consequences of being without political power. In the old days, loss of an election (to praetorship or consulship, for example) meant loss of face, but no long term loss of status for one's family (we return to this topic in Chapter I of Volume Two). Towards the end of the Republic, loss of an election could mean bankruptcy; loss of political power could mean, as it did in Cicero's case, exile and later execution. Political competition had become fiercer because the rewards of gaining office, at home or in the provinces, and the disadvantages of missing office had become greater. The use of violence by armies and by armed gangs had eroded, even though they did not destroy the rule of law. Romans in the last decades of the Republic began again to walk in city streets carrying arms, or accompanied by armed retainers. In their fight for victory or survival, political factions felt themselves forced to use any weapon which came to hand; they used especially those institutions which had been forged in the process of structural differentiation, and which were not yet firmly embedded in the social order. Hence criminal charges against political enemies in the jury-courts, judicial murders by 'proscription' (the publication of lists of enemies of the state who could be lawfully murdered for a reward), attacks by the army on the capital and civil wars. As the power of the state (measured in taxes gathered, coins minted, men employed or range of laws passed) increased, so it became crucial for faction leaders to make sure that they and not others controlled the state.

Fifth and finally, if the Roman state was to persist as a single entity, then it needed new institutions, new norms and values which would help integrate the newly differentiated parts. The main new integrative institution was the Principate, the name we give to the patrimonial monarchy which was forged by Augustus and which in its essentials persisted for close on three hundred years. This new political order represented the increased power of the state. It deserves and has received whole volumes of description and discussion. For our present purposes, it is enough very briefly to describe several constituents which distinguished the Principate from the Republic.

The emperors' power clearly rested on control of the professional, long-service army. The legions were relocated outside Italy on the frontiers of the empire at a comforting distance from the scene of active politics at Rome. Legionaries' pay had been significantly increased by Julius Caesar; Augustus added a bounty to be paid on satisfactory completion of sixteen, later twenty years' military service. Such regular payments, which accounted for almost half of the total imperial budget, depended upon the regular and predictable payment and collection of taxes. They also depended upon the increased monetarisation of the imperial economy. Under the Republic there had already been substantial increases in the volume of coins minted at Rome; but under the Principate, the whole empire was for the first time given a nearly unified system of coinage, which in turn reflected a partial unification of the whole monetary economy. This partial unification of the monetary economy was achieved largely by the interaction of tax and trade. Money taxes were exacted in the core provinces (such as Gaul, Spain and Asia) and were mostly spent in Italy or on army pay in the frontier provinces; core provinces then had to export goods in order to buy back the money with which to pay taxes.[113] This simplified model goes some way towards explaining why Italy under the Principate was such a heavy net importer of provincial goods.

Another constituent of the new imperial order was its legitimacy. This legitimacy had several facets: the conscious restoration of tradition, the extension of political support beyond the metropolis to the elites of Italian and of provincial towns, and the enforcement of the rule of law. Augustus, the first emperor, ostantatiously set about restoring the old Republican constitution. It was a surprising act for a monarch. But the traditional oligarchic constitution was designed to ensure (for example, through collegiate tenure and short periods of holding office) that no aristocrat got too much power. With a monarch

[113] On the growth in money supply at Rome under the Republic, see M. H. Crawford, *Roman Republican Coinage* (Cambridge, 1974) 696ff.; on the reciprocity of tax and trade, see briefly K. Hopkins (1978: 39ff.).

superimposed to see that all the rules were obeyed, the traditional Republican constitution worked in the monarch's favour. One important change was necessary: aristocrats' access to the metropolitan populace in elections was blocked. The metropolitan poor were effectively disfranchised; but the citizen army was no longer sufficiently identified with them to protect their ancient privileges. They were left with bread and circuses. Meanwhile the basis of the emperor's own political support had been widened (this had been particularly necessary in the bitter civil war against Antony) to include the elites of Italian towns, and then later of provincial towns also. In Chapter v, we examine some of the beliefs and rituals which heightened the emperor's legitimacy and which helped many subjects throughout the empire to identify with the new regime. Legitimacy also rested upon the rule of law. Indeed, in many history books, Augustus' power is described as resting on the legal regulation of his constitutional powers (his consular *imperium*, his tribunician power); no doubt, these were important props for Romans, as well as for modern scholars. But the rule of law also signified a widespread retreat from violence in interpersonal relations, and even more important a predictability of outcome in many political, social and business arrangements.

The Augustan settlement broke two vicious circles. The first vicious circle we set out in Figure 1.1; it was a sequence of conquest and plunder, the import of booty and slaves into Italy, the impoverishment of Italian peasants and their extrusion from their farms, their recruitment to the army (or their migration to the city of Rome) and their subsequent demands for Italian farms of their own. The break in this chain reaction, as we have seen, was the mass emigration of Italian peasants, mostly ex-soldiers, to settle in colonies on northern Italian or provincial land. By the end of Augustus' long reign (31 BC–AD 14), the territorial expansion of the empire had virtually stopped, and the volume of slave imports had, in my view, considerably diminished. A second vicious circle affecting aristocrats and other wealthy Italian land-owners was also broken. The massive emigration of soldier colonists had eased the competition between rich and poor for Italian land; the peaceful conditions of the Principate and the gradual unification of the monetary economy of the empire as a whole made it easier for rich Romans, including senators, to own estates overseas in the provinces, and to have their cash rents safely transmitted over long distances to be spent in the city of Rome.

This rapid characterisation of some of the differences between Republic and Principate and of the process of change in the late Republic has captured some but only some aspects of a complex reality. Structural differentiation has two particular disadvantages: first, it does not form part of an effective, large-scale theory of social change; in this respect, it is not like the concept 'mode of production' within a Marxist theory; secondly, structural differentiation is a modern, non-Roman concept (like social mobility or economic growth), superimposed on Roman history, and independent of the perceptions of Roman actors. Neither disadvantage is overwhelming. And of course, using a modern concept does not preclude consideration of actors' perceptions and intentions. Indeed in later chapters, I shall try explicitly to enter into the perceptual world of Romans and hold a counterpoint between my and their perceptions of various problems, from winning freedom for a slave to worshipping the emperor as a god. The point I want to make is that all approaches, bourgeois, Marxist, annalistic, prosopographical, are necessarily selective and partial.[114] A change in perspective or the use of a different concept leads us to select different facts or to present the same facts in a different light. In this sense, concepts are intellectually prior to the evidence and demand as much skill and attention as does the evidence itself.

APPENDIX

On the probable size of the population of the city of Rome

The size of the population of the city of Rome has often been disputed. There is not enough evidence from which to deduce secure conclusions. However, it seems worth outlining such evidence as does exist and some of the problems surrounding it, since an estimate of the city's size plays a significant part in any estimate of the population of Italy as a whole and its distribution.

The main basis for estimating the size of the city of Rome's population is the recorded number of recipients of the free wheat dole and/or the money gifts (*congiaria*) occasionally handed out in the city of Rome. These were recorded as numbering 320,000 in 46 BC; but they were then immediately reduced to 150,000 by Julius Caesar who organised emigration to the provinces and a careful block by block registration of those qualified (Suetonius, *Julius Caesar* 41–2). This reduction gives ground for thinking that the official number of recipients was swollen at other times also by malpractice or inefficiency. Augustus himself in his record of his achievements claimed that the recipients of his money gifts and/or wheat doles in the city of Rome numbered 250,000 or more on five occasions (in 44, 29, 24, 23, and 12 BC); in 5 BC, the number of recipients rose again to 320,000 but then sank in 2 BC to 'just over 200,000' (*Res Gestae* 15). Although the distribution was formally limited to those living in the city of Rome, it would have been worthwhile for peasants living nearby to walk to the city and claim a sizeable free ration of wheat (33 kg per month).

---

[114] I do not mean by this to imply that since all approaches are partial, no choice can be made between them. Far from it. Such choices are repeatedly made.

Appendix

Perhaps we should make some allowance for this. Even so all the recorded numbers indicate a very large city by pre-industrial European standards.

All the recipients were male and of citizen status; we must therefore add women, children, resident aliens without citizenship, slaves and soldiers. We do not know how many. We also do not know how old males of citizen status had to be to qualify for the wheat dole. Suetonius (*Augustus* 41) stated that Augustus in his distribution of money included young boys, even though they customarily received largesse only when they reached the age of ten. Beloch (1886: 392ff.), whose discussion of the ancient evidence still seems best, deduced from this that boys also normally received the wheat dole from the age of ten onwards. This assumption may not be right, since Suetonius was writing about money gifts, but it significantly lessens the multiplier which we have to use in order to account for women and children. For example, the number of 250,000 male recipients aged ten years and older implies a total population (if sex ratios were balanced and the population was self-reproducing – these are simplifying assumptions only, not statements of fact) of about 670,000 (at $e_0 = 25$). Alternative assumptions of higher mortality ($e_0 = 20$) or a higher age of qualification for the wheat dole (say age fifteen and $e_0 = 25$) produce total populations of about 690,000 and 770,000 respectively. In fact, the proportion of women and young children in the city may have been less than in the population at large.

To these figures we should then add resident aliens, soldiers and slaves, and subtract the outlying citizens who walked to the city to collect their dole. This is pure guess work. Beloch reckoned that to take account of them all, we should add roughly a further 300,000 to make a total population for the city of between 800,000 and just under one million.

Other evidence can also be used to help us: the built-up area of the city, the quantity of wheat imported and the number of houses listed. This information serves as a check on the estimates we have just made. The area inside the city walls which were built in the third century AD was 1,373 hectares (Meier 1953/4: 329): this area corresponded roughly with the estimated area of the city in the time of Augustus (Friendländer 1921[10], vol. 4, 117). If the population of this area had been one million, then the average density would have been about 730 persons per hectare. This was certainly possible; the density in the poorest districts of Rome and Naples in 1881 were over 800 and almost 1,500 persons per hectare respectively (Beloch 1886: 409). And I myself have seen squatter settlements in Hong Kong, comprising one- or two-storey ramshackle huts, built of bamboo and tin-sheeting, with densities considerably higher (up to 2,500 per hectare). But such a high average density for the whole city of Rome, once allowance is made for public spaces, roads, gardens, temples, markets and the houses of the rich, seems improbable. On this crude reckoning, therefore, the population of ancient Rome within the boundary of the third-century walls was somewhat less than a million in the time of Augustus.

This rough order of magnitude is corroborated by what we know of wheat imports. As usual the evidence is disputed. I follow Beloch and Kahrstedt (1921: 11ff.) in dismissing the evidence of Josephus (*Jewish War* 2.383 and 386) and the Epitome (*On the Caesars* 1.6), which taken together suggest that Rome's annual consumption of wheat totalled 60 million *modii* = 390,000 tons per year. This would have been enough to feed almost two million people at 200 kg wheat per person year. This is a high but not impossible rate of consumption, if we allow for spoilage and loss. But the conclusions on population size are incredible.

Another generally unreliable source (*SHA, Septimius Severus* 23) informs us that in about the year AD 200, daily consumption in the city of Rome was 75,000 *modii* (= 180,000 tons per year), less than half the figure cited above. A similar figure, 80,000 *modii* per day, is given by an ancient commentator, a scholiast, on Lucan (ad *Pharsalia* 1.319; ed. C. F. Weber (Leipzig, 1831) vol. 3, 53). These two figures could imply populations of about 900,000 at the rather high rates of consumption cited above.

Finally, the number of houses, as listed in a fourth-century topography for each region of the city of Rome (see R. Valentino, *Codice topografico della città di Roma* (Rome, 1940) 89ff., and 161–2; and Zacharias of Mytilene, *ibid.* 331). Depending on which text one uses, there were about 44,000, 46,000 or 47,000 *insulae* and about 1,800 *domus*. The *domus* were clearly grand houses, *palazzi*. What *insulae* were is disputed.

Authority can be found for two meanings: single residential units like the mediaeval hearths, or houses, some of which were subdivided and let to different families and individuals. The meaning *house* seems more common, and even a very modest multiplier, such as only ten persons per house (*insula*) gives a total population of close on half a million. But clearly we do not know anything certain about occupancy rates in Roman *insulae*.

In sum, precision is impossible. But all the figures cited suggest that the city of Rome had a very large population, almost certainly above 500,000 in the reign of Augustus, and probably less than one million. I agree with Beloch, that the most probable guess is in the region 800,000–1,000,000. But it is only a guess. Finally, I should add that such a large metropolitan population was possible only because of the sophisticated system of water supply (eventually water was brought by nineteen aqueducts from as far as 90 km (56 miles) away), and also because of the less visible but equally impressive system of main drainage.

The literature on this subject is extensive. K. J. Beloch, *Die Bevölkerung der griechisch-römischen Welt* (Leipzig, 1886) 392 ff. seems best; the discussion by U. Kahrstedt in L. Friedländer, *Sittengeschichte Roms* (Leipzig[10], 1921) vol. 4, 11ff. adds something to this. F. G. Maier, 'Römische Bevölkerungsgeschichte und Inschriftenstatistik', *Historia* 2 (1953/4) 318ff. is oversceptical.

The best discussion in English is perhaps by W. J. Oates, 'The population of Rome', *Classical Philology* 29 (1934) 101ff.; that by P. A. Brunt (1971: 376ff.) is too much influenced by his views on the preponderance of ex-slaves in the city's population.

II

THE GROWTH AND PRACTICE OF
SLAVERY IN ROMAN TIMES

THE GROWTH OF A SLAVE SOCIETY

It's no fun being a slave. And it's not just the work
But knowing that you're a slave, and that nothing can change it.
                    Slave character in Plautus, *Amphitryo* (*c.* 200 BC)

Only a handful of human societies can properly be called 'slave societies', if by slave society we mean a society in which slaves play an important part in production and form a high proportion (say over 20%) of the population.[1] There are only two well established cases from antiquity: classical Athens and Roman Italy; but perhaps other Greek districts (such as central Greece around Delphi) or the Greek cities on the Asia Minor seaboard (such as Ephesus and Pergamum) were also slave societies in this sense. To be safe, we should call the two antique cases: Greece understood liberally to include Greek settlements overseas and Roman Italy. Yet even this loose formulation is important since it implies that in most parts of the Roman empire slavery was of minor importance in production.[2] From the early modern period,

[1] Twenty per cent is obviously an arbitrary cut-off point, but it marks a discontinuity between slave societies as defined here and other slave-owning societies. In other words, I am claiming that the number of slave societies would not be increased if the dividing line were fifteen per cent or even ten per cent.

[2] Marxists in particular have been keen to think that slavery predominated throughout the Roman empire, primarily because that was the received opinion when Marx wrote. Recently, however, the discovery and acceptance of the Asiatic mode of production as an alternative link in the social evolutionary chain has diverted attention from slaves to other forms of dependency. The literature is enormous, but see F. Vitinghoff, 'Die Theorie des historischen Materialismus über den antiken Sklavenhalterstaat', *Saeculum* 11 (1960) 89–131, E. Mandel, *Marxist Economic Theory* (London, 1968) 86ff., and E. Varga, 'Über die asiatische Produktionsweise', *Jahrbuch f. Wirtschaftsgeschichte* (1967, 4) 181ff., a journal which regularly carries good articles by East German marxists about ancient history. See also P. Anderson, *Lineages of the Absolutist State* (London, 1974) 462ff. The ancient evidence on slavery in the Roman empire outside Italy is so thin that it seems compatible with many theories. Incidentally the single passing statement by Galen (ed. Kühn, vol. 5, 49) that there were roughly equal numbers of (*a*) citizens, (*b*) women, (*c*) slaves in Pergamum is surely best understood not as a census statistic, but as meaning 'lots of slaves'. We know so little of rural:urban populations that this single statement by itself is difficult to interpret.

99

only three more cases are known, the West Indian Islands, Brazil and the southern states of the USA.[3] These five societies in which slaves played a considerable role in production (and in ostentatious consumption) form a distinct category of 'slave society'.

This definition of slave society is admittedly arbitrary, but it may be useful, because it underlines how rare such 'slave societies' have been, and the marked discontinuity between them and the numerous tribal and pre-industrial slave-owning societies, in which a small proportion of men and women were kept as slaves. The *Human Relations Area Files* record the presence of some slaves in nearly half out of 800 societies studied.[4] But sacrificial slavery among the Kwakiutl, for example, or domestic 'slavery' in traditional China, or the presence of several thousand black slaves in England in the eighteenth century was on a completely different scale from slavery in slave societies as defined above. Among the Kwakiutl, in traditional China and in England, slaves were a negligible factor in production. In Roman Italy, the southern states of the USA and Brazil, slavery was a very large factor in production (see Table II.1).

The similar importance of slavery in the five slave societies makes comparisons between them seem attractive. Obviously, comparison of slavery within the Americas is easier. Whatever the differences in culture, all American slave societies were the product of similar conditions: European expansion into spacious and uncultivated territories, the absence of an easily available and effective labour force, the mass import of black Africans to provide labour, and finally the close links between production by slaves and the economically developed non-slave societies, which provided both tools of production and markets in which the slaves' surplus produce was sold.

In this chapter, few explicit comparisons are to be made between

---

3   For present purposes it seems reasonable to treat the West Indies as a single case. The West African kingdoms at the other end of the slave trade present a difficult case; there seems to be evidence of significant levels of slavery; in some kingdoms slaves probably accounted for fifty per cent of the total population according to nineteenth-century travellers' reports; but the functions of slavery and the treatment of slaves seem remarkably different from those we find in other slave societies. I have therefore, tentatively, not included them as slave societies. This may be wrong. See further the essays in C. Meillassoux, *L'esclavage en Afrique précoloniale* (Paris, 1975) and A. G. B. Fisher and H. J. Fisher, *Slavery and Muslim Society in Africa* (London, 1970).

4   Evidence of the presence or absence of slavery was available from 808 societies. Of 387 societies with some slavery, hereditary slavery was certainly attested in only 165 societies. But the quality of such data is inevitably uneven. See G. P. Murdock, 'Ethnographic atlas: a summary', *Ethnology* 6 (1967) 109ff. The distinction between a slave-owning society and what I call here a 'slave society' is adapted from M. I. Finley, *sv* Slavery in *The International Encyclopaedia of the Social Sciences* (New York, 1968).

Table II.1. *The population of five slave societies*

	Estimated total population ('000,000)	Estimated number of slaves ('000,000)	Slaves as a proportion of the population (about)
Athens[a]			
c. 400 BC	(0.2)*	(0.06)	30%
Roman Italy			
225 BC[b]	(4)	(0.6)	15%
31 BC[c]	(5–6)	(2)	35%
Brazil[d]			
1800	3	1	33%
1850	8	2.5	30%
USA, southern states			
1820[e]	4.5	1.5	33%
1860[f]	12	4	33%
Cuba			
1804	0.5	0.18	28%
1861	1.4	0.4	30%

* Figures in parentheses indicates a considerable degree of doubt.

Sources to Table II.1

(a) R. L. Sargent, *The Size of the Slave Population at Athens* (Urbana, Ill., 1924) 63, 127; (b) derived from P. A. Brunt, *Italian Manpower* (Oxford, 1971) 60 (excluding northern Italy) – a rough guess; (c) K. J. Beloch, *Die Bevölkerung der gr.-röm. Welt* (Leipzig, 1886) 418, 435–6; (d) C. Prado, *História Econômica do Brasil* (São Paolo[8], 1963), appendix; (e) S. E. Morrison et al., *The Growth of the American Republic* (New York, sixth edition 1969) 262, 499, 861; (f) K. M. Stampp, *The Peculiar Institution* (London, 1964) 39; (g) H. S. Klein, *Slavery in the Americas* (London, 1967) 202. The slave population of other islands in the West Indies was smaller.

Roman slavery and slavery in the other 'slave societies'.[5] But comparisons is implicit, in that the argument concentrates on four important aspects of Roman slavery, which seem exceptional by comparison with the southern states of the USA. Three of these factors hang together: the high status of an important body of professional and skilled slaves in Rome, the high rate of slave manu-

[5] Explicit comparisons have been rare, but see particularly J. Vogt, *Sklaverei und Humanität*, Historia Einzelschrift 8 (Wiesbaden[2], 1972), esp. 97ff. (now translated as *Ancient Slavery and the Ideal of Man* (Oxford, 1974) 170ff.); D. B. Davis, *The Problem of Slavery in Western Culture* (Ithaca, N.Y., 1966); Finley (1968); C. A. Yeo, 'The economics of Roman and American slavery', *Finanzarchiv* 13 (1952) 445–83 is now somewhat dated.

mission, and the assimilation of former slaves into citizen society on terms of near equality with native-born Roman citizens. The fourth factor is more complex, and again in stark contrast with southern slavery: the Romans imported a massive number of agricultural slaves into Italy in order to cultivate land which was *already* being cultivated by citizens. We have to explain not only the importation of slaves, but the extrusion of citizens. And we have to fit the growth of slavery into its historical context, concentrating on structure and process in the political economy of Rome during its imperial expansion. Let us tackle this last problem first; we can do it quite rapidly, but some repetition of arguments from the last chapter is unavoidable.

Slavery and the expansion of empire

Mass slavery in Roman Italy (including Sicily) was a product of conquest. In just over two hundred years, the Romans conquered the whole of the Mediterranean basin. In 260 BC, Rome was a poor but politically powerful city-state with control over central and southern Italy. By the end of the first century BC, Rome controlled an empire which stretched from the English Channel to the Red Sea and from Algeria to the Black Sea. It covered a land area equal to more than half the USA, and contained a population which is conventionally estimated at fifty or sixty million, which was (again by conventional estimates) about one fifth of the world population at that time.[6]

Slaves were concentrated in Roman Italy, the heartland of the empire. Most of them were probably captured in battle, after sieges or in the immediate aftermath of conquest;[7] among agricultural slaves, males predominated; while the empire was being expanded, they were replaced by fresh captives, supplemented by trade and breeding. The evidence on slave numbers is slight and disputed; but it is commonly agreed that there was a huge increase in the slave population in the period of expansion, and it seems likely that by the end of the first century BC there were about two million slaves in Italy out of a total population of six million.[8]

---

[6] K. J. Beloch, *Die Bevölkerung der gr.-röm. Welt* (Leipzig, 1886) 507; United Nations, *Determinants and Consequences of Population Trends* (New York, 1953) 8; D. M. Heer, *Society and Population* (Englewood Cliffs, N.J., 1968) 2.

[7] This is disputed, but wrongly, I think, by E. M. Schtaerman, *Die Blütezeit der Sklavenwirtschaft in der römischen Republik* (Wiesbaden, 1969) 36–70; she thinks that even in the period of imperial expansion most slaves in Italy were bought or bred. Of course, war captives too were traded.

[8] I follow Beloch (1886: 418, 435–6) rather than P. A. Brunt, *Italian Manpower* (Oxford, 1971) 124, who thinks in terms of about three million slaves out of a total Italian population of seven and a half million. These differences give some idea of the inadequate evidence.

The growth of a slave society

The conquest, plunder and administration of a huge empire transformed the old political order. The traditional oligarchy had long been entrenched but its power (measured in taxes or in the number of officials) was limited by the lack of governmental resources and by an electorate of armed citizen peasants. The new prosperity destroyed its stability. A series of bitter and destructive civil wars between rival generals led to the establishment of a powerful monarchy strongly based on exclusive control of a professional army. In a parallel process, the intrusion of a large number of slaves transformed the traditional system of production. Peasants who often grew barely enough to feed themselves were evicted to make room for slaves who produced a surplus for sale in the market. The displacement of citizen peasants by slaves, of conquerors by their captives embittered the poor, and from the end of the second century BC exacerbated a series of political disruptions.[9] As soldiers and city proletariat, the landless peasants were an important factor both in fomenting and in providing fodder for the civil wars which marked the demise of the Republic (133 BC–31 BC).

The provision of food and work for two million slaves imported to live side by side with four million citizens implied radical changes in economic and political organisation. It is important to see the interdependence of these changes, and so to be able to set them in a framework which in some way transcends the specific circumstances of any one event. This view complements the historians' normal focus on particular men and their actions ordered primarily by time. Figure 1.1 (p. 12) illustrates the interdependence of *some* of the factors which affected the growth of slavery in Roman Italy. As before, I must stress that the diagram is selective and schematic, but it may be helpful in providing a guide to the discussion. I shall begin from the top left-hand corner.

The Romans conquered the whole of the Mediterranean basin only by a fanatical dedication to fighting wars. This can be seen as a product of the warrior ideology, embedded in the nobility and shared by citizen soldiers. It is difficult to find adequate criteria of militarism. We can see it reflected in Roman folk-heroes such as Fabius the Delayer who refused to fight Hannibal in open battle, or in their later imitators such as Pompey the Great or Julius Caesar, and in the names adopted by Roman nobles to commemorate the regions which they had conquered (e.g. Africanus, Asiaticus), and in the belligerent behaviour of Roman generals. The Roman senate was once dismayed to find that a general assigned to a region in which 'he had not

9 For the most perceptive ancient comments on these developments, see Appian, *Civil Wars* 1.7ff.

accomplished anything memorable' had marched several hundred kilometres to fight an unprovoked war, presumably in the hope of winning glory (Livy 43.1; 171 BC). From the middle of the second century BC onwards, the goddess Victory riding in a chariot and brandishing a whip became a common symbol stamped on Roman silver coins. But the most powerful index of the importance of war in Rome is the numbers of soldiers enlisted. For two centuries, the Romans typically mobilied about one eighth of all adult male citizens, and a much higher proportion of young males.[10] This was greater and more sustained military effort than I have found recorded in any other pre-industrial state.

Economically, foreign wars were disastrous for many of the Roman poor and profitable for the rich. There is an element of crude simplification and tautology in this statement: even so, it seems worth saying. Through death in battle, injuries and prolonged absence, wars created vacancies on Italian agricultural land, which the rich were only too anxious to occupy. War deprived poor families of male labour (and in Roman law, land neglected by its owner could be legally claimed by anyone),[11] while victory provided rich Romans with the alternative labour of slaves. Poor soldiers were engaged in capturing their own replacements.

Frequent victories enabled the Romans to bring back to Italy huge quantities of booty in the form of treasure, money and slaves. The accumulated wealth of the kingdoms of the eastern Mediterranean was brought back to Rome. Provinces were first plundered then taxed; the rapacity of many provincial governors was notorious, and largely unchecked. Some of the booty was spent in turning the city of Rome into a resplendent capital city. Aristocrats displayed their booty in triumphal processions, spent their incomes in the city and competed with each other in ostentatious luxury. This lavish private expenditure, together with government expenditure on public works and on gifts of wheat distributed to Roman citizens living in the city of Rome, all helped encourage the migration of peasants to the city (just as heavy expenditure in capital cities in developing countries nowadays pulls in peasants from the countryside). In addition, the urban population was swollen by slaves imported to work in workshops and to serve the rich in their palaces. By the middle of the first century BC, the

[10] Brunt (1971: 391ff.) reveals and tabulates the extent of this military effort.
[11] '...a man may without violence take possession of another's land, which is lying vacant either because of the owner's neglect, or because the owner had died without a successor or has been absent for a long time' Gaius, *Institutes* 2.51 – a text-book of the second century AD, but I assume that the laws derived from earlier times.

population of the city of Rome was probably well over three quarters of a million.[12] (Rome was thus one of the largest pre-industrial cities ever created.\

The rich invested a considerable part of their new wealth in agricultural land in Italy. Land was the only safe and prestigious large-scale investment available. But fertile land around Rome was already densely occupied by citizen peasants. The rich bought up peasants' land, or took possession of it by violence. They reorganised small-holdings into larger and more profitable farms. The existing pattern of landholdings prevented nobles from creating huge single estates in Italy; their total land-holdings were large, but were typically made up of several properties. There is almost no evidence of estates owned by Roman nobles in the provinces until the end of the Republican period of conquest.[13]

Large numbers of the peasants who had been displaced by slaves migrated to the city of Rome to take advantage of the increased expenditure there and to other Italian towns, or they joined the army, or they migrated to the newly pacified north Italian plains. The reaction to displacement was often bitter and provided a plank for political activists, of whom Tiberius Gracchus is the best known example. As we have seen, he tried to limit the amount of public land (*ager publicus*) which could be cultivated by the rich and proposed that the remainder be distributed to the poor. He was assassinated by conservative nobles, though his plans were, in the short run, modestly successful. In the course of the next century, soldiers repeatedly appealed to their generals for land to settle on and they were willing to fight for what they wanted. As a result, small-holders were often displaced by veterans, since large estates generally escaped seizure and

---

[12] This figure is based primarily on the figures of male recipients of free wheat in the late Republic: 320,000, 150,000, 250,000; add females, children, free non-citizens and slaves. The best discussion of the evidence still seems to be by U. Kahrstedt, in L. Friendländer, *Sittengeschichte Roms* (Leipzig[10], 1921) vol. 4, 11–21 (in detail, see Appendix 1.1, pp. 96–8).

[13] See E. Rawson in M. I. Finley ed., *Studies in Roman Property* (Cambridge, 1976) 85ff. R. P. Duncan-Jones, *The Economy of the Roman Empire* (Cambridge, 1974) 324–33, has collected much of the relevant ancient evidence on estate size and farm size and on labour input from the Roman agricultural writers, and has tackled the problem again in Finley ed., *op. cit.* 8ff. His methods sometimes give a spurious precision to data of varying reliability, without providing criteria by which the plausibility of our records can be tested. There are other problems; estate and farm sizes varied; we need to know how much they varied, and how the variation changed over time. The Roman agricultural writers tried to overcome the variation in the real world by using formal modules of 25–60 hectares (according to crop), and these have sometimes been incautiously used as evidence of actual farm size. The classification of farm size by H. Dohr, *Die Italischen Gutshöfe* (Cologne, 1965) 11ff. is arbitrary and misleading.

were given to rich favourites. The combined pressure of peasants, ex-soldiers and slaves on Italian land was finally relieved by the emigration of several hundred thousand soldiers and civilians to provincial colonies, set up by Julius Caesar and Augustus (*c.* 50–10 BC), and by the further settlement of north Italy.[14]

The Economic Structure of Slave-Holdings

Economically, many of these changes in land use and movements of population may be seen simply as the simultaneous creation of a new surplus and a new market for its consumption. The new slave farms of Italy produced a surplus of marketable crops on land which had previously supported only peasants near the level of subsistence. Land-owners must have achieved this surplus primarily by raising the productivity of labour. Fewer men produced more food. Under-employed peasants (typically providing enough food for themselves and their families with less than one hundred man-days labour a year) were expelled from their family plots and replaced by a smaller number of slaves.[15] The Roman writers of treatises on agriculture imply that in the period of expansion agricultural slaves were usually male and celibate.[16] Providing a single male with food cost substantially less than a family; the difference was one source of the slave-owner's profit. For example, Columella (*On Agriculture* 2.12) recommended that an arable farm of 200 *iugera* (50 ha) could be cultivated by eight adult male slaves. This contrasts with the median size of farms allotted

[14] Brunt (1971: 262–4); I think that he underestimated peasant migration to the city of Rome; see also A. J. N. Wilson, *Emigration from Italy in the Republican Age of Rome* (Manchester, 1966).

[15] Estimates of underemployment in dry-farming for Roman peasants may be based (*a*) on the known size of colonial allotments to Romans (see conveniently E. T. Salmon, *Roman Colonization under the Republic* (London, 1969) or *ESAR* vol. 1, 123); (*b*) on the labour input indicated in ancient sources (see best Columella, *On Agriculture* 2.12 but see also Book 11 for the two-year cycle of cultivation; (*c*) on comparative evidence, see, for example, O. S. Morgan ed., *Agricultural Systems of Modern Europe* (New York, 1933). K. D. White, 'The productivity of labour in Roman agriculture', *Antiquity* 39 (1965) 102ff., contains several significant errors. I shall deal with this problem of labour input and farm size at length in a subsequent publication.

[16] As so often, the evidence is ambiguous. In some passages, the Roman agricultural writers Cato, Varro and Columella seem to take it for granted that only overseers had female partners; but in other passages (for example, Varro 2.10.6 and Columella 1.8.19), it seems clear that slave offspring were encouraged. It is clear from the West Indies that it is possible to run an economy with a predominantly male labour-force, high mortality and a high rate of imports. Much depends on the relative cost of adult slaves and of breeding plus maintenance. Cf. O. Patterson, *The Sociology of Slavery* (London, 1967) 107. For a slightly apologistic account of some ancient evidence, see K. D. White, *Roman Farming* (London, 1970) 370.

to ordinary Roman settlers in twelve colonies in the early second century BC – the only period from which we have such evidence; they were only 10 *iugera* (2.5 ha). This suggests that the same area of land could support either twenty free colonists' families, comprising some eighty men, women and children or just eight adult male slaves. Unfortunately, this evidence poses several problems of credibility which we cannot go into here.[17] But there can be no doubt that the man-power saving made by changing from peasant to slave farming was substantial.

An increase in productivity would have been useless without its reciprocal: the creation of a market. Land-owners needed to sell the newly created surplus so that they could make a return on their investment in land and slaves. The peasants who migrated to Rome (and other Italian towns) and the new urban slaves together provided this market; they consumed the surplus food which was transported from the Italian slave estates. Too much is sometimes made of the heavy cost of overland transport in Roman Italy. In so far as the rich owned surplus-producing farms distant from Rome, they must have sold the surplus, whatever the transport cost. In the sixteenth century, when the population of the city of Rome was under 200,000, wheat was regularly brought from the east coast of Italy around Ancona to Rome – partly by way of the Tiber.[18] In so far as the increased wealth of the Roman elite was based on the ownership of land, then a surplus produced on that land must have been sold. Most of it was probably sold to the largest market, the city of Rome. To the elite whose writings survive, the Roman proletariat seemed impoverished. But they must have earned enough money to buy food.[19] This analysis cannot be authenticated in the conventional way by citations from ancient authors; ancient authors did not conceive contemporary changes in economic terms. But modern history-writing should not be limited to what the ancients themselves perceived. After all, it is commonly agreed that there was a great increase in the production of wine and olive oil in Italy during the last two centuries BC. This increase in production must have been based on an increase in the purchasing power of Roman consumers; and by far the single biggest market was the city of Rome.

17 Cf. Brunt (1971: 194ff.) for some doubts and explanations and *ESAR* vol. 1, 114ff.
18 See J. Delumeau, *La vie économique et sociale de Rome* (Paris, 1959) vol. 2, 521ff.
19 What did the urban proletariat do? We do not know. In contemporary under-developed economies, there is often in the capitals what is called a bazaar economy, a fantastic fragmentation of services and retail sales. Expenditure by rich Romans must have had a considerable multiplier effect, as those who received money spent it – a process which was then repeated.

The growth and practice of slavery

The provision of subsidised and then free wheat to citizens living in the city of Rome must have provided important support to the market. It underwrote the capacity of the free poor to buy food produced on estates owned by nobles and worked by slaves, although there is no evidence that contemporary Romans perceived this function of the wheat dole. To be sure, some of the wheat was imported from the provinces as tax, especially from Sicily and North Africa. But the urban poor could still spend the money, which they would have spent on bread, on wine and oil instead. After all, the rich did not consume all the wine and oil produced on their own estates.

Why slaves and not citizens?

There is one problem about the growth of slavery in Roman Italy which seems particularly puzzling. Why did Roman landowners get rid of citizen peasants and put slaves in their place? At first sight, this may seem like making a mountain out of a molehill. The expansion of slavery may seem to need no explanation. It might be said that the conquering Romans simply took advantage of their victories, enslaved the defeated and carted them off to Italy to work their farms; after all, enslaving captives was an old trandition in the Mediterranean world. But then so was killing captives, putting them to ransom, sparing them, exacting a single indemnity from them, forcibly evicting them and taxing them. Of all these solutions to the problems of victory, slavery was one of the least common, and usually reserved for particularly obstinate or treacherous enemies. After all, the Romans conquered lands occupied by about fifty million people and had only about two million slaves. In a subsistence economy, not everyone wants a slave. Poor Italian peasants might well look the gift of a slave in the mouth, as someone extra to feed. Poor peasants with only small plots of land could not benefit from another pair of hands. They could not afford to maintain a slave.

The rich used slaves instead of free men as dependent workers, because slaves had advantages which outweighed their obvious disadvantages. Slaves cost money and were often, even usually expensive (see below, pp. 110, 161); unlike wage labourers or tenants, they were probably unwilling to work hard or efficiently, and were costly to supervise. On the other hand, slaves, unlike citizens, were not liable to be called away for several years on military service, they were at their master's beck and call and could be forced to work long hours throughout the whole year. Slavery allowed masters to sell land with an adequate supply of labour attached. Above all, unlike peasant families, slaves could be formed into permanent work-gangs several times the size of a family. Columella, for example, recommended gangs of ten male slaves spread over a large farm (*On Agriculture* 1.9.7). Slaves could thus be made to cooperate in working the large farms of nobles who had grown rich on the profits of empire. Slaves were the fuel of an agrarian revolution,[20] a means of organising labour in an economy without a labour market. In modern societies, we take the relationship of employer to employees for granted and sugar the pill of wage-slavery with political democracy.[21] The Romans had no tradition which legitimated the regular employment of free men; in Roman law (the evidence comes from the High Empire), employees in the household were considered as slaves (*loco servorum*) for the duration of their service.[22] Free citizens therefore tried to avoid such work. In the period of imperial expansion, continuous war made slavery seem an easy and attractive way for rich men to organise labour on farms which were much too large to be cultivated by a free family.

Slavery was by no means an obvious solution to the elite's need for agricultural labour. The extrusion of free peasants created a large pool of landless or underemployed citizens. The rich could have employed them to work their estates either as tenants or as day-wage labourers. Some did; Cato, who wrote on farming in the second century BC, advised that the manager of an estate should not employ the same labourers for more than one day, and so assumed a large pool of free labourers (*On Agriculture* 5); Julius Caesar passed a law (which like most Roman laws could not be enforced) that at least one third of men employed as herdsmen should be free citizens (Suetonius, *Julis Caesar* 42). Similarly, our sources generally assumed that most work on the

---

[20] 'The ancient slave estate devours human beings as the modern blast-furnace devours coal.' So Max Weber, 'The social causes of the decay of ancient civilization' trans. in J. E. T. Eldridge, *Max Weber* (London, 1971) 263 or M. Weber, *The Agrarian Sociology of Ancient Civilizations*, trans. R. I. Frank (London, 1976) 398.

[21] The long distance between production and consumption in industrial societies allows the growth of institutions and values which disguise the degree to which manual workers are exploited by the prosperous. In pre-industrial societies, exploitation was more likely to be face-to-face. I use the word exploitation, insofar as possible, neutrally to describe the process by which the product of one man's manual labour is consumed by someone else.

[22] A typical legal text is D. 43.16.1.16–20: '...the term household (*familia*), includes slaves...and those whom we keep like slaves (*loco servorum*)', on which see the commentary of F. M. de Robertis, *Lavoro e lavoratori nel mondo romano* (Bari, 1963) 101–42. The arguments of D. Nörr, 'Zur Bewertung der Arbeit in Rom', *ZSS* (*rom. Abt.*) 82 (1965) 90ff. are a useful corrective to those of de Robertis. The sophisticated discussion about whether a debtor was really a slave (Quintilian, *Institutes* 7.3.26; Ps. Quintilian, *Declamations* 311) is evidence of their assimilation. See the arguments of E. M. Schtaerman and M. K. Trophimova, *Slave ownership in the Early Roman Empire* (*Italy*) (Moscow, 1971) 21 (in Russian).

estates of the wealthy was done by slaves, helped out (for example, at harvest time) by free men.

Why did land-owners not make more use of free men? Free workers have obvious advantages. They can be paid wages out of current income, as and when they are needed; free tenants have an interest in productivity and cost much less than slaves to supervise. Throughout world history, tenancy has been a much more common method of exploitation than slavery. Tenancy was already well established in Roman Italy, and it was always much more important than slavery in the provinces. Its availability intensifies the difficulty of understanding why rich Romans preferred to buy slaves.

The chief disadvantage of slaves was their high capital cost, all the more so if we include the cost of buying the slaves who normally supervised other slaves. This assertion contradicts the common assumption by modern historians that Roman slaves were cheap. They probably were after a battle or in moments of glut in a conquered province. But such fragmentary evidence as we do have suggests that, at the end of the period of expansion, adult male unskilled slaves cost as much as would support an average peasant family for four years (2,000 HS = four tons of wheat equivalent at a conventional price for wheat of 3 HS per *modius*). At that price, slave-owners would have had to keep their slaves at work for at least two hundred days per year in order to make a profit.[23] That is, more than twice as long as most subsistence farmers in Mediterranean (i.e. dry) farming normally work. Moreover, in conditions of high mortality, such as were prevalent in the ancient world, a slave owner risked the sudden death of the slaves he had bought and the immediate liquidation of his asset.

I do not mean by all this to question the profitability of Roman slavery in the period of expansion. Slavery lasted too long for that to

[23] The demand price for slaves should reflect their marginal profitability; it is therefore misleading to concentrate on knockdown slave prices ruling at moments of over-supply. The common price (500 *dn* = 2,000 HS) used here is the one given by A. H. M. Jones, 'Slavery in the ancient World', in M. I. Finley ed., *Slavery in Classical Antiquity* (Cambridge, 1960), 9–10, admittedly on exiguous evidence, mostly chance remarks in poems; it is corroborated by a second-century inscription from Africa (*CIL* 8.23956): 'the price of a slave according to the census scale is 500 dn'. So also D. 4.4.31: Papinian; D. 5.2.8.17: Ulpian', D. 5.2.9: Paul. And see the prices for release cited in Chapter III. The calculation of days' work is based on the amortisation of capital cost over twenty years, plus the cost of feeding, plus interest at 6% on capital invested against the cost of day wage labourers, derived from Diocletian's *Edict on Maximum Prices* at 2.5 kg wheat equivalent per person per day plus food (*ESAR* vol. 5, 336); I follow R. P. Duncan-Jones' persuasive argument that the *castrensis modius* used in the Edict equalled 1½ regular *modii* (each of 6.5 kg wheat), *ZPE* (1976). These data are crude, but the best we have, and give rough orders of magnitude. They would have to be absurdly wrong to upset the general conclusion advanced here.

be a realistic problem. Rather I want to stress the economic logic of slavery. The importation of a large number of agricultural slaves into central Italy necessarily implied a drastic reorganisation of land holdings. In a system of small family farms, slaves could not be adequately exploited. If slaves were to be properly supervised in gangs, then small family farms had to be amalgamated into larger holdings. The high capital cost of slaves led to the creation of units large enough to provide them with work throughout the year. Moreover, large farms, especially those which concentrated on herding, olives or viticulture, could have yielded some economies of scale. Put another way, owners could afford to pay high prices for slaves, precisely because of the high productivity which could be forced out of them on larger farms.

For the owners of large farms, slaves offered several advantages over free labour. Slave-ownership conferred status. Slaves could be completely controlled by the master. They could be forced to work long hours throughout the year: Cato allowed oxen holidays on feast days unless there was grain to be stored, or firewood was needed; but mules and donkeys (and presumably the slaves working with them) got no holidays, except for family festivals (*On Agriculture* 138; cf. Columella 2.21). And slaves could be organised in gangs, in a way which cut across the traditional family organisation of free labour,[24] and allowed some agricultural specialisation (such as ox-drivers, and vine-dressers). In a society without a market in free labour, recruitment by force (i.e. slavery) was probably the only method of securing large numbers of full-time dependants with particular skills. Finally, in the exceptional circumstances of imperial conquest, Roman nobles could afford the high capital cost of slaves. They had massive spoils from the provinces at their disposal, and a shortage of opportunies for their profitable investment.[25] At the same time they faced a shortage of amenable free labour. Slavery was one solution to this predicament.

Slavery and politics

Mass slavery in Rome should also be seen as a product of Roman politics. In the Roman political system, aristocrats depended for their status and power on election to political office, which they solicited from the plebs. To be sure, aristocrats manipulated the electorate.

24 Gangs of itinerant free labourers were available for specific agricultural tasks, such as the olive harvest, but not all the year round.
25 These spoils were archetypal 'free floating resources', rare in pre-industrial societies in which the surplus is usually committed to a narrow range of conventional expenditures. For this idea, see S. N. Eisenstadt, *The Political System of Empires* (New York, 1963), 76ff.

Nevertheless, the political power of the citizen body significantly limited the extent to which rich Romans could systematically exploit free Roman citizens as overt dependants. Roman histories preserved the proud tradition of how, in the past, the armed plebs had marched out of the city of Rome in protest against aristocratic misrule and had won important concessions. An aristocrat who was shaking the hands of the people before an election once commented laughingly on the horny hand of a peasant; the rumour went round the rural tribes that he despised peasants for their poverty, and he lost the election.[26]

This story is only one illustration of the fact that throughout the period of conquest, portions of the Roman plebs had sufficient political and military power to limit the power of nobles and to secure a share in the imperial booty for themselves. Roman citizens living in Italy were exempted from direct taxes (after 167 BC); citizens living in the city of Rome received subsidised (from 122 BC) and eventually free wheat (from 58 BC); citizens and ex-soldiers received land-grants in colonies established outside central Italy and in the provinces. One function of all these developments was to allow the rich to occupy more land in central Italy because the state was providing alternative supplementary benefits for the free poor.

Slaves were forcibly imported aliens who were exploited to a degree and in a way which citizens would not allow. Moreover, slavery fed on itself. The presence of a substantial number of slaves in Roman society defined free citizens, even if they were poor, as superior. At the same time, free citizens' sense of superiority probably limited their willingness to compete with slaves, to work full time as the overt dependants of other citizens.[27] Yet rich men, by definition, need dependants. Slavery permitted the ostentatious display of wealth in the palaces of the rich without involving the direct degradation of the free poor. Indeed slavery persisted as a method of displaying wealth in the Roman empire long after it had ceased to be a major method of producing wealth. Slavery allowed an increase in the discrepancy between the living-styles of rich and poor, while the traditional independence of the citizens was apparently preserved. It was important for the state that citizens should not be alienated from their willingness to fight as soldiers, for the further extension of the empire and the capture of more slaves. Even so, it is worth noting that, although slaves were often a significant element in war booty for both soldiers and

---

[26] Valerius Maximus 7.5.2.

[27] This is a core argument of M. I. Finley, *The Ancient Economy* (London, 1972) 76ff. I am not sure that the resistance to working for someone else persisted among the proletariat or peasantry after the fall of the Republic; cf. n. 22 above and D. Nörr (1965: esp. 75ff.).

generals, there is no evidence that the capture of slaves was a primary objective of warfare. Slaves were an important but incidental product of empire.

The sudden influx of huge wealth disrupted long-established patterns of production, consumption and exploitation. The elite converted their new-found wealth into the only asset which conventionally gave high status, Italian land. Compared with public office, landownership gave a steady income. Roman nobles did not become feudal lords or satraps, each ruling one sector of the conquered domain; oligarchic control of nobles by each other and by citizen soldiers was too strong. The central government, after a severe struggle throughout the last century of the Republic, survived as a strong force which controlled the power of individual nobles. Even so, Roman nobles increased their wealth towards a level commensurate with their control over a huge empire. But they kept their main source of wealth, the private ownership of land in the home country.

The preservation of these political and economic boundaries determined the developments already outlined. The nobles dispossessed large numbers of peasants of their land and replaced them by slaves. This led to the mass emigration of peasants. They went to the army and to the towns (and much later went to settle in the provinces). As soldiers, they provided the means of new conquests; as plebs, they formed a market for the consumption of the produce grown by slaves on the farms of the rich. The forcible intrusion of so many slaves into the peasant economy precipitated the repeated civil disturbances of the last century of the Republic. Even so, slavery was probably less disruptive than some of its alternatives, such as feudal fragmentation or the sudden transformation of Roman citizens into serfs.

This analysis suggests some of the aspects of slavery which have been common to the five 'slave societies'. In Rome and the Americas, and perhaps in Athens too, mass slavery was a direct consequence of imperial expansion. The purchase price of slaves was largely funded from outside the slave societies. In the southern states and in the West Indies, the growth of slavery can be seen as only one point in a triangle of extensive economic development. North-western Europe and the northern states of the USA provided both capital and a market; Africa provided labour; the slave states produced staples for export. The Roman economy was less differentiated; slavery was more directly a product of war: booty capitalism, as Weber called it, instead of industrial capitalism.

In both Athens and Rome, the mass participation of citizens in prolonged fighting was to some extent dependent on the labour of slaves. Large numbers of citizens could fight, simply because slaves were producing food or goods (wheat, wine, armour, ships). In both societies, the rights of citizenship were secured by the military power of citizens; these same rights prevented the full exploitation of citizens by each other. The rich were driven to exploit imported aliens as well or instead. Democracy in Athens and plebeian privileges in Rome were made possible by the combination of imperial conquest and slavery. It is interesting that slavery was also an important part of the economic network of democratic England and the northern states of the USA; but the connection between them is obscured by the fact that slavery was geographically located outside the boundaries of democratic society.[28]

It is tempting to use these selected common characteristics of mass slavery as part of an explanation of its rarity. Conquest seems to have been a prerequisite, since most pre-industrial societies do not by themselves generate a sufficient surplus to pay for the capital purchase of a large alien labour force. The predominance of the subsistence sector precludes the sudden expansion of production, if only because there is no market for the consumption of a surplus. A similar vicious circle still binds economically underdeveloped societies today.

But when conquest had occurred, slavery was only one of several possible forms of exploitation: feudal fragmentation, the colonisation of populated territories (which requires the conquerors to live in the conquered lands) or dependence on tax revenues (which presupposes a stable fiscal system and bureaucracy), each lessens the need to purchase and transport a slave labour force to the home country. Mass chattel slavery has arisen only where there was either a shortage of a local labour force in the conquered territory, or some effective limitation on the number and degree to which conquerors could themselves be exploited; or both.[29] In Athens and Rome, the rich remained in the home-country; their exploitation of fellow-citizens was constrained by the norms of citizenship and by their continued dependence on citizens as soldiers, In a simple economy, where ownership of land was the chief basis of wealth, the distance between production and consumption was so short that effective disguise of exploitation was difficult. Exploitation was mostly face-to-face. You knew who was profiting from your labour. Slavery allowed the rich

[28] The part played by slavery in the economic development of the first industrial nations is provocatively stressed by E. Williams, *Capitalism and Slavery* (London, 1964).

[29] This analysis is derived in part from H. J. Nieboer, *Slavery as an Industrial System* (The Hague², 1910); cf. for an interesting comparative discussion A. Sio, 'Interpretations of slavery', *Comp. Stud. Soc. Hist.* 7 (1964–5) 289–308.

to enjoy the fruits of conquest by exploiting outsiders i
insiders, without provoking a sharp break in the political cult
else could the elite take advantage of a rapid increase in th
of being rich?

WHY DID THE ROMANS FREE SO MANY SLAVES?

I took care that he would not die a slave, when a fatal fever held him burning
in its grip. I resigned all my rights as a master to the sick man – he deserved
my gift and to get better. Dying, he was conscious of his reward, and called
me 'patron' [not master], as he began his journey to the underworld waters,
a free man. (Martial 1.101.5–10)
Freedom conferred at the end of life. . . is of no importance. (Julian – a Roman
lawyer second century AD (D 40.4.17))

On the number of ex-slaves and the high status of some

One of the most striking aspects of Roman slavery was the frequency
with which slaves were freed by their masters. The impression one gets
from the sources is of a large number (i.e. tens of thousands) of ex-slaves
mingled with the free-born population in the city of Rome. It is
important to note that we have clues rather than precise numbers of
ex-slaves in the total population. For example, one successful political
general in the late Republic (Sulla) is said to have freed ten thousand
slaves (Appian, *Civil Wars* 1.100 and 104); the fire-brigade of seven
thousand men, formed in AD 6, was initially recruited only from
ex-slaves (Dio 55.26); under Augustus, a law was passed prohibiting
a master from freeing more than a hundred slaves in his will (Gaius,
Institutes 1.42–3), although no effective limit was placed on the number
of slaves whom he could free during his life-time.[30] About seven
thousand tombstone inscriptions from the city of Rome clearly indicate
the dead person's status; of these, three times as many commemorate
ex-slaves as free-born.[31] We should not conclude from this that most

[30] See S. Treggiari, *Roman Freedmen during the Late Republic* (Oxford, 1969) 31–6; and
A. N. Sherwin White, *The Roman Citizenship* (Oxford², 1973), 322–34; and on the
ineffectiveness of laws restricting manumission see G. Alföldy, 'Die Freilassung von
Sklaven', *Rivista storica dell' antichità* 2 (1972) 97–129; he shows that a high proportion
of ex-slaves, whose ages at death were recorded and who were freed, died before
the age of thirty. But such slaves are probably not a random sample of all slaves
or ex-slaves, so that his conclusion that *most slaves* were freed before the age of thirty
is obviously illegitimate (see note 63 below).

[31] On Republican tombstones from the city of Rome recording the death of slaves (N
= 650), see Treggiari (1969) 32; for later evidence see L. R. Taylor, 'Freedmen and
freeborn in the epitaphs of imperial Rome', *Amer. J. Phil.* 82 (1961) 113–32. It is very
important to note that only about one third of 22,000 tombstone-inscriptions from
the city of Rome provide clear indication of the dead person's status, whether slave,

citizens living in the city of Rome had once been slaves or were the offspring of slaves.[32] But it seems reasonable to think that the numbers of ex-slaves were substantial.

Almost all ex-slaves freed by Roman masters received Roman citizenship (but see Gaius, *Institutes* 1.12ff.). Some ex-slaves gained considerable wealth and social prominence. In a debate in the Roman senate, it was reportedly said that many knights and some senators were descended from ex-slaves (Tacitus, *Annals* 13.27). Throughout the first century AD, ex-slaves of the emperor's household filled important posts as secretaries of state (of the treasury, appeals etc.) in the central administration. They were the confidants of emperors, resentfully flattered and courted for favours by free-born nobles. Pallas, the ex-slave of the emperor Claudius, for example, was given the rank of praetor; and in a fulsome decree the senate offered him fifteen times the minimum fortune of a senator. 'Pallas, to whom all to the utmost of their ability acknowledge their obligation, should reap the just reward of his outstanding loyalty and devotion to duty' (Pliny, *Letters* 8.6). To add insult to injury, he refused the offer.[33]

In the provinces, ex-slaves of the emperor supervised the collection of taxes and kept an eye for the emperor on the activities of senatorial governors.[34] Sometimes, ex-slaves governed a province; for example, Felix, the procurator of Judaea who judged St Paul, was an ex-slave. Ex-slaves were sometimes admirals in charge of the Roman navy. Slaves of the emperor frequently married women of free birth and

ex-slave, free citizen or alien. Their status was clearly not as important to them as to us. On the basis of names typically given to slaves (for example, Eutyches), and from the marriage of men and women with the same name taken from their common master, Taylor deduced that among those whose death was recorded and whose status is uncertain the proportion of slaves and ex-slaves was as high as among the minority whose status was certain. But what about the descendants of ex-slaves, who were freeborn? T. Frank ('Race mixture in the Roman empire', *Amer. Hist Rev.* 21 (1916) 689–708) concluded that most people living in Rome, including the descendants of ex-slaves, were of slave extraction.

[32] Brunt (1971: 377, 386) concluded on even worse evidence that in the late Republic most people living in the city of Rome were either slaves, ex-slaves or their descendants. *Prima facie*, this is improbable; it presupposes a *cordon sanitaire* around Rome preventing the immigration of landless citizen-peasants. It seems clear to me that the surviving tombstones are unrepresentative of the total city population; that said, the explanation for the preponderance of tombstone inscriptions set up to or by ex-slaves escapes me.

[33] Other notable flatteries by free men of ex-slaves are in Statius, *Silvae* 5.1 and 3.3 (the latter addressed to the son of an ex-slave married to a woman of noble birth); Seneca, *To Polybius, On Consolation* – addressed by a senator to an ex-slave high official of the emperor.

[34] For a very good general discussion see A. M. Duff, *Freedmen in the Early Roman Empire* (repr. Cambridge, 1958) 143–86; for detailed footnotes, see G. Boulvert, *Esclaves et affranchis impériaux* (Naples, 1970), esp. 107ff. on ex-slave provincial procurators.

themselves owned slaves.[35] Private owners used slaves as business agents, confidential secretaries and farm bailiffs. Such slaves were put in charge of other slaves, as overseers, and unlike practice in the American south, they were, at least ideally, specially trained for the task (Columella, *On Agriculture* 11.1). Education and literacy were in no sense thought of as subverting slavery. Many skilled slaves gained their freedom. A few amassed huge fortunes and set up magnificent monuments; the wealth of ex-slaves became notorious, a subject of satire on the decadence of old free Roman virtues.[36] One ex-slave at his death owned over 4,000 slaves, 7,200 oxen and 60 million HS in cash (sixty times the minimum fortune of a senator) (Pliny, *Natural History* 33.135). Our sources give the impression that at humbler levels of society ex-slaves dominated commercial life in the city of Rome. Nor was it only commercial life which they dominated. Ex-slaves commonly became leaders of religious cult-groups, apparently on equal terms with free citizens.[37]

The large number of ex-slaves and the high status of some pose a problem. Why did Roman masters free so many slaves? At first sight, it seems amazing. Slaves cost money. Skilled or talented slaves apparently stood the best chance of securing their freedom, and they cost a lot of money.[38] By buying a slave in the first place, a master had acquired the right to all the slave's labour and produce for the rest of his life, without further payment. Why did he surrender these rights? Roman society was not marked by altruism.

Historians of ancient slavery have usually described the emancipation of slaves from a humanitarian point of view; they have seen it as a softening element in a harsh system. It is true that for the individual slave, manumission was an act of generosity by the master

[35] P. R. C. Weaver, *Familia Caesaris* (Cambridge, 1972) 114. Of 462 known wives of imperial slaves, only a quarter were themselves slaves.

[36] The archetypal rich ex-slave is Trimalchio, Petronius' satirical fiction in the *Satyricon*. He made his money through inheritance from his master and by risky trade. For other ex-slaves' wealth, see Martial 5.13; Pliny, *Natural History* 33.134–5; Seneca, *Letters* 27.5 and 86.7.

[37] One inscription (*ILS* 6073) from the second century AD shows that 229 (86%) out of 275 district officials (*magistri vicorum*) connected with the imperial cult in the city of Rome were ex-slaves; see Duff (1958: 132). In many religious cults there was no strict dividing line between slaves, ex-slaves and free. Indeed slaves were sometimes cult-masters (*magistri*) with free men as cult 'servants' (*ministri*). See F. Bömer, *Untersuchungen über der Religion der Sklaven in Griechenland und Rom*, part 1 (Wiesbaden, 1958) *passim*.

[38] Columella (*On Agriculture* 3.3.8) advised the purchase of a skilled vine-dresser at 6–8,000 HS, that is three-four times the 'normal' (see n. 23) price for an unskilled adult male slave. At the conventional wheat price of 3 HS per *modius* of 6.5 kg, 6,000 HS = 13 tons of wheat equivalent, roughly enough to support a peasant family at minimum subsistence for thirteen years.

which allowed him to escape from servitude. Ex-slaves presumably felt, and in the surviving records frequently expressed their gratitude to their masters – a feeling for which we have the flattering mirror-image in Martial's poem on the liberation of his own dying slave, quoted at the beginning of this section.

Such descriptions of individual feelings have biased the discussion of slave emancipation. If we consider slavery as a system, then the liberation of slaves, whatever blessings it brought to individuals, acted not as a solvent of the slave system, but as a major reinforcement. Emancipation reinforced slavery as a system because Roman slaves, frequently, even customarily in my view, paid substantial sums for their freedom. The prospect of becoming free kept a slave under control and hard at work, while the exaction of a market price as the cost of liberty enabled the master to buy a younger replacement. Humanity was complemented by self-interest.

Misery, cruelty, rebellion and philosophy

Both views of slave manumission, the humanitarian and the economic, require some qualification and elaboration. Most Roman slaves were freed only by death.[39] Roman writers on agriculture took it for granted that their readers' land would normally be worked by gangs of chained slaves.[40] Such slaves presumably had no realistic prospect of liberty. Cato recommended that slaves worn out with work should be sold (*On Agriculture* 2.7). And we know that some masters in the first century AD left their sick slaves to fend for themselves in public places dedicated to the god of healing, only to reclaim them if they recovered (Suetonius, *Claudius* 25; D. 40.8.2); the emperor denied the master's right to recover slaves neglected in this way.

Roman literature abounds with examples of incidental cruelty to individual domestic slaves. The emperor Augustus, for example, ordered that the legs of a trusted slave be broken because he had taken a bribe and revealed the contents of a letter (Suetonius, *Augustus* 67). The physician Galen reported that the emperor Hadrian once in anger stabbed a slave in the eye with a stylus. He later regretted it and asked the slave to choose a gift in recompense. The slave was silent. The emperor pressed him for a reply. The slave said that all he wanted was his eye back (ed. Kühn, vol. 5, 17–18). Seneca portrayed a master at dinner, surrounded by slaves: 'The unfortunate slaves are not

---

[39] This assumes an egalitarian heaven.
[40] Pliny (*Letters* 3.19) made a special point of the fact that he and neighbouring land-owners did not use chained gangs. This makes sense only if it was common in some other places – for which see Columella, *On Agriculture* 1.6.3; 1.8.15ff.; 1.9.4.

allowed to move their lips, let alone talk; the birch keeps murmuring down. A cough, a sneeze, a hiccup is rewarded by a flogging, with no exceptions. Any break in the silence is severely punished. They stand at the ready all night, tense and mute' (*Moral Letters* 47)[41]

Gladiatorial shows in which slaves were publicly killed for the pleasure of the free, and the legal fiction in criminal cases that the evidence of slaves could be trusted only if it was exacted under torture are two symptoms of the customary cruelty of Roman masters to their slaves. Ancient descriptions of working conditions for slaves in quicksilver mines in central Asia Minor, or gold mines in Egypt make it clear that slave miners there did not survive long.[42] In the Spanish silver mines, forty thousand slaves were said to have worked:

The slaves... produce incredible profit for their masters, but they themselves wear out their bodies, digging underground by day and by night, and many of them die under the strain of such terrible conditions. They are not allowed any pause or rest from their work, but are forced by the blows of their overseers to endure sheer misery. (Diodorus 5.38)

'All slaves are enemies' (*quot servi, tot hostes*) went a Roman proverb.[43] Tens of thousands of slaves were systematically exploited on farms and in mines; even talented and responsible slaves in the households of senators and knights were liable to suffer from the cruel caprice or normal disciplinary practices of a master.[44] Slaves were at

[41] Augustus was also said to have punished an ex-slave procurator in Egypt, who ate a prize-fighting quail, by having him nailed to a ship's mast (Plutarch, *Sayings of the Romans* 207B). Beating slaves was routine; philosophers merely advised that it should not be done in anger (Galen, ed. Kühn, vol. 5, 17–18; Seneca, *On Anger* 3.32ff.).

[42] For the realgar (?quicksilver) mines, see Strabo 12.3.40 '...in addition to the harshness of the work, it is said that the air in the mines is deadly...so that workmen very soon die'. Cf. Cyprian, *Letter* 76 (Budé) for a rhetorical account of conditions in mines for condemned Christians. For numbers in the Spanish silver mines in the second century BC, see Strabo 3.2.10 citing Polybius. For Egyptian gold-mines in the second century BC, see C. Müller, *Geographi Graeci Minores* vol. 1, 123ff., and Diodorus 3.12–14. For an overview, cf. O. Davies, *Roman Mines in Europe* (Oxford, 1935).

[43] Festus 314L; Seneca, *Moral Letters* 47.5; Macrobius, *Saturnalia* 1.11.13; all call it a proverb. Seneca (*loc. cit.*) preached that masters alienated slaves by their cruelty and abuses; Macrobius similarly: 'At home we become tyrants and want to exercise power over slaves, constrained not by decency but capacity'.

[44] It is of course difficult to tell what was normal. Ancient sources provide no systematic account of slavery; there are no slave autobiographies, no abolitionist tracts – because no one questioned the institution of slavery. The occasional glimpses provided by ancient authors, however, fit in well enough with the full and very interesting accounts provided by, for example, Frederick Douglass, *My Bondage and My Freedom* (New York, 1855), and G. Osofsky, *Puttin' on Ole Massa* (New York, 1969) respectively the best and a collection of slave autobiographies from the American south. See also the detailed eye-witness accounts in *The Minutes of the Evidence taken before a Committee of the Whole House* (the British House of Commons on slavery in the West Indies) 1789–91, and the discussion by G. Freyre, *Masters and Slaves* (New York, 1946) on Brazilian slavery.

the mercy of their masters. They could be overworked, neglected, thrown out when old, beaten, or even killed, and mostly had no realistic chance of protecting themselves (but see below, p. 222). To be sure slaves had no monopoly of misery. The free poor did most of the jobs which slaves did; they worked in mines and on farms, though less often as domestics. Indeed, the economic value of slaves to their masters sometimes protected them. In Roman Italy, as in the southern states, masters on occasion gave dangerous jobs to free men explicitly in order to safeguard their slaves (see Varro, *On Agriculture* 1.17). Even so, slaves must often have feared maltreatment, and that fear must have affected even more than those who actually suffered.

The mutual hostility of master and slave, which slavery inevitably evokes, showed through both collectively and individually. Between 135 and 70 BC, there were three major slave rebellions in Sicily and Italy, which were apparently fostered by the concentration and neglect of thousands of newly enslaved. The slaves' initial success against Roman legions was not maintained; eventually the slave armies were defeated and ruthlessly crushed.[45] It is worth noting that rebel slaves never aimed at the abolition of slavery, only at the exchange of roles with their masters or at escape to their home country; after 70 BC, we hear of no serious, large-scale slave revolts, though minor outbreaks occasionally threatened (Tacitus, *Annals* 4.27; *Histories* 3.47; *ILS* 961).

The hostility of masters to their slaves ran just below the surface of Roman civilisation. It erupted in the law and the practice that all the slaves living in the house of a master killed by one of his own slaves should be tortured and executed.[46] In one notorious case (AD 61), four hundred household slaves were executed, though only after a debate in the senate and in the teeth of popular outcry. According to Tacitus, the clinching argument in the senate was:

...do you believe that a slave made up his mind to kill his master without an ominous phrase escaping him, without one word uttered rashly? Assume however that he kept quiet, that he procured his weapon in an unsuspecting household. Could he pass the watch, carry in his light, and perpetrate his murder without an accomplice? A crime has many antecedent symptoms.

So long as our slaves act as informers, we may live a minority amid their mass, secure while they fear, and finally, if we die, certain of vengeance against the guilty. Our ancestors always suspected slaves...

[45] The road from Capua to Rome was lined with 6,000 crucified slaves captured from the remnants of Spartacus' rebellion. In general, see J. Vogt, *Struktur der antiken Sklavenkriege* (Wiesbaden, 1957) now translated in J. Vogt, *Ancient Slavery and the Ideal of Man* (Oxford, 1974) 39ff.

[46] By a senatorial decree of AD 10 (*SC Silanianum*), if a master was killed, and the murderer could not be found, all the household slaves were tortured and executed.

Why did the Romans free so many slaves?

Now that our households comprise tribes with customs the opposite of our own, with strange cults or with none, you will never coerce such a mixture of humanity, except by terror. (*Annals* 14.44, cf. 13.32); trans adapted from the Loeb Classical Library)

Most slave resistance involved neither open rebellion nor murder. It probably took the form of guile, deceit, lying and indolence. This can be documented only from incidental remarks in Roman and Greek literature, which of course reflect the masters' stereotype of their slaves. Yet it is interesting that the character of slaves in Roman comedy has a lot in common with the American stereotypical slave Sambo: impudent, gossiping, lazy, deceitful, light-fingered, unscrupulous. It seems reasonable to suppose that the stereotype was based in reality; many slaves' characters were moulded by their overt powerlessness.[47]

Roman slaves had one decisive advantage over American black slaves; they had no obvious distinguishing marks. Proposals to make them wear special dress were rejected out of fear that they would then realise the strength of their numbers (Seneca, *On Mercy* 1.24). Both as slaves and as freed men they could merge with the rest of the population. In a society without photographs, it was relatively easy for slaves to run away. The emperor Augustus recorded in his list of achievements that during the civil wars he had returned 30,000 runaway slaves to their masters for punishment.[48] Conditions during the civil wars were exceptional; but the problem was recurrent, witness the iron slave-collars excavated by archaeologists. Several are inscribed; for example. 'I have escaped; arrest me; take me back to my master Zoninus and you will be rewarded with a gold piece' (*CIL* 15.7194).

The viciousness of Roman slavery, the exploitation, cruelty and mutual hostility are worth stressing because modern accounts often focus instead on those elements in Roman philosophy, literature and law which point to the humanitarian treatment of slaves, and to the willing loyalty of some slaves to their masters.[49] Stoic philosophers stressed the common humanity of slaves and free men: the master buys and sells only the slave's body; 'only their body is at the mercy and disposition of the master; the mind is its own master, and is free...' (Seneca, *On Benefits* 3.20); the slave can be free in spirit, just as the

---

[47] G. E. Duckworth, *The Nature of Roman Comedy* (Princeton, 1952) 249ff.; S. M. Elkins, *Slavery* (New York, 1963) 81–139.

[48] *My Achievements* 25; those for whom no master could be found were impaled, so Dio 49.12.5. See now also H. Bellen, *Studien zur Sklavenflucht im römischen Kaiserreich* (Wiesbaden, 1971).

[49] On loyal slaves, see J. Vogt on *Sklaventreue* (1972) 83–96; (1974) 129.

free men can be a slave to ambition, fear, grief or gluttony. Man is by nature free, not a slave.[50] But for all their enlightened views on slavery, Stoic philosophers were not social reformers. They objected to cruelty, but they never aimed at abolishing slavery. The elevation of moral freedom above the slavery of the body relieved them of any pressure to change the social order. Christians similarly, by their emphasis on rewards in heaven partly in compensation for sufferings on earth, accepted slavery.[51]

Slaves, give entire obedience to your earthly masters, not merely with an outward show of service, to curry favour with men, but with single-mindedness out of reverence for the Lord...knowing that there is a Master who will give you your heritage as a reward for your service. Christ is the Master whose slaves you must be. (Paul, Colossians 3.22–4; The New English Bible, 1961)

Within these rigid lines of accepting slavery, philosophy and later Christianity both helped to soften the rigours of Roman law concerning slaves. It was forbidden to sell slaves as gladiators or prostitutes without stating specific cause (*SHA, Hadrian* 18); masters were not allowed to punish slaves excessively or to kill them (unless they died as a result of reasonable punishment!); the separation of slave wives and children was discouraged; slaves who thought that they were unjustly treated could seek asylum at the emperor's statue, in a temple, or later in a Christian church; a magistrate could order maltreated slaves to be sold to another master.[52] In some borderline cases, the law gave the benefit of doubt to the slave and upheld his right to be freed. Slavery was even defined by an academic jurist as 'a practice of the law of nations, by which one person is subjected to the dominion of another, contrary to nature' (D. 1.5.4.1 Florentinus). Yet for all this, it is doubtful that the Roman government ensured that its laws were executed systematically, let alone in favour of slaves. Rather, we should understand the laws as reflecting a desire of the ruling class to see that the worst excesses of masters were checked. 'Masters, be just and fair to your slaves, knowing that you too have a Master in Heaven'

---

50 Seneca, *On Benefits* 3.18ff.; Epictetus, *Discourses* 1.29; 3.24; Dio Chrysostom, *Discourses* 14–15 which (in fifteen pages) form the longest treatment of slavery in classical literature.
51 Still the best discussion of Christian and philosophical attitudes is H. Wallon, *Histoire de l'esclavage dans l'antiquité* (Paris, 1879) vol. 3, 1–46; more recently, H. Gülzow, *Christentum und Sklaverei* (Bonn, 1969).
52 Gaius, *Institutes* 1, 53; D. 1.6.2: Ulpian; Paul, *Sententiae* 5.23.6; D. 33.7.12.7: Ulpian; Wallon (1879) vol. 3, 62ff.; W. L. Westermann, *The Slave Systems of Greek and Roman Antiquity* (Philadelphia, 1955) 114ff.

(Colossians 4.1).[53] Ideals no doubt affected practice; but moral prescription is usually weak evidence of actual behaviour. Evidence from elsewhere suggests that laws and social values deprecating cruelty failed to prevent excesses.[54] The mitigation of slavery by philosophical belief and imperial decree probably made little impression on the routine corruption implicit in an elite culture which took the massed subservience of slaves for granted.

The legal and social status of slaves and ex-slaves

In Roman law, slaves were treated more as things than as persons. According to the Roman senator Varro, agricultural slaves were 'articulate tools' (*instrumentum vocale*) as distinct from 'semi-articulate tools' such as oxen, or 'dumb tools' such as carts.[55] These definitions are yet further symptoms of the powerlessness and suffering of many slaves in Roman Italy. Yet the starkness of the legal definition is too persuasive; it tempts us to think of slaves as forming unequivocally the lowest stratum in the Roman social pyramid.

But an important minority of slaves had considerable prestige, social power and influence. Their social status conflicted with their legal status as slaves. I am not thinking here of masters' pet slaves, concubines or nannies. As in Brazil and the southern states, their privileges implied a dent in the stratification system, but their deferential dependence on their masters kept them in their place. However, there were other slaves whose value to their masters lay in the fact that they were able to take responsibility as *thinking persons*, not things. These were slave doctors, teachers, writers, accountants, agents, bailiffs, overseers, secretaries, and sea-captains. Why did the Romans give such jobs to slaves?

Part of the answer lay in the cultural and administrative implications of conquering an empire. The Romans admired and wanted to imitate the culture of the conquered East. But imitation required refined education and the exercise of skills, in which Romans had no experience. To fill the gap, Greek-speaking philosophers, teachers and

---

53 Cf. Seneca, *On Mercy* 1.18: 'It is praiseworthy to be moderate in what you tell slaves to do. Even with slaves, one ought to consider not how much you can make them suffer without fearing revenge, but how much justice and goodness allow; both enjoin mercy on captives and bought slaves.'

54 See Douglass (1855) and *Minutes* (1789–91) cited in note 44; poor masters did maltreat their only valuable slave. Occasionally Roman slaves succeeded in invoking the law in their favour; I suspect they had powerful patronage.

55 *On Agriculture* 1.17; but see D. 1.6.2: Ulpian; Gaius, *Institutes* 1.53.

doctors were brought to Rome.[56] Slavery was one of the chief methods of recruiting the highly cultured to work in Roman Italy. The sophistication of Rome as the cultural capital of the empire depended considerably on educated, foreign-born slaves. Similarly, the administration of a huge empire under a single stable government required the development of a bureaucracy. As we have seen, free-born Roman citizens traditionally disliked the idea of working as long-term employees at the beck and call of other free men (except in the army). The second-century satirist Lucian has left an amusing account of the servitude implicit for a free man working as a 'professor' or litterateur in the house of a noble Roman (*On Salaried Posts in Great Houses*, esp. 23–4). In a later essay, he justified his own actions in taking a salaried post in the provincial administration, on the grounds that working for the emperor did not involve the same servitude (*Apology* 11). It seems amazing that this had to be argued, even for amusement, in the second century. Free men apparently felt that a permanent job restricted their freedom of choice, constrained them like slaves. Faced by this prejudice, provincial governors in the Republic and then emperors staffed their administration predominantly with slaves and ex-slaves, and not with free born citizens.[57]

The slaves and ex-slaves of the emperor formed an especially privileged and powerful group. The status and power of their master inevitably rubbed off on them.[58] Unlike nobles, slaves' tenure of office was not restricted to short periods. They had time to accumulate power. Several top slaves and ex-slaves had privileged access to the emperor; they provided him with, or cut him off from information; they were his trusted confidants. But their inferior legal status was still important; they were at the emperors' mercy, even more than senators; because they were slaves, or ex-slaves, they could easily be punished and they were not rivals for imperial power. In many other monarchies, lower-class servants have been similarly used in positions of power (see below, Chapter IV).

In the imperial household, and in private households too, the discrepancy between the legal status of cultured slaves and their actual power and responsibility was repeatedly solved by giving them

[56] On slave litterateurs, see for example those listed by Suetonius, *On Grammarians*. Both Terence and Aesop, for example, were slaves. A notable ex-slave doctor was Antonius Musa, physician to the emperor Augustus. Many such skilled men were freed.

[57] Freeborn citizens served as lieutenants or aides-de-camp of the governor; as such they were subordinates, but only temporarily and they saw themselves ideally as men of independence. For a Republican example of the power of a slave assistant to the governor, see Cicero, *Letters to his brother Quintus* 1.1.17.

[58] On the influence of the emperors' slaves and ex-slaves, see Boulvert (1970: 335ff.).

freedom. But it was only a partial solution. First, even the insignia of high rank, commensurate with actual power (for example, a few imperial ex-slaves were given senatorial insignia, several the status of knights) could not erase the stigma of previous slavery. Secondly, the emancipation of imperial administrative slaves did not generally raise the status of administrative jobs in the eyes of many free men sufficiently to make them attractive; the attitudes of Lucian cited above show this clearly. Throughout the High Empire, many important posts remained the preserve of slaves and ex-slaves, although in the course of the first century AD the highest positions in the central and provincial administration (such as head of the central government secretariat or of indirect taxes in the provinces), were increasingly filled by free-born knights.[59]

The regular use by Romans of skilled and highly cultured slaves in responsible positions (which contrasts so markedly with common practice in the American southern states) induced a series of flexible compromises with the weaknesses and rigidity of chattel slavery. For example, by a legal fiction, an agreement made by a slave acting as his master's accredited agent was binding on the master; the slave was assumed to be an extension of the master's body, working with his master's mind.[60] The master thus revoked total control of the slave and gave him discretion in bargaining. In other cases, the master explicitly limited his liability to the extent of the slave's own 'private purse' (*peculium*).

The concept '*peculium*' applied originally to the money which a father allowed a son, who was still under his authority; in our sources, however, it is most commonly used to describe a slave's possessions. The institution of *peculium* allowed the slave a working capital, 'borrowed' from his master. The use by slaves and ex-slaves of their master's capital gave them a decisive advantage over the free poor, and must have been an important factor underlying the prominence of slave and ex-slave enterprises in Roman commerce and manufacture. The manumission of slaves engaged in commerce or manufacture, with finance derived from their masters, symptomised the fragmentation of production and trade in the Roman world and the predominance of the family as the unit of labour. In the Roman world, slavery was almost the only mechanism which allowed the aggregation of labour into units larger than the family. But manumission split large units owned by a capitalist master back into smaller,

---

[59] On the rise of knights, see H. G. Pflaum, *Les procurateurs équestres sous le haut-empire romain* (Paris, 1950).
[60] W. W. Buckland, *The Roman Law of Slavery* (Cambridge, 1908) 131ff.

family units, based on the ex-slave. In the process, the master sacrificed any economies of scale for lower costs of supervision and smaller risk. In return, he presumably got from his ex-slaves, either interest on loans or a share in the ex-slaves' profits, or both. The devolution of risk and control in commerce to individual ex-slaves was similar to the growing preference of Italian landlords in the High Empire for tenancies rather than large directly-controlled farms.

The very idea that slaves could *de facto* control their own property, including their own slaves, implied independence of action. The *peculium* was the institutional expression of that freedom of action. Although even privileged slaves were not always able to sell their labour on the market as they chose, many of them worked in positions in which they were able to make a profit for themselves. Indeed, there is evidence that masters paid some of their slaves a regular monthly wage.[61] Slaves could save out of their earnings. And eventually they could use their savings to buy their freedom.

The slave's desire to buy his freedom was the master's protection against laziness and shoddy work – although the slave might also cheat his master to speed his chances of buying freedom. The slave had freedom to work for. The master held out the carrot as well as the stick; the stick by itself, as the American experience showed, was ineffectual. The cost of providing an incentive for good work was liberty. But the regular emancipation of slaves subverted the original unconditional purchase of a slave's total life-long labour. For skilled slaves, chattel slavery was effectively transformed into a medium-term labour 'contract'. Of course, it was not a legal contract; it could not be enforced by individual slaves; slaves had no such legal rights; but in general, the 'contract' was honoured. The slave who killed his master and so brought about the execution of four hundred fellow slaves may have been provoked, according to Tacitus (*Annals* 14.42) by his master's refusal to grant him liberty, after a price had been fixed. Cicero once implied (*Philippics* 8.32) that 'diligent and honest' slaves could reckon on liberty within seven years.[62] Among the ex-slaves of private owners

---

[61] Seneca, *Moral Letters* 80.7 indicated that urban slaves got 5 *modii* (33 kg) of wheat and 20 HS cash per month. Lucian (*On Salaried Posts in Great Houses* 23) made it clear that slaves there got monthly pay. Roman manumissions were not unique. Some slaves were freed in the American south, and a great number of slaves were freed in Cuba, through the bridging institution of *coartación* (H. S. Klein, *Slavery in the Americas* (London, 1967) 197). However, the scale of manumission in Rome, the high status of some ex-slaves and their assimilation into the free population, all seem exceptional.

[62] In other passing remarks, Cicero implied that freedom was regularly granted to slaves (*Pro Balbo* 24), and that without the prospect of freedom slavery would be intolerable (*Rab. Perd.* 15 and 16). It is likely that he was thinking of a narrow range of slaves such as those with whom he himself came into contact. Even then his perceptions may not have been realistic for all masters.

whose age at death was recorded on tombstones in the western half of the empire, over three fifths had been freed before the age of thirty (N = 1,201).[63] Among ex-slaves belonging to the emperor, the proportion was lower, but clearly freedom was granted to most of those commemorated before the age of forty.[64] Such evidence is difficult to interpret because slaves and ex-slaves with inscribed stone memorials were unlikely to have been typical of all slaves, or perhaps even of all ex-slaves. Yet this evidence does corroborate the general impression we get from the sources. A substantial body of skilled slaves secured their freedom at an age when they were still valuable to their masters. Why?

Analytically, we can separate the various reasons for freeing slaves, but in reality the reasons were probably mixed. Some masters freed their slaves predominantly out of affection. Three fifths of the ex-slaves, commemorated as dying before the age of thirty, were female (N = 768),[65] and we find a similarly high proportion of females among the slaves freed at Delphi (Chapter III). A fair number of tombstones record marriages between a master and his ex-slave. Admittedly, tombstone inscriptions invite pious over-statement; still, full legal marriages between master and ex-slave, publicly acknowledged, bespeak a paternalism quite different in quality from what is known from the southern states of the USA. Slaves were not considered slaves by nature; they had no distinguishing racial characteristics and so could easily become free parents of free citizens. Other surviving tombstones record affection between a master and the slave he had found, reared (*alumnus*) and then freed. The law codes preserve dozens of legacies by which a master provided for the benefit or maintenance of ex-slaves

---

[63] This is based on G. Alföldy's (1972) analysis of 1,201 ages at death of ex-slaves from the city of Rome, Italy, Spain and the Danubian provinces, excluding the emperors' ex-slaves. He drew attention to the fact that only 14% (N = 644) of slaves, as against 38% of ex-slaves are recorded as dying over the age of thirty. He concluded that therefore most slaves, except those living in the countryside, were released before the age of thirty. But those who had their age at death recorded by patrons, masters or fellow slaves may have been a biased sample of all slaves and ex-slaves dying; for example, young highly valued slaves, of a quality such that they might later be freed, were presumably more likely to be commemorated if they died young, than dull slaves who would never be freed. For a discussion and analysis of uncorrectable bias in ages of death recorded on Roman tombstones see Volume Two. But even though Alföldy overstated his case, it does seem that manumission before the age of thirty was common for those 'privileged' ex-slaves commemorated on tombstones. Moreover, ex-slaves who died at ages greater than thirty may have been freed before they reached thirty.

[64] Among imperial ex-slaves, only 24% (N = 173) are recorded as freed and dead before the age of thirty, while 47% (N = 440) of imperial slaves died over the age of thirty while still slaves. Overall, Weaver (1972: 100–4) plausibly concluded that imperial slaves were often manumitted at ages 30–40.

[65] G. Alföldy (1972) 111.

after his death (for example D. 33.1; 34.1 and 40.4). Moreover, it became common to allow ex-slaves to be buried together with the ex-master's wife and children in the family tomb. For example, a tombstone inscription from the city of Rome reads: 'To the Gods of the Underworld. Q. Alfidius Apolaustrus to his revered wife Turrania Satulla with whom he lived for 45 years and to his son Q. Alfidius Apolaustrus who lived 27 years...and to their ex-slaves and their descendants' (*CIL* 6.11439).

Masters also freed slaves as an ostentatious token of their wealth and power. Dionysius of Halicarnassus wrote of conditions in the late Republic, before Augustus limited the number of slaves who could be freed by will: 'I know of some who have allowed all their slaves to be freed at their death in the hope of being called good men when they are dead, and of having a large funeral procession of ex-slaves wearing the cap of freedom on their heads' (*Roman Antiquities* 4.24). Perhaps some prominent citizens freed their slaves to swell the numbers of their clients (though I don't know whom they would have impressed); and it is said that others freed their slaves to take advantage of the free wheat distributed to citizens. Emancipation of this kind caused something of a scandal in the time of Julius Caesar and Augustus, but it seems doubtful that the numbers involved were really as great as the objectors implied.

In the final analysis, the liberation of so many slaves was acceptable to masters only because it was profitable. As we have seen, masters derived some of their profit from the extra work which favoured slaves did under the spur of freedom enticingly visible on the horizon. This prospect of freedom was underpinned by yet another subversion of pure chattel slavery: such slaves were paid a wage. If the slave died before he bought his freedom, which must have happened often in the conditions of high mortality prevalent in Rome, then in law his savings automatically went to the master. Generous masters might waive their rights in favour of the slave's wife or children (Pliny, *Letters* 8.16), but that was mentioned presumably because it was exceptional. The sum which the slave paid, or contracted to pay out of his future earnings, was the master's chief source of profit from manumission. With this money he could replace an old slave with a young one.

These arguments are plausible, but they do not constitute proof. Unfortunately, the Roman evidence for frequent self-purchase of manumission is only circumstantial. The frequency with which the practice was mentioned in the Roman law codes (I have found over

seventy references) suggests that the practice was common.[66] (
in the law codes confirm also that the slave's purchase of free
compatible with other forms of release. For example, a mas
will commonly gave a slave permission to buy his freedo
formula: 'If he gives *n denarii* to my heir, let him be free.' Lawyers
sometimes just took it for granted that a slave had to pay his market
value to the ex-master's estate.[67] Many slaves would have been grateful
for such an opportunity; yet literary sources have understandably
concentrated on the axis of generosity and gratitude, rather than on
the cash paid. All in all, it seems reasonable to argue that slaves'
purchase of their own freedom was very common. In the manumissions from Delphi in Greece which we examine in Chapter III,
purchase of freedom was almost universal. Passing references in
literature took it for granted that slaves were saving up to buy their
liberty. 'The money which slaves have saved up by robbing their
stomachs, they hand over as the price of liberty' (Seneca, *Moral Letters*
80.4).

Sale was not the only source of profit. By custom, the ex-slave owed
his former master, his patron, a whole set of unspecified obligations
(*obsequium, reverentia, officium*); the ex-slave was expected to be at his
patron's service until his death, and when he died at his children's;
he was generally precluded from doing anything to put his former
master in disrepute (for example, by suing him at law); and he was
expected to help maintain his former master if he fell on hard times.[68]

---

[66] Frequency of mention is a risky criterion. Buckland (1908: 496), considered that
payment of money by the slave was the most common condition exacted in testamentary manumission. There seems to be no handy compendium of wills. The
references are mostly to be found in the Digest, Bks 30ff., and see M. Amelotti, *Il
testamento romano* (Florence, 1966).

[67] See D. 40.7.3 (Ulpian) and ff. for several variations on the formula and Buckland
(1908: 496ff.) for comments. When a will was technically void, but by the ruling in
favour of freedom (*favor libertatis*), liberty was still granted to those named in the
will, they were required to pay 20 *aurei* = 500 *dn* (so D. 5.2.8.17: Ulpian). These 500
dn equalled the 'normal' value of a slave fixed in the census (see note 23). It is worth
adding that in the Principate the 5% tax on manumissions was well-conceived only
if it was common for the slave to buy his freedom in a publicly declared act which
specified the price. Otherwise, the master and slave could collude to defraud the
tax collector by fixing a low value on the slave. The tax would certainly make more
sense if slaves normally bought rather than were given their freedom.

[68] See M. Kaser, *Das römische Privatrecht* (Munich², 1971) 298–9, and in greater detail
his 'Die Geschichte der Patronatsgewalt über Freigelassene', *ZSS* 58 (1938) 88–135.
Three legal opinions on ex-slaves' duties are worth citing: 'ex-slaves shall give
support in accordance with the resources they possess to their former masters, when
they are in need (*egentibus*)' (D. 25.3.5.19: Ulpian). 'Former masters and their
children have absolutely no rights over the possessions of their ex-slaves unless they
have proved before the governors that they are sick or poverty-stricken as to merit

It became a commonplace in ruling circles to complain of the 'insolence and ingratitude, of some ex-slaves nowadays'; the senate in AD 56 debated the proposal that masters should have the right to re-enslave. According to Tacitus some senators argued that 'it would be no great burden for a freed slave to keep his freedom by the same obedience which had earned it' (*Annals* 13.26). The emperor Nero rejected the proposal because it threatened too large a class of ex-slaves. However, magistrates still had the power to punish 'ungrateful ex-slaves' by fine or whipping, and in exceptional cases by re-enslavement.[69]

In addition, as a condition of freedom, slave-owners often stipulated specific duties (*operae*) which the ex-slave had to undertake for the benefit of his former master and if specified, for his heirs. The Roman evidence on these duties is unfortunately sketchy. According to one distinguished lawyer in the late Republic, masters 'customarily made very stringent demands on their ex-slaves' (Servius cited in D. 38.2.1). Surprisingly, the praetor eventually limited this form of exploitation by law, 'because it had grown excessively, so that ex-slaves were burdened and oppressed' (D. 38.1.2). It usually takes considerable excesses to persuade an unselfconscious ruling class to limit its exploitation of the powerless.

From the Principate, legal opinions are preserved which insisted, for example, that the specific duties (*operae*) required of an ex-slave should suit his health and status; that no such jobs be required of women over the age of fifty; and significantly, that the ex-slave either be given enough time to earn his own food, or be fed while working for his former owner.[70] Of course, such legal regulations were for the most part unenforceable; but they reflect both the sympathetic concern of lawyers and the actual burdens imposed on ex-slaves by exploitative masters.

We know very little of the variety of terms imposed by Roman masters on their ex-slaves; it is tempting therefore to supplement our knowledge with the rich details about manumission available from central Greece (see Chapter III). But to what extent can we infer Roman practices from Greek, even though for most of this period Greece was

aid from their ex-slaves in the form of monthly maintenance' (D. 25.3.9: Paul). Ulpian also ruled that a slave's purchase of his own liberty reduced the master's claim on an ex-slave's general obligations (D. 25.3.5.22). It is worth noting that a patron also owed his ex-slave a general obligation to help.

[69] Buckland (1908: 422ff.); see also Suetonius, *Claudius* 25.

[70] See particularly, D. 38.1 and 2. In general, manual duties (*operae fabriles*) could be willed to heirs, service duties (*operae officiales*) could be willed only if that had been stipulated on manumission (Ulpian, D. 38.1.5–6).

part of the Roman empire? There are similarities: for example, in Roman law (D. 48.19.11.1: Marcian) as in central Greek practice, an ex-slave who continued to live in his master's household was subject to his master's discipline like a slave. One difference was that Roman masters often seem to have stipulated specific, rather than open-ended obligations for their ex-slaves. Moreover, Augustus in his social legislation on the family, legally undercut the Roman system by offering ex-slaves release from their specific obligations to their former masters if they bore two children by a free spouse (D. 38.1.37 *pr.* Paul). This suggests that such services were a marginal not a major factor in a slave-owner's recompense for granting freedom.

CONCLUSIONS

Our clear distinction between slave and free, indeed the clear legal distinction between slave and free in Roman law cannot do justice to much Roman practice.[71] The Roman system of slavery, like the Greek, worked by adulterating slavery with some of the privileges which we normally associate with freedom (such as giving slaves the right to make contracts, and to receive wages and to save); on the other hand, the Romans often extended a slave's servitude into the period when he had become legally free.

The prospects of emancipation served as an incentive for many slaves, including perhaps many slaves who never succeeded in getting their freedom. For the masters, manumission was economically rational, partly because it tempted slaves to increase their productivity and lowered the cost to the master of supervising his slaves at work, and partly because the slave's purchase of freedom recapitalised his value and enabled the master to replace an older slave with a younger one. In some cases the contract of manumission also provided an additional source of income even after the slave had been freed. Manumission, for all the benefit which it gave to individual ex-slaves, thus served to strengthen slavery as a system.

Roman slavery was a cruel system of extreme exploitation. Its cruelty was attacked, and for some slaves perhaps even mitigated, by philosophers and philanthropists. Manumission offered a channel of escape. The evidence suggests that the number of freed slaves was absolutely large; we have little idea and can only guess that slaves who secured freedom constituted a minority, though perhaps a substantial minority of all slaves. We have concentrated on the economic under-

---

[71] See particularly, M. I. Finley, 'Between slavery and freedom', *Comp. Stud. Soc. Hist.* 6 (1964) 233–49.

pinning of manumissions. Masters could afford to be generous with liberty, because they benefited from giving it. But we should also remember the non-economic factors which may have determined their actions. Some Roman masters freed their slaves by will and did not exact compensation. Their wishes took effect only when they themselves had died. What did they hope to gain from this public dissipation of the family wealth, which worked only to the detriment of their heirs? Was it merely a desire for social ostentation, or an attempt to secure an easier path to quick salvation in purgatory? We do not know. Many other slaves were freed without charge by living masters, sometimes out of love or gratitude or kindliness. Slaves often felt and expressed their gratitude to their masters. Masters who manumitted their slaves liberally, and who acted as considerate patrons to their ex-slaves received their social reward from heightened prestige, and no doubt got personal rewards from a favourable self-image. These human factors have often been exaggerated, but they should not be ignored.

[·]·[·]

BETWEEN SLAVERY AND FREEDOM:
ON FREEING SLAVES AT DELPHI
Written in collaboration with P. J. Roscoe

THE BACKGROUND

The purpose of this chapter is to describe and analyse changes in the practice of freeing slaves at Delphi in central Greece in the last two centuries before Christ. It is based on roughly one thousand recorded acts of slave manumission, involving over twelve hundred slaves. Most of these records were carved on the smoothed polygonal blocks which make up the retaining wall for the terrace on which the temple of Apollo at Delphi was built; others were carved in the base of prominent public monuments by the side of the Sacred Way which led to the temple.

These inscriptions provide some of the fullest information which we have from the ancient world on the price which slaves paid to their masters for full freedom. The inscriptions also cast light on a curious institution called *paramonē*, which we translate rather loosely as conditional release; perhaps suspended release would be better. By this institution, slaves bought formal freedom but contractually bound themselves to stay with and to continue serving their former owners even after they were freed, just as though they were still slaves, usually until the former owner's death. Conditional release was a twilight state of juridical freedom combined with slave-like service, a state which overlapped both slavery and freedom. It is found elsewhere in Greece, besides Delphi, as well as in other parts of the Roman world; parallels have also been found in the ancient Near East. But the Delphic inscriptions, with their amazing variety of specified conditions, reveal more than all the evidence from elsewhere the ties which bound ex-slaves to their former owners.

Our study shows that the prices which slaves paid for their freedom rose in the last two centuries before Christ. And as the prices of full freedom rose, a higher proportion of slaves bought conditional release. The price of conditional release remained fairly stable, but the conditions of release contractually agreed were increasingly to the slaves' disadvantage; some ex-slaves were even required to hand over their babies as replacement slaves. We argue that one of the functions of manumission, particularly if a slave bought full freedom, was that it enabled masters to recapitalise the value of older slaves and to replace them with younger ones. Finally, we argue that the prices which slaves paid for release approximated the market price for slaves and that market forces both systematically overrode affective ties between masters and slaves and disrupted the slaves' ties with their families.

Excavations at Delphi yield information about over twelve hundred slaves freed in the period 201 BC–AD 100. Over two thirds (71%) of these were freed in the second century BC; less than one tenth (9%) were freed in the first century AD (see Table III.1). Rostovtzeff once argued that this decline in the number of recorded and surviving manumissions from Delphi reflected a general decline in the Greek economy under Roman rule.[1] This deduction seems wrong, partly because we know nothing about manumissions at Delphi before 201 BC, and partly because the manumissions in neighbouring Thessaly show clearly that the rate of recorded and surviving manumissions rose in Thessaly during the last century BC, that is when recorded manumissions at Delphi declined; and they were still at a high level in Thessaly in the early second century AD, when no manumissions were apparently recorded at Delphi. It seems likely therefore that the number of manumission tablets at Delphi reflects local developments in the social history of Apollo's shrine rather than rates of manumission in Greece as a whole. This conclusion poses difficulties. The surviving manumissions fit somewhat awkwardly with what else we know about the Delphic oracle, although our knowledge of that too is patchy. The peak of Delphi's glory and prosperity was much earlier and its fame endured much later than the manumissions. A brief overview of Delphi's history will give some background to the manumissions.

According to ancient myth, Delphi was situated at the centre of the earth (Strabo 9.3.6).[2] In its golden age, that is in the sixth and fifth centuries BC, the Delphic oracle had given its enigmatic prophecies to ambitious generals and kings from all over Greece and even from Asia Minor. Its blessing was regularly sought to ensure the appropriate

[1] M. I. Rostovtzeff, *Social and Economic History of the Hellenistic World* (Oxford, 1941) vol. 2, 625–6. And on manumissions in Thessaly, see K. Hopkins and P. J. Roscoe, *Manumissions in Thessaly* (forthcoming).

[2] The brief account of Delphi depends on H. W. Parke and D. E. W. Wormell, *The Delphic Oracle* (Oxford², 1956), G. Daux, *Delphes au IIe et Ier siècle* (Paris, 1936) and R. Flacelière, *Greek Oracles* (London, 1965) 33ff.

religious rites and propitious timings for the foundation of new colonies sent out from Greece to southern Italy and Asia Minor. City states appealed to the priestess at Delphi for decisions on disputes, both military and religious, which could not be resolved at home. The temple of Apollo at Delphi was in some sense a ritual centre for Greeks from all the different city states. The gratitude which the oracle inspired in its devotees was reflected in the wealth, grandeur and beauty of the buildings, monuments and dedications at Delphi, and presumably in the prosperity of its citizens (priests, guides, hoteliers).

The political role of Delphi changed as the larger kingdoms created in the wake of Alexander's conquests robbed small city states of their political independence. In the third century BC, Delphi fell under the political control of the local Aetolian League. In general, the oracle became less concerned with affairs of state, although great kings still occasionally made flattering dedications. The Roman senate, after a crushing defeat in the war against Carthage (216 BC), sent an official delegate to consult the Delphic oracle (Livy 22.57; 23.11); and eventually, when the Romans defeated Carthage, the shrine was richly rewarded (Livy 28.45). A few years later, when the Romans were fighting the Macedonians in Greece, both sides used Delphi as a place to publicise their claims or to proclaim their victories (Plutarch, *Flamininus* 12; *Aemilius Paullus* 28 and 36; Polybius 25.3.2; Livy 41.22). But Roman domination of Greece ended both the Aetolian League's control over Delphi (191/190 BC) and the oracle's own role as a mediator in interstate politics. Even so, Delphi continued to engage occasionally and profitably in relationships with the kings of Pergamum, Syria and Egypt; and the Amphictionic Council, which represented Greek states from a wide area around, continued to meet regularly at Delphi.

The oracle retained some of its old prestige. Important persons consulted it. Sulla, for example, asked for the interpretation of a dream; but that did not prevent him from robbing the shrine when he needed money for a military campaign (Plutarch, *Sulla* 12 and 19); Appius Claudius consulted the oracle on the outcome of the Roman civil wars (Valerius Maximus 1.8.10); Cicero called Delphi the oracle of the whole world (*Pro Fonteio* 30). The recorded visits by famous men serve as one index of the continued high reputation of Delphi, which presumably at once reflected and increased the flow of lesser visitors. Important men paid more for their consultations, but it was ordinary folk and dignitaries from surrounding towns, with their anxieties about marriage, voyages and loans (Plutarch 408c) who presumably provided priests and temple guardians with their regular basic income.

According to Plutarch, cities still consulted the oracle officially not on matters of state but about the size of crops and public health (408c).

It is difficult to know how much these changes, the growth of Roman power and the domestication of the oracle, affected Delphi's prosperity. The evidence is ambiguous. The geographer Strabo, writing at the end of the last century BC stated that the temple was then very poor compared with older times (9.3.8).[3] But there is considerable evidence that Delphi continued to be a tourist attraction with impressive buildings, thousands of statues (Nero removed 500, but 3,000 statues remained), professional guides and occasional royal patronage (Pausanias, *Description of Greece* 10.7; Pliny, *Natural History* 34.36). Nero's patronage was a mixed blessing; Hadrian visited the shrine and asked the oracle the old chestnut about where Homer came from and he got a stunning reply: Homer was the grandson of Odysseus (*Contest of Homer and Hesiod* 314). Plutarch, writing at the end of the first century AD, in an essay *On the Obsolescence of Oracles* (*Moralia* 409ff.), stated that Delphi employed only one priestess; formerly, there had been two with a third in reserve. He attributed the decline of oracles to a general decline in the population of Greece (414A). But he also noted that many shrines at Delphi were new or restored, and that its affluence had spread even to its suburb (409A). Pausanias, who wrote in the second century AD, devoted the best part of a book in his *Description of Greece* to the artistic wonders of Delphi.[4] In sum, although our knowledge of Delphi is scanty, we should not expect from what we know that manumissions would begin to be recorded about 201 BC (ten years before the Roman domination) nor that they would peak in the second century BC, nor that they would stop before the end of the first century AD. To be sure, such expectations do not help; but it seems worth saying that the limitation of recorded manumissions to this period (201 BC–AD 100) is puzzling.

[3] Delphi had been attacked by barbarians in the beginning of the last century BC (Appian, *Illyrian Wars* 5) before its despoliation by Sulla, who made some reparations (Plutarch, *Sulla* 19). According to some interpretations of a sentence in Plutarch, (*Antony* 23), the temple at Delphi was not rebuilt for forty years; this may serve as a symptom of Delphi's decline, but this interpretation is speculative (see Daux, 1936: 410). The previous wealth of Delphi was mythical, so a decline may have been imagined (cf. Dio Chrysostom, *Discourses* 37.36).

[4] It seems customary but dangerous for scholars to equate dated mentions of Delphi with temporary efflorescence and decline. A visit by the emperor Hadrian or Julian in the mid-fourth century is not good evidence of prosperity; nor is silence in the sources good evidence of decline. The local council of Delphi was apparently in difficulties about providing games as late as AD 424 (C.Th. 15.5.4).

The background

These Delphic manumissions have often been studied.[5] Since Calderini's basic work of 1908, most scholars have concentrated on religious and legal aspects of manumission. They have been fascinated by the role played in manumission by the priests of Apollo, and by the so-called holy or temple slavery which existed elsewhere in the ancient world. They have attempted to sort out the exact legal status and implications of the conditional or suspended release (*paramonē*), for which there is comparable evidence from the pre-classical Near East and from several areas of the classical world outside Greece.[6] Westermann and Finley have used this intermediate stage of conditional release to create the concept of a spectrum of statuses between slave and free.[7] This idea seems now to have won general acceptance among ancient historians and has undermined the old, strict dichotomy, slave–free. Recently, some Russian research, notably by Zel'in and Marinovich, has combined Marxist theoretical sophistication with careful deductions from fragmentary evidence and an empathy with the oppressed; this constitutes a real advance over the strictly juridical approach which has guided many Western studies.[8]

[5] The basic work is A. Calderini, *La manomissione e la condizione dei liberti in Grecia* (Milan, 1908); W. L. Westermann, *The Slave Systems of Greek and Roman Antiquity* (Philadelphia, 1955: 18ff.) gave not only a sympathetic account of the Delphic manumission inscriptions, but also briefly described comparable Semitic-Oriental practices; he also reanalysed Calderini's data on freed slaves' origins. P. Foucart, *Mémoire sur l'affranchissement des esclaves* (Paris, 1867) gave the most colourful account of the detailed variations in Delphic manumissions, and we have benefited a lot from his ideas. The review by H. Rädle, *Untersuchungen zum griechischen Freilassungswesen* (Diss. Munich, 1969) is somewhat legal but careful and useful, except on prices. M. Bloch, *Die Freilassungsbedingungen der Delphischen Freilassungsurkunden* (Diss. Strasburg, 1914) presented the best statistical analysis.

[6] On temple slavery, see F. Bömer, 'Die sogenannte sakrale Freilassung', *Abhandlungen der Akad. Mainz, geistes- und sozialwiss. Kl.* (1960, 1), A. Cameron, 'Sacral manumission and confession', *Harvard Theological Review* 32 (1939) 148ff. and P. Koschaker, 'Über einige griechische Rechtsurkunden aus der östlichen Randgebieten des Hellenismus', *Abhandlungen Sächs. Akad. Wiss. phil.-hist. Kl.* 42 (1931) 1ff. On *paramonē*, see W. L. Westermann, 'The Paramone as a general service contract', *Journal of Juristic Papyrology* 2 (1948) 9–50, and A. E. Samuel, 'The role of paramone clauses in ancient documents', *ibid.* 15 (1965) 221–311, especially 221–9 and 256ff. – this is the fullest account of *paramonē* clauses in English, but some of his main conclusions concentrate on legal clarification without taking account of social practices or pressures: in short, one has to ask not merely what the law was, but also whether people obeyed it.

[7] W. L. Westermann, 'Between slavery and freedom', *American Historical Review* 50 (1945) 213ff; M. I. Finley, 'Between slavery and freedom', *Comparative Studies in Society and History* 6 (1964) 233–49, 'The servile statuses of ancient Greece', *Revue internationale des droits de l'antiquité* 7 (1960) 165ff, and *The Ancient Economy* (London, 1973) 62ff.

[8] See particularly K. K. Zel'in in K. K. Zel'in and M. K. Trophimova, *Forms of Dependency in the Eastern Mediterranean in the Hellenistic Period* (in Russian; Moscow, 1969) 119–87 and L. P. Marinovich, 'Paramone in Delphic manumissions of the Roman

We thought that it would be worthwhile to analyse the manumission inscriptions from Delphi once again to see if we could squeeze anything further out of them. We used the chronological list of priesthoods and inscriptions published by Daux (1943) and followed the example of Westermann (1955: 32) in splitting the data into fifty-year periods to coincide with priesthoods.[9] But first a note of caution. The surviving inscriptions were merely the last part, the by-product of a religious ritual, in which the master set the slave free solemnly and publicly before the god Apollo, his priests and civil witnesses and guarantors. Only those masters, and slaves, who set store by a solemn act of manumission validated by a religious ceremony and by a public record of the act took the trouble to manumit and to be manumitted at a prestigious shrine. The ceremony must have cost money; the priests must have expected something in return for their involvement; inscribing a detailed record of the act on stone and on papyrus cost money. All these factors probably made these Delphic manumissions a biased sample of all manumissions. We cannot correct the bias, since we know little or nothing of other manumissions. We do know that in the beginning of the second century BC the majority of manumittors recorded at Delphi came from the towns surrounding Delphi, convincing evidence of the shrine's extra-local prestige. We assume that they were typically visitors to the shrine rather than resident aliens. But from the middle of the second century BC onwards, slave-owners from other towns apparently freed their slaves in their home-towns, and the majority of manumittors at Delphi came from Delphi itself.[10]

period', *Vestnik Drevnei Istorii* 118 (1971) 27–46. Marinovich's concentration on manumissions after 20 BC is slightly odd; the numbers of manumissions surviving from this period are too small to justify some of his tabulations. But his findings reinforce our view, which perhaps we should have put more forcefully, that the manumissions of the first century AD are, for reasons unknown, significantly different from the earlier manumissions.

9   G. Daux, *Chronologie Delphique* (Paris, 1943); the date ordering of the inscriptions is fairly secure, especially in the second century BC; but we do not know the exact dates of later priesthoods, so that the dates used in the text are only rough. Period A (201–153 BC) covers priesthoods I–V; period B (153–*c*. 100 BC) covers priesthoods VI–XII[1]; period c_1 (*c*. 100–53 BC) covers priesthoods XII[2]–XVI; period c_2 (*c*. 53–1 BC) covers priesthoods XVII–XXV; period D_1 (*c*. AD 1–47) covers priesthoods XXVI–XXVIII; period D_2 (*c*. AD 48–100) covers priesthoods XXIX–XXXIV. The dates of the later periods are approximate only.

10   On the origins of manumittors from towns near Delphi see G. Daux (1936: 490–6). We supplemented these conclusions with three systematic samples of fifty inscriptions, complete with the relevant data, taken from the periods 201–174 BC, 152–125 BC, 100–53 BC; the proportions of known non-Delphic manumittors fell from 55% to 22% to 16% respectively. In the later inscriptions, the custom of stating explicitly that a manumittor came from Delphi, which was prevalent in the earliest period, fell into disuse; we assume that this was because the vast majority of manumittors in the later periods did come from Delphi.

And the great majority of Delphic manumissions recorded in these inscriptions came from a narrow interrelated circle of priests, town-councillors and guarantors.[11] This suggests that the Delphic material is surprisingly complete, and not just a tiny surviving sample of a vast mass of lost inscriptions. However that may be, in the rest of this chapter when we write of manumissions at Delphi we mean only those which were recorded and have survived. Finally, we should stress that freed slaves were probably only a small minority of all slaves. Most slaves, we think, were never freed. Therefore, we cannot properly make deductions about all slaves from those slaves who were fortunate enough to buy liberty.

A preliminary analysis is set out in Table III.1.[12] We apologise for the mass of numbers in it. Let us glance quickly at three factors: age, sex and origins. In a significant minority of cases (17%), the inscriptions record that the freed slave was a young boy (*paidarion*) or a young girl (*korasion*). These categories are never explicitly defined and may not have meant anything precise.[13] We necessarily assume that all the remaining freed slaves were adults. Of these, a majority (63%) were female; that implies a sex ratio of only 59 male freed slaves for every 100 female slaves freed. This high proportion of females among freed slaves is found elsewhere in the Roman world, but that does not make it easier to understand.[14] Since slaves paid considerable sums for their freedom, we have to ask what opportunities these female slaves had for acquiring money.

Finally, origins; in one half of the inscriptions, no mention was made of a slave's origins.[15] The other half can be divided into home-born

11 According to Zel'in (1969: 185), 75% of the manumittors who came from Delphi itself (N = 452) between 180 and 120 BC were archons, councillors, priests, guarantors, or close relatives of such; the circle of known manumittors from Delphi was thus quite small.

12 The inscriptions come from two prime collections: H. Collitz, J. Baunack et al., *Sammlung der griechischen Dialekt–Inschriften* (Göttingen, 1899) vol. 2, 1683ff; and G. Daux, ed., *Fouilles de Delphes* vol. 3 (Paris, 1922–70) in six parts. Hereafter they are called *GDI* and *FD* respectively. Many of the works cited in the last few notes are cited hereafter only by author and date.

13 In the newly discovered fragments of Diocletian's *Edict on Maximum Prices* from Aphrodisias, kindly shown to us by Michael Crawford and Joyce Reynolds, slave prices of youths were split into age groups 0–7, 7–15 years (by English reckoning); adults began at age 15; we do not know if these practices have any relevance to what happened at Delphi.

14 See Hopkins and Roscoe (forthcoming), and G. Alföldy, 'Die Freilassung von Sklaven', *Rivista storica dell' antichità* 2 (1972) 109–14, and Chapter II above, notes 30 and 63.

15 Westermann's influential reanalysis of slaves' origins (1955: 32–3) depended effectively on ignoring those ex-slaves whose origins were unknown and concentrated on the ratios of home-born ex-slaves to *known* aliens. Thus in his and our first three periods (ABC₁ in Table III.1) home-born ex-slaves constituted successively 28%, 61%

Table III.1. *Preliminary analysis of 1,237 manumissions recorded and surviving from Delphi*

	a	b	c	d	e	f	g	h	k	l	m	n
		Adults*		Children		Origins						
	Slaves freed	Male	Female	Male	Female	Not known	Home-born	Known aliens†	Slaves conditionally released‡	Acts of manumission	Acts of multiple manumission§	Slaves multiply manumitted
Approximate dates	(Number)	(%)		(Number)		%	%	(Number)	(%)	(Number)	(%)	(%)
A 201–153 BC	495	61	39	23	17	62	11	27	30	411	14	29
B 153–100 BC	378	63	37	38	32	27	44	29	25	303	14	27
C₁ 100–53 BC	123	64	36	15	19	46	46	8	37	93	19	39
C₂ 53–1 BC	128	59	41	16	23	62	36	2	52	96	21	39
D₁ AD 1–47	63	75	25	9	16	56	41	3	61	45	24	46
D₂ AD 48–100	50	77	23	4	3	82	18	0	40	26	35	66
Total %	–	63	37	–	–	50	29	21	32	–	16	33
Total numbers	1,237	627	371	105	110	621	357	259	400	974	159	404

* 24 ex-slaves of unknown sex are excluded.

† Known aliens were from a wide variety of places, especially the Balkans, Asia Minor, Syria, Palestine and other regions in Greece.

‡ The conditions of release were not known for 45 slaves (3.6% of the total) and are excluded.

§ Acts of multiple manumission were acts in which more than one slave was released by an owner at one time.

140

slaves (*oikogeneis, endogeneis*) and 'known aliens', that is those for whom a specific ethnic origin was given; they came from Asia Minor, Syria and the Balkans as well as from other parts of Greece. Overall, 29% of freed slaves are known to have been home-born, but in some periods the proportion was much higher (153–100 BC: 44%). This, as Westermann argued (1955: 32–3), is an important finding. These figures constitute the only hard evidence which we have from the classical world on rates of slave reproduction.[16] But they are under-estimates. We must also take into account the actual origins of those slaves whose origins are unknown;[17] evidence on prices (which we present later) suggests that many of them were in fact home-born. Indeed it seems safe to conclude that from 153 BC to AD 47, over half of the slaves freed were home-born.

This conclusion poses a problem of succession. If home-born slaves were freed, who then were the home-born slaves freed in the next generation? Two complementary answers are obviously possible: first those freed were only a small proportion of all slaves;[18] and secondly, slaves were typically freed only when they had left children behind them in slavery to take their place. We shall explore this problem later in greater detail.

FULL FREEDOM AND CONDITIONAL RELEASE

Most (72%) of the slaves freed at Delphi in the second century BC were freed unconditionally; they were given full freedom. As soon as they had paid, their masters declared them free in a formal act which took

and 84% of those whose origins are known (these proportions are based on Westermann's figures which are very slightly different from ours). But those of unknown origins should not be so cavalierly ignored. It seems safer to argue for a real fall in the proportion of known aliens in period c than for a real increase in the proportion of home-born slaves in period B (see note 17).

16 The argument that slaves' children were a major source of slaves is put strongly for Roman Italy in the late Republic, perhaps too strongly by E. M. Schtaerman, *Die Blütezeit der Sklavenwirtschaft in der römischen Republik* (Wiesbaden, 1969) 36–70.

17 Changes in the recorded proportion of home-born slaves may have resulted from a change in what was conventionally recorded rather than from a revolution in slave imports or slave reproduction. We can date the transition to a twenty-year period 157–139 BC (Delphic priesthoods v–viii). The proportions of slaves who were recorded as home-born by priesthoods was as follows: i–iv 10% (N = 449); v 17% (N = 46); vi 36% (N = 144); vii–viii 50% (N = 56). In priesthood ix (*c.* 139–122 BC) the proportion of recorded home-born ex-slaves was 49% (N = 120). For the evidence on prices see below, note 55.

18 G. Alföldy (1972) has argued from Roman data that most slaves were freed; but in our view his arguments are unconvincing. He ignores the probability that only a small proportion of all slaves and ex-slaves were commemorated on inscribed stone memorials; cf. p. 127, note 63.

the form of a fictional sale to the god Apollo. We quote from a second-century BC inscription, which is typical:

A	date	In the Magistracy of Damosthenes, in the month of Poitropios, when Philaitolos the son of Phainis and Timokles the son of Thraslas were councillors for the first half of the year, and when Anaxandridas the son of Aiakidas was scribe,
B	sale to the god	Polemarchos, the son of Polemon, with the agreement of his son Polemon, sold to Phythian Apollo, the female body [slave] whose name is Pistis, home-born, on the following conditions for a
C	full freedom	price of four and a half *mnae* [450 *drachmae*]. Accordingly, Pistis has entrusted the sale price to the god, on condition that she is free and cannot be claimed as a slave by anyone for all her life; she can do whatever she wants, and she can run off to whom she chooses.
D	guarantee of free status	Guarantor in accord with the law of the city. . . (*GDI* 2187)

The slave became juridically free; she was her own mistress, free from arbitrary seizure, doing what she wanted, and going where she chose. These were the four aspects of freedom repeatedly emphasised in these inscriptions. But in the second century BC, a substantial minority, and before the end of the first century BC a majority (52 %) of slaves were freed conditionally.[19] There was some considerable variety in the conditions specified, but for us the definitive condition was that the ex-slave, although juridically free, should stay and serve (*paramenein*) her former owner, usually until the owner's death. An illustrative example dating from the first century BC is on the page opposite.

The formula discussed

Several points in this formulaic record deserve our attention. The temptation to dismiss formulas, simply because they are repetitive, should be resisted. The inscription begins with the date (A) and then records the sale of the slave to the god, Pythian Apollo. The sale was fictitious in that its function was not to transfer the ownership of the slave to the god, but to give a religious sanction to the slave's freedom.

[19] We are making a statement about social relations here, not about law. In law perhaps, as Samuel (1965: 282–4) argued, all ex-slaves were fully free; some then entered into contractual obligations similar to those into which originally free-born persons had entered; these obligations did not affect their juridical status as free men. In fact, the obligations taken on by ex-slaves in *paramonē* clauses severely restricted their actions and status; socially, therefore, we think that it is proper to see them as conditionally freed, in the sense that they were freed and then bound by conditions. We leave legal debate to others.

A typical manumission giving conditional release

A	date	In the magistracy of Antipholos son of Gorgilos, in the month of Enduspoitropios [April/May], when Aristokles son of Philoneikos, and Damon son of Polemarchos were councillors,
B	sale to the god	on the following conditions Eurydika daughter of Archidamos sold to Pythian Apollo, so that he would free them, two female bodies [slaves] whose names are Onasiphoron and Sotero, home-born for a price of eight *mnae* [800 *drachmae*], and I have received the whole price. The guarantor in accord with the laws of the city is Stratagos son of Philon.
C	the *paramonē* clause	The two aforementioned bodies are to stay and serve Euridika the whole time so long as Euridika lives and are to do everything she orders without giving cause for complaint. If either or both of the aforementioned bodies disobeys or does not do what she is ordered by Euridika, Euridika may punish them in whatever way she wishes. When Euridika dies, let the aforementioned slaves be free, never to be claimed by anyone for all time, belonging to no one in any way.
D	a release clause	But if one of the aforementioned bodies wishes to be freed from staying and serving (*paramonē*) at an earlier time, let her give on the spot whatever price for release she may persuade [her mistress to accept] and let her be released from staying and serving (*paramonē*) just as she would also be freed after the death of the woman who gave her conditional release (*paramonē*).
E	security of status	And if anyone lays a hand on the aforementioned bodies after their [release] from staying and serving (*paramonē*), let the seller and the guarantor make the sale to the god secure. Similarly, let anyone have the right to rescue and set the aforementioned bodies free, without incurring punishment or trial, free from all legal action and penalties.
F	witnesses	Witnesses: the priests of Pythian Apollo, Philon, son of Stratagos, Polemarchos, son of Damon, and private citizens Kleon..., Pason, son of Polemarchos, Diolkes son of Philistion, Agon son of Poplios, Theokles son of Kaloklidas, Antigonos son of Babylos. (G. Daux ed., *Fouilles de Delphes* 3.3.313; end of first century BC)

The role of the god in maintaining the slave's freedom against all-comers is reaffirmed in the last section of the record.

Even at the moment of their freedom, the slaves were called bodies (*somata*). In law slaves were regarded in some ways as things not persons; but it still comes as a shock to see how depersonalised, how degraded slaves were, not men or women, but bodies male or female. And just as in the American south, masters called slaves by their given names. This was another social stigma of slavery. A free person had a socially recognised father (Euridika daughter of Archidamus); the father of the slave was not socially recognised; the slave was simply Zoila.[20] Just because stigma is commonplace, that is no reason for us to take it for granted.

We shall be discussing conditional release in some detail below, so for the moment let us merely stress two aspects of the *paramonē* clause (c) in the formula; first the tension between what we might call the ex-slave's juridical freedom given in the previous paragraph (B) and the contractual restraints of conditional release. In numerous Delphic inscriptions, this contrast was even starker than in the example quoted; the slave was first explicitly given full freedom, then contractually constrained:

Accordingly Athenaïs has entrusted the sale price to the god on condition that she is free, never to be claimed by anyone for all time, doing what she wants and running off to whomever she wants...
But let Athenaïs stay and serve [her mistress] Klyta as long as Klyta lives... (*GDI* 1925)

Secondly, let us stress that the master, anxious to secure good performance of the contract from the freed slave, found his chief answer in punishment. If the freed slave did not do what she was told, the mistress had power to punish her in whatever way she wished. Westermann (1955: 22 and 41) has written of the general leniency shown towards slaves in classical Athens and, individual abuses apart, of the non-oppressive nature of Hellenistic slavery; perhaps Greek slavery was lenient, if it is compared with Roman slavery in mines or on large estates. But we should beware of masters' idealisation (Ps. Xenophon, *The Constitution of the Athenians* 1.10), and we doubt if any chattel slavery can in general be humane, in any normal meaning of that word. The Delphic inscriptions make it quite clear that punish-

[20] All discussions of classical slavery take place in the shadow of American slavery. Indeed one of the purposes of the present chapter is to stress some areas of difference between Greek and American slavery. For slave institutions, see still K. M. Stampp, *The Peculiar Institution* (London, 1964); for colour and much else, see E. D. Genovese, *Roll Jordan Roll* (London, 1975).

ment, at the complete discretion of the master, was central to the owners' perception of the slave system, and that the threat of punishment persisted in conditional releases, even after the slave was freed.[21]

In the final sections of the formula (EF), the seller, the guarantor, the priests of Apollo and other witnesses joined forces in assuring the ex-slave that his newly won freedom would be protected. This clause reflected the history of the institution of manumission: in most Greek city-states, manumission was originally a private act, of no formal interest to the state authority, and in theory susceptible to easy upset. If a rich citizen laid hands on a poor non-citizen claiming him as a slave, the poor man needed both protection and evidence that he was indeed free. Hence the public record of manumission – in the theatre, in a temple, on papyrus, on stone; the slave needed reassurance that all the effort expended on winning his release would not arbitrarily be lost. The guarantor and witnesses were meant to ensure that. But at the same time the formula recognised the violability and uncertain status of the unprivileged outsider in Greek city-states. Changes of Fortune and Death were prominent in ancient life, not just in ancient literature and philosophy.[22] We should stress two conclusions: first, conditional release as an institution depended upon the probability that the master would die soon, even if soon meant a decade; secondly, both masters and slaves sought through religious sanctions to give the ex-slave a security of status which civil authorities were too weak to ensure.

Our present-day scepticism should not lead us to underestimate the god Apollo's power. Manumission was a religious ceremony held 'in the middle of the temple by the altar' (*GDI* 2010). The following inscription from the shrine of Apollo the Sun God at Dionysopolis (in modern Turkey) reveals the public abasement which transgression against the god could induce. It was put up by an ex-slave:

I confess that I have perjured myself...and that I have transgressed and forcibly entered the (holy) precinct...and although the god commanded me not to give up the document of manumission to my master, when I was pressed from all sides, I gave it up.

And I was punished by the god greatly, and he appeared unto me in dreams and stood over me and said 'I shall take my slave by the feet, even if he were sitting at the gates (of Hell) and shall bring him back up from there.'

---

[21] On the centrality of punishment in the American south see perhaps best the collection of autobiographical accounts by ex-slaves, collected in the 1930s edited with an interpretative summary by G. P. Rawick, *The American Slave, From Sundown to Sunup* (Westport, Conn., 1972) especially 55–7, and Genovese (1975) *passim*.

[22] This point is well made by A. Gouldner, *Enter Plato* (New York, 1965) 24ff.

And I command that no one shall scorn the god of the Sun Apollo, when he shall have this monument as a reminder.[23]

In sum, four elements of the formula are striking: first, the role of the god Apollo as guardian of liberty for the ex-slave; secondly, the danger that the ex-slave might lose his status through arbitrary seizure; thirdly, the centrality of punishment; and finally the severity of the contractual obligations which some slaves entered as soon as they were formally free.

The problem

Conditional release posed three obvious problems. First, why did slaves scrimp and save sizeable sums of money merely to change their legal status? To all appearances, conditional release obliged the slave to remain in a slave-like condition, liable to work and punishment just like a slave, with only the indeterminate prospect of full freedom when her former owner died. There were some advantages: in most cases we think that children born to the freed slave during this protracted service were free; that was one of the obvious advantages to the slave of securing conditional release; but several scholars (cf. Zel'in 1969; 148) have assumed the opposite; no one knows for sure. Above all, the ex-slave would have the feeling that she was free. But the price paid for this illusion was considerable. At conventional wheat prices, the sum of 400 *drachmae* which was commonly paid for conditional release (cf. Table III.4) equalled some three and a half tons of wheat equivalent, enough to feed a poor peasant family for over three years.[24] Such a calculation is inevitably crude and gives only a rough order of magnitude. Yet halve or double the price of wheat, and the sum still

---

[23] The text is edited by Cameron (1939: 155ff.) with an interpretation of possible meanings and this is the text which we translate as best we can here.

[24] We know only seven Greek wheat prices from the second century BC. Four of these come from the small island of Delos between 190 and 169 BC; the most common price was 10 *drachmae* presumably for one *medimnos* conventionally estimated at 52 litres = 39 kg wheat. This seems high for three reasons: first, the price of barley meal from Delos in the same period, which should be higher than for barley grain, was only 3–5 *drachmae* per *medimnos* (N = 5) – see J. A. O. Larsen, 'Roman Greece' in *ESAR* vol. 4, 385–6; secondly, in Egypt and elsewhere, barley prices were normally about three fifths of wheat prices; thirdly, Delos wheat prices also look high if we compare them with the conventional Roman price for wheat (3 HS per *modius* of 6.5 kg = 4.5 *drachmae* per *medimnos*). The three other prices for wheat (*SIG* 976 Samos; *IG* 5.2.437 Megalopolis; *Inschriften von Priene* 108.46) were not market prices but administered prices: for example, the price fixed by a public benefactor in a famine. They were 5⅓, 5½ and 4 *drachmae* per *medimnos* respectively, all much closer to the conventional price of wheat at Rome than to the price of wheat at Delos. Whether we take the wheat prices from Delos or Rome, the 400 *drachmae* paid by a slave equalled 1½ to 3½ tons of wheat equivalent. We think the latter price more plausible. A poor peasant family needed one ton of wheat equivalent for minimum subsistence, which includes a bare allowance for heat, housing and clothing.

remains sizeable, difficult enough for a peasant, let alone a slave to accumulate.

This leads to our second problem, which we have already raised: how did slaves, perhaps especially female slaves, acquire such sums of money? In the cities of Rome and classical Athens, both trading centres and capitals of empire, it is easy enough to understand that there were spaces in the economy in which outsiders, aliens, even slaves, could acquire small fortunes. Indeed perhaps because they were outsiders, like the Chinese in south-east Asia or Indians in East Africa, they had more social space in which to make a profit, exactly because they were outsiders, free from the constraints which compelled citizens to give their kin-folk and fellow citizens a bargain. But all that does not explain why large-scale manumission, based on cash accumulations, was possible in the relatively rural and economically under-developed area around Delphi (and in Thessaly). To be sure, business derived from the oracle and Apollo's temple accounted for some economic activity, but they do not fully explain the high level of release prices paid by slaves, and of course they do not explain the high rate of manumission in Thessaly.

Our third problem is why did slave-owners free their slaves conditionally. Perhaps an answer to this problem presupposes an answer to the broader problem: why did masters allow slaves to buy their freedom at all? Let us discuss that briefly; two arguments seem important.

First, it was sensible for masters to opt for the carrot rather than or in addition to the stick. The prospect of buying freedom encouraged a slave to show both initiative and parsimony. Ideally, the slave both sought to make a profit and to save. If the slave died before achieving liberty, the master pocketed his savings; in strict law, they belonged to the master anyhow. If the slave later bought full freedom, the master had recapitalised the slave's value and with the purchase money he could buy a younger slave to replace him. The second argument is complementary: as the adult slave grew older, the chances of death and sickness increased; insofar as release prices were related to market prices, it was better for the master at some stage to capitalise the slave's current value than to go on risking total loss or to keep on a declining asset.[25] It was the paradox of classical slavery that a master maximised his profit from a valuable slave by selling him freedom.

We do not assume that all or even most masters and slaves perceived manumission in this light, or that all masters maximised their profit.

[25] It might be particularly in the master's interest to sell a slave freedom, if the slave borrowed some part of the capital costs of liberty from someone else, for example from her father or husband-to-be. Borrowing transferred the risk of death or of non-repayment from the master to outsiders.

But doubtless some did; and it seems probable that some such rationale underlay the institution of manumission as a whole. Very few slaves were given freedom without payment; a small minority bought release at well below average prices (for reasons unknown), and as we shall see, home-born slaves paid on average about 6% less for their freedom than foreign-born slaves. Some exploitation was coated over with a veneer of paternalism and of its reciprocal, loyalty, and even with affection. From the individual's point of view, whether master or slave, the master's agreement to release a slave counted as generosity. The master had given away his right to the slave's life-long labour. But from the point of view of the system, if that makes sense, manumission reinforced slavery as an institution. It allowed ambitious slaves a focus for their ambitions; it gave them the possibility of being released, and it gave them the crowning prize of eventual success, with all its implications of virtue rewarded. Finally, manumission provided slave-owners with the working capital to buy new slaves; manumission gave strength to the slave market. But manumission also transformed slavery, at least for some, from the inescapable hereditary caste which it might have become, into a temporary servitude.[26]

In the light of this discussion, let us take another look at conditional release. Clearly it was a compromise between slavery and freedom, between what the master wanted and what the slave wanted. The master capitalised some part of the slave's value, and yet retained a lien on the slave's services. He did not have to buy a new slave or to break him in; he simply kept the old slave on. The slave too gained something. He paid only part of his market value; indeed, as we shall see, the average prices paid for conditional release remained fairly steady throughout the last two centuries BC, while the cost of full freedom rose sharply, so that the difference in the price paid for each became substantial (see Table III.4). The ex-slave on conditional release also remained secure in the socio-economic role which he had occupied as a slave; he did not have to leave the house and find a new niche. Juridical freedom probably made very little difference to his way of life; nor was that necessarily to the slave's disadvantage. We imagine that he continued to receive food and clothing from the ex-owner, whom he continued to live with and serve. Conditional release was an insurance against the harsh risks of independence.[27] Epictetus presents a

---

[26] Not that slavery in the American south, still less in Brazil or Cuba, was an inescapable caste (for manumissions in Cuba see H. S. Klein, *Slavery in the Americas* (Chicago, 1967) 62ff.). But the existence of colour difference reinforced hereditary status; the low visibility of status distinctions in the classical world must have helped manumissions.

[27] The shock of independence recurs in the autobiographical accounts collected by G. P. Rawick, *The American Slave, A Composite Autobiography* (Westport, Conn., 1972–) 19 vols.

colourful picture of the slave putting all his hopes and fantasies in freedom:

'If I am set free', he says, 'immediately everything will be fine...I shall talk as an equal on equal terms with everyone; I shall go where I please'...Then he is freed, and immediately he has nowhere to eat; he looks for someone to flatter at whose table he can eat...he falls into harsher slavery than before...and yearns for his old slavery. 'What was wrong with it? Someone else clothed me, shod me, fed me, looked after me when I was ill: and I didn't do much for him'...(*Discourses* 4.1.33)

Yet there were difficulties on conditional release; three seem particularly worth stressing. First, the master committed himself to wasting a valuable asset; as soon as the master died, the ex-slave became completely free and the loss of the slave fell on the master's heirs. Secondly, giving the slave the status of a free person made it difficult to exact from the ex-slave, now formally free, punctilious performance of slave-like duties; from the master's point of view, the slave became less reliable. Thirdly, conditional release gave the slave an active interest in his master's early death, which occasionally must have made the master feel uncomfortable. Given these disadvantages, it is interesting that conditional release survived and was not displaced by manumission by sealed will, which was so common in Rome, and perhaps had fewer drawbacks.[28] Manumission by will was known in post-classical Athens (Diogenes Laertius 5.55 and 72–3), and in neighbouring Thessaly (e.g. *IG* 9.3.1118); but it is only once recorded in Delphi and then by an outsider (*GDI* 2101). Finally, from the slave's point of view, the main disadvantage of conditional release was that he remained at his master's beck and call while his master went on living, sometimes for years on end. Greek masters and slaves were clearly aware of all these problems. The variations of conditions which we shall now discuss under the three headings 'Length of service', 'Performance', 'Loss of an asset' reflect their attempts to tackle them.

Length of service after manumission – fixed term and doubled obligations

The majority of conditionally freed slaves were obliged to stay and serve either their former master or their former mistress, until the old owner died. We do not know how long on average this service lasted, because we do not know how old manumittors typically were. But if we assume that most manumittors were mature adults, we can use life

[28] Manumission by will did not necessarily preclude the slave from paying the master's heirs for his release. W. W. Buckland (*The Roman Law of Slavery* (Cambridge, 1908) 496) considered that the payment of money by slaves was the most common of the conditions exacted in Roman testamentary manumissions.

tables to get a general idea of the average length of a slave's post-manumission service. At levels of mortality most probably prevalent among slave owners in the classical world (an average expectation of life at birth of 25–30 years), half the men aged forty survived a further 17–20 years, and half the men aged sixty survived a further 8–10 years.[29] Female owners would have survived marginally longer. If these projections based on historical data from comparable societies are a good guide, then in general and on average, slaves released conditionally to serve oldish owners could still expect to continue in service for a substantial term. Of course, each slave was interested not in the average, but in his own length of service. The sheer fact that he did not know how long it would last was probably a continual source of irritation. Some slaves must have developed a ghoulish interest in their master's every illness.

A substantial minority of conditionally released slaves were obliged to serve both master and mistress until both had died. The chances of protracted service were doubled. The obligation to serve both master and mistress as a condition of release became increasingly common during the last two centuries BC (see Table III.2: col. *c*.); from 201 to 153 BC, only a tenth of conditionally released slaves were exploited in this way; but in the last century BC, the proportion rose to one third.

This double obligation was merely one aspect of a general deterioration in the conditions of release which slaves got from their owners. Over time, as we have already seen (Table III.1, col. *k*), progressively fewer slaves were given full freedom, and those who were given it paid steeply higher prices (see Table III.4). In the second century BC, a small minority of slaves (13% of those conditionally released 201–153 BC) negotiated a fixed term with their masters, similar to the old English indenture; on average, it lasted six years (N = 25). But by the first century BC, according to these inscriptions, the practice had died out completely (Table III.2: col. *d*).[30]

The fixed term was replaced, again for the few, by manumission in stages. As the price of full freedom rose, more slaves bought conditional release; if they were lucky, this was only the first step. Instead of waiting for their old owner(s) to die, they bought full freedom with a second and often sizeable payment (av. = 388 drachmae; N = 12). We can trace this two-stage purchase of freedom for forty-four slaves, who

[29] United Nations, 'Methods for Population Projection by Sex and Age', *Population Studies* (New York, 1956) 70ff.

[30] In a few cases the year limit was used to protect the owner's interest. For example, in one case (*GDI* 2084 cf. 1742) a female ex-slave was required to serve her master until his death, and to serve his wife if he died before eight years had passed.

Table III.2. *Conditionally
freed slaves were increasingly exploited*

Conditionally freed slaves were required to stay and serve until				
a	*b*	*c*	*d*	*e*
One master died	One mistress died	Both died*	Fixed term†	Total number of cases
		(%)		
A 201–153 BC	49	27	11	13	142
B 153–101 BC	38	31	24	8	88
C 101–1 BC	24	41	35	0	107

* The great majority of these paired owners were apparently husband and wife – but in some cases they were brother and sister, mother and daughter, etc.

† The average length of fixed term service was 6 years.

constituted a small but steadily increasing proportion (it eventually affected one quarter) of those conditionally freed.[31] We can also tell, though only somewhat roughly, how long their service after manumission lasted. Most of them (59% N = 41) secured full freedom during the same Delphic priesthood in which they had been conditionally freed; the duration of priesthoods varied, on average they lasted ten years; the average length of conditional service within one priesthood was probably significantly shorter. But a few (20%) had to wait several priesthoods, in some cases for twenty years or more, before they secured the second stage of full freedom (cf. *FD* 3.3.43; 340–1).[32]

The increasing frequency of two-stage manumissions is corro-

[31] The successive proportions of conditionally freed slaves who were released from service in periods A B c_1 c_2 and D (see Table III.1) were 4%, 2%, 10%, 26%, and 27%; NB the base numbers in the later periods are small – c. fifty per period. In one case, in the second century BC, a master who gave a slave release from service without charging her a fee, explicitly declared himself to be sound in mind and body (*GDI* 1751). This suggests that charging a fee was normal; but in the formula for release which became established about the time of Christ, the price paid was rarely mentioned; occasionally (e.g. *FD* 3.3.333) it was stated that the money had been paid as arranged; indeed in this example, it was paid in spite of the fact that the ex-slave was clearly the mother of the slave-owner's son. We doubt if silence about price meant that the second release was usually free. Samuel (1965: 265) came to a similar conclusion after an excellent discussion of the evidence.

[32] We can trace these two stages of release for forty-one ex-slaves. Twenty-four were fully freed in the same priesthood, nine in the next priesthood and eight several priesthoods after their first manumission.

borated by the standardisation of the formula giving release from conditional service. In the second century BC, release from service had been recorded in a form similar to the first fictive sale to the god; but by the first century BC it was recorded in a distinctive, standard and brief formula (contrast *GDI* 2015/1868 with *FD* 3.3.398 and 419). This standardisation strongly suggests that formal release from service before the owner's death had become common.[33] And in the first century BC it also apparently became common to make specific provision in the first manumission contract for a slave to buy himself, or more often herself, out of service, sometimes at the death of one of two joint manumittors, sometimes whenever the ex-slave wished (eg. *FD* 3.3.351). There had been occasional provision for this early release (eg *FD* 3.2.243; *GDI* 1717) in the second century BC, but in the first century BC the two-stage releases (which we know to have been successful) and the provisions for slaves to buy early release (about whose outcome we are ignorant) cover a third (33%; N = 109) of all the slaves conditionally freed.[34] Thus although the Greeks adopted an institution of conditional release (seemingly from the Near East) which catered for slave-owners until their death, they adapted it and allowed a significant proportion of ex-slaves to escape from service before the owners had died.[35]

Performance

Up to now we have taken for granted that masters and slaves had conflicting interests, as did the former owners and the ex-slaves still serving them. We have assumed that the ex-slaves wanted speedy release into full freedom, while the masters wanted sterling performance of all duties both from slaves and from the ex-slaves serving them. Punishment was as central to this intermediate institution of conditional service as it was to slavery itself. The tension between the ex-slave's formal status as a free man and the contractual obligations

---

[33] This point is made by Daux (1936: 615) but his list of releases from conditional service stops in the middle of the last century BC and is therefore shorter than ours.

[34] The 36 cases of potential or actual two-stage release from service may be subdivided as follows: (*a*) 11 slaves were freed in two stages, (*b*) six more slaves were offered the option of early release and we know that they took it, (*c*) six slaves were obliged to stay with their owner(s) until death and then could buy freedom with a second payment (this may be considered to belong to another category, since it was in the owner's interest to exact a second fee), but the slave may have seen it as early release, (*d*) thirteen slaves were given an option to get early release, usually when they wished, but subject to the agreement of their master and the payment of a fixed fee. Please note that in the second century BC, similar provisions, excluding those who received fixed term contracts, covered less than 5% of the conditionally freed.

[35] See I. Mendelsohn, *Slavery in the Ancient Near East* (New York, 1949) especially pp. 10ff. and 74ff. Samuel (1965: 255) attributed the creation of the legal concept of *paramonē* to the third century BC.

into which he entered when he was first freed, was solved in the master's favour. In some manumission contracts, ex-slaves were explicitly required to go on working after manumission, 'like slaves' (*douleuonta* – FD 3.3.337 cf. 6.51). Such requirements, which have parallels in Roman practice, make nonsense of the conventional dichotomy, dominant in the sociological literature, between slave and free; in the classical world, the two categories had a significant overlap.[36]

Masters usually took the right in conditional manumissions to punish ex-slaves as they chose, if the ex-slave did not do what he was told or did not stay and serve. 'If Eisias does not stay and serve or does not do as she is ordered let Kleomantis have power to punish her in any way he wishes; he may beat her, chain her or sell her' (*FD* 3.3.329). Of course, formal contracts do not tell us how people, ex-masters and ex-slaves behaved. Legal documents often merely set limits, which are not necessarily tested. Yet they do betray each party's fears and give clues about actual behaviour. After all, the centrality of punishment in the manumission records reflected not only the owners' power, but also their fear that ex-slaves might not do what they were told, neither stay nor serve.

At one extreme, then, the master could legally punish the ex-slave's disobedience by selling him, presumably as a slave, to someone else; in other words, the master could, unilaterally, void the sale to the god and revoke the freedom which the slave had paid for: 'but if he does not stay and serve, the sale is void and without effect' (*GDI* 1721 – there are a dozen similar instances; cf. *FD* 3.3.6). In this respect, the institution of *paramonē* gave Greek slave-holders more power than Roman manumission did. This may have been partly because the act of manumission at Delphi, although it was carried out in public, was a private act, in the sense that state authorities were not involved.[37]

---

[36] In formal law, Roman ex-slaves could not be slaves: 'the praetor does not allow the manumitted slave to serve as a slave, unless he is bound under another law' (Dositheus, frag. 12, *FIRA* vol. 2, 620). But Roman freedmen owed their masters the general duties of clients to patrons and could be contractually bound at manumission to perform specific services. Moreover, ex-slaves who stayed in their master's household after manumission were subject to his disciplinary power, to some extent like slaves (D. 48.19.11.1: Marcian) while free men who worked for a period in a household were also like slaves (D. 43.16.1.16–20: Ulpian). See F. M. Robertis, *Lavoro e lavoratori nel mondo romano* (Bari, 1963) 101–42; D. Nörr, 'Zur Bewertung der freien Arbeit in Rom', *ZSS (rom. Abt.)* 82 (1965) 90ff. and M. Kaser, 'Die Geschichte des Patronatsgewalt über Freigelassene', *ZSS* 58 (1938) 88–135 and S. Treggiari, *Roman Freedmen during the Late Republic* (Oxford, 1969) 75ff.

[37] Rädle (1969) analysed very well the progression of manumission from private acts done in private to private acts proclaimed and recorded in public to acts in which the state took an active interest. However, his proffered explanations, namely that literacy was increasing and that ex-slaves wanted to preserve their free status, are plausible, but surely insufficient.

At Rome by contrast, slaves who were properly manumitted before a magistrate became Roman citizens; they lost citizenship only rarely and by official action. In sum, Greek masters sought to secure high performance from their freed slaves who stayed with them by threats of punishment, sale and the loss of freedom.

This was not true of all conditional manumissions. In several cases the master's power was restricted.[38] The single most common limitation (N = 26) was that the master could not sell the ex-slave. He could punish as he wished but not sell. Slaves wanted to avoid sale, not merely because sale would sever the slave from his or her family but also because it would presumably destroy the rights which the slave had acquired at manumission. In a few cases at Delphi, the restriction on a master's power was considerably greater; masters and freed slaves agreed to resolve any differences about the quality of the ex-slaves' work through arbitrators (*GDI* 1832, cf. 1694, 1696, 1874). This provision implicitly recognised a measure of equality between master and freed slave. But most contracts of conditional release were unequal; the legal force of contract was being used to get ex-slaves to agree to their own exploitation.

Masters and slaves were not always at loggerheads. In some cases, a slave was acknowledged as the owner's foundling (*idion threpton*: *FD* 3.6.37 and eleven similar instances), reared by him, presumably with some affection. We should stress again that neither this tie nor the obvious parentage by the owner of a slave (such parentage was never made explicit but it can be deduced from names; for example, Kleomantis changed the name of his slave's son to Kleomantis – *FD* 3.3.333) led to any obvious reduction in the fees which child or foundling paid for freedom. But it is clear that in some cases the ex-slave was the master's only or main helper, obliged to care for him 'day and night' (*FD* 3.6.57), provide all bodily services (*FD* 3.2.169), and look after him in old age (*GDI* 1723, 1731). When the master died, the ex-slave, in a dozen surviving instances, was charged with the care of the funeral, so important in Greek life, and even inherited the owner's property (*FD* 3.2.172 and five other cases). As in other slave societies, the tie between master and slave could be warm; this warmth did not necessarily lessen exploitation, though it may have softened the slave's feelings about it.

---

[38] The following sketch of various conditions is necessarily selective. Please note that the universe is 289 conditional manumissions involving 400 slaves. From a statistical point of view, therefore, none of the conditions discussed is important, though several seem intrinsically interesting. These two dimensions of analysis, incidence and interest, have sometimes been confused.

Full freedom and conditional release

How to lessen the loss of an asset

From the slave-owner's point of view, there were two main arguments against conditional release. First, freeing a slave, even when he was kept on in service, weakened the master's control over him, and made it more difficult to get good work out of him. We have already dealt with these problems at some length. Secondly, freeing a slave conditionally might cost the slave-owner money. Conditionally freed slaves paid considerably less for the change of juridical status than those who bought immediate and full freedom. But when the owner died, the conditionally freed slave became completely free. The master's heirs had lost an asset. We have seen how a minority of owners struggled against this loss, whether by doubling a slave's obligations so that he served both his former owner and his mistress, until both had died, or by exacting an additional payment from the ex-slave when one of his owners died.

Two further sets of conditions revealed in the inscriptions deserve our attention, since they highlight interesting aspects of exploitation. The first is familiar because it has a direct parallel in Roman law. In these cases, the slave-owners freed a slave but kept a lien on the ex-slave's property even after he had gained full freedom, by stipulating that when the ex-slave died, especially if he had no issue, all his property reverted to his erstwhile owner, or to his owner's heirs. He was not allowed to give anything away or to adopt an heir (see for example, *GDI* 1891, 2097, 2202). The savings of these freed slaves, just like the savings of a slave, were claimed by the master. But in other cases, owners explicitly allowed their conditionally freed slaves to take their savings away with them when they left service (*FD* 3.3.37 and 205).

The second set is more dramatic. It concerns the children born to conditionally freed slave-women during their service. Were their children to be slave or free? We assume that in most cases, children born during service were free, but we really cannot know for certain, since up to 50 BC explicit provision was rarely made (but see *GDI* 2136, 2171 and perhaps 1719). But towards the end of the last century BC and in the first century AD, it became increasingly common for masters to make explicit provision in the manumission contract about the status of children born during service. The number of inscriptions surviving from the first century AD is small, so that any conclusions must be very tentative; moreover the provisions are polarised, and split evenly between slave-women whose children born during service were free (N = 9/27), and those who were required to hand over a child or children as slaves usually to the heir, son or daughter, of their former

owner (N = 10/27).[39] In extreme cases, the master specified that although the children of his ex-slave were formally free, he reserved the
right to sell them if the need arose (*FD* 3.6.39), or that children born
during service belonged to the master, and once again, if the need
arose, they could be sold by the master (*FD* 3.3.306). But the most
common stipulation was that the female slave who had already bought
her freedom at a price should serve her owner until he died and in
addition should surrender a baby or babies, one or two years old, to
the master's heir. It was not enough for the master to get money from
his former slave with which to buy a new slave; he wanted the slave's
own flesh and blood, and was knowledgeable enough to wait until the
child was weaned and the risks of mortality had diminished.

The development of this new institutional form of hereditary slavery
and its ironical creation within the framework of manumission are
extremely interesting. And although the number of instances known
from Delphi is limited, many similar cases have been found from the
same period, the first century AD, in Calymna, a tiny Greek island near
Cos.[40] Perhaps this development can be partly explained by the
increasingly peaceful conditions of the early first century AD, which
drastically reduced the numbers of prisoners of war enslaved. The fall
in slave supplies may have forced masters to seek replacement slaves
outside the market, from among the children of their own slaves.
Rather than prevent manumission, they compromised and got the best
of both worlds by giving the appearance of freedom and by demanding
child replacements for the adults freed.

The following is an illustrative example from Delphi:

...Euphoria sold to Pythian Apollo two bodies called Epiphanea and Epaphro
for the price of six *mnae* [600 *drachmae*], and I have received the whole
sum...on the following conditions: they [the ex-slaves] shall remain with
Euphoria as long as she lives and are to do everything she orders without giving
cause for complaint. If they do not do what they are told, let Euphoria have
the power to punish them in whatever way she wishes.

And after my death, let Epaphro give to my grandson Glaukias, son of
Lyson, three babies (*brephē*), each two years old. If she does not have any
children, let her give 200 *denarii* (= 200 *drachmae*).

And let Epiphanea give to my son Sostratos one three-year-old child

---

[39] The requirement to produce children for the former master gained momentum only
in the first century AD. In the second half of the last century BC, only one out of
twenty-seven conditionally freed adult women was required to surrender a child or
pay a fee of 300 *drachmae* to her previous owner's heir (*FD* 3.3.291), although two
out of twelve conditionally freed young girls were so required (*FD* 3.3.273 and 332).

[40] See M. Segré ed: 'Tituli Calymnii', *Annuario della Scuola archeologica di Atene* 22/3
(1944–5) 169ff.; his introduction to these inscriptions is very useful.

(*paidion*) after five years, and another three-year-old child to my grandson Glaukias after three years.

And then let Epaphro and Epiphanea be free...(*FD* 3.6.38 – *c*. AD 20)

The Calymna inscriptions show that the institution of service after manumission was not limited to central Greece; they also suggest that the development of demands for young replacement slave children was widespread, a response to developments within slave society at large.[41] The following is a typical example from Calymna:

In Asklepios' third monarchy [of Cos] in the month of Hyacinth...Asphales and Menodotos freed their own foundling slave Monarchia on condition that she stays and serves Asphales for the rest of her life. And if she does not stay and serve him, she shall pay for each day's absence 4 *asses* [> 2 kg wheat equivalent]. And she shall bear and rear for the sons of Menodotos a male child [and hand him over] when he is two years old, or pay 50 *denarii*. After the death of Asphales, she shall be freedwoman to no one. (*Tituli Calymnii* 176a; ed. M. Segré (1944/5))

As at Delphi in this period, most of the slaves (for whom a record survives at Calymna) were freed conditionally (56/68) and of these, half were apparently released only for service during the lifetime of one owner, less often of two owners. The other half of the conditionally freed slaves (28/56) were required to stay and serve their masters and to produce one, and less often two children for their owner or his heirs; in a few cases (6/28), children only were required, apparently without service.[42]

One difference between Calymna and Delphi is striking: at Calymna,

---

[41] W. L. Westermann (1948) reported about sixty instances of *paramonē* from documents found in Roman Egypt; but these do not seem to be connected with release from chattel slavery. They are general service contracts, usually associated with a loan to the servitor or to his family. There are several isolated examples of conditional service, as discussed in this paper from elsewhere, but not in sets of data comparable with those from Delphi and Calymna. See, for example, in other parts of central Greece, *IG* 9.1.36–42 and 189–94, especially 193 (second century AD) in which an ex-slave was required to hand over a two-year-old child at the end of service or 200 *dn*; the prices charged in these inscriptions were very high (6/7: 1,000 *drachmae* or more); cf. *IG* 9.1.318 (Amphissa), 350–1 (Physkus) and 379ff. (Naupaktus), and *SEG* 25 (1971) 640 and 23 (1968) 352–3, where the prices read by the editor E. Mastrokostas are difficult to believe. See also *PSI* 1263 (Egypt, second century AD) and Gregory Nazianzen's will (*PG* 37.392b: Asia Minor, fourth, century AD).

[42] Several of these inscriptions are fragmentary; the analysis of conditions which is set out in Appendix III.1 may overestimate numbers in the short categories, such as 'no conditions' (rows A B E F). We distrust Segré's conclusion (175ff.) that all ex-slaves were *legally* bound to provide (*a*) service after manumission and (*b*) one replacement slave child. He deduced this from the fact that the phrase 'in accord with the manumission laws' only once occurred when these two conditions were explicit, and argued therefore that these were the conditions which the manumission laws prescribed. G. Klaffenbach (*Gnomon* 25 (1953) 459) also disagreed with Segré.

male as well as female slaves were conditionally freed with an obligation to produce issue for their previous owners. If they did not meet these requirements, they were often liable to pay money instead. But we are not told whether or how much they paid for their first formal liberation. It was usually specified that the child should be male and two years old when it was handed over to the former owners to start a new generation of foundlings (*threptoi*).[43] This category of foundlings of which there are 23 examples from Calymna (out of less than 75 possible cases) seems to have replaced the older category – home-born.

Overall the purposes of these chilling practices seem clear. The old stock of slaves was given formal freedom with residual duties of service until the owner died, and at the same time the slave stock was updated; adults were replaced by children within the framework of a quasi-familial relationship. For the owners, foundlings were better than slaves bought in the market.

PRICES

The prices which slaves paid for their freedom at Delphi form the single largest series of prices over time which we have from the classical world. For that reason alone, they deserve more attention than they have received. To be sure, many of the prices seem conventional: prices of 300, 400 and 500 *drachmae* were very common. But when we analysed the prices in terms of the other variables known: sex, age-group, conditions of release, origins and date, significant patterns emerged.

Table III.3 shows what we think no one has previously argued from this evidence, namely that there was a steady rise in slave prices in the last two centuries before Christ.[44] Average prices of all slaves rose by

---

[43] It seems likely that the ownership of the baby by the ex-slave's master was confirmed formally, rather than that the baby was actually handed over to be cared for in the master's household. The whole institution of service after freedom and of found-lings' slavery presupposes a close settled community in which the slaves, the ex-slaves and the enslaved children of the ex-slaves lived in various shades of dependence on the master. The classic but opaque article on foundlings is by A. Cameron, 'Threptos and related terms in the inscriptions of Asia Minor', *Studies presented to W. H. Buckler*, ed. W. M. Calder and J. Keil (Manchester 1939) 27–62; see also A. N. Sherwin-White, *The Letters of Pliny* (Oxford, 1966) 650.

[44] The prices in Tables III.3 and III.4 are for slaves freed singly. We excluded the multiply manumitted slaves because most of their prices are given in combinations (for example, an adult male and an adult female freed together for 1,000 *drachmae* – *GDI* 2158) which we do not know how to split. Occasionally, prices for slaves freed together were given separately, or for pairs of slaves of the same sex. However, we decided not to include these prices as and when they occurred lest there was a systematic difference between the prices paid by slaves freed singly and multiply,

Table III.3. *The average prices (drachmae) paid by slaves for freedom at Delphi (201–1 BC)*

Approximate dates	a Adult males	b Adult females	c Boys	d Girls	e Rough ratios*
A 201–153 BC	403	376	235	160	100
B 153–100 BC	510	428	276	244	125
C_1 100–53 BC	566	470	319	287	140
C_2 53–1 BC	641	437	330	333	150
Rough ratios	100	80	55	50	
		Number of cases			
A	130	190	11	9	
B	83	128	19	18	
C_1	9	27	8	15	
C_2	19	19	10	15	

* The vertical ratios indicate the relative cost over time of one man, one woman, one boy and one girl. The horizontal ratios indicate the relative cost over time of four men to four women, etc.

roughly 50% (Table III.3 col. *e.*). One explanation which immediately comes to mind is that the demand for slaves in Roman Italy outran supply, in spite of the thousands of prisoners captured in war and enslaved. Central Greece was hooked by Roman conquest into a pan-Mediterranean economy, and so slave prices rose.

Table III.3 also shows fairly steady rises in release price over two centuries for adult males, adult females, boys and girls. It is impressive to find steady price rises (only two figures are awry) for each category. The rough ratio of release-price paid by adult male and adult female slaves (100:80) and the lower prices paid by children (55:50) seem to rule out prostitution associated with Apollo's temple (for which there is no evidence) as a major source of slaves' income. The steep rise in release-price for adult males (from an average of 403 *drachmae* to 641 *drachmae*) may reflect demand for adult male slave labour in Italy.

or lest the master was more interested in the total price than in its allocation between those freed together – for example between a mother and her child. In fact, there was no significant difference in prices paid by those multiply freed, and their exclusion or inclusion makes only slight differences to the profile. This is illustrated in Appendix III.1, where Table III.4 is recast to include the multiply freed. The only exception we made was to include in Table III.3, cols. *cd* 18 boys and girls released in pairs or trios of one sex without an adult; their inclusion increased the base numbers significantly, although the profile was not much changed.

In most cases, presumably the grant of full freedom to a slave involved the owner in buying a new slave to replace the slave who had been freed.[45] Insofar as this was true, it is therefore probable that the prices which slaves paid for manumission bore a close relationship to what it would cost to buy replacement-slaves in the market. Indeed in one manumission inscription, replacement was specified: a conditionally freed slave was to be allowed full freedom if she provided a slave of similar age instead of herself (*GDI* 1717). Of course, it is possible that many slaves paid more for their freedom than the market price.[46] Masters had power to impose their own terms; and they were often harsh. But it was also in the masters' interests to keep within reason. In general, they wanted slaves to accumulate savings; freedom had to appear reasonably achievable. In sum, we conclude that release prices approximated market prices.

Table III.3 prompts two questions. First, did the rise in release prices reflect a general rise in prices throughout the Greek world, or a specific rise in slave prices? Unfortunately we do not know enough about prices in the rest of the Greek world to make any firm statement about price trends in the last two centuries BC. But Table III.4 solves part of the problem. Secondly, can we properly combine prices for full freedom with prices for conditional release? That depends on the problem being considered. Prices for full freedom and conditional release can be amalgamated, if what we want to know is how much slaves paid for release of any type. And it is worth stressing that on average they paid a high price, and that the price during the last two centuries BC rose. But the price of full freedom was significantly higher

[45] Alternatively manumission led to a reduction in the number of slaves, or slaves left replacement slave children behind them in slavery; but the latter alternative would work easily only if slave holdings were very large.

[46] Westermann (1955: 36) doubted that manumission prices were closely tied to market prices. We have no firm information on Greek slave market prices for this period; contemporary data from Greek Egypt are exiguous and difficult to compare with Greek prices; but they seem to confirm that prices paid by slaves at Delphi were high. Rädle (1969: 165–7) argued and Bloch (1914: 21) noted in passing that the *mna* at Delphi was divided into 35 *staters* = 70 *drachmae*, and so was worth only 70/100 of the Attic *mna* (100 *drachmae*). By no means all the evidence fits this assertion (see *GDI* 1951, 2001, 2082) and what does (for example, three manumission prices including the figure 17½ *staters*) can easily be explained as survival from the fourth century BC (when there is apparently evidence of a *mna* of 70 *drachmae*) rather than as current practice in the second century BC. We have willingly followed the dominant convention: one Delphic *mna* equals one Attic *mna*. The only problem is what to do with the 38 prices which include *staters* and/or *drachmae*. We have counted them in the Attic style, as equally 1/50 and 1/100 of a *mna*. If we had treated them as 1/35 and 1/70 of a *mna*, it would have altered the average prices paid by slaves for freedom by 0.01 drachma or less in each period. We thank Mr M. Crawford for advice on these points.

Table III.4. *The cost of full freedom increased, but the cost of conditional release held steady at Delphi (201–1 BC)*

| | Average prices (in *drachmae*) | | | |
| | Adult males | | Adult females | |
Approximate dates	Full freedom	Conditional release	Full freedom	Conditional release
A 201–153 BC	405	396	390	337
B 153–100 BC	532	422	440	372
C_1 100–53 BC	641	(300)	500	367
C_2 53–1 BC	827	433	485	383
	Numbers			
A	107	23	140	50
B	67	16	106	22
C_1	7	2	21	6
C_2	10	9	10	9

than for conditional release, so that we are mixing two different entities. Table III.4 provides some answers.

Table III.4 is extremely interesting. It shows that the price of conditional release remained fairly constant, while the price of full freedom soared. Indeed for adult males, the average price of full freedom doubled (from 405 to 827 *drachmae*) while the price of conditional release increased by only 10% (from 396 to 433 *drachmae*). The changes in the average price paid for freedom by adult females were significant but less striking; their average price for full freedom rose by a maximum of 28% from 390 to 500 *drachmae* while the price of conditional release rose by only 14%. These differences in the increase of prices make it unlikely that general inflation is the correct explanation. If there had been inflation, the price of both full and conditional freedom for adult males and females should have increased similarly.[47]

As the price of full freedom rose, the proportion of slaves who could afford it fell (from about three quarters of those freed in the second century BC to under half at the end of the last century BC – see Table

---

[47] At first we were tempted to see the markets for full and conditional freedom as somehow belonging to different circuits of the economy, to different markets, Mediterranean and local. Perhaps they did, but please note that although the price of conditional release remained roughly constant, the terms of conditional release became tougher, so that slaves received less for their money. The cost of conditional release rose even though the price did not.

III.1, col. *k*). Complementarily, since the average price of conditional release remained fairly steady for two centuries (at 396–433 *drachmae* for adult males and 337–383 *drachmae* for adult females), more slaves compromised and bought conditional release. Again from Table III.1 (col. *k*) we know that between the second century BC and the second half of the last century BC the proportion of slaves having to be satisfied with conditional release almost doubled (from 27% to 52%). It was all that they could afford.

At the beginning of the second century BC, there was only a very small difference between the cost of full freedom and conditional release; indeed for adult male slaves, the average difference (9 *drachmae*) was negligible. Why? Surely it makes sense only if there was little practical difference between the actual consequences of the two types of freedom.[48] We suggest that in the early period most ex-slaves continued to live in the same socio-economic roles which they had fulfilled as slaves. In a stable, local economy, the juridical status of workers made only a slight objective difference to their other social and economic ties; most ex-slaves, once freed, continued to depend on their former owners for patronage, for the preservation of their new status, for the sale of produce, for loans in times of famine or family crisis.

The integration of central Greece into the Roman world, the prolonged upsets which followed the Roman conquest, the imposition of taxes, the migration of slaves and of ex-slaves to Roman Italy stirred up local economies throughout the entire Mediterranean basin.[49] By the last century BC, owners who gave slaves their full freedom not only changed the slaves' status, but also ran the real risk of losing the ex-slaves' services. Moreover, replacement slaves had to be bought in a slave market, whose tentacles now stretched from the rich market of Italy as far as Greece. We think that is why the price of full freedom rose, and that is why it increased more steeply for men than for women slaves – because men could more easily take advantage of the expanding economy by personal mobility.

But why did the price of conditional release remain relatively stable? Once again we can only speculate, but the principal reason must surely

[48] Rädle (1969: 134ff.) argued, as others have done, that Plato's *Laws* (11.915) reflected current Athenian practice and that ex-slaves there owed their former master serious obligations. It does seem likely that *paramonē* as an institution grew up out of practice. What we see in these Delphic inscriptions is the codification and development of those practices, and the bifurcation of *paramonē* as an institution from full freedom. It is of course possible, though we know nothing of it, that the two forms of freedom were reserved for distinct categories of slaves.

[49] This process in Greece is described in Rostovtzeff (1941: vol. 2, 610ff.).

be that the slaves who bought conditional release secured only a change in status; they had no chance of changing their socio-economic roles. As ex-slaves they continued to stay with and serve their former owner, until his death. Therefore the price of conditional release was relatively unaffected by increases in the price of full freedom and of new slaves. In short, the price of conditional release was fixed in a different, completely local market. But the two markets did influence each other. As the price of full freedom rose, and so became more difficult to acquire, so some masters, as we have seen, felt able to squeeze conditionally-freed slaves harder: they doubled their obligations by requiring them to serve during the lives of both master and mistress, or they exacted an extra payment for full freedom. Similarly, as the cost of replacement slaves increased, so masters exacted new slaves – infants – from a significant minority of the conditionally freed. The increasing harshness of conditional freedom was a consequence of the higher cost of full freedom.[50]

FAMILY TIES AMONG THE FREED

One stark contrast between slave and free was in family relations. In the American south, free persons were married in church 'until death do us part'; slaves were married by ceremonially jumping over a broomstick in the master's house, and the marriage was scheduled to last, the cynics said, until *buckra* [master] sold one of them.[51] Surviving classical evidence cannot match the American south for richness of detail; we have to be satisfied with glimpses. But even the lapidary inscriptions from Delphi reveal many of the family ties between free manumittors, and also between the freed slaves.

As we have seen, husbands and wives often jointly required conditionally-freed slaves to serve them until they both died (see Table III.2). A free manumittor also often secured the formal consent of a relative to the manumission; this collaboration was not required by law, but since relatives were potential heirs they had an interest in the family property and so bore witness to the renunciation of a shared good.[52]

---

50 A somewhat similar conclusion, reached in a different way by Rädle (1969: 152), relied too much on the ratio of home-born slaves to the known aliens; but see Bloch (1914: 25 and 37–8).
51 Genovese (1975: 481).
52 Collaboration may not have been related only to property but may also have helped guarantee the ex-slave's freedom. In this respect, collaboration especially by sons who might outlive the prime manumittor was particularly helpful (so Calderini 1908: 190ff.). We should stress that although women had collaborators more often than men, they also acted singly; and many men had women as collaborators.

Table III.5. *Manumissions by male slave-owners decreased; manumissions by female slave-owners increased. Manumissions in which relatives formally collaborated increased**

| | Proportions (%) of cases in which a slave was released by | | | |
| | *a* | *b* | *c* | *d* |
	Male manumittor	Female manumittor	Joint manumittors†	Collaborative manumissions‡
A 201–153 B	68	17	15	19
B 153–101 BC	52	30	18	58
C 101–1 BC	35	32	32	56

* These data are based on systematic samples of 100 inscriptions from each period.
† Joint manumittors are manumittors who released a slave together, equally (*x* and *y* freed the slave *z*). Please note that the figures in columns *a*+*b*+*c* horizontally add up to 100%. The figures in column *d* are separate.
‡ By collaborative manumissions, we mean manumissions in which the manumittor explicitly indicated that the manumission was undertaken with the agreement of relative(s) (*x* with the agreement of *y* freed *z*).

Husbands agreed to manumissions by wives (*GDI* 1697) and more surprisingly wives formally consented to the acts of husbands (*FD* 3.3.295 and 394); sons and daughters agreed to the acts of fathers and mothers (*GDI* 2062, 2212, 2245); less often mothers (*FD* 3.3.375), brothers (*FD* 3.3.433) and grandchildren (*GDI* 2188) signified their agreement. What is more, the custom of collaborative release became increasingly common, for reasons which may be connected with, but which are not fully explained by the increase in the number of manumissions performed by women (cf. Tables III.2 and III.5). But for our present purposes, all we need to stress is that these brief inscriptions recorded a wide variety of family relationships among free slave-owners.

Among slaves, matters stood differently, at least as far as their owners were concerned. We can see this particularly in the large number of multiple manumussions which occurred in the last two centuries BC (133 acts analysed, involving 323 slaves). By multiple manumissions we mean those manumissions in which more than one slave was freed. *A priori*, we might expect such multiple manumissions explicitly to include slave husbands and wives freed together, or slave fathers and sons, brothers and sisters. But they do not. The only relationship among slaves repeatedly recognised in these Delphic inscriptions was that between slave mother and child (in 29 out of 133 multiple manumissions). The law, of course, did not recognise the capacity of slaves as persons to have husbands or wives; this was true in Roman law as well, but in Roman practice slave mates were frequently commemorated. We suspect that slave mothers were explicitly recognised as mothers, both because slave status derived from the mother, and because it was in the slave-owners' interest that slave children should be nurtured. Even among slaves, motherhood was a valued role.

The recognition of lateral kin among slaves, whether husbands, wives or brothers (or even fathers) would have limited masters' freedom to split families by sale. This judgement may sound harsh. But how else can we explain the virtual absence of any other acknowledged relationship in the large number of slaves freed in multiple or single manumissions.[53] Only once in a thousand (N = 978) manumissions, single or multiple, was the tie between slave husband and slave wife explicitly recognised (*GDI* 2183); and only once was a slave's father acknowledged (*GDI* 1708). Chattel slavery depends upon the market. The market operates best by denying family ties, partly because buyers do not necessarily want to purchase a whole family unit, partly because slaves themselves might not be able to pay for the release of all family members at one time. The tie between slave mother and slave child was the only tie which partly withstood these forces of separation.

Most (80%; N = 215) of the slaves freed as children were freed separately from their mothers (a few of these (10%) were freed with apparently unrelated adults). Apparently the pressure of increased prices for full freedom paid by adult slaves induced an increasing proportion of slave parents to buy their own liberty first and to leave their children behind them in slavery, perhaps with the hope of buying them out later. And then the increased cost of manumission induced more and more parents to rest satisfied with the cheaper intermediate stage of conditional freedom. This pressure was probably highest when an ex-slave tried to free a mother and child, or children, altogether at the same time. Table III.6 shows the trends: the proportion of child slaves released alone, without an adult, rose during the last two centuries BC from 50% to 85% (Table III.6, col. *a*); the proportion of children conditionally freed, which was initially the same

---

[53] In six cases, we can deduce relationships from the similarity of names of slaves freed together; they are probably sibs: for example, Kleo, Kleonika (*GDI* 1977): Boiska, Boiskos (*GDI* 1837; cf. 1836). Fatherhood is probably implied by the joint release of an adult male and a one-year-old child (*FD* 3.6.12), but it is the only such case.

Table III.6. *Slave families were split by manumission*

	a Slave children freed without an adult	b Slave children freed conditionally	c Adults freed conditionally	d Number of slave children recorded
	(%)			
A 201–153 BC	50	30	29	40
B 153–101 BC	63	46	19	70
C 101–1 BC	85	56	38	73

as for adults (cf. col. *b* with col. *c*), became significantly higher and eventually accounted for half of the slave children whose manumission is recorded at Delphi in the last century BC (Table III.6, col. *b* and col. *c*: 56% for children as against 38% for adults). Thus many ex-slave parents succeeded in securing their children's full or partial freedom only by the successive manumission of family members (father, then mother, then child). It must have taken years of struggle. But our figures, especially the overall ratios of adults to children (*c.* 4:1) and the high proportion of home-born slaves who bought freedom only as adults, suggest that most parents failed to free their children. Parents left children behind in slavery to win freedom for themselves as adults.[54]

Slave-owners also developed family ties with slaves. Masters had children by their female slaves; and they probably established affectionate ties with some of the slaves who had been members of the household since birth. As in several other slave societies, the category 'home-born' (*oikogenēs*) grew out of this recognition that home-bred slaves were different from the aliens bought in the market place. We can see the impact of these affections both statistically and by illustrative example. First, statistically: there are over five hundred prices for singly freed adult slaves from the second century BC, enough to run a series of paired comparisons between the prices paid by home-born and by known alien slaves (for example, from 201 to 153 BC the average prices paid by adult males for full freedom were:

[54] The overall proportion of children among the freed slaves at Delphi (17%) is the product of some uneven sub-totals. In 201–153 BC, the proportion was only 8%; from 153–100 BC, it was 19%; and in the last century BC, it was 29%. These figures perhaps support the idea that the proportion of home-born slaves was increasing; just as the high proportion of home-born slaves among those freed suggests that freed slaves left slave children behind them.

home-born: 350; known aliens: 410 *drachmae*). The average price paid by home-born slaves was lower in six out of eight such paired comparisons, and the (unweighted) average price-advantage to home-born slaves was 6%. Put another way, being home-born counted for little when the master fixed the price of a slave's release.[55]

Some masters may have been more generous than we know about. After all, there were many factors affecting price; we do not know which slaves were ugly, handsome, attractive, hard-working, lazy, clever or dull. Less a dozen inscriptions record that a slave had a particular skill, such as embroiderer (*FD* 3.3.230) or bronze worker (*FD* 3.1.565), skills which elevated the cost of their freedom well above the norm. This may mean that such skills were not usual; we cannot tell. Nor can we tell from the prices alone which slaves their masters loved, or which they were pleased to see go. The overwhelming majority of slaves paid sizeable sums for their freedom. We noted only two slaves who were explicitly given their freedom free of charge (*FD* 3.3.45 and 364), and each had to stay on with her previous mistress and serve her as long as the mistress lived. Some gift. In addition over thirty slaves, less than 3% of the total, paid what we may call a concessionary price of 100 *drachmae* or less; most of these were children; and in any case the top limit, 100 *drachmae*, was equal at conventional wheat prices to 850 kg wheat equivalent, somewhat less than a year's maintenance for a poor family; this was surely not a token sum to most slaves.

A few masters, as we have seen, relied on an ex-slave to look after them in old age, to arrange the funeral; some masters made their ex-slaves heirs, a measure of loneliness but also of affection. In 172 BC, for example, one girl was freed by her master and was to be 'considered the daughter' of his daughter Dorema 'doing all that children properly do for their parents' (*GDI* 1803; cf. 1806, 1945). For this privilege the girl called Hedula paid 350 *drachmae*; her real parents probably paid it on her behalf. The matter apparently ended well: fifteen years later,

---

[55] Other paired comparisons, for example, are (201–153 BC):

males with *paramonē*	home-born 333 *drachmae*;	known-aliens 357 *drachmae*
females without *paramonē*	home-born 363 *drachmae*;	known-aliens 404 *drachmae*
females with *paramonē*	home-born 300 *drachmae*;	known-aliens 346 *drachmae*

Those whose origins were not given tended to pay a price between the home-born and the aliens, but the pattern was not as even as in the home-born/known aliens comparisons. Nonetheless, it suggests that many of those whose origins were not given, were in fact home-born. Such analyses were not practicable for the slaves freed in the last century BC, because the numbers involved were too small.

another inscription records the manumission of a slave by Dorema 'with the approval of her daughter Hedula' (*FD* 3.3.8). In another case (*GDI* 1715), a master Agamestor, son of Telestas, released a woman and two house-born males called Agamestor and Telestas; the names certainly suggest that they were the owner's own sons. Yet the trio paid 700 *drachmae* for conditional freedom (for similar cases see *GDI* 2144; *FD* 3.3.372). In the southern states of the USA, similar instances are recorded in which masters acknowledged the paternity of slaves; but that paternity only mitigated slavery, it did not eliminate slave status.

CONCLUSIONS

Finally, we should return to a basic problem which we raised earlier and never solved. How did slaves, perhaps especially female slaves, acquire the very considerable sums necessary for buying their freedom? The straightforward answer is that we do not know, and in the absence of knowledge, we shall be reduced to speculation. Several points are worth making. First, the average prices paid by slaves for their freedom at Delphi were high – roughly equal (at 400 *drachmae*) to a family's sustenance for three years. Many paid substantially more. This suggests that those slaves who were freed lived at well above the level of minimum subsistence. During their time as slaves, they accumulated sizeable capital sums. They were not an underclass; they must have been richer than many free peasants. We do not know what they did. It seems unlikely that they were typically tenant farmers, because the region around Delphi is not agriculturally rich. Very few of the slaves freed (less than a dozen) are explicitly stated to have been craftsmen. We have excluded temple prostitution as a typical characteristic of the slaves freed, because men paid more for their freedom than women and boys or girls. It seems likely that many of the slaves freed were in some way connected with the prosperity derived from the Delphic shrine. And we should stress once again that these slaves, freed by special ritual, are likely to have been an unrepresentative sample of all slaves freed, and a minority of all slaves most of whom, we suspect, were never freed.

Secondly, we may have been wrong to assume that all slaves paid for their own freedom. We cannot help wondering whether money for the purchase of freedom was sometimes put up by someone else. Perhaps the best way to broach this speculation is by posing another problem. By and large most masters in Delphi released a single slave; admittedly this was partly a function of the style of record: one inscription per act of manumission. We know that some masters freed more than one slave in the same year (*GDI* 2169, 2187) or freed several slaves in several years (*GDI* 1783, 1888; *FD* 3.3.37); but such cases are rare. And when masters did release more than one slave in a single act of manumission, then by and large the number of slaves released in each multiple manumission was small (the average was 2.54 slaves in 159 acts).[56] Typically most masters released only one slave at a time. We deduce that most slave-holdings were small.

Small slave-holdings face a special problem of reproduction. Each slave household is unlikely to contain a marriageable male and a nubile female. Among free persons in free societies, the circulation of females, if we can look at it in this crude way, so that each adult female goes to one adult male, takes up a lot of social time, emotion, ritual and expense. Perhaps then, some of the release money for female slaves may have been paid by males, whether free or slave, who wished to marry them. Freedom, full or conditional, may have been the only path by which slaves mates could be provided.

Why did masters not sell their slaves outright to the owners of male slaves? Perhaps they did, and if they did, we should know nothing of it from manumission documents. But we can easily envisage a situation in which the owners of a young single female slave, acknowledging her wish to marry, sold her partial freedom, which both allowed her to marry an outsider and yet retained a lien on her services. Eventually in a number of cases, owners even demanded a share in their former slaves' offspring. Of course, this reconstruction is only speculation. But even so, understanding intermarriage between small slave households and their reproduction remains a real problem. And there are eleven cases in the Delphi manumission in which the ex-slave was conditionally released and required to serve someone other than her former owner. Probably not all those who paid for a slave's liberation had marriage in mind. But it is worth stressing that in this tiny minority of cases the purchaser of liberty was not the slave herself but some one else.

Thirdly, slavery in central Greece, like slavery in Roman Italy, seems to have been only a temporary servitude, at least for some slaves. Greek slavery, even the slave-like service of conditional release, was usually indeterminate; its period was decided either by the master's 'genero-

---

[56] Over the whole period, covered by the manumission at Delphi (201 BC–AD 100), both the proportion of all manumissions which were multiple, and the proportions of slaves freed in multiple manumissions doubled (see Table III.1, cols *mn*: 14% to 35%, and 29% to 66%). It seems reasonable to deduce from this that the size of slave-holdings among those who freed slaves at Delphi was increasing. We reached a similar conclusion in our study of Thessalian inscriptions (see note 1 above).

sity' in allowing the slave to buy his freedom at a price, or by the ex-master's death. But in spite of this uncertainty, numerous slaves became free. This system worked for masters because it made slaves work harder and because the money which slaves saved and gave to their masters paid for new slaves. Manumission and the slave market grew hand in hand.

Finally, our data have allowed us to trace changes both in the price which slaves paid for freedom and in the degree of exploitation implicit in the institution of conditional release (*paramonē*). While the price of full freedom rose, the price of conditional release remained nearly constant; but for a significant minority of conditionally freed slaves the terms of their release deteriorated; they received less for what they paid; they either had to serve two owners for their life-times instead of one, or to pay a second fee to win full freedom, or to surrender one or two of their children as replacements for themselves. Thus their own escape was tempered by a child's enslavement. We have discussed these developments in detail; the point we wish to make here is that the institutions of slavery, manumission and conditional release are too often treated as monolithic, unchanging. It will come as no surprise to historians, that they changed.

APPENDIX III.1

Conditions of release in manumissions from Calymna (see note 42)

Conditions of release	Male slaves	Female slaves	Sex not known	Total
A No conditions	5	7	–	12
B *Paramonē* only	13	13	2	28
C *Paramonē* only, one child	8	8	–	16
D *Paramonē* only, two children	2	4	–	6
E One child only	1	1	2	4
F Two children only	1	1	–	2
G Conditions not known	3	3	1	7
Totals	33	37	5	75

Conclusions

Table III.4. – *bis. Recast to include prices paid by slaves multiply freed**

Approximate dates	Adult males		Adult females	
	Full freedom	Conditional release	Full freedom	Conditional release
A 201–153 BC	409	375	387	330
B 153–100 BC	528	413	431	369
C₁ 100–53 BC	765	(300)	478	367
C₂ 53–1 BC	794	409	467	356
Numbers				
A	112	34	151	65
B	72	19	116	25
C₁	9	4	23	6
C₂	14	11	13	17

* By 'multiply freed' we mean those slaves who were freed together by one owner.

IV

THE POLITICAL POWER OF EUNUCHS[1]

THE POWER AND THE PRIVILEGES OF THE COURT EUNUCHS

Why Eunuchs? Primarily because they were important. No one who has waded through the church histories of the fourth and fifth centuries or the numerous later Byzantine chronicles, or those lives of the saints which touch upon court life, can have failed to be struck by the frequent imputation that, in the Eastern Empire especially, the real power lay in the hands not of the emperor nor of his aristocrats, but of his chief eunuch;[2] or alternatively that the corps of eunuchs as a group wielded considerable if not predominant power at court.[3] Yet the eunuchs were barbarians by birth and slaves into the bargain.[4] The purpose of this chapter is to explain why slave eunuchs and particularly ex-slave eunuchs held so much power in the imperial and aristocratic society of Eastern Rome, to put this power in the context of the socio-political developments of the later empire, and to analyse some of the social functions of this power.

[1] This chapter owes a huge amount to the kindness and encouragement of my then supervisor Professor A. H. M. Jones, and to his great work *The Later Roman Empire* (Oxford, 1964). An earlier version of this chapter was published in the *Proceedings of the Cambridge Philological Society* 189 (1963) 62–80. I am grateful to the society for permission to publish this version.

[2] For the power of chief eunuchs under various emperors see, for example, Libanius, *Speeches* 18.152; Malalas 340; Olympiodorus, frag. 13; Priscus, frag. 7; Cedrenus 1.587 and 626 (Byzantine annalists are cited from the texts published in the *Corpus Scriptorum Historiae Byzantinae – CSHB*).

[3] Again for eunuchs' collective power under different emperors, see Sozomen, *History of the Church* 3.1; Zosimus 4.22–3 and 28; Suidas, *sv thladias*; John of Antioch, *frag.* 191, 194. The fragments of John of Antioch, Olympiodorus and Priscus may be found in C. Müller, ed. *Fragmenta Historicorum Graecorum* vol. 4 (Paris, 1885).

[4] Castration was forbidden on Roman soil (*CJ* 4.42.1–2) and the penalties were severe; Justinian made the penalty fit the crime (*NJ* 142). Most eunuchs apparently came from outside the empire (Cedrenus 1.601; Theophanes 1.154), especially from the Abasgi (Procopius, *Gothic Wars* 8.3.15–17 and 19), at least until the sixth century. But in times of famine some parents are said to have castrated their children and sold them (Cedrenus 1.590); moreover general laws like this could not be rigorously enforced, so that some eunuchs may have been from inside the empire.

Here, right at the beginning, the objection might be raised that we are faced with nothing but a problem of historiography. Eunuchs might have been to Byzantine historians nothing more than women and gods were to Herodotus, convenient personal pegs to hang historical causes on. In itself this would not be without its interest. Eunuchs served as scapegoats. They were like Court Jews in German states in the seventeenth and eighteenth centuries.[5] They were subjected to similar obloquy and similar characteristics were attributed to them by contemporaries. This comparison suggests, what we should have suspected, that these characteristics (ambition, emotional instability, arrogance and avarice) were the product of a position within the structure of power, common to both court eunuchs and Court Jews, rather than a direct consequence of castration. Being a scapegoat was one of the eunuch's functions at court. But above and beyond this, I hope to show that ex-slave eunuchs did in fact exercise real power; that people who wanted important tasks immediately executed with the support of imperial authority regularly approached the court eunuchs rather than any other imperial officer or indeed the emperor himself. People believed that eunuchs exercised power and acted upon that assumption.

But were court eunuchs actually responsible for the acts attributed to them by historians in antiquity, or were these acts instituted by the emperor himself with the ex-slave eunuch as a front? What were the motives of each in effecting a particular policy? Such questions can never, with our sources as they are, be finally answered. It was difficult enough at the time. For example, the emperor Julian did not really know whether it was the Grand Chamberlain Eusebius alone who had prevented him from having audiences with the then emperor Constantius II, or whether Constantius himself also did not want to see him.[6] Eunuchs were unpopular. Even an intelligent and well-informed contemporary like the historian Ammianus Marcellinus took a somewhat prejudiced view. He believed that his hero and commander Ursicinus had been insufficiently recognised and rewarded. He put the blame on the palace intrigues of malicious eunuchs,

---

[5] See S. Stern, *The Court Jew* (Philadelphia, 1950) 4–49, 245ff., and H. Schnee, *Die Hoffinanz und die moderne Staat* (Berlin, 1953–5) vol. 3, 172ff. In many interesting ways the Court Jews paralleled court eunuchs. They were dependent on the favour of the prince, but their rise to power was independent of the characteristics of any particular prince and often took place in the context of the struggle between the ruler and the Estates. The rulers needed servants who were free from attachments to religious and corporate associations. And Court Jews like eunuchs had relatively free private access to rulers.

[6] Julian, *To the Athenians* 274AB.

and on one eunuch Grand Chamberlain in particular. But a modern scholar has argued convincingly that there may have been a serious and well-considered purpose behind this policy;[7] the Grand Chamberlain may simply have been responsible for executing this policy and not acting out of self-interest.

The problem is more difficult with the annalistic compilers of the later Byzantine period. Many of their stories have an apocryphal ring about them. Anything strange or wrong was attributed to the court eunuchs; above all, anything unpopular. This may be valuable in showing the common attitude to eunuchs or for the analysis of their usefulness in soaking up criticisms which might otherwise have fallen upon the emperor. But it makes an accurate estimate of their powers difficult. Once again the function of court eunuchs seems similar to that of Court Jews, who received some of the unpopularity caused by political acts which had been initiated by the ruler; the Court Jews were rewarded with great wealth, but at the cost of increased social isolation; and like ex-slave eunuchs, Court Jews ran the risk of sudden denunciation.[8] Many of the acts which the Grand Chamberlain executed on the emperor's behalf and in response to his instructions must have been debited to the Grand Chamberlain's account. We cannot say, of course, which particular actions come under this category; we cannot say with certainty that any did; but it is unlikely that most writers had any accurate inside information. In this quandary we shall have to turn not only to historical anecdotes, but to the development of certain institutions which reflect the real and increasing power of eunuchs.

Whatever may have been the prestige of eunuchs in society at large, the rank which they held at court was almost the highest in the land; and if anything the court eunuchs improved their rank during the fourth and fifth centuries, as the depreciation and inflation of titles produced yet more formal differentiation within the central elite. In the first part of the fourth century, the Grand Chamberlain (*praepositus sacri cubiculi*) seems to have been of senatorial rank (*CIL* 6.31946). In the second half of the fourth century, the title of *clarissimus* attached to senators had so depreciated as to make necessary the institutionalisation of two new and superior titles for court nobles, those of Respectable (*spectabilis*) and Illustrious (*illustris*). The highest title, that of Illustrious, was restricted at first to a very small group of prefects

[7]   Ammianus 18.4.3 and E. A. Thompson, *The Historical Works of Ammianus Marcellinus* (Cambridge, 1947) 42–5.
[8]   See note 5 above.

and generals, and members of the 'Privy Council' (consistorian counts). By AD 384 the Grand Chamberlain was also reckoned 'among those of the first rank'.[9] In the established order of precedence of the Eastern Empire, the Grand Chamberlain, eunuch and ex-slave, held the fourth rank in the realm, coming after the Praetorian Prefects, the Prefect of the City and the Masters of the Soldiers.[10] A similar ranking was given in a Western law of AD 412 (*C.Th.* 11.18.1). This is interesting because it shows that the rank achieved by Grand Chamberlains in general was independent of the great individual power of the Eastern Grand Chamberlain, Eutropius. In AD 422 the grade *illustris* was already depreciated and was split into two. The Grand Chamberlain was classed with the upper group which consisted of the prefects and the masters of the soldiers (*C.Th.* 6.8.1). And at the end of the fifth century the Grand Chamberlain was still an official of the highest rank (*CJ* 3.24.3 (AD 485/6) and 12.5.5 (Anastasius).

The Grand Chamberlain was not the only court eunuch to hold high rank, although he was in a special position because his tenure continued at the emperor's pleasure and often lasted longer than the three years thought to be normal for praetorian prefects.[11] Beneath the Grand Chamberlain, two other eunuch ex-slaves, the Superintendent of the Sacred Bedchamber (*primicerius sacri cubiculi*) and the Chief Steward of the Sacred Palace (*castrensis sacri palatii*) were probably recruited from the corps of eunuchs and held their offices for a statutory two years.[12] The very names of their titles and their close association with the emperor's private person recall the high status of similar functions in the courts of European monarchs (for example, the English Lord High Chamberlain and the pages, grooms and Ladies of the Bedchamber); but in European courts these duties were

[9] *C.Th.* 7.8.3 (AD 384); but cf. *C.Th.* 11.16.15 (AD 382) which Ensslin (*RE* Suppl. 8, 558) interprets wrongly; see rather J. E. Dunlap, *The Office of the Grand Chamberlain in the Later Roman and Byzantine Empires* (University of Michigan, Humanistic Series, 14; New York, 1924) 184.

[10] *Notitia Dignitatum*, ed. O. Seeck, *Or.* 1, index; cf. *Occ.* 1, index.

[11] Cf. for example, Socrates, *History of the Church* 2.2; Sozomen, *History of the Church* 3.1; Ammianus 21.15.4 for the long tenure of Eusebius; and Theophanes, 1.125 and 127 for Antiochus.

[12] It could be inferred from *CJ* 12.5.2 (AD 428) that promotions to three of the four top jobs held by eunuchs: *primicerius*, *castrensis* and *comes domorum* went by seniority. This is partially confirmed by John of Ephesus (*Lives of the Eastern Saints*, trans. from the Syriac by E. W. Brooks, *P.O.* 19.202) who wrote that Theodore retired before his time, as *castrensis*; and that *castrenses* normally retired after two years (*C.Th.* 6.32.1 (AD 416)). But there are difficulties about ranks; E. A. Costa ('The Castrensis Sacri Palatii', *Byzantion* 42 (1972) 358–87) argues convincingly that in the early fourth century, the *castrensis* was superior to the Grand Chamberlain and may not have been a eunuch; by the end of the fourth century, the Grand Chamberlain was certainly superior. See also for other difficulties, Hopkins (1963) 65 n.6.

performed by nobles or gentlefolk of high status, not by castrated ex-slaves. The closest parallel to these late Roman practices can be found in the Chinese and Ottoman courts; the latter probably inherited or copied Byzantine habits. According to the Roman book of precedence (the *Notitia Dignitum*), the Superintendent of the Sacred Bedchamber and the Chief Steward of the Sacred Palace both ranked as Respectables (*spectabiles*) and thus were equal in rank, in spite of their origins, to high nobles.[13] In the late fourth and during the fifth century, four further posts of high rank were created and filled exclusively by eunuchs.[14] The number of high positions open to them was still further increased when it became customary for the empress to have a separate Bedchamber with its own complement of high officers.[15] Nothing reflects more clearly the tremendous and sustained influence which court eunuchs were able to bring to bear upon a whole succession of emperors than their occupation of a regularly increasing number of offices, and the high rank which went with them.

In the early days of the Roman monarchy, in the first century AD, some ex-slaves of the emperor exercised considerable power as heads of administrative bureaux; and they were given the insignia of high rank (*inter praetores*). But the chief eunuchs in the later Empire continuously achieved rank superior to the vast majority of nobles, and quite out of proportion to the formal duties of palace organisation.

[13] *Notitia Dignitatum Or.* 17; *Occ.* 14–15; *C.Th.* 6.32.1 (AD 416).

[14] In sum, the chief positions held by eunuchs in the palace and the earliest known date of their tenure were: (i) Grand Chamberlain (*praepositus sacri cubiculi*) AD 326; Codinus, *On the Origins of Constantinople* 18. (ii) Superintendent of the Sacred Bedchamber (*primicerius sacri cubiculi*) perhaps by AD 312, more certainly by AD 326; *ib.* 18 and 21. (iii) Chief Steward of the Sacred Palace (*castrensis sacri palatii*) *c.* AD 343; Athanasius, *History of the Arians* 15; *Apologia against the Arians* 36. (iv) Count of the Imperial Estates in Cappadocia (*comes domorum per Cappadociam*) between AD 379 and AD 414; *CTh.* 6.30.2 (AD 379); 11.28.9 subscript (AD 414); *Not. Dign. Or.* 10; Dunlap (1924) 187. (v) Count of the Imperial Wardrobe (*comes sacrae vestis*) AD 412; *C.Th.* 11.18.1. (vi) Captain of the Bodyguard (*spatharius*) AD 447; Theodoret, *Letters* 110. (vii) Keeper of the Purse (*sacellarius*) AD 474–91; John of Antioch, frag. 214.4. NB: offices may well have existed before these dates and may also have been occupied by non-eunuchs.

[15] Already by the reign of Constantine, the empress was attended by eunuchs (Philostorgius, *History of the Church* 2.4, and Codinus, *On the Origins of Constantinople* 18 and 21) mentions two Grand Chamberlains in Constantine's court, though Ensslin doubts that any firm conclusion about their rank may be drawn from so late a source (*RE* Suppl. 8, 557). Certainly in AD 400, Amantius was Chief Steward to the empress Eudoxia (Marcus Diaconus, *Life of Porphyry* 36–7, 40), and by the reign of Theodosius II, and again at the coronation of Leo I and in the reign of Anastasius, there is evidence of separate Bedchambers (Theophanes 1.151–2; Constantine Porphyrogenitus, *On Ceremonies* 1.91 (416 *CSHB*); *CJ* 3.24.3 (AD 485/6) and 12.5.5). In AD 536 the empress had her own Keeper of the Purse (John of Ephesus, *P.O.* 18.630, n.1). In fact the two Caesars, Gallus and Julian, both had their own Grand Chamberlains in the middle of the fourth century (Ammianus 15.2.10; 16.7.2).

Power and privileges of court eunuchs

In the highly centralised system of the later Empire, with its detailed and established order of precedence, the exercise of informal power without formal recognition would have been very difficult. Besides, however important the rights of aristocratic birth and of wealth, and no one can deny that they were important, what gave most power at court in the later Empire was the degree of association with the emperor. And the exercise of office near to the sacred person of the emperor entitled even eunuchs to honour and acknowledgement.

This proximity to the emperor and the assurance of his favour was the sole firm basis of court eunuchs' power.[16] Their duty to protect the emperor from intruders was of great importance in this respect. It served to emphasise the eunuchs' own freedom of access and their opportunities for informal persuasion.[17] And it gave them the formalised right of controlling audiences (Constantine Porphyrogenitus, *On Ceremonies* 1.87). It was Gallicanus, the Grand Chamberlain of the usurper Maximus, who apparently decided that St Ambrose should be received in formal council and so wrecked his diplomatic mission (Ambrose, *Letters* 24). On a humbler level it was through the services of Amantius, the Chief Steward of the empress Eudoxia, that Porphyry bishop of Gaza gained an imperial order against pagans still practising in his home town (Mark the Deacon, *Life of Porphyry* 36ff.).

A further product of the eunuchs' closeness to the emperor was that those who wanted favours, either positions or policies, found it advisable to grease the palm of the court eunuchs and to get them to espouse their cause.[18] Several stories illustrate this point. When one governor of a province was accused of corruption, he only just managed to escape by putting his whole future at the disposal of the court eunuchs (Zosimus 4.40.8). When the Arian sect wanted support from the new emperor Constantius, they found it easiest to get at him by winning over the Grand Chamberlain Eusebius first. The lesser eunuchs and the empress followed suit, and the emperor was surrounded (Socrates, *History of the Church* 2.2). To be sure we must be careful in the evaluation of these stories. Many of them may have been based upon hearsay. However that may be, there is enough reliable evidence that men of importance were willing to stake very consid-

---

16 On occasions the emperor seems to have been surrounded by eunuchs alone (Cedrenus 1.622); certainly even the Grand Chamberlain was within calling distance while the emperor was asleep (Theophanes 1.253).

17 The Grand Chamberlain could enter the presence freely (Constantine Porphyrogenitus, *On Ceremonies* 1.97 (442 *CSHB*); the other chamberlains could gossip with the emperor while performing intimate tasks (Ammianus 14.11.3; 18.4.2; Suidas, *sv. thladias*; Zosimus 5.1.4).

18 Libanius, *Speeches* 18.149; Ammianus 18.4.3. Cf. also Sozomen, *History of the Church* 4.12.16; Mark the Deacon, *Life of Porphyry* 26–7.

erable sums on the assumption that the persuasive powers of eunuchs were paramount. When Cyril, bishop of Alexandria, wanted to win the emperor over to his cause, he distributed considerable bribes both to the wife of the Praetorian Prefect and to the Master of Offices: each got 100 Roman pounds of gold and sumptuous furnishings. A similar amount went to the chief legal officer, the *quaestor* of the palace. But one of the two chief eunuchs received twice as much gold, and a further seven chamberlains shared between them similar furnishings and 380 Roman pounds of gold in cash (*Acts of the Ecumenical Councils*, ed. E. Schwartz (Berlin, 1922–) vol. 1.4, 224 and 293).

In addition to favours for others, eunuchs were not slow to gain privileges for themselves. They exacted fees for audiences;[19] and by the fifth century they exacted a sizeable commission from everyone appointed to public office. It was a token of their influence in the process of selection. The eunuch Chrysaphius demanded a payment even from a newly appointed patriarch of Constantinople; nor was he put off by the archbishop's plea that in order to pay up, church plate would have to be sold. (Evagrius, *History of the Church* 2.2; Theophanes 1.150–1). Justinian, even when he abolished payment for office, allowed the fees of eunuchs to survive. And there is further evidence for the privileged position of eunuchs to be found in a law of AD 430; if the emperor made a grant of confiscated land, eunuch chamberlains alone were allowed to keep the whole grant; everyone else had to surrender half to the treasury.[20] Some of them, Ammianus claimed (18.4.3), were not above plotting against those whose possessions they coveted.

The consistent exploitation of these opportunities led eunuchs to consolidate usage into privilege; such privileges brought wealth, and wealth can be considered as both an index of their power and a reinforcement of it. The fortunes accumulated by eunuchs, even by ones not noted for their avarice, were enormous (John of Ephesus, *Lives, P.O.* 19.202; Zosimus 4.5.3–4). The wealth of the eunuch Narses was legendary;[21] the bequests of the eunuch chamberlains Calapodius and Antiochus to the Church survived as entities for near on two centuries, and were so large that they required the services of twelve full-time accountants (*chartularii*) to manage them (*CJ* 1.2.24.11; AD 530). The fortune of Theodore, a pious eunuch who retired before his time, as Steward of the Sacred Palace, is illustrative. His fortune amounted to 1,500–2,000 Roman pounds of gold, plus silver, slaves and rich clothing (John of Ephesus, *Lives, P.O.* 19.200–5). One hesitates to

---

[19] *Life of Melania (Analecta Bollandiana* 8 (1889) 29), 1.11.

[20] *C.Th.* 10.10.34; eunuchs had various other privileges: *CJ* 12.5.2 (AD 428); *C.Th.* 7.8.16 (AD 435).

[21] *Liber Pontificalis* 63 (ed. L. Duchesne (Paris, 1886) 1.306); Gregory of Tours, *History of the Franks* 5.13 (19).

think what an impious eunuch could have acquired. For this fortune alone was equal to that of a very wealthy eastern senator. It can do nothing but reflect the socio-political power of eunuchs that they managed to expropriate so large a slice of the economic surplus and accumulated wealth.[22]

Proximity to the emperor had yet another consequence. It led to the selection of eunuchs for special tasks. Invested with imperial authority and high rank, eunuchs were sent on special missions.[23] The Grand Chamberlain, Eusebius, was sent to quell an incipient revolt in the Gallic army by bribing the rebel leaders (Ammianus 14.10.5). And later in his career he was given the delicate duty of persuading the pope, Liberius, to condone Arianism (Athanasius, *History of the Arians* 35–8). The future Grand Chamberlain, Eutropius, was sent by Theodosius the Great to consult a holy hermit in Egypt about the outcome of his battle against the usurper Eugenius (Sozomen, *History of the Church* 7.22). Another eunuch chamberlain, Chrysaphius, was instrumental in organising a plot to assassinate the king of the Huns Attila, and the eunuchs' power is reflected in the fact that when Attila uncovered the conspiracy and demanded the surrender of Chrysaphius on the threat of invasion, there was sufficient support at court for Chrysaphius for the emperor to run the risk of calling Attila's bluff (Priscus, frag. 7–8, 12–13).

Certainly Eusebius, Eutropius and Chrysaphius were exceptional. In their time they wielded nearly absolute power. But there are many other humbler examples.[24] And it was this consistent exploitation of the emperor's need for servants he could trust,[25] and the loose demarcation of jurisdiction typical of a patrimonial bureaucracy, which together paved the way for the extensive informal powers of eunuchs, many of which crystallised into exclusive privileges. This is not to say that eunuchs considered as a body, let along as individuals, were the major political force in the state. Their power rested upon their personal contact with the emperor, and was usually confined to palace politics. In the provinces the hereditary and traditionally

---

22 The same Theodore was given a pension of 1,000 *solidi* p.a. when he had dispersed his capital in charity (John of Ephesus, *Lives P.O.* 19.205). This was more than the entire annual salary of a governor of a small province (*NJ* 24–7).

23 There are many examples; e.g. *Vitae vivorum apud monophysitas celeberrimorum*, ed. E. W. Brooks in *CSCO*, scr. syr., ser. 3, vol. 25, 9; Cedrenus 1.581; Jordanes, *Getica* 42.224; Ammianus 20.8.4. These tell of rather less famous eunuchs than those mentioned in the text.

24 Cf. Marcellinus Comes, *Chronicon* (*MGH. AA* XI) 83, a.449; 101, a.519. Constantine Porphyrogenitus, *On Ceremonies* 1.92 (421–2), and 1.93 (428 *CSHB*); two attempts at king-making.

25 E.g. Ammianus (21.16.8) speaks of Constantius' fear of conspiracy and his tireless investigation of the slightest suspicion.

legitimate powers of the aristocracy, church, and army were paramount; and at court too their representatives competed for the emperor's favour. Yet the power of eunuchs was both great and significant enough to pose a problem. It was so firmly entrenched that the two upstart emperors (Julian and Maximus) who attempted to do away with eunuchs, both failed to establish an effective alternative.

Julian executed the Grand Chamberlain Eusebius and his followers for their part in the prosecution of the Caesar Gallus, and dismissed eunuchs and other palace attendants from service. His pretext for the dismissal of the eunuchs was that, since he was celibate, he had no need of eunuchs. More likely the real motive was to show that he was not subject to the same influences as his predecessor Constantius (Socrates, *History of the Church* 3.1). Julian's policy was surprisingly unpopular; if we can believe a Christian historian, people thought that he was stripping the monarchy of its necessary pomp (Socrates, *History of the Church* 3.1). But the reversal of Julian's policy was easy, because eunuchs fulfilled a vital function. They acted as a lubricant preventing too much friction between the emperor and the other forces of the state which threatened his superiority. Constantius, with the eunuch Eusebius as his chief executive, managed both to keep the army from getting above itself, as Ammianus says (21.16.1–2), and to avoid giving too many honours to the nobility. The several accounts of plots against over-powerful generals, often attributed to emperors but engineered by eunuchs, are symptomatic of the same conflict and the eunuchs' role in it.[26]

A sociological dimension

The problem of the ancient power of eunuchs was never been adequately tackled, either because historians until recently thought that it offended propriety or because the position of eunuchs could be superficially explained in psychological terms. Eunuchs exercised their power, the traditional view maintained, under 'weak' emperors, by means of 'subtle flattery', oily insinuation and unsavoury ambition reinforced by their sexual frustration. Over the long road from Ammianus Marcellinus in the fourth century through Gibbon in the eighteenth to Hug, Dunlap and Herter in the twentieth century this has been thought sufficient.[27]

---

[26] Theophanes 1.197; Marcellinus, *op. cit.* 90, a.471; John of Antioch, frag. 201.2; 201.4; Zosimus 4.23.5.

[27] Ammianus 18.5.4; Gibbon, *Decline and Fall*, ed. Bury, vol. 2, 245; Hug, *RE* Suppl. 3, col. 454; Dunlap (1924: 180); Herter, *R.A.C. sv Effeminatus*. But for more sensible views cf. S. Runciman, *Byzantine Civilisation* (London, 1933) 203–4, and best of all K. A. Wittfogel, *Oriental Despotism* (Yale, 1957) 354–8.

What can be said against this explanation is not so much that it is untrue, but that it is inadequate. The most significant aspect of the power held by eunuchs is its consistency, its repetitiveness from the middle of the fourth century onwards. No sooner had one eunuch been burnt because of his arrogance, or executed after a battle because his power threatened all other forces in the state, or compulsorily retired to a monastery as the result of political intrigue,[28] than another took his place at the apex of formal power. Within a few years either he, his successor, or the eunuchs as a body had accumulated considerable informal influence as well. We should be wary of evaluations of emperors as 'weak', which are based exclusively or mainly on whether eunuchs held power in their reign. For eunuchs flourished under powerful soldier emperors like Valentinian I, even under Theodosius the Great, just as under an idle fop like Theodosius II[29]

We are confronted here with something more than the weakness and virtues of individual emperors. To be sure, it is not only fruitful but indispensable to view history in this dimension, as a mosaic of the individual actions of separate individuals; without a doubt we can profitably discuss the personalities and achievements of individual actors. But there is another dimension. Emperors as individuals delegated power to different barbarian, ex-slave eunuchs, but the whole series of eunuchs cannot be explained satisfactorily exclusively in terms of their individual actions. It was not merely coincidental that all emperors appointed eunuchs to positions of power, nor was the power of eunuchs determined exclusively by the psychological make-up of each emperor. The continuing power position of eunuchs must be considered rather as a socio-political institution in itself, a patterned regularity, a phenomenon to be explained not only by its individual manifestations but with reference to other broad social factors. It is this generality which we shall now discuss.[30]

CHANGES IN THE POWER STRUCTURE

Political eunuchism as an institution arose in response to and gained a new weight in society because of changes in the power structure of society as a whole. Political development in the Roman Empire can

---

[28] Cf. the fates of Rhodanus: Malalas 339–40; Eutropius: Philostorgius, *History of the Church* 11.6; Antiochus: Cedrenus 1.600. A similar recurrence in the wealth and power of imperial ex-slaves in spite of individuals' demise is noted by Tacitus, *Histories* 1.37 and 2.95.

[29] Malalas 340; Zosimus 4.28; Cedrenus 1.587.

[30] Cf. N. Elias, *Uber den Prozess der Zivilisation* (Basel, 1939), vol. 2, 2 – in my view a neglected sociological masterpiece; but now see his *Die höfische Gesellschaft* (Berlin, 1969) especially the chapters on sociology and history, and on court etiquette as a restriction on the king's freedom of action.

be seen as the gradual concentration of power in the hands of the emperor, and of his direct nominees holding office in the patrimonial bureaucracy.

In the early days of the principate, wide areas of self-government were left to the cities through the unpaid services of avocational (non-professional) notables. Taxation was light. The senate ruled the internal provinces of the empire by means of its appointees. The emperor was only first among equals, and often had friendly and personal relations with his aristocratic peers. Trajan's surviving correspondence with his provincial governor Pliny and Hadrian's dinner parties for senators can not be paralleled in the later Empire, the so-called dominate, because by then the emperor was removed from fellows mortals not only by elaborate court ceremonial, but also by the general idea that he was sacred. A weak point of the monarchy in the first three centuries after Christ lay in its failure to legitimate among aristocrats the supremacy of any particular man or family. The first emperor Augustus had originally made monarchy tolerable to republican aristocrats by proclaiming that emperor and aristocrats were social equals; this inevitably led to the idea that any one noble might replace or succeed the ruling emperor. To confirm his position, therefore, the emperor had to restrict the power of aristocrats and to secure the loyalty of the standing army, paid from taxes raised by his bureaucracy. The bureaucracy was at first the extension of the administration of the emperor's private household and estates: a classic case of what Max Weber called patrimonial bureaucracy. It was staffed by slaves and headed by ex-slaves. The hierarchic organisation of the bureaucracy, and the long working career which alone enabled expertise in it, implied a submissiveness which in the beginning excluded aristocrats.[31] However, because of the increasing prestige associated with wielding the delegated power of the ruler, the bureaucracy came by the end of the first century AD to be headed by equestrians or knights, drawn from the second estate of the empire, though the emperor's slaves and ex-slaves were still powerful.

In sum, we can enumerate the constituent elements in the power constellation of the High Empire as follows:

(1) the emperor;

(2) his patrimonial bureaucracy headed by personal appointees with the social status of knights but largely manned by imperial slaves and ex-slaves;

---

[31] For an apology by a litterateur for working in the imperial bureaucracy see Lucian, *Apology* 10. On patrimonial bureaucracy, see M. Weber, *Economy and Society* (New York, 1968) vol. 3.

(3) the army, recruited from the peasantry and officered by regulars with the social status of knights and access on retirement to the bureaucracy;

(4) the peasants who paid taxes and rents and so supported the whole empire on their backs;

(5) the small urban population, both slave and free, which manu-factured goods and provided services for landlords, army and peasants;

(6) the cities administered locally by notables with access in recognition of services to the status of knights or senators;

(7) the senators themselves, the political elite of the hereditary landowners.

First a few words about senators. Some of them renewed their social position in each generation by holding offices for a short term only (rarely more than two years) in an area where they had no possessions, or as supreme military generals with an under-staff of professionals. Most members of the senatorial stratum inherited status by virtue of their inherited wealth; only a minority of them entered active politics. But senators, individually and collectively, were the greatest threat to the emperor's position; and senatorial status was the prime objective of many men's ambitions; promotion to the senate was in the emperor's and his servants' estimation the highest reward. The organisation of the political system which gave senators the positions of greatest honour, but restricted their tenure of office and exposed them to persecution, confiscation of goods and execution, is sufficient evidence of the tension in the power structure (see further in Volume Two, Chapter 11 of this work).

The emperor maintained his position only by maintaining a balance of power between constituent elements. The appointment of the praetorian prefect as chief executive of the government from the equestrian estate, and his combination of military and fiscal authority were significant indications of which way the balance was turning: away from the senatorial aristocracy towards the consolidation of the emperor's supremacy over his social rivals. In the crises of the third century brought about by the barbarian invasions, it was the technical efficiency of the bureaucratically organised army and administration which saved the empire. To minimise risks of amateurish defeat in battle, the emperor increasingly excluded senators from responsible gubernatorial or military positions and arranged for the collection of taxes from cities by way of professional tax collectors under the general supervision of the traditional local gentry. In spite of numerous barbarian attacks and civil wars, the empire was saved both from barbarians and from regional fragmentation.

The winner of the last scrimmage of the third century, a soldier of obscure origins from the north Balkans (Eutropius, *Breviarium* 9.19), Diocletian, was faced with a different balance of power from that of the Principate. The senatorial aristocracy had high social esteem, but had only localised power. Its individual members were by lack of training excluded from the efficient exercise of military or bureaucratic command. The bureaucracy had grown beyond the palace, and was headed by equestrians and divided into separate ministries with an organised jurisdiction and an established order of promotion. The army officered exclusively by equestrians offered the greatest chance of social mobility, and the biggest threat to established authority.

Diocletian and his successor Constantine together by their reforms established a system by which the equestrian order was assimilated to the old senatorial order; military power was divided between palace and local troops, and military power was separated from fiscal power, while the size of individual commands was greatly decreased. Similar developments took place in the bureaucracy. Staff was increased to gain greater control over the populace and greater revenues, but the area of individual authority was diminished. The legitimation of the emperor was heightened by symbols and rituals which asserted his close association with god.

The elements in the new power situation of the later empire thus were

(1) the emperor deified or in Christian times, the vice-gerent of God on earth;[32]
(2) a large and by former standards very efficient professional bureaucracy, separate from the army and divided into ministeries; the lower ranks were hereditary occupations; the upper ranks, upon retirement only, gave access to the new nobility (which was a significant separation of administrative power and social prestige);
(3) the army, recruited from the peasantry and from barbarians living on the borders of the empire, divided into border troops, heavy reserve and imperial guard, organised in small units and officered by professionals, who on retirement received ennoblement;
(4) the peasantry as before were so diffused that they lacked any organisation by which they could express effective objections to the

[32] Cf. e.g. 'The emperor is one, image of the one all-ruling God', Eusebius, *In Praise of Constantine* 7 (*GCS* 7.215), and K. M. Setton, *Christian Attitudes towards the Emperor in the Fourth Century* (New York, 1941), for the interrelation of the Christian idea of the emperor and of God.

increased taxation which supported the larger army and bureau-cracy or to the deterioration of their status *vis-à-vis* land-owners;

(5) the urban population in the later Empire was probably smaller than in the High Empire and probably contained significantly fewer slaves; some manufacturing for the army was carried on by here-ditary workers in state factories;

(6) the cities, much fallen in prestige, with vestigial autonomy and a hereditary local gentry who were dragooned into being collectively responsible for the payment of taxes which were high;

(7) a new nobility made up of: (*a*) great landlords and their immediate descendants, who might be invited by the emperor to fill office for a very short period, (*b*) upwardly mobile lesser landlords, origina-ting in the local gentry, who served semi-professionally as provin-cial governors or bureaucratic executives, (*c*) high army officers both serving and retired, often of barbarian origin, (*d*) retired professional bureaucrats.

The tensions at work in this constellation may be seen from the developments which actually took place over the next two centuries, Whereas previously the emperor had been able to control the aristocracy by the persecution of individuals, and by means of the professional equestrians in the army and in the bureaucracy, the complete victory of the equestrians and the eclipse of the cities had left only one unified upper order. To be sure entry into this order was controlled by the emperor and given only upon office, that is, upon the performance of certain services. But there was a constant and powerful tendency in both East and West for the aristocracy to expect to hold office as a matter of birthright and as a profitable sinecure. The second tendency, one reinforced by the high level of taxation, was centrifugal in direction: a tendency for the local land-owners to resist the tax-collecting claims of the bureaucrats. On the other side of the balance sheet, the division of the army into different corps of differing prestige and smaller units, plus the theocratic (or more correctly caesaropapist) legitimation of the new order, reduced considerably but by no means eradicated rebellions and usurpations. The unified honour system, which gave everyone of importance an exact position in the hierarchy, emphasised the overall superiority of the emperor. But it also accen-tuated the major problem which the emperor had to face. In so far as efficiency in executing the major tasks of government, that is, the collection of taxes, the administration of justice, the supply of the army, and its command, depended upon the skill and experience of his chief officers, any step the emperor might take towards the lengthening of their service to increase their experience, or any reward he might give them in terms of wealth or prestige in the only way available to him, and in the only way they wanted, was likely to increase the threat they represented to his survival as sole emperor.[33]

THE STRATEGIC POSITION OF EUNUCHS

In other societies a similar general problem has occured; namely the problem of conflict between an autocratic government aided by a patrimonial bureaucracy on the one hand, and on the other the military power of a professional army and a centrifugally inclined hereditary aristocracy. Yet in by no means all such societies have eunuchs risen to power. A structural analysis of developments in the power structure of the Roman Empire is indispensable. Without it we cannot delineate the functions of political eunuchism; we cannot analyse its contribution to the maintenance of the socio-political order of the Roman Empire; nor can we show why eunuchs came to power in the fourth and fifth centuries rather than before or after. Nevertheless, such an analysis cannot by itself explain the rise and survival of political eunuchism rather than of any other institution with the same function. It does not explain the question: Why eunuchs in particular rather than any other analogous group? For this we shall have to turn to a more detailed examination of the specific traits of eunuchs and of Roman culture.

Eunuchs, in the later Han and T'ang dynasties, were able to rise to positions of power when the emperor was deified and the executive ministers were excluded from intimacy.[34] It was in the same conditions that eunuchs became powerful in the later Roman Empire. The ritual of an audience became elaborate and compared with republican times servile.[35] It was a mark of humility on the part of Valentinian II that he forgot his imperial dignity sufficiently to kiss the head and hands

---

[33] This rather abstract analysis should be supplemented by the basic chapters on Government, Administration and Senators in A. H. M. Jones, *The Later Roman Empire* (Oxford, 1964) 321ff. or the splendidly written evocation of J. F. Matthews, *Western Aristocracies and Imperial Court* (Oxford, 1975).

[34] Ch'ien, T-S., *The Government and Politics of China* (Harvard, 1950) 31.

[35] Cf. A. Alföldi, 'Die Ausgestaltung des monarchischen Zeremoniells', *Mitt. des deutschen arch. Instituts* 49 (1934) 1–117, reprinted in *Die monarchische Repräsentation im römischen Kaiserreiche* (Darmstadt, 1970). Alföldi argues forcibly for the gradual development of elaborate ritual and exposes the general attribution of its introduction to Diocletian as little more than a literary *topos*. But then how does one explain the fact that the literary *topos* centres so frequently around Diocletian? The two views are not irreconcilable: a general development of ritual with additions by Diocletian.

of his sisters.[36] To kiss the bottom of the emperor's robes was the peak of some men's careers (*adoratio*).[37] The emperor's *consilium* changed its name and its tenor. It became at first the *consistorium* and finally the *silentium*.[38] St Ambrose on a diplomatic mission for Valentinian II objected strongly to being received in such a formal atmosphere (*Letters* 24). Negotiation was impossible, persuasion out of the question. By keeping to himself the emperor gained in prestige but lost in contact with his subjects. Synesius of Cyrene complained bitterly about this to the emperor Arcadius. Nothing, he said, is so bad as shutting the emperor away from public sight. The emperor should lead his troops in·person as he used to do; he should travel around the provinces in person and see for himself how his people are faring (*On Kingship PG* 66: 1076, 1080, 1100).

In many cases the exercise of power leads to isolation. This is to the leader's advantage when, like the captain of a ship, he is secure in the legitimacy of his authority. But the Roman emperors had to reaffirm their legitimacy by their divinity, reinforce it with a ritual which served to emphasise their superiority over humans, and each rebellion or palace plot served only to emphasise their insecurity. Absolute power is correlated with absolute isolation. There is no need to exaggerate, but the atmosphere in which nobles could mix with the emperor was completely different in the fourth century from the first. Gallus Caesar like Harun al Raschid wandered in disguise through the streets and inns of Antioch, asking people what they thought of him (*Ammianus* 14.1.9).[39] The comparison of the Byzantine empire with the Abbasid Caliphate and the very fact that a Caesar had to go to such lengths are not without their significance. Most emperors did not have Gallus' sense of adventure. And to rule effectively the man at the top needs information. The rise of eunuchs is not to be attributed to their 'skilful flattery and shrewd insinuation'.[40] There is more to it than that. Eunuchs met a distinct need, the need of a divine emperor for human information and contact.[41]

---

[36] Ambrose, *de obitu Valentiniani* 36. Cf. the story of a doctor who sat down to treat a bedridden emperor without permission by Marcellinus Comes, *Chronicon* (*MGH AA* XI), 88, a.462.

[37] It was also customary to kiss the emperors slippers, see Constantine Porphyrogenitus, *On Ceremonies* 1.84 and 86 (*CSHB* 387, 392).

[38] Cf. *NJ* 62.1–2, where both terms are used; cf. Constantine Porphyrogenitus, *On Ceremonies* 1.86 (*CSHB* 393).

[39] So too did Nero, but on drunken sprees (Suetonius, *Nero* 26).

[40] Dunlap (1924: 180).

[41] Insofar as the *Scriptores Historiae Augustae* reflected fourth-century conditions and allowed their opinions to enter their historical judgements, the following passage might be of interest: 'under Elagabalus, when everything was sold by the eunuchs

The political power of eunuchs

The power position of eunuchs stemmed in the first place then from their intermediary position between a sacred and isolated emperor and those about whom the emperor wanted information or who wanted favours from the emperor. Governors and bishops, nobles and vicars who wanted strings pulled had access to the emperor only through the Grand Chamberlain, the chief eunuch, and his services had to be paid for. From being a mere channel of information, through the exploitation of informal influences such as the patrimonial bureaucracy permitted, the Grand Chamberlain in particular and the corps of eunuchs in general expanded their power well beyond the formal confines of palace administration. But the continuity of their power as individuals depended upon the direct patronage of the emperor, and the sphere of their power was limited as it radiated from the court.

Secondly, eunuchs' power depended upon the tension between the autocratic emperor and the other power elements in the state whose exercise of power threatened the emperor's supremacy.[42] Yet the emperor had to entrust the execution of his commands to some of his subjects and the exercise of imperial authority inevitably invested its bearers with high status. The traditional bearers of this delegated authority, backed by the system of imperial justice (i.e. the systematic protection of traditional property rights), were precisely the people who most threatened the emperor's legitimacy and his universal power. Aristocrats had to be given power. But in the fourth century there were no equestrians to counterbalance them. Aristocratic power was limited by collegiality and short tenure, but the danger implicit in the situation can be seen in the growth of proto-feudal large land-owners (*potentiores*) in the western empire and in their resistance to taxation and to the levy of recruits for the army.

Since power, and especially that power whose major source is derived from the centre, is fixed, any exercise of power by non-aristocrats limited the power of aristocrats. Indeed the authority exercised by eunuchs not only by-passed the aristocracy but also served to supervise them.[43] The search for executives of lowly or foreign

– a class of men who desire that all the palace-affairs should be kept secret, solely in order that they alone may seem to have knowledge of them and thus possess the means of obtaining influence or money' (SHA, *Severus Alexander* 45.4–5, Loeb Classical Library translation).

[42] The power of eunuchs is put in the same context in other studies of comparable societies, namely the emperor's desire to liquidate rival political cliques. Cf. H. S. Levy, *Harem Favorites of an Illustrious Celestial* (Taichung, 1958) 17–18. P. A. Tschepe, S.J., *Histoire du royaume de Ts'in (777–207 av.J.-C.)* (Shanghai, 1909) 360; and cf. Zosimus 2.55.

[43] 'Since his castration deprived him of hopes of the purple, he persuaded the emperor to make him patrician and consul.' So Philostorgius (*History of the Church* 11.4) of Eutropius.

origin free from aristocratic ties and dependent upon royal favour has been common to many kings and most notable in those who have struggled against the traditional or hereditary interests of the aristocracy. But whether we take the service nobility of Peter the Great, the incipient bureaucracy of Prussia, or the commoners of Henry II, none wielded delegated imperial authority so much in the emperor's interest as the eunuchs of the Chinese and early Byzantine empires.[44]

There is no specific ancient evidence that early Byzantine emperors used eunuchs with a clear vision of their superiority over functionally comparable groups. Yet the very fact that eunuchs, in spite of their unpopularity with the aristocracy, in spite of their despised status, were constantly invested by emperors with high rank and great power, does in some measure confirm the hypothesis that this was done to counteract the power of the nobles. Nonetheless, the following analysis is not presented on the assumption that it was directly perceived by contemporaries, but that, whether it was perceived or not, the qualities of eunuchs could not but have influenced the role they played in politics.

This may appear in its sharpest light when eunuchs are compared with other groups. Let us take for example the Imperial Secretaries (*notarii*), a body of short-hand writers who took notes at meetings of the imperial council. They were recruited in the first half of the fourth century from outside the elite, probably because the long training needed to acquire manual skill was traditionally despised. Yet their knowledge of state secrets acquired in the course of their job and their personal contact with the emperor made them suitable for executive and supervisory jobs. They gained power and prestige. And by the end of the fourth century they had already become little more than a fashionable body ignorant of short-hand and holding sinecures, with the status of ordinary senators (*CIL* 6.1710). They had to be rewarded in conventional terms of high status and rank, and were thus assimilated to the aristocracy; they both penetrated into and were penetrated by the aristocracy.

By contrast the corps of eunuch chamberlains could never be assimilated into the aristocracy. Their origin as slaves and barbarians, their physical deformity and the emotions it aroused, their easy recognisability, were all against it. They were completely dependent upon the emperor and had no natural allies in society, no other retreat than his protection.[45] Nor could they, unlike others, gain acceptance by the

---

[44] Wittfogel (1957) sees the rise of eunuchs in the T'ang and Ming dynasties as coinciding significantly with the attacks upon the hereditary power of nobles through the establishment of the examination system and the restriction of *yin* prerogatives.

[45] Their barbarian origins robbed them of support outside the court. Cf. Claudian, *In Eutropium* 1.187.

social mobility of their sons.[46] In this respect they were like the clergy of the Middle Ages; but unlike them they had no corporate existence by which they could transmit inherited wealth.[47] The existence of a strong clergy might preclude the extensive use of eunuchs, but the non-corporative character of eunuchism was much more favourable to the maintenance of the emperor's power.

The complete dependence of eunuchs as individuals upon the emperor made their exercise of power more tolerable to all parties. Like Court Jews in German states they took the blame for many unpopular actions, and like Court Jews they could be sacrificed when the outcry was too great.[48] Their accumulated wealth, often enormous, could then be redistributed by the emperor to his favourite supporters; the aristocracy would breathe more easily now that a threat to their power and honour had been dramatically removed. The official decree dismissing the Grand Chamberlain Eusebius went as follows:

He shall be stripped of his splendour and the consulship is to be freed from the foul stain, the memory and the sordid dirt of his name; all his acts are to be annulled, so that all ages will pass him over in silence, and a blot will not appear in the history of our times... We command that all his statues, all his images, in bronze and marble... shall be destroyed in all cities, towns, private and public places, so that the blemish, as it were, of our age may not pollute the sight of onlookers... (C. Th. 9.40.17 (AD 399))[49]

The exclusion which eunuchs faced, the hatred they met all around them, cut them off from the rest of the Court and must have strengthened their cohesion as brothers in misfortune: '...those whom nature or bodily disaster has separated from the common lot of humanity and exiled from either sex' (Claudius Mamertinus, *Panegyric* 11.19.4).[50] And compared with ambitious aristocrats who were ama-

---

[46] Eunuchs seem to have a desire for wives and children. Their acquisition by purchase of both in China was a sign of their power, an attempt both at evading the appearance of being a eunuch and at transmitting wealth. Acolius, Grand Chamberlain under Valentinian III, had an adopted son (Constantius, *Vita Germani* 39 (*MGH SRM.* 7.279)).

[47] Eunuchs by a decree of Constantius were allowed to make wills (*CJ* 6.22.5 (352)), but even so they could hardly be compared to the institution of the Church. Cf. Procopius, *Anecdota* 29.13.

[48] Schnee, 1953–5: vol. 3, 190ff.

[49] See also the brilliant homily on vanity of vanities, preached by John Chrysostom over the quaking prostrate Eutropius who had sought asylum in his church (*PG* 52.392f.).

[50] The trauma of castration itself might also have strengthened their ties. Justinian cited one instance in which 87 out of 90 boys died from the operation (*NJ* 142). If this was the normal rate of loss we should expect to find it reflected in the price; slave prices given in a law (*CJ* 7.7.1 (AD 530)) reveal a sizeable premium for eunuchs but nothing of the above order; newly discovered fragments of the Diocletianic *Edict on Maximum Prices* kindly shown me by Mr M. Crawford and Miss J. M. Reynolds do not give eunuch slaves any special price.

teurs fighting their way competitively to the top as individuals, at best with patronage, and who held office only for short periods, eunuchs were lifetime professionals, *habitués* of court ceremonial, and furthermore with unrivalled opportunities of free access to the emperor (Constantine Porphyrogenitus, *On Ceremonies* 1.97). Insofar as eunuchs stuck together, they did not cater to the emperor's best interests. In combination, they can be seen less as intermediaries and more as an independent force with its own interests, and not always on the emperor's side. We can see them, for example, in action as a group, hammering away at the emperor to secure the execution of the Caesar Gallus, in support of the policy of the Grand Chamberlain Eusebius (Ammianus 14.11.3–5), just as we can see them collectively protecting Gorgonius, Gallus' Grand Chamberlain, from the fate of his master (Ammianus 15.2.10).

To recapitulate: the tension between an absolutist monarch and the other powers of the state; the seclusion of a sacred emperor behind a highly formalised court ritual; the need of both parties for intermediaries; the exploitation by eunuchs of this channel for the appropriation to themselves of some of the power of controlling the distribution of favours; the non-assimilability of eunuchs into the aristocracy; the cohesive but non-corporate nature of their corps; and the expertise which resulted from the permanence of their positions as compared with the amateurish, rivalrous and individualistic strivings of aristocrats; all these factors in combination and in interaction can account for the increasing power with which eunuchs were invested, and the continuity with which they, as a body, held it.

Eunuchs and chamberlains: the convergence of two traditions

Such general considerations as these, however, though they help to account for the continuity of eunuchs' power and the gradual increase in their rank and influence, can hardly explain their introduction into the palace and their rise to power. For this we have to look at the convergence of two traditions and an external catalyst. The position of chamberlain, *cubicularius*, involving general duties of personal attendance upon a Roman nobleman and the surveillance of visitors, is first recorded in our sources in the first century BC (Cicero, *Against Verres* 2.3.8). Its appearance was in line with the progressive specialisation of duties within wealthy households. Like aristocrats, the early emperors had chamberlains, and some like Helicon under Caligula and Parthenius under Domitian achieved considerable influence, but their power was never institutionalised as it was in the later Empire.

Apparently very few of the chamberlains known to us from the Principate were eunuchs.[51] In sum, the position of chamberlain was well established, and the chamberlains of the later Empire fulfilled similar duties to those of their predecessors; but it was new to use castrated servants in the bedchamber.

Eunuchs had been known to the Mediterranean world from the earliest times.[52] They were associated in classical times with certain priesthoods, such as that of Cybele, or with harems such as that of the Persian king (Herodotus 3.48; 8.104ff.). In the early Roman Empire their use does not seem to have been widespread, though there are an increasing number of references to them in the literature.[53] Occasionally, for example under the emperor Claudius, a eunuch is said to have been influential (Suetonius, *Claudius* 28). By the early third century, there is evidence that they were increasingly being employed in private households, probably as attendants upon women. Dio noted with shock (75.14) that a contemporary praetorian prefect under Septimius Severus had a hundred free Romans castrated so that only eunuchs should wait upon his daughter; and according to a rather doubtful source, the emperor Aurelian limited the number of eunuchs a noble might own.[54] The position of eunuchs at court in the third century thus seems to have been insecure; except under the mad Elagabalus, there is no evidence to suggest that eunuchs wielded power or consistently filled the post of chamberlain before the reign of Diocletian.[55]

It is my suggestion, therefore, that the consistent use of eunuchs as court chamberlains and their repeated exercise of power were probably connected with the elaboration of court ritual, which can be roughly dated to the end of the third century. There is evidence from a variety of sources that there were eunuchs at work in the palace of Diocletian, and also a suggestion that they were powerful.[56] I cannot help wondering whether the capture of the Persian king's harem by Galerius

---

[51] Dunlap, 1924: 166–9; and F. Millar, *The Emperor in the Roman World* (London, 1977) 74–83 goes through the evidence on the early powerful chamberlains. Parthenius, the chamberlain of Domitian, had a son (Martial, *Epigrams* 4.45), and so did Cleander, the powerful chamberlain of Commodus (Dio 72.13), so they were not eunuchs. Such chamberlains had huge influence and wealth and were occasionally assimilated to the formal status hierarchy (*AE* 1952, 6), but not as a matter of course. And see Dio 76.14 and 77.17.

[52] Wittfogel (1957: 354–5) for references.

[53] Hug, *RE* Suppl. 3, col. 451.

[54] SHA, *Aurelian* 49.8. Cf. *Alex. Sev.* 23.5f., but see also Clement of Alexandria, *Paidagogus* 3.26.

[55] SHA, *Gordiani III* 23.7f.; but *Carus* 8.7.

[56] B. de Gaiffier, 'Palatins et eunuques dans quelques documents hagiographiques', *Analecta Bollandiana* 75 (1957) 17–46; Lactantius, *de mortibus persecutorum* 15.

in AD 298 led to a proliferation of eunuchs in the Roman court.[57] Their presence may have acted as the catalyst for the separate traditions of chamberlains and eunuchs. The new emperors may well have felt the need for a ritual which elevated them above their courtiers, and for these purposes what servitors could be better than eunuchs acquainted with the elaborate ritual of the Persian court? Lactantius certainly accused Galerius of imitating the Persian king.[58] In any case eunuchs, wherever they came from, became the proper appurtenance of an emperor, and once established, their power increased for the reasons which we have already analysed.

The eunuch image

The full paradox of the political power of eunuchs cannot be complete without a description of their public image. To some extent, of course, their stereotype was built up as part of the aristocratic objection to the power which eunuchs wielded. But it also reflected the residual characteristics of eunuchs, and the roles they played in social life. It appears from modern comparative studies that eunuchs have a normal range of intelligence, but that as with domestic animals castration leads in many cases to docility, though a small proportion of hypogonads have compensating aggressiveness.[59] Eunuchs have high-pitched voices, and faces with smooth glossy skins covered with a network of

[57] Theophanes 1.11–13 (*CSHB*). On the Persian campaigns see T. D. Barnes, 'Imperial campaigns 285–311', *Phoenix* 30 (1976) 182ff.

[58] *de mortibus persecutorum* 21; Theophanes (1.11–12) connected Diocletian's elation at the success of Galerius' Persian campaign with the introduction of prostration (*proskynesis*). Cf. Aurelis Victor, *de Caes.* 39.2–4; Claudian, *In Eutropium* 1.415; but contra Alföldi, 1970 and see note 35 above.

[59] R. I. Dorfman and R. A. Shipley, *The Androgens* (New York, 1936) 319; J. Kasanin and G. R. Biskind, 'Personality changes following substitution therapy in pre-adolescent eunuchoidism', *J. Amer. Med. Assoc.* (1943) 1317–21; S. L. Simpson, 'Hormones and behavior patterns', *BMJ* (1957) 839. Hypogonads may not be strictly comparable to eunuchs in their social situation, but the sense of deprivation may be a significant common factor. J. J. Matignon, a doctor at the French legation in Peking, who had opportunities to study court eunuchs at first hand, wrote 'C'est à tort qu'on a representé l'eunuque comme sanguinaire et violent. Il est plutôt doux, conciliant, conscient de son infériorité', 'Les eunuques du palais impérial à Pékin', *Bull. de la soc. d'anthropologie de Paris*, 4 sér. 7 (1896) 334. J. J. Bremer, in a comprehensive recent study of the castration of adult sex criminals, etc., wrote of a 'peculiar emotional lability' among castrates and of an endocrine psychosyndrome (usually of an asthenic and dysphoric-depressive nature) which affected 25% of his sample. He did not find a general pacifying effect in many cases in social behaviour; one cannot tell how far this was affected by the psychopathology of his subjects (*Asexualisation* (Oslo, 1958) 25, 159f., 309). The same lability is remarked by A. Mez, *Die-Renaissance des Islams* (Heidelberg, 1922) 336.

fine wrinkles; they tend to run to fat.[60] Their physical distinctiveness must have reinforced their group solidarity and separateness.

What makes eunuchs' exercise of political power at court even more remarkable is the type of occupations with which eunuchs were normally associated. Hordes of them, wrote Ammianus (14.6.17),[61] looking sallow and misshapen (*obluridi, deformes*) cleared the way for the sedan chairs of noble Roman women. They were increasingly used as private attendants upon women,[62] and were clearly intended to be their ineluctably safe guardians. But humans are resourceful, and we are told that even eunuchs were occasionally exploited to satisfy their mistresses' appetites;[63] sexual intercourse could have occurred to any serious extent only with post-adolescent castrates. And there is evidence to suggest that most boys were castrated young.[64] These young *castrati* seem to have been often used as catamites by men, who took advantage of the fact that eunuchs preserved their freshness longer than boys passing through puberty.[65] To these indignities were added the performances by eunuchs of lewd dances in theatres (Prudentius, *Hamartigenia* 309–10); and in private service too, part of their attraction, as with the hunch-backed jesters of medieval courts, lay in the freakish piquancy of their deformity.

In the descriptions of court eunuchs which survive, these general associations were rarely forgotten. Eutropius was alleged to have progressed from catamite to pander in private service before his elevation to Grand Chamberlain under the emperor Arcadius (AD 395–408 BC, cf. Claudian, *Against Eutropius* 1.62–150). True, the poet Claudian had a particular axe to grind, and perhaps the eunuchs Eusebius and Chrysaphius would not have suffered so much if they had been on the side of victorious orthodoxy. But perhaps most revealing is the way in which Ammianus hedged his praise of the chamberlain Eutherius:

If a Numa Pompilius or a Socrates should give any good report of a eunuch and should back their statement by a solemn oath, they would be charged

---

[60] Bremer, 1958: 109–11.

[61] Cf. Jerome, *Letters* 22.16 and 32; 54.13; 66.13.

[62] *Life of Melania* 1.5 (*Anal. Boll.* 8 (1889) 23); Cyril of Alexandria, *Sermon against Eunuchs*, PG 77.1108; Palladius, *Historia Lausiaca* 35 (ed. Butler, 106); *ibid.* 61.157; Malchus, frag. 8.

[63] Cyril of Alexandria, *Sermon against Eunuchs*, PG 77.1108–9, for a catalogue of their activities; Jerome, *In Jovinianum* 1.47 and cf. Juvenal 6.366f.

[64] Claudian, *In Eutropium* 1.45–6; Basil, *Letters* 115; *CJ* 7.7.1 (AD 530); Petronius, *Satyricon* 119. Cf. the Chinese custom of early castration: S. W. Williams, *The Middle Kingdom* (New York, 1904) vol. 1, 408; and the Spanish: R. P. A. Dozy, *Spanish Islam* (trans. London, 1913) 430. The eunuchs had to be trained and educated for the palace service.

[65] Theophanes 1.79; Cyril of Alexandria, *op. cit.* PG 77.1108.

with having departed from the truth. But among the brambles roses spring up, and among the savage beasts some are tamed...In unrolling many records of the past, to see which of the eunuchs of old I ought to compare him to, I could find none. True there were in times gone by those that were loyal and virtuous (although very few), but they were stained by some vice or other. (16.7.4 and 8 – Loeb Classical Library translation)[66]

Praise was the exception; more typical of fourth- and fifth-century attitudes, if more than usually vituperative, was the view attributed to St Basil:

...lizards and toads...the dishonest race of detestable eunuchs, neither men nor women, but made with lust for women, jealous, corruptible, quick-tempered, effeminate, slaves of the belly, avaricious, cruel, fastidious, temperamental, niggardly, grasping, insatiable, savage and envious. What else can I say? Born to the knife, how can their judgement be straight when their legs are crooked? They do not pay for their chastity; the knife has done it. Without a hope of fulfilment they are made with desires which spring from a natural dirtiness. (*Letters* 115)

One can only imagine the horror with which a blue-blooded aristocrat must have approached such tainted upstarts to beg for favours (cf. Sozomen, *History of the Church* 4.16).

It was easier to curse court eunuchs behind their backs than to their faces. A considerable part of the objection made to their power arose from the lowness of their origins (Ammianus 22.3.12). Roman eunuchs deserved the soubriquet of eunuchs in China, 'the lucky risers'.[67] But social mobility in so stable a society offended the interests and the outlook of hereditary aristocrats; and the literature which survives stems mostly from the aristocracy, or reflects their prejudices. Nothing shows the dislike of eunuchs more clearly than their behaviour on retirement. Sundered from the protection of the emperor's favour, they lurked, wrote Ammianus, like bats in secret hiding places (16.7.7). At court it was a different story. Their non-assimilability to the aristocracy left them isolated, not as individuals but as a group. And it was as a group that they exercised power. The Grand Chamberlain and the high officers stole the limelight, but beneath them there must have been a substantial number of chamberlains of all ages gradually progressing upwards through the ranks.[68] Their survival depended

---

[66] There is a fulsome dedication to the chamberlain Lausus in Palladius' history, but Butler considers it a later bombastic redaction (E. C. Butler, *Historia Lausiaca* (Cambridge, 1904) 4). Priscus (frag. 13) says that all men held Chrysaphius in high regard, but this was not a view shared by all (John of Antioch, frag. 198).

[67] Yang, L.-S., 'Great families of eastern Han', trans. in *Chinese Social History* (Washington, 1956) 122.

[68] There is no accurate indication of number. Libanius says they were 'more numerous than flies on sheep in the spring' (*Speeches* 18.130). As an impression only, I should

upon the emperor's favour; the price was that they served his interests;[69] the rewards were great wealth and high rank; though the greater the power, the higher the risks of sudden demotion and execution.

The violent criticism directed against eunuchs diverted dissatisfaction which might otherwise have been aimed at the emperor. But this was not their only or their most important function. By acting as intermediaries they made the emperor's isolation viable. To be sure other groups as well were used as lubricants for the system, but as in the case of the Imperial Secretaries and the Companions (*comites*), they were rapidly assimilated to the aristocracy. As can be seen from the rise in eunuchs' rank and from the increase in the number of offices which they filled, eunuchs also progressed by this process of consolidation of privileges, which seems endemic to a patrimonial bureaucracy. Thus their powers can be understood only in the context of their non-assimilability and their consequent continuity. This applies to the Grand Chamberlains with exceptional powers as well as to the run-of-the-mill Superintendents and Stewards of the Sacred Bedchambers. The one was inconceivable without the other. Finally, the exercise of power by eunuchs limited the power of centrifugal forces in the state. Eunuchs' influence in the Eastern Empire was one of the major interacting factors (partly cause, partly result) in the preservation of central monarchic authority. In the Western Empire, there was a polarisation of power between the army which dominated the emperor and the aristocracy which avoided tax payments, whether of men or money. In the East, the eunuchs were at the very balance of power between these constituents. Paradoxically, the political power of eunuchs in general, far from being a sign of the emperor's weakness, was, in the Byzantine empire of the fourth and fifth centuries, a token of, and a factor in, the survival of the emperor as an effective ruler.

say there were hundreds rather than thousands. If they were taken in young, and given education, and there is evidence that they were (Ammianus 17.7.5, and no accusation of illiteracy), given the high rates of mortality prevalent in the Roman empire, a fairly large base number would be needed to fill seven top posts with reasonably efficient eunuchs.

[69] Certainly eunuchs feathered their own nests, but they were not exclusively self-interested. Cf. Ammianus 21.15.4; Malchus, frag. 2a; Ambrose, *Letters* 20.28: Calligonus, the Grand Chamberlain of Valentinian II, said to the great bishop Ambrose: 'While I am alive, do you criticise Valentinian? I'll have your head off.'

V

DIVINE EMPERORS OR THE SYMBOLIC UNITY OF THE ROMAN EMPIRE

INTRODUCTION

Absolutist kings of large pre-industrial states have almost always ruled with divine aid. The nature and degree of their divinity have varied: for example, the Pharaohs of Egypt were god-kings, Chinese emperors ruled by the mandate of heaven, Abbasid Caliphs called themselves Shadows of God on Earth, Byzantine emperors ruled as the vice-gerents of god on earth, English and French kings claimed divine right.[1] The list could be extended; but the basic point is clear. The king of a large empire, never seen by most of his subjects, legitimates his power by associating himself and his regime with the mystic powers of the universe. Reciprocally, subjects who rarely see an emperor come to terms with his grandeur and power by associating him with the divine.

The first part of this chapter is concerned with emperor worship, but emperor worship is only one way of approaching a wider problem. The problem is: How did the Romans know that they were living in the Roman empire? In what sense was the Roman empire a single political system? One obvious answer is that the inhabitants of the empire shared an emperor. In many rituals and public celebrations the emperor was declared to be divine, a god or the son of god, or he was closely associated with a god. The diffusion of emperor cults, their acceptance in once Republican Rome, and philosophical resistance to the idea of human divinity have fascinated many scholars. I too have succumbed. But I have also tried in the second half of the chapter to look beyond the direct evidence, which consists mostly of

---

[1] 'The state of monarchy is the supremest thing on earth, because kings are not only God's lieutenants here below and sit upon God's thrones, but even by God himself are called gods' (from a speech by James I of England in 1609; see C. W. McIlwain, *The Political Works of James I* (New York, 1965) 306ff.). The literature on the religious legitimation of rulers is enormous, but see M. Weber, *Economy and Society* (New York, 1968) vol. 3; P. Anderson, *Lineages of the Absolutist State* (London, 1974); and the different perspective of S. N. Eisenstadt, *The Political Systems of Empires* (New York, 1963) 50ff.

honorary inscriptions, to the rituals which created the evidence. And
I began wondering about the significance of stories or myths which,
although they were untrue, had considerable currency in Roman
circles. Sober historians are interested primarily, sometimes exclusively, in the truth; they therefore usually ignore untrue stories. Indeed
as one reads an ancient source, there is a temptation, rooted perhaps
in modern scientific rationalism, to pass over these fabrications,
roughly as most readers turn over a page which contains statistical
tables, with barely a glance. But political power and legitimacy rest not
only in taxes and armies, but also in the perceptions and beliefs of men.
The stories told about emperors were part of the mystification which
elevated emperors and the political sphere above everyday life. Stories
circulated. They were the currency of the political system, just as coins
were the currency of the fiscal system. Their truth or untruth is only
a secondary problem.

Power is a two-way process; the motive force for the attachment
between the king and the gods does not come from the ruler alone.
His aides and his lowest subjects, since they cannot usually change the
social order, wish to justify, indeed they often wish to glorify, the *status
quo* and their own place within it. The attachment of the people is not
necessarily to a particular king, but to an ideal king, who symbolises
the fixed order of the world. When the king dies or is deposed, the
people's loyalty is automatically transferred to the new king. The close
association of the king with god or gods, the sacred rites performed
in his honour, the laudatory rhetoric, the similarity of attributes of
god and king (such as Omniscience, Justice, Omnipresence), all stem
from the belief that the emperor like god represents the moral order,
and that the emperor, as the best of men, stands between ordinary
men and the gods. This view is most clearly expressed, if clearly is the
right word, in semi-philosophical writings:

Of all that is most honoured in nature, god is greatest; so too, in earthly and
human matters the king is greatest. As god rules the universe, so the king rules
the state. As the state is to the universe, so the king is to god. The state is
a harmony of many different elements and so imitates the order and harmony
of the universe; since the king has absolute power and is living law, he is
transformed into a god among men. (From Diotogenes, *On Kingship* cited in
Stobaeus, *Anthologium* 7.61 = Wachsmuth and Hense eds., vol. 4, 265).[2]

[2] Diotogenes is unknown except from the citations in Stobaeus dating from the fifth
     century AD. According to L. Delatte (*Les traités de la Royauté* (Liège, 1942) 284ff.),
     Diotogenes' vocabulary, style and ideas date him to the first or second century AD;
     this is hotly disputed by H. Thesleff, *An Introduction to the Pythagorean Writings of
     the Hellenistic Period* (Abo, 1961) 65ff.; see also F. Taeger, *Charisma* (Stuttgart, 1957–60)
     vol. 2, 616ff. and E. R. Goodenough, 'The political philosophy of Hellenistic king-
     ship', *Yale Classical Studies* 1 (1928) 55ff. for commentaries on these philosophical
     excerpts.

Introduction

This formulation is regrettably abstract, but the underlying problem is clear enough. How and why did Roman emperors reinforce the political system by associating themselves with gods? Why did local leaders of towns in Italy and in the provinces honour emperors in the elevated language of prayer and call emperors, like gods: Saviour, Benefactor of the Whole World, Defender from Evil, Lord of all mankind?[3] It is not enough to say that the practice originated in the east and spread to the west, because that begs the question: Why did it spread? Nor is it enough to say that professional orators elaborated the language of panegyric, so that it took on an academic life of its own, divorced from reality. That is true as far as it goes; but why did subjects and kings spend long hours listening to this inflated rhetoric of praise? What meaning did they attach to the extravagant metaphors and similes scattered through honorary decrees and speeches? These rococo figures of speech recurred too often to be simply meaningless or hypocritical.

The following extravaganza is taken from a formal speech of welcome delivered in the presence of the emperors Diocletian and Maximian (*alias* Jupiter and Hercules) in Milan in AD 291.[4]

...while other men and places were frozen and overcome by the bitter cold, you were followed by gentle breezes and spring winds, and the rays of the sun...shone on your path. With the greatest of ease, you overcame obstacles which others would find unsurmountable. One of you crossed the Julian, the other the Cottian Alps, as though they were beaches on the open shore when the tide is out...You, invincible emperors, almost single-handed with your divine steps like Hercules...opened up the path across the Alps blocked by winter snows...

Then, as your divinity shone from the ridge of each of the Alps, a brighter light shone over the whole of Italy and all who looked up were struck with wonder and doubt as to whether the gods had risen to the mountains or whether they had descended to earth from the sky.

[3] The parallelism between the cults of emperor and Christ is striking: the following terms were used frequently of both: god (*theos*), Son of god, god made manifest, lord (*Kurios*), lord of the whole world, lord's day (Sebaste – pagan, Kuriake – Christian), saviour of the world, epiphany, imperator, sacred writings. See the superb discussion by A. Deissman, *Light from the Ancient East* (tr. London, 1910), 346–84, and more recently K. M. Setton, *Christian Attitudes Towards the Emperor in the Fourth Century* (New York, 1941).

[4] It may seem dangerous to use evidence from the late third century to cast light on attitudes in the Principate. Yet there seems to be a similarity in thought and expression between the extract cited and Greek honorary decrees and, for example, the speeches of Aelius Aristides (second century). The only surviving Latin panegyric from a significantly earlier period is by Pliny (AD100). It is less floridly fanciful, but dates from a time when the emperor Trajan was consciously trying to play down imperial power. Imagine the panegyrics delivered by Roman senators to Caligula, Nero and Domitian; and besides, the idea of Jupiter and Hercules as especially associated with Roman rulers dates back at least to Trajan, see J. Beaujeu, *La religion romaine à l'apogée de l'empire* (Paris, 1955) 71ff.

But as you came nearer, people began to recognise you. All the fields were filled not only with men rushing to see you, but also by the herds of cattle which abandoned their distant pastures and glades. In all the villages, farmers rushed to spread the news...altars were lit, incense put in place, libations of wine were poured, victims sacrificed. Everywhere ardent joy was felt, everywhere applause resounded. Praises and thanksgiving were sung to the immortal gods. Jupiter was invoked...as visible and present; Hercules was worshipped...as an emperor. (*Panégyriques latines* 3.9–10 ed. Galletier)

In modern societies, similarly inflated language is heard at alumni reunions, retirement banquets and at political rallies, though the metaphors are different: 'Brethren, let us keep alive the white hot fires of Socialism' – UK 1975; 'May Chairman Mao Live for Ever.' These are ritual occasions during which the evocation of sentiment induces feelings of camaraderie, necessary for the success of a large and mixed social occasion. The language reflects a search for symbols, redolent with shared associations, which will suspend criticism and unite divergent groups. The mystical elements in Roman decrees to the emperor may have served a similar function. The fusion of god and emperor reflected the coalescence of the moral and political order.

THE BEGINNINGS OF EMPEROR WORSHIP IN ROME, ITS ESTABLISHMENT AND DIFFUSION

Originally, the divinity of the living emperor was alien both to traditional Roman religion and to Roman oligarchic politics. Its eventual acceptance even by the elite in the city of Rome was a symptom of the growth of emperors' power and of the changes which took place in Roman political culture; these changes made it possible to express individual emperors' political power in religious terms. But the emperor's divinity was only one aspect, albeit the most impressive aspect of the emperors' association with the gods. The intricate relationship of emperors and gods and its political significance can be understood only against the backcloth of Roman religious beliefs and rituals. Religion and politics were intertwined.

In metaphors, myths and sacred rites, Romans frequently bridged the great divide which in puritan Christianity separates man from God. The every-day world of the Romans (not simply their mystic world) was populated by a host of divine intermediaries who stood between men and the great gods of Heaven and Hades. They ranged from demi-gods and divine heroes such as Castor and Hercules to divine forces such as Victory, Fortune and Hope and even to portents and omens of good and evil. Each household had its private cults in which men placated the spirits of the living (*Genius*) and the dead (*Lares*) with sacrifice and ritual, and invested them with such divinity as they chose. Cicero, for example, wanted to build a shrine, not a tomb to his dead daughter in order 'to achieve deification as far as possible' (*Letters to Atticus* 12.36). This was a private act, and therefore consistent with his violent public objection to the official deification of Julius Caesar.[5]

Earlier in the Republic, Romans had associated several of their leaders with gods, but not in the state cult. For example, after the political murder of the Gracchi brothers, statues of them were set up in a prominent place in the city of Rome; 'many people sacrificed at and worshipped their statues every day, as though they were visiting the shrines of the gods' (Plutarch, *Gaius Gracchus* 18). Other leaders were similarly honoured, while they were still alive. For example in 102–101 BC, the general Marius achieved a crushing victory over the Celtic tribes which had for several years defeated Roman armies in northern Italy. He was honoured in the city of Rome with libations 'just like the immortal gods' (Valerius Maximus 8.15.7). Exceptional ability or success or the spark of genius was commonly recognised as having something divine about it. The dictator Sulla took the soubriquet *Felix*, Fortunate, to reflect his protection by divine forces. Republican poets such as Ennius, Lucretius and the early Virgil each referred to great men (Scipio, Epicurus and Octavian) as though they were gods or god-like.[6]

Emperor worship involved the transfer of what had previously been private and unofficial rites to the public domain; it involved the inclusion of the emperor in private household rites; and it involves paying honours to the living which had customarily, though not exclusively, been given to the dead. For example, a wall painting has been discovered in a private house in Pompeii, which shows the spirit (*Genius*) of the head of the household, surrounded by his family, pouring a libation; a second figure was added to this picture, and was carefully

---

[5] The background to Julius Caesar's deification is discussed by L. R. Taylor, *The Divinity of the Roman Emperor* (Middletown, Connecticut 1931) 42ff. and at length by S. Weinstock, *Divus Julius* (Oxford, 1971) – on which see J. A. North, *JRS* 65 (1975) 171ff. Cicero violently objected to Caesar's public and official deification: 'Do you think, conscript fathers, that I would have voted for the decree which you have reluctantly passed and which associates a cult of the dead with prayers, introduces sacrilegious practices into state religion and decrees prayers to the dead? I deny that honour to anyone, even to Brutus, who liberated the state from monarchy...I cannot accept that I should associate any dead man with the worship of the immortal gods...May the immortal gods pardon the Roman people who did not approve the decree and voted it unwillingly...' (*Philippics* 1.13).

[6] Scipio: Seneca, *Moral Letters* 108, 33–4; Epicurus: Lucretius, *On the Nature of the Universe* 5.8; *deus ille fuit, deus*; Octavian: Virgil, *Eclogues* 1.6–7. Cf. Weinstock (1971: 294–6).

preserved in ancient times. Mau interpreted this figure as the Genius of the emperor Augustus, since beneath the picture were the letters EX SC 'by decree of the senate', which Mau took to be the decree of the senate which ordained that a libation should be poured to the emperor at all public and private meals (Dio 51.19) – like a Christian grace or an English royal toast.[7] And we know from literary sources that this toast: 'To Augustus, Father of the Fatherland, hail' (*feliciter*) became common practice (Petronius, *Satyricon* 60).[8]

Julius Caesar was the first Roman to be recognised as a god in a public state cult. He had also been more powerful than any Roman before him. His divinity followed from his political power. Julius Caesar had also been the first living Roman noble to claim descent from a god, through Aeneas from Venus. Even during his life-time, when he was dictator, he was given honours similar to those given to a god. For example, a statue of Caesar was set up in the temple of Quirinus with the inscription 'To the Unconquered God' (Dio 43.45). At the circus games, an ivory statue of Caesar was carried in solemn procession along with those of the gods (*ibid.*). The senate ordered that a temple be built 'To Julius Caesar and his Clemency', and that a special priesthood be instituted in his honour similar to Jupiter's (Dio 44.6). But his elevation provoked opposition. He was assassinated by a band of nobles who could not endure his supreme power and quasi-divinity.

Julius Caesar's deification after his death was partly a legitimating manoeuvre by his political successors, particularly by his adopted son and heir Octavian, who thus became 'Son of God' (*divi filius*).[9] Deification after death was also a continuation of Caesar's life-time ambitions and of popular belief. An angry crowd reacted to his assassination by burning down the senate-house in which he had been murdered and then attempted 'to bury his body in the temple [of

---

[7] This interpretation seems bold but justifiable. Mau cites two other instances in which the Genius of the emperor may have been portrayed in private shrines. Cf. A. Mau, *Pompeii in Leben und Kunst* (Leipzig, 1908) 278; G. K. Boyce, 'Corpus of the Lararia of Pompeii', *Memoirs of the American Academy at Rome* 14 (1937) no. 466. 'A genius is a god, the same as a *lar*, as many ancient authorities such as Granius Flaccus [? first century BC] have said...A genius constantly observes us and is not away from us even for a second, but stays with us from the moment of birth until our dying day' (Censorinus, *On The Birthday* 3).

[8] Horace described how the peasant on his return from the fields had dinner and invoked Augustus as a god: 'he prays to you, honours you with unmixed wine and joins your divine spirit (*numen*) to his household gods' (*Odes* 4.5.29ff.).

[9] In Latin there was a distinction between *deus* and *divus* (Weinstock (1971) 391–2). Strictly, *deus* was used for the immortal gods and *divus* for gods who had been men (Servius on *Aeneid* 5.45); in Greek, both were called *Theos* and the Greek equivalent of *divi filius* was *theou huios*, son of god.

Emperor worship

Jupiter on the Capitol] along with the gods' (Appian, *Civil Wars* 2.148). The priests turned the crowd back and so they burnt the body on a hastily built pyre in the Forum. Caesar's power, his popularity, the manner of his death and the political sagacity of his heir, all combined to make his funeral and his memory more a public than a private family matter. Julius Caesar was numbered among the state gods, wrote Suetonius,

not only by public decree but also by popular belief. At the first games, which his heir Augustus gave in honour of his consecration, a comet shone for seven successive days...it was believed to be the soul of Julius Caesar, which had been taken to heaven. And this is why a star is set at the top of his statue. (*Julius Caesar* 88)[10]

Augustus and the emperors who succeeded him were the first Romans to be widely acknowledged as gods during their life-time. Several emperors found this personally embarrassing, and in the city of Rome it was politically awkward; it cut across the constitutional mask which disguised the emperors' supremacy. They did not want to be assassinated. Members of the elite, who suffered most from the emperor's human weaknesses, were most sceptical of his divinity. Hence, for example, Seneca's savage skit on dead Claudius' arrival in heaven and his open scorn for the senators who had seen the soul of the imperial dead rising in the sky and had been richly rewarded for the speed of their vision (*The Pumpkinification of Claudius* 1; Dio 56.46; 59.11).

Emperors were caught in a cleft stick. In the eastern provinces rulers were traditionally honoured as gods. Emperors could not refuse the honours and prayers of the eastern provincials without giving gratuitous offence which might undermine the provincials' loyalty. Equally, they could not afford to be seen, especially by the Roman elite, to welcome divinity. Augustus and his immediate successors tried to cope with this clash of cultures by a compromise which they enforced in the provincial state cults; in these, they allowed temples and priests

[10] The separation of the divine spirit from an obviously dead body is always an awkward moment in the apotheosis of a human; cf. the Christian account of Jesus' death/ascension. On this problem for the Romans, see E. Bickerman in *Le culte des souverains dans l'empire romain*, Fondation Hardt, *Entretiens* 19 (Geneva, 1972) 3–37 (the essays in this collection are excellent) and the dramatic account of the ritual of apotheosis at Rome by Herodian (see below, p. 214). Julius Caesar's deification became a noted motif in Roman state art. See, for example, the picture of four horses pulling a chariot carrying Caesar's soul, steeply rising into the sky, depicted on an Augustan altar from the city of Rome (I. Scott Ryberg, 'Rites of the state religion in Roman art', *Memoirs of the American Academy in Rome* 22 (1955) fig. 28a); also the Augustan silver coin from Spain (19–15 BC) which showed a comet with eight rays and a tail and bore the legend *Divus Julius* (*BMCRE* 1.63).

to be established in their honour, but only in association with an established deity, usually *Roma*. Or they diverted the direct imputation of personal divinity by allowing sacrifices only to the living or divine spirit of the emperor (*Genius, Numen Augusti*). In this way, religious rites and feelings were harnessed to the political order as well as to the individual emperor.

Several sources reveal the awkwardness of this solution, as emperors rejected unwanted honours proffered by deferential provincials or defended themselves to Romans for the honours which they had accepted. The extract which follows is from a papyrus, first published in 1924, which contained a letter from the emperor Claudius to the Alexandrians sent in AD 41:

...First, I allow you to keep my birthday as a sacred day as you have requested, and I permit you to erect...a statue of me and my family...But I decline the establishment of a high-priest and temples to myself, not wishing to be offensive to my contemporaries and in the belief that temples and the like have been set apart in all ages for the gods alone. (*P. Lond.* 1912 = *Corp. Pap. Jud.* 153 = Loeb Classical Library, *Select Papyri* 212)[11]

But in the proclamation publicising this very letter, the Roman prefect of Egypt referred to 'the Greatness of our God Caesar', apparently in direct defiance of the emperor's explicit wishes. The conventional explanation of this inconsistency is persuasively simple; it was considered all right publicly to entitle Caesar 'God', provided it happened in the provinces. But decisions about emperor worship in the provincial state cults were often made in the city of Rome. The contradictory expectations of Roman aristocrats and of provincials therefore could not be segregated.[12] And when a decision was made in public in the city of Rome, the emperor often took the Roman elite's view into account. Besides the emperor was a member of that elite. Tacitus records the following debate which took place in the senate in AD 25:

Farther Spain sent a delegation...(which applied) to follow Asia's example and built a shrine to Tiberius and his mother. Disdainful of compliment,

---

[11] Claudius' refusal was made at Rome, which partly explains its tone. In Egypt itself, temples had been set up to Augustus during his life-time, and we know from one (at Philae) that he was depicted as Pharaoh God (cf. Taylor (1931) 143-4, fig. 22). A Greek epigram to Octavian from the same place, inscribed on stone, identified him with Zeus: 'To Caesar, Lord of the Sea and Ruler of the Universe, Zeus the Liberator, born of Zeus the Father, Lord of Europe and Asia...' (*CIG* 4923 = G. Kaibel, *Epigrammata graeca* 978).

[12] I follow here the conventional distinction between the provincial state cults and individual or town cults, but without much conviction. Perhaps the place where the decision was made about the cult's form was more important than whether the cult was provincial or municipal.

Tiberius saw an opportunity to refute rumours of his increasing self-importance.

'I am aware, senators', he said, 'that my present opposition has been widely regarded as inconsistent with my agreement to a similar proposal by the cities of Asia. So I will justify my silence then and my intentions from now on.

'The divine Augustus did not refuse a temple at Pergamum to himself and the city of Rome. So I, who regard his every action and word as law, followed the precedent thus established, the more since the senate was to be worshipped together with myself. One such acceptance may be pardoned. But to have my statue worshipped among the gods in every province would be presumptuous and arrogant...senators, I emphasise to you that I am human, performing human tasks. I am content to occupy the first place among men.'

Later too, even in private conversation, (Tiberius) persisted in rejecting such veneration. Some attributed this to modesty, but most people thought it was uneasiness. (*Annals* 4.37–8 tr. slightly adapted from M. Grant, Penguin books)

Such public protestations had little effect, in Italy or the provinces. We can see this, for example, in the public proclamation made by Germanicus Caesar, the nephew and adopted son of Tiberius, in Alexandria in AD 19. He refused divine honours for himself, although the offer was very restrained by Egyptian standards.

I welcome the good-will which you always display when you see me, but I totally reject your acclamations which are invidious and appropriate to the gods. They belong exclusively to the real Saviour and Benefactor of the Human Race, my father [the emperor Tiberius], and to his mother, my grandmother [Livia]...(Loeb Classical Library, *Select Papyri* 211)

He was perhaps afraid that exaggerated reports of the honours accepted by him would reach the jealous emperor's ears.

Emperor worship in a broad sense, that is the public association of emperors with gods, divine forces, sacred rites, altars and temples, flourished almost everywhere. Even the elite in the city of Rome repeatedly elevated living emperors to the level of a god. The list of honours voted to Octavian is extraordinary: in 29 BC, the senate decreed that his name be included in its hymns equally with the gods (Dio 51.19–20). They decreed 'that a tribe should be called the Julian tribe after him, that he should wear the triumphal crown at all festivals...that the day on which he entered the city of Rome should be honoured with sacrifices by the whole population and be held sacred for evermore' (Dio 51.20). In 27 BC, he took the name Augustus, which like *divi filius* – *theou huios* (Son of God) – symbolised his superiority over the mass of humanity. An altar was set up in Rome to his Victory, temples were built to Fortune which vouchsafed his Safe Return (*Fortuna Redux*), and to the Augustan Peace. His statue was placed in the entrance to the Pantheon while another statue of him, dressed in all the insignia of Apollo was set up in the library attached to the new temple of Apollo (Ps. Acro on Horace, *Epistles* 1.3.17).

Stories about the connections between Augustus and Apollo circulated even in sophisticated circles and have survived in the histories of Suetonius and Dio. In the book *About the Gods* by Asklepias of Mendes, the story was told that Augustus' mother once spent the night in the temple of Apollo with other matrons. While she slept, a snake came to her (by Roman convention, a snake was apparently used on household altars to represent the Genius – but Freudians will also make speculations about the imagery in the story); when she awoke, she washed herself as though after intercourse with her husband, but she could not wash away the mark of the snake which she found on her body. In the tenth month afterwards, Augustus was born and was therefore considered to be the son of Apollo (Suetonius, *Augustus* 94; Dio 45.1).

To continue the saga, Augustus eventually in 12 BC became High Priest. He did not move into the traditional High Priest's house, but gave it to the Vestal Virgins. In compensation he made part of his own house into a public shrine with an ever burning fire. In this way the household gods of the state and Augustus's own household gods were under the same roof. Augustus was Father of the Fatherland (*pater patriae*) as well as head of his own family (*paterfamilias*). The headship of state was fused with the office of High Priest; the regime had the ostensible support of the gods.

Outside Rome, in Italy and in the provinces, eastern and western towns and town-councillors competed in their search for the appropriate honours to pay their monarch. They looked for honours which would cast most glory upon themselves, in their own eyes, in the eyes of the distant monarch,[13] and in the eyes of the common folk who watched the sacrifices and participated in the festivals held in the emperor's honour. The emperor's birthday and other anniversaries were celebrated by public games and in other ways. In 9 BC, for

[13] The vote of honours by a municipal council was often marked by the dispatch of a legation to inform the emperor. This provided towns with an opportunity for self-advertisement and gave ambassadors a legitimate excuse for a trip to court with the prospect of an audience, with enhanced kudos on their return home. On the accession of Caligula, in AD 37, the small town of Assos (in western Asia Minor) swore an oath of loyalty to Caligula 'by Zeus the Saviour, the God Caesar Augustus and the ancestral Holy Virgin [Athene]...It was decreed by the town council and by the Roman businessmen among us and by the people of Assos to appoint an embassy chosen from the foremost and best Romans and Greeks to seek an audience and congratulate him and to beg him to remember the city with solicitude, as he himself promised when he first visited our city's province with his father Germanicus...' (when Caligula was aged six!) (*SIG* 797).

example, 'the cities of Asia [Minor] decreed...that a crown be awarded to the person suggesting the highest honours for the god [Augustus]...' (*OGIS* 458). Discreetly enough, they then awarded the prize to the Roman governor of the province for suggesting 'an honour for Augustus hitherto unknown among the Greeks, namely to start the year on his birthday' (*ibid.*). The idea was taken up with public enthusiasm. 'The birthday of the most divine emperor is the fount of every public and private good. Justly would one take this day to be the beginning of the Whole Universe... Justly would one take this day to be the beginning of Life and Living for everyone...' (*CIG* 3957b – Apamea Cibotus).

In other cities also, the emperor's birthday and other anniversaries were publicly celebrated by sacrifice, rituals, ceremonies and games. Three more examples will be enough to give the flavour, and to illustrate the variety. The following is a brief extract from a calendar inscribed on stone from Cumae in the bay of Naples; it listed public festivals and is one of a number found in Rome and nearby towns:[14]

January 7   On that day Caesar first held high office. Public prayers to Eternal Jupiter.

January 16   On that day Caesar was called Augustus. Public prayers to Augustus.

January 30   On that day the Altar of the Augustan Peace was dedicated. Public prayers to the rule of Caesar Augustus, guardian of Roman citizens and the whole world.

(*CIL* 10.8375: heavily restored = A. Degrassi, *Inscriptiones Italiae* 13.2 (Rome, 1963) 279)[15]

[14] Fragments of nearly forty calendars inscribed on stone have survived, nearly all from the city of Rome and the surrounding towns. They date from after Julius Caesar's calendar reforms to the end of the first century AD. They listed public and sacred festivals. Unfortunately, the fragments allow us to assess uniformity and diversity only in about ten towns and not in all of them for the same months. For some festivals (such as Augustus' victory in Spain or his deification) there was considerable uniformity; but in other cases there were discrepancies; for example, the anniversary of the assumption of the title Augustus was recorded as a festival in only three out of five towns; the consecration of the Altar of the Augustan Peace was celebrated in only four out of six towns, and of the Altar of Victory in only one out of three towns for which the calendar is complete. This diversity is interesting and shows how unrealistic it is to create single calendars, as though all festivals were celebrated everywhere. The evidence is collected by A. Degrassi, *Inscriptiones Italiae* 13.2 (Rome, 1963) and collated by J. Marquardt, *Römische Staatsverwaltung* (repr. Darmstadt, 1957) vol. 3, 567ff.

[15] The cumulative impact of celebrating imperial achievements can be seen in the calendar of festivals of the 20th Palmyrene cohort stationed at Dura (Syria) dating probably from AD 225–7. By then 21 deified emperors and empresses were still recognised; and of 41 festival days recorded for this military unit, 27 were connected with the imperial cult. By then also most of these imperial festivals were celebrated expensively by the sacrifice of animals (usually an ox), rather than by the simpler

Secondly, in AD 11, the town council of Narbonne in southern France had a marble altar erected to Augustus and dedicated it in perpetuity to Augustus' divine spirit (*numen*). They put it there so that 'each year on this altar on 23 September, the day when he [Augustus] was brought forth to be ruler of the world for the happiness of the age, three Roman knights chosen by the people and three ex-slaves will each sacrifice a (sheep) and...will provide the colonists and the other inhabitants with incense and wine for the cult worship of his spirit' (*CIL* 12.4333). Similar celebrations were to take place at the expense of the chosen six on four other days of the year, while another inscription on a bronze plaque probably from the same period records the establishment of a provincial priesthood of Augustus – the priest to have the right to set up a statue of himself with the name of his father and his year of office and the obligation to set up statues of the emperor with surplus temple money (*CIL* 12.6038).

The third example comes from Naples: in 2 BC, the citizens there voted to establish games sacred to Augustus, 'ostensibly because Augustus had restored the town after it had been laid flat by earthquake and fire, but in reality because its inhabitants...emulated Greek customs' (Dio 55.10). The games were grandiosely called *Italica Romaia Sebasta Isolympica* and to drive the point home the Neapolitans built a temple to Augustus, the first temple to a living emperor on Italian soil. Augustus must have approved, since he attended the fourth games in AD 14 (Dio 56.29).

These examples illustrate three general points. First, the style of public celebrations held in honour of the emperor varied considerably from town to town, as it did between provinces.[16] This variety demonstrates that the festivals were not instituted by Augustus himself or by the dictate of the central government. The varied arrangements reflected local initiatives or competitive innovations rather than imperial decree. The strength of local feelings and beliefs, the sense of

offering of wine and incense which dominated (15:1) the Cumaean calendar cited above. But then one would expect the imperial cult to be more effusively celebrated in the army than elsewhere – it was in the emperors' interest to invest heavily in the army's loyalty to their image. See R. O. Fink, A. S. Hoey and W. F. Snyder, 'The Feriale Duranum', *Yale Classical Studies* 7 (1940) esp. 23ff., 173ff. We can compare the festivals at Dura with those at Theveste (Algeria) from an inscription (*ILAlg* 3041) dated AD 214. Of 15 imperial festivals listed at Theveste, 12 were also celebrated at Dura, but N.B. 16 out of 36 festivals certainly dated from Theveste are of no known public significance (Snyder *op. cit.* 1940: 299ff.). Thus in the early third century, there was a central core of uniformity in imperial festivals between a military unit in Syria and an African colony, and considerable local variation as well.

16 An additional example: the imperial cult was joined with that of Roma in only one (Tarraconensis) of the three Spanish provinces – see R. Etienne, *Le culte impérial dans la péninsule ibérique* (Paris, 1958) 293, cf. 231.

obligation to the emperor, the belief in the benefits to be derived from his propitiation far outweighed the effect of any imperial regulation. The evidence simply does not match the model which consciously or unconsciously still seems to underlie some modern discussions of the imperial cult, especially in the western provinces: namely that it was initiated, licensed, controlled and maintained primarily by the emperors themselves in the interest of some overall policy of political control, and that western provincials were far too sensible to believe in such eastern superstititions.

Sometimes local leaders spontaneously initiated their own rites in honour of the emperor; at other times, especially in the western provinces, emperors themselves or their delegates did play an important role in initiating and organising the cult of the emperor. For example, Drusus, Augustus' stepson, is said to have forced a meeting of the chiefs of sixty Gallic tribes, at a time when they were reportedly dissatisfied with Roman administration. Apparently, he won them over and instituted the cult of Rome and Augustus, with a great altar and a provincial high priest chosen annually from amongst them (Livy, *Summary of Book* 139; Strabo 4.3.2). This official promotion of the state cult is often considered as overt political manipulation. And so it was. But the cult would have been of no use to the emperor, nor would the provincial leaders have kept it alive unless they had quasi-religious feelings or beliefs which could be harnessed.

At other times, emperors responded to provincials' requests that they approve certain honours. Emperors' replies to these requests, together with competitive imitation between towns and the common cultural traditions which existed within provinces, combined to create distinct patterns of emperor worship: statues, processions, games, altars, arches, temples, sacrifices in commemoration of birthdays, victories and of each new emperor's accession. But within and around this common core there was always variation which reflected the uncontrollability or spontaneity of local demonstrations of loyalty to the emperors.[17] For example, it is impossible to imagine that the

[17] Sometimes provincials and provincial governors behaved contrary to the emperor's declared wishes, often because they did not know better. For example, the senate pressed Tiberius to have his birth-month November named after him as Julius Caesar had done before him. He refused the honour scathingly: 'What will you do when you get to the thirteenth Caesar?' (Dio 57.18). But in Smyrna and Calymna, for example, November was called Tiberion (A. E. Samuel, *Greek and Roman Chronology* (Munich, 1972) 175) and in Egypt this month was called Neos Sebastos – New Augustus – and the name stuck through the second century (K. Scott, 'Honorific months', *Yale Classical Studies* 2 (1931) 243–4). So much for control by the emperor. The Cypriot calendar of 15 BC was exclusively honorific, with months named after the following: Augustus, Agrippa, Livia, Octavia, Julia, Nero, Drusus, Aphrodite, Anchises, Rome, Aeneas, Capitol (*ibid.* 183).

following script for a public presentation celebrating the accession of the new emperor Hadrian in AD 117, which was found on a papyrus fragment from a district capital in upper Egypt, was anything but local. The two characters in the dialogue represent the sun god Phoebus Apollo and the People:

Phoebus: With Trajan in my chariot of white horses I have just climbed aloft to heaven; and now I come to you, oh people, I Phoebus, by no means an unknown god to proclaim the new ruler Hadrian. All things serve him on account of his virtue and the Genius of his Divine Father.

People: Let us make merry, let us kindle our hearths in sacrifice, let us surrender our souls to laughter, to the wines of the fountain and the unguents of the gymnasia. For all these we are indebted to the reverence of our governor [*strategos*] towards our Lord [Hadrian] and to his zeal on our behalf.

(*P. Giss.* 3 adapted from the translation by P. J. Alexander, *Harvard Studies in Classical Philology* 49 (1938) 143–4.)

One of the main functions of these celebrations was that they confirmed the prominence of local leaders. Emperors and the feelings which they evoked served as the pretext for ceremonial display, for the expense and the fun. But it was also more serious than that. The processions, dedications and sacrifices were the symbolic forms by which the local elite and the local populace of free men and slaves, townsmen and peasants, reaffirmed their relative positions and their subordination, however they perceived it, to their distant emperor. How else would anyone have known that he ruled?

Secondly, participation by the poor must have been encouraged by the gift of free wine and incense, and by the prospect of a share in the meat from the sacrifice.[18] The gods got only the entrails. In a poor society, hunger was endemic; food was a recurrent subject for art in rich men's houses; eating meat was a treat. The sense of occasion was heightened by the dramatic slaughter of the choice victim and by the anticipation of eating. In surviving carved altar panels, the sacrificial victims figure prominently (for example, a bull for the Genius of Augustus, a hog for his Lares). At the celebration of games or at the dedication of a statue to the emperor, rich men often gave banquets to their social equals. Scores of inscriptions, mostly from Italy, also

[18] It is clear that sacrifices were sometimes made the excuse for eating meat. For example, Titus in thanksgiving for his victory in Judaea 'sacrificed a vast number of oxen...and distributed them all to the army to feast on' (Josephus, *Jewish War* 7.16). For a similar equation, sacrifice equalled a meat feast, see Ammianus Marcellinus 22.12. However examples illustrate but do not prove my point that sacrifice was an important source of meat for the urban poor.

record that occasionally they also gave money or a feast, or meat (*visceratio*), sometimes just rusks and mead (*crustum et mulsum*) to all the citizens.

Sacred to Apollo Augustus, for the safety of the Emperor
Marcus Aurelius Commodus Antoninus Augustus,
Conqueror of the Sarmatians and of the Germans,
Son of the divine Marcus Antoninus Pius,
Conqueror of the Germans and of the Sarmatians,
Grandson of the divine Pius, Great-grandson of the divine Hadrian,
Great-great grandson of the divine Trajan,
Great-great-great grandson of the divine Nerva,
High Priest, in the seventh year of his Tribunician Power,
Victor for the fourth time, in his third Consulship,
Father of the Fatherland, Quintus Abonius Secundus son of [?]
in honour of his (priesthood)
which the order (of decurions) decreed to him of its own accord, has set up
this statue with a donation of 4,000 HS of his own money over and above the
legal sum required, and on the occasion of the dedication [has donated] gifts
of money to the decurions and a feast [to the people].
(Inscribed on a statue base from a small town in north Africa – *CIL* 8.14791)

The role of ex-slaves in the imperial cult

The cult rules from Narbonne also show that ex-slaves played a prominent part in the celebration of the imperial cult. Why did ex-slaves
take a leading part in the worship of the emperor? To be sure,
some of them were rich; but all of them bore the stigma of their
foreign origin, captivity and enslavement. Yet in spite of their low
origins, ex-slaves held office as organisers and celebrants, *Augustales*,
of the rites associated with the family spirits of Augustus, held at the
cross-roads (*compitalia*) in the city of Rome and throughout Italy and
the western provinces.[19]

An explanation is difficult to find. The rites were partly an Augustan
innovation built on a traditional base. In Republican Rome, the two
guardian spirits of the cross-roads (*Lares compitales*) had been pro-
pitiated in local festivals and sacrifices provided by district leaders
(*vicomagistri*) (Asconius, p. 7 ed. Clark). Slaves and ex-slaves had always

[19] For a detailed analysis of hundreds of inscriptions recording the existence and
functions of Augustales, see A. von Premerstein, *DE sv. Augustales*. In central and
southern Italy, nearly all the Augustales whose status is known were ex-slaves, but
in northern Italy several free-born Augustales are known (*ibid.* cf. *CIL* 5.1765).
Leading Augustales (usually *seviri*) gave money for the celebration of games as well
as animals for sacrifices. See also now R. Duthey, 'La fonction sociale de l'Augustalité', *Epigraphica* 36 (1974) 134–54, but his deductions about those whose status is
unrecorded should be treated with caution.

played a prominent part in this ritual and for the duration of the festival they were traditionally freed from all slavish stigmata and got extra wine rations (Dionysius Halicarnassus, *Roman Antiquities* 4.14; Cato, *On Agriculture* 57). Interestingly enough, the cult leaders were also allowed for the duration to wear senatorial dress of purple-bordered toga, and like magistrates, were accompanied by two lictors (Dio 55.8). Our sources tell us that Augustus revived this cult along with other parts of the traditional religion which were dying (Suetonius, *Augustus* 31) and transformed it by adding his Genius to the two Lares of the cross-roads; the three were thereafter called the Lares Augusti.[20]

I looked for images of the twin gods,
But they had decayed with the force of time.
The City now has a thousand Lares and the Genius of our Leader;
He gave them to us; and the districts worship three divinities.
(Ovid; *Fasti* 5.143–6)

Several finely sculpted altars to the Augustan Lares, nearly all of them set up by district leaders, survive from the city of Rome and confirm the transformation of the cult. Like other monuments of the period, they depict scenes which glorify the virtues of Augustus and his family: for example, a chariot carrying the soul of Julius Caesar to the sky, winged victories, and Augustus in priestly garb handing over to other men, presumably district priests, a statuette of a Lar.[21]

Augustus cannot have created this cult from nothing. It seems more likely that in the course of his long reign, ex-slaves had begun to celebrate the emperor's power in the traditional local festivities and rites; when Augustus reorganised the districts in the city of Rome and was High Priest, he legitimated and institutionalised these local celebrations, which had been till then only informal, and they became the rites of his cult. The cult of the emperor's Genius and his guardian spirits persisted over the next two centuries, as the evidence of more than a thousand surviving inscriptions shows. The cult provided rich

[20] Excavations at Pompeii show that it was common for Roman households to have niches or shrines (like saints' wayside shrines in rural Italy or Greece recently) which contained a statuette or portrait of a Lar (or portrait of the Genius – for their fused identity see note 7 above) and two Penates – household gods. Shrines at the cross-roads traditionally held only two Lares, one for each road – Augustus made it a trio – and at least in some minds Penates equalled Lares. 'Augustus had ordered household-gods (*Penates*) to be set up in the cross-roads. . . The priests were ex-slaves called Augustales' (Ps.-Acro on Horace, *Satires* 2.3.281); cf. the oath 'by Jupiter and divine Augustus. . .the genius of the [living] emperor and the household gods (*Penates*)' (*CIL* 2.1963).

[21] Ryberg (1955) has the best pictures; but the discussion by Taylor (1931) 186 is as interesting as ever; cf. *CAH*, plates vol. iv, 128ff.

ex-slaves, as organisers of the cult, with a prestigious and public outlet for social display. And it allowed emperor worship to flourish at street level.

The emperor's divinity won some acceptance even in the elite. It may seem surprising that leading Romans gave even grudging acceptance to the idea that their human emperor and his father were divine. It seems surprising partly because it contrasts with earlier Republican sentiments, and partly because it contradicts our own modern notions of humanity, divinity and rationality. As a consequence, several modern historians of Rome have dismissed the evidence of our sources as glib flattery or as insincere exaggeration. Perhaps much was, but that does not explain it away. The idea of the emperor's divinity and close association with the divine persisted and was fostered by Roman notables.

Sometimes emperors demanded, and sometimes the Roman senate volunteered, an extra token of its belief that the emperor was a favourite of the gods. For example, at the beginning of the New Year in AD 40, the senate in a body went to the Capitol and offered the regular sacrifices; and then because the emperor was away from Rome, they abased themselves (*prosekunēson*) before his empty throne in the temple of Jupiter. Roman senators, grandchildren of the generation in which the heroes of the Republic, Brutus and Cassius had assassinated Caesar, returned to the senate house and 'spent the whole day in praising the emperor and saying prayers on his behalf' (Dio 59.24)[22] In AD 65, the consul-designate proposed that a temple should immediately be built to the divine Nero, because Nero had earned the worship of mortals. Nero refused the honour as an unwelcome presage of his death (since in the city of Rome emperors had been openly deified in a state cult only when dead) and was content to rename the month of April Neroneus (Tacitus, *Annals* 15.74 and 16.12) and planned to rename Rome Neropolis (Suetonius, *Nero* 55). Perhaps fear prompted the senators to humble themselves with flattery, but fear does not explain the form which their flattery took. Nor was it fear which induced the 'richest citizens to use all their influence to compete with each other to obtain the priesthoods' of the temple to Caligula (Suetonius, *Caligula* 22). The emperor's divinity was created by the deference of subjects to a visibly powerful ruler more than by the emperors' own policy.

[22] Caligula was particularly extravagant in his demands; in the temple, which he had set up to his own divine spirit (*numen*), 'there was a life-size statue of the emperor made of gold, which was dressed every day in clothes similar to those he was wearing' (Suetonius, *Caligula* 22). But the ceremonies recorded here by Dio seem to have been initiated by the senators themselves.

These developments can be illustrated from Roman art. Plate 2*a* shows the magnificent panel which celebrated the ascent to heaven and deification of the emperor Antoninus Pius and his wife Faustina. It formed one side of the pedestal which supported a high funerary column, set up in the city of Rome to commemorate the emperor's death. The panel portrays the emperor's ascent to heaven on the back of a winged Genius, watched by two seated figures. The beautiful young man on the left, holding the whole column in his lap, represents Mars, the god of war, in whose field (the Campus Martius) the monument was built and Roman emperors were solemnly cremated in effigy. The female on the right is the goddess Roma. The imperial couple is seated; each is carrying a sceptre and is flanked by an imperial eagle; traditionally the eagle was believed to carry the imperial soul to heaven and of course signified Roman power.[23] Plates 1 and 2*b* show other scenes of deification, one of the empress Sabina, who died in AD 136/7, the other a beautiful cameo, said to be of either Germanicus (Tiberius' adopted son) or of the emperor Claudius. For our present purposes it does not matter which; what matters is that in Roman art, seen by people who never read a literary text, the Roman emperor was portrayed as a favoured inhabitant of heaven.

Deification was not merely a subject for sculpture, however brilliantly executed. It was also the end process of lively and impressive rituals with a cast of thousands. The historian Herodian, who wrote in the early third century, has left a good account of the elaborate ceremonies which in the city of Rome surrounded the emperor's death and elevation to Heaven.

It is normal Roman practice to deify emperors who die. . .All over the city, expressions of grief are displayed, but they are combined with a festival and a religious ceremony. The body of the dead emperor is buried in a normal way with a very expensive funeral. But then they make a wax model exactly like the dead man and lay it on an enormous ivory couch raised up on high legs at the entry to the palace, and spread golden drapes under the effigy.

The model lies there pale, like a sick man, and on either side of the couch people sit for most of the day. On the left is the entire senate dressed in black cloaks and on the right all the women who hold a position of high honour because of the distinction of their husbands or fathers. None of these women appear wearing gold ornaments or necklaces; they wear only a plain white dress to show they are in mourning.

For seven days these ceremonies continue. Each day the doctors come and go up to the couch, and each day they pretend to examine the patient and make an announcement that his condition is deteriorating. Then, when it appears that he is dead, the noblest members of the equestrian order and

[23] I rely here on L. Vogel, *The Column of Antoninus Pius* (Cambridge, Mass.; 1973) 32ff.

picked young men from the senatorial order lift the couch up and take it . . . out of the city to the Campus Martius, where . . . a square building made of vast wooden beams has been constructed in the shape of a house (with several storeys). Inside, the building is completely filled with brushwood, and outside it is decorated with gold-embroidered drapery, ivory carvings and a variety of paintings. . . .

The bier is taken up and placed on the second storey. Every perfume and incense on earth and all the aromatic fruits and herbs and juices are collected in great heaps. There is no tribe or city or prominent person who does not compete in sending these last gifts in honour of the emperor. When an enormous heap of these aromatic spices has filled the entire space, a cavalry procession around the pyre begins; the whole equestrian order rides in a circle round and round in a fixed formation, following the movement and rhythm of the Pyrrhic dance. Chariots circle round in the same formation . . . carrying figures which wear masks of all the famous Roman generals and emperors.

When this part of the ceremony is over, the heir to the throne takes a torch and puts it to the built-up pyre. The whole structure easily catches fire because of the large amount of dry wood and aromatic spices which have been piled high inside. Then from the highest and topmost storey an eagle is released . . . and soars up into the sky with the flames, taking the soul of the emperor from earth to Heaven, as the Roman believe. After that he is worshipped with the rest of the gods.

(Herodian 4.2 adapted and abbreviated from the translation by C. R. Whittaker, Loeb Classical Library)

SOME FUNCTIONS OF BELIEF – THE LIVING PRESENCE

Did sensible educated men really believe that a man was a god, or did they merely mouth these empty metaphors and put on a polite face through the formal ritual of singing the emperor's praises? Did they do it only because it brought them political advantage or social prestige, while it left their hearts and minds untouched? In short, was emperor worship political rather than religious?

No single answer to this question can be found; the surviving literary evidence relates only or predominantly to educated men; surviving memorials were put up mainly by the prosperous. And it is difficult to deduce feelings from artefacts. We know little of the actions and feelings of the lower classes. In a society as large and as culturally varied as the Roman empire, the range of cult practices was immense. Add the dimension of time stretching over three centuries, and it becomes painfully obvious that historians are forced to impose plausible and simplifying fictions on a complex and largely irrecoverable past. Besides, the question is itself misconceived, since it treats the two categories of politics and religion as separate. Even in modern, relatively irreligious societies, the two are often intertwined (for example, at ceremonies commemorating those killed in war, or at the installation of new heads of state). But in classical Rome, religion and politics often overlapped and were fused.

There was a wide spectrum of values, beliefs and attitudes. At a rational level, several of them were probably incompatible, yet in fact held by the same people simultaneously. Indeed, people often pick values, beliefs and attitudes from a common social stock and give them different emphasis and expression according to the demands of social circumstances. For example, different values and beliefs are expressed at cocktail parties or stag parties and in church, in public and in private, at the emperor's court, in the royal presence, and in a philosophical discussion. It is both impracticable and undesirable to compress this huge variety into a single historical account, whether our subject is beliefs in contemporary England, America or in ancient Rome. Nor can we discover what the Romans really believed, any more than we can give a single account of what really happened. What we can do is to illustrate the variety of Roman religious values, beliefs and practices, and consider particular social contexts (such as public processions in provincial towns, appeals to the emperor by maltreated slaves, or the prosecution of Christians) which moulded the expression of beliefs in the emperor's divinity. Our task ideally is to show the relationship between beliefs, social processes and the political structure. That is a tall order, and I shall tackle it selectively, choosing evidence from a variety of places and periods, so that we can draw on the full inventory of Roman beliefs and practices.[24]

In the sophisticated circles of philosophers, courtiers and historians, cynical scepticism about the divinity of a human emperor was readily available. Roman emperors themselves manifestly distrusted or rejected as absurd some of the honours wished on them by flattering admirers. The emperor Vespasian, for example, on his death-bed was reported to have said: 'Alas, I think I am becoming a god', a story told then, as now, in mockery of his impending deification (Suetonius, *Vespasian* 23).[25] A panegyrist, Aelius Aristides, in a letter to the

[24] This concentration on structure and process has its costs. In this case, by drawing on a wide variety of evidence from different places and periods, I somewhat ignore the canons of time and place, which are the prime ordinands of most history-writing. In other words, for these purposes, I treat the Roman empire statically as a single entity, when clearly there was both change over time and variation between regions. Obviously, I regret this; as I show elsewhere in this book, this is not a strategy imposed by my methods, only a tactic in this chapter.

[25] When the citizens of Tarraco reported to Augustus that a palm tree had magically grown on his altar, he is said to have quipped: 'That shows how often you light fires on it' (Quintilian, *Institutes* 6.3.77). But the most notable satire on deification is by Seneca, *The Pumpkinification of Claudius* – an eye-witness account of the new god's arrival in heaven.

emperors (AD 178), when Smyrna was in ruins after an earthquake, made a clear distinction between the gods to whom men pray, and 'the most divine rulers' from whom men beg favours (*Speech* 19.5, ed. Keil). He clearly did not intend any disrespect; we can assume that his distinction was acceptable and did not cause offence. Whatever men said, at least some knew that the emperor was not a real god.[26] Indeed after the excesses of the emperor Domitian, there was a period of reaction in which emperors emphasised their humanity not their divinity, at least at court in Rome (Pliny, *Panegyric* 2). Speculative philosophers often made fine distinctions:

The emperor is the last of the gods...but the first of men. As long as he remains on earth he is separate from his true divinity, but in relation to men he has something exceptional, which is akin to the divine. His soul within him comes from a higher place than the souls of men. (*Corpus Hermeticum*, ed. Festugière (Paris, 1954) vol. 4, 53; frag. 24.3)

We simply do not know how widespread such sophisticated distinctions were either among intellectuals or common folk. Nor does it matter much. After all, in the contemporary world, it is quite possible to find cynical unbelievers who participate in religious rituals of marriage and death, and who listen to the rhetoric of Christian prayer and gain a certain satisfaction or pleasure from their participation, without feeling that it challenges their disbelief. We do not have to choose between politics and religion, between hypocrites and true believers. The rituals themselves, the symbolic acts of priests and congregation, the words of prayer are all redolent with associations, whether from childhood or a historical past. They bring a message which transcends the actual meaning of the words.

Immortal Nature, after Overwhelming Benefactions, has Bestowed on Men the Greatest Good of all. She has given us the Emperor Augustus, who is not only the Father of his Country, Rome, Giver of Happiness to our Lives, but also the Fatherly God and Saviour of all Mankind. It is He whose Providence has not only Fulfilled but even Surpassed the Prayers of all. For Land and Sea lie at Peace and the Cities bloom with the Flowers of Order, Concord and Prosperity... (*Greek Inscriptions in the British Museum* 894)[27]

---

[26] I owe this point to G. W. Bowersock, 'Greek intellectuals and the imperial cult' in *Le culte des souverains* (see note 10) 179ff., who amply illustrates the scepticism of philosophers. I think however that he underestimates the probability that philosophers' acts differed from their thoughts. J. R. Fears (*Princeps a Diis Electus* (Rome, 1977) 10) makes a distinction between the 'official ideology of the principate' and the metaphorical language of men of letters. But he puts too much weight upon it; it is only one of several plausible distinctions. Otherwise this seems a very good guide to the evidence.

[27] It is a pity that classical epigraphers have concentrated exclusively on the transcription of discovered texts and have done so little to present a synoptic picture which

This was a decree of the local senate of Halicarnassus in Caria inscribed on stone for the occasion of a visit by the emperor's grandson in 1 BC. To the rationalistic prejudice of moderns, the language may seem hopelessly inflated, reminiscent of English tombstone encomia in the eighteenth century. But statements which do not mean exactly what they say, should not be summarily dismissed as meaningless. Honorary decrees recur much too often for that; the hundred which survive must reflect many thousands ever drafted, intoned or carved.

It is clear from these surviving decrees that in the East the emperor was widely acknowledged in public as a god. The following is a fragmentary extract from a decree set up early in the first century in a small town (Tlo) in Asia Minor, to mark the establishment of a cult in honour of Livia, the wife of Augustus, the mother of the emperor Tiberius:

...since She had established the family of the Augusti through the most Holy Succession of the Gods Manifest, the Incorruptible and Immortal House for Time Everlasting, the Lycians in their Piety to the Goddess [Livia] have decided to institute Processions, Sacrifices and Banquets to Her in Perpetuity...(*TAM* 2.549)

To catch the true flavour, such passages should not be read softly to oneself; they should be intoned aloud, at half an octave above or below one's normal speaking pitch. Each of these two extracts has some uncanny echoes of later Christian prayer; they belong to the same genus.

We should not be too impressed by the evidence which happens to survive. Words cut in stone stand a good chance of survival; the memory of 'Processions, Sacrifices and Banquests' fades. Yet to the provincial notable who played a prominent part in the processions, and paid for them, and certainly to the men in the street who watched and cheered, the actions of the day mattered more than their record for posterity.[28] Cult acts, sacrifices, ritual, public games, feasts all underwrote the conception of the emperor's supremacy and the benefits derived from the existing order. The following description,

highlights the importance of their hard work, unifies the texts with the monuments on which they were inscribed, and which explicates the culture which shaped the ceremonies which prompted the inscriptions. Credit in the profession apparently goes to those who transcribe new texts, however similar to those already found.

[28] Of course, both mattered. That is why men spent money on inscriptions for posterity. I wonder how long the interval was between the erection of a monument and its displacement. Tombs often declared fines against violators in perpetuity. Statue bases did not, and we know that new heads were sometimes fitted onto old torsos.

although it is of an emperor's proud entry into the city of **Rome**, and comes from the fourth century, gives a good idea of how impressive such processions were, and were intended to be.[29]

...[the emperor] sat alone in a gold chariot in the resplendent blaze of various precious stones, whose mingled glittering seemed to form a second daylight...He was surrounded by dragons which were woven from purple thread and attached to golden and jewelled spearheads, their gaping mouths exposed to the breeze so that they hissed as though in anger, while their tails whirled behind them in the wind.

...when he was hailed as Augustus with shouts of approval...he never moved, but showed that imperturbability which had been apparent in the provinces...he gazed straight ahead as if his neck was in a vice, and turned his face neither to right nor left...nor did he nod when the wheel jolted, and not once was he seen to wipe his face or nose, or to spit...and although this was affectation on his part, nevertheless...[it was also] an indication of considerable endurance granted, it was thought, to him alone. (Ammianus Marcellinus 16.10)

The emperor's progress, like the king's progress in post-feudal Europe, was only one aspect of royal grandeur.[30] Since most emperors in the High Empire visited few cities outside central Italy, the towns which were visited by the emperor often tried to immortalise their transient glory by erecting commemorative arches, temples and columns or even by starting the calendar year or an era from the date of the emperor's visit ('in the 69th year from the first visit of the god Hadrian in Greece' = AD 101/2; one of several such decrees from Tegea, *IG* 5.2.52).[31]

In daily life, there were repeated reminders of the emperor, and of his close association with the gods. All coins carried a picture of the emperor's head and name, the reverse showed portraits of symbols illustrating the emperor's success or power such as, for example, the personification of Victory, Rome or Justice together with varied

---

[29] On such processions see S. MacCormack, 'Change and continuity in late antiquity: the ceremony of *adventus*', *Historia* 21 (1972) 721–52; T. E. V. Pearce, *Classical Quarterly* 20 (1970) 313–16.

[30] I am very grateful to C. Geertz who first persuaded me of the significance of such processions and the symbols of power, and gave me his then unpublished article to read, 'Centers, Kings and Charisma' in J. Ben-David and T. Clark, eds., *Culture and Its Creations* (Chicago, 1977).

[31] 'Some Italian towns made the day on which (Augustus) visited them the beginning of their year' (Suetonius, *Augustus* 59). In Thessaly, Greece, the era of Claudius was apparently dated from a visit to Greece in AD 10/11 as well as by the years of his reign: 'in the seventh year of Caesar Germanicus Augustus and the 37th year' = AD 47/8 (*IG* 9.2.13). See H. Kramolisch, *Chiron* 5 (1975) 343ff.

slogans reminding people of the benefits of imperial rule (such as LIBERTY RESTORED, CONCORD, JOY, LOYALTY OF THE ARMIES).[32]

In city streets, squares and temples, prosperous citizens erected statues of the emperor, usually to commemorate their own tenure of local office. The dedication inscribed on the statue base recorded the formal titles of the emperor and often the exact sums spent. For example:

Anicia Pudentilla in her will ordered two statues to be erected at a cost of 30,000 HS
Manlia Marcina her mother and heir had that done, adding 8,000 HS of her own
G. Manilius Manilianus her son-in-law executor.
(*The Inscriptions of Roman Tripolitania* 22, from Sabratha)

In some provincial towns, statues of the emperors were highly standardised. At Bulla Regia in north Africa, for example, statues of the joint emperors Marcus Aurelius and Lucius Verus were almost identical except for a higher brow on one (Marcus Aurelius), a detail which may have been copied from a coin. In other towns, statues of emperors portrayed as gods have been found (for example the face of Hadrian with the body of Mars at Carthage).

In the city of Rome in the fourth or fifth century there were said to be close on 4,000 bronze statues of emperors in public places and an unknown number of stone or marble;[33] excavations at Lyttos, an undistinguished town in Crete, have yielded thirty-two bases of emperor's statues from a single century (*Inscriptiones Creticae* 1.18.15–46); in a medium-sized north African town (Leptis Magna), archaeologists have found over eighty statue-bases with inscriptions

[32] Too much is often made of these slogans as a means of communication. After all most coins circulated for decades so that most messages were passé. That said, the symbols are sometimes very striking, much more raised than in modern coins, and the messages were probably more prominent in popular consciousness then than they would be nowadays, when we suffer from mass communications pollution. The Roman coin slogans reflect most on their composers whoever they were. In several reigns, there were too many issues for the emperor to have supervised them personally.

[33] Two late Syriac epitomes perhaps from the chronicle of Zachariah Rhetor, who wrote in the late fifth century, preserve the number of bronze statues in Rome, and much other such information; they probably derive from Greek versions of the earlier (fourth-century *Curiosum urbis Romae*. See R. Valentini and G. Zucchetti, *Codice topografico della città di Roma* (Rome, 1940) vol. 1, 320–34 with an Italian translation. For Leptis, see J. M. Reynolds and J. B. Ward Perkins, *The Inscriptions of Roman Tripolitania* 316ff. My thanks to Joyce Reynolds for information about excavations in Leptis. But apparently almost no statues of emperors have been found in private houses, so E. Bickerman in *Le culte des souverains* (see note 10 above) 5–6; emperors were public gods who protected the public good; for private benefits, men prayed to other gods.

to emperors. To be sure this number represents the accretions of four centuries – by no means all would have been on display at the same time. On the other hand, the whole of the public area has not yet been excavated and many statues and bases must have been lost. However, the exact number does not matter too much. The point I want to stress is that public places were filled with or dominated by representations of royalty, most of them put there by private citizens. In a letter to Marcus Aurelius, then heir to the throne, his former tutor Fronto wrote: 'You know how in all the money changers' shops, in booths and bookstalls, eaves, porches, anywhere and everywhere, people have put up busts of you, badly enough painted to be sure, indeed for the most part modelled or sculpted in a crass, cheap style...' Even so, Fronto went on, however bad the likeness, the sight made him remember his royal pupil with a private smile (Fronto, Loeb Classical Library vol. 1, 207 translation adapted).

The emperor's statue (see Plates 3 and 4)

The emperor's statue was not just a lifeless monument, an aesthetic adornment to a public square. Slaves, litigants and even magistrates in times of trouble fled to the emperor's statue, as though it stood for the emperor himself, as though it could provide the protection and justice which ideally the emperor would himself dispense – if only he were present and knew the facts. Once in Aspendos (in southern Turkey) in the reign of Tiberius, during a food shortage '...an excited crowd was infuriated with the chief magistrate and was lighting a fire to burn him alive, even though he was clinging to the statue of the emperor, which at that time was more feared and venerated than the statue of Zeus at Olympia' (Philostratus, *Life of Apollonius* 1.15).

In the Greek East, the right of asylum in certain temples, such as the temple of Artemis at Ephesus, had long been recognised. But the idea of asylum was alien to traditional Roman law, since it seemed to offer an extra-judicial escape from deserved punishment. And it was open to abuse. In AD 22, the Roman senate received a report (which may well have been exaggerated) that: 'Throughout the Greek cities, there was a growing laxity in granting rights of asylum, so that criminals escaped punishment. Temples were filled with the dregs of slaves, the same asylum was granted to debtors escaping their creditors, and to men suspected of capital offences' (Tacitus, *Annals* 3.60). The senate determined to restrict the number of sanctuaries, and with that in mind, investigated the rights of various cities. Some sanctuaries were said to stretch back centuries to a mythical past, while the Cretans

...ed rights of sanctuary for a statue of Augustus (Tacitus, *ibid.*).

The very existence of a supreme emperor tempted appeals to the ...ghest authority. In both civil and criminal cases, Roman citizens even ...n the provinces could appeal to Caesar. If they were lucky, like St Paul, they were sent to Rome for trial. But citizenship did not always afford protection. The town magistrates at Philippi (northern Greece) had St Paul flogged and imprisoned; next day, when they discovered that he was a Roman citizen, they apologised (Acts 16).[34] In Jerusalem, St Paul saved himself from another flogging by declaring his citizenship immediately to the centurion in charge (Acts 22.25). He spent two years in captivity, while his case was being considered; it was said that the governor hoped for a bribe (Acts 24.26). Eventually when a new governor came, St Paul extricated himself from prosecution by Jewish leaders by appealing to Caesar. 'Then Festus [the governor], after conferring with his advisers, replied: "You have appealed to Caesar; to Caesar you shall go" (Acts 25.12). But when a murderer pleaded his Roman citizenship to another provincial governor, all he got for his trouble was an extra high white-washed cross to be crucified on (Suetonius, *Galba* 9). Several such cases show how erratically legal privileges were honoured.

What concerns us here is not only the access to higher authority which some citizens gained through their right of appeal to Caesar, but also the feeling that Caesar was there to protect the rights of the underprivileged against injustice. It was this feeling which underwrote the extraordinary development by which slaves, the least privileged stratum in Roman society, could appeal against malreatment by their masters to the statue of Caesar (Seneca, *On Mercy* 1.18). By the middle of the first century AD, slaves in Rome had an established right to flee to the statue of the emperor to complain against outrageous cruelty; starvation or enforced prostitution (Ulpian, D. 1.12.1.8; Labeo and Sabinus (consul in AD 69) cited in Ulpian, D. 21.1.17.12). If their case was upheld, they were sold to another master. Emperors had to steer a delicate course. They did not wish to undermine the slave-owners' traditional rights: 'the powers of masters over their slaves should not be diminished' (decree of Antoninus Pius, D. 1.6.2); after all, emperors' own power rested upon respect for tradition. At the same time, with the plea of public interest, emperors sought to earn their reputation for all-seeing justice by checking outrageous abuses. 'If you exercise authority with revolting cruelty, the provincial governor may be forced

---

[34] I follow here Jones (1960: 53–65). On slaves' appeals, see H. Bellen, *Studien zur Sklavenflucht im römischen Kaiserreich* (Wiesbaden, 1971) 64–78.

1   The deification of the empress Sabina, carried to heaven from her funeral
pyre on the back of a winged *genius* (like an angel)

2a Above: the ascent to heaven of the emperor Antoninus Pius and the empress Faustina

2b Below: the deification of the emperor Claudius or perhaps of Germanicus, the adopted son of the emperor Tiberius

3a Above left: the face of concern – the emperor Maximin the Thracian
3b Above right: the emperor naked – Domitian as a god

3c Below left: the emperor as handsome philosopher – Marcus Aurelius
3d Below right: the emperor as handsome general – Lucius Verus

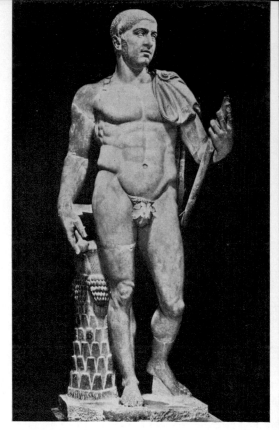

4a   Above left: the emperor as conqueror with foot on a captured boy, perhaps a Jew – Hadrian

4b   Above right: the emperor almost naked – Severus Alexander

4c   Below left: the emperor on horseback – Marcus Aurelius
4d   Below right: the emperor as far-seeing ruler – Augustus

to prevent a possible breach of the peace by taking away your slaves with my authority' (decree of Antoninus Pius, *Comparison of the Laws of Moses and the Romans* 3.3.6). We do not know how many slaves managed to exercise their rights by fleeing to the statue of Caesar; success must have been even more difficult for them than for Roman citizens. The difficulty of bringing off an appeal to Caesar successfully is caught beautifully by Apuleius in his satirical story, *The Golden Ass.* The author had just been turned into an ass by a magical error, when robbers broke into the magician's house in a small town in Greece and used the author-ass to carry away their booty:

I was almost dead with the weight. . . I decided to appeal to the civil authorities, by invoking the venerable name of the emperor, and so deliver myself from so many miseries. . . I tried to call on the August name of Caesar in Greek, I called out 'O', cleverly and loudly, but as for the rest of Caesar's name I just could not get it out. And the thieves were furious with me for braying and slashed my poor skin until it wasn't fit for anything. (3.29)

In real life, the appeals of many slaves must have been similarly frustrated by their owners' violent punishment.

But the mere possibility of making an appeal, even dreaming about it or telling stories about how others had successfully done it, must have been important, just as the myth of the poor man becoming the President of the USA has been more important in fantasy than in reality. Yet, in fact, it was significant that the sellers of slaves in Rome reassured buyers by claiming that the slave was 'neither a gambler, nor a thief, nor had he ever fled to [Caesar's] statue' (Ulpian, D. 21.1.19.1). The statues were a silent court of appeal against injustice, and not merely for slaves. An unsuccessful claimant in Egypt, disappointed in his appeals to the local bureaucrat, finally deposited his petition 'in the temple of Augustus at the feet of our Lord and most divinely favoured emperor Gaius. . . Trajan Decius' (*CPR* 20, AD 250). The statue of the emperor was the only court of appeal available to him.

The statues and portraits of the emperors helped maintain a living presence of the emperors in public places and in the consciousness of subjects.[35] These statues were not necessarily objects of worship, especially as worship is commonly understood in our culture; rather the emperor's statues and portraits were objects of homage or respect, symbols of the emperors' legitimate authority. This point is well made by a bishop called Severian, who preached at the end of the fourth century.

[35] See H. Kruse, *Studien zur offiziellen Geltung der Kaiserbildes im römischen Reiche* (Paderborn, 1934).

Consider how many governors there are in all the world. Since the emperor is not with them all, the emperor's picture has to be put up in courts of justice, in market places, in meeting-houses, in theatres. The emperor's picture must be put in every place in which the governor exercises power, in order to give his acts authority. (*Sermons on the Creation of the World* 6.5 = *PG* 56.489)

I do not know how far back this practice went or how widespread it was in the early Roman Empire, but there is one instance recorded from north Africa in the second century in which the defendant appealed to the emperor's statue in the court room as the final arbiter of propriety (Apuleius, *Apology* 85). And the custom persists even today: portraits of the President of the USA, of British monarchs and of Chairman Mao Tse-tung adorn different court-rooms and public offices throughout the world.

The cult of the emperor, alone or associated with other gods, was particularly important to the authorities in the Roman army. Emperors continued the Republican tradition of taking titles (such as Germanicus, Parthicus) to celebrate the victories of their armies, and were ever conscious of the need to foster a special relationship with the army – as Commander in Chief (*Imperator*), as leader in battle (a role played by Caligula and Claudius as well as by Vespasian, Trajan and Marcus Aurelius among others), and as benefactor, donor and paymaster. Soldiers' loyalty and their will to fight bravely were enhanced by having their minds fixed on the greatness and glory of the ruler of the known world, the divine emperor in Rome. From the first century onwards, the emperor's portrait was carried (like a flag or in medallions) along with the other military standards (Tacitus, *Histories* 1.41 and 4.62). Indeed a special soldier (the *imaginifer* – *CIL* 13.1895) was entrusted with the task of carrying this royal standard for each unit. Reverence was given to the emperor, or to his Genius, alongside the military standards, and emperors were worshipped or closely associated with divinity on altars set up by officers in military camps throughout the empire. For example, in a British fort near Hadrian's wall, two altars have been found inscribed: 'To the Genius of our Lord and of the standards of the first cohort of the Vardulli and the Unit of Scouts...' (*RIB* 1262) and 'To the God Matunus for the welfare of Marcus Aurelius who reigns for the good of the human race' (*RIB* 1265).[36]

In other contexts too, the presence or power of the emperors was recognised in the custom of swearing oaths by the emperor, or by the emperor's Genius (or *Tyche*), just as, in other circumstances, men swore, as they still do, by a god (Jupiter, God, Christ). Of course, there

[36] On the importance of the imperial cult in the army, see Fink, Hoey and Snyder (1940).

was an element of formulaic repetitiveness in oaths; but nonetheless, the style of such formalities has to be taken seriously. For example, on the accession of the emperor Caligula in AD 37, the inhabitants of Aritium in Portugal swore the following oath of loyalty: '. . . If consciously I swear falsely or am proved false, may Jupiter the Best and Greatest and the deified Augustus and all the other immortal Gods punish me and my children with loss of my homeland, with loss of security and of all my fortune' (*CIL* 2.172: adapted from the translation in *Ancient Roman Statutes*). It is noteworthy that the deified ancestor of the new emperor kept the highest company.

In less formal acts, it also became common practice to swear what came to be known as 'the divine oath' (*P. Oxy.* 85). For example, in a will made in the second century AD in Italy, the testator appealed to the local town-councillors: 'I ask and beg you by the welfare of the most holy (*sacratissimi*) emperor' (*ILS* 6468) to keep the terms of the will. In Egypt, many papyri show that statements made in court, routine statements of tax obligations, and even of record-keeping were sworn to be true 'By the Fortune of the Emperor' (e.g. *P. Oxy.* 77), or by the emperor himself: 'I swear by the Emperor Caesar Marcus Aurelius Commodus Antoninus Augustus that the above statements are correct' (AD 180–92 – *P. Oxy.* 79 cf. 246). And a master manumitting a slave in central Greece did it 'in the presence of the priest of Sarapis and of Isis, and before the aforesaid Gods and the Augustus Trajan Caesar Germanicus' (*IG* 9.1.86 Hyampolis). Since the emperor Trajan himself was certainly not there in person, the manumittor was either relating to a statue or to a metaphorical presence, which gave his act supreme validity. In consequence, the violation of the oath involved the law-breaker, or tax defrauder not merely in crime, but also in sacrilege. The oaths of subjects, voluntarily undertaken, legitimated aspects of the political order by appeals to the religious and moral order.

Romans did not always think well of their emperors. The ubiquitous imperial statues were also targets for attack. They were exposed to popular hostility as well as to admiration. Indeed, at times of riot or rebellion, the emperors' statues were often the prime target, much easier to overthrow than the emperor himself. For example, a crowd of rioters in Antioch objected violently to an increase in taxation in AD 387:

. . . seeing the many images (of the emperor) on painted panels, they committed blasphemy by throwing stones at them, and jeered at them as they were smashed. / The statues of the emperor and of the empress were thrown down and dragged through the city, and as is usual on such occasions, the enraged multitude uttered every insult which passion could suggest. (Libanius, *Speech* 22.7 / Sozomen, *History of the Church* 7,23)

On other occasions the rioters indulged in ostentatious hostility, maltreating the statue of the emperor like a common criminal. Libanius against tells how once the citizens of Edessa pulled down a bronze statue of the emperor Constantine and dragged it through the streets face downwards, hitting it like a school-boy as it went with straps 'on the back and the parts below as befitted someone furthest removed from royalty' (Libanius, *Speech* 19.48). In this way, the populace exorcised their anger and then spent anxious days in trepidation, awaiting condign punishment, while officials diplomatically pleaded their basic innocence, since only the statues and not the emperor himself had been harmed (John Chrysostom, *Homilies on the Statues, PG* 49, 73 and 216).

The destruction of the image sometimes symbolised, not merely discontent, but rebellion. For example, the end of Galba's regime was dramatically signalled, when the colour-bearer of the imperial escort, at the approach of rebel troops, tore the portrait of Galba from its standard and dashed it to the ground (Tacitus, *Histories* 1.41; cf. Plutarch, *Galba* 26). Once an unpopular emperor had been dethroned and killed, the desecration of his statues, the erasure of his name from the historical record, in short, the damnation of his memory, invited widespread and uninhibited participation. The staid senator Pliny recalled the delight with which Domitian's golden statues had been deposed after his assassination.

It was our delight to dash those proud faces to the ground, to smite them with the sword and savage them with the axe, as if blood and agony could follow from every blow. Our transports of joy, so long deferred, were unrestrained; all sought a form of vengeance in beholding those mutilated bodies, limbs hacked in pieces, and finally that baleful, fearsome visage cast into the fire, to be melted down...(Pliny, *Panegyric* 52, trans by B. Radice, Loeb Classical Library)

The violence of the hatred, almost primitive in its intensity, is surprising. It indicates, perhaps better than eulogy, the high hopes which men had of their ideal emperors. Deification was merely one ritual expression of such hopes. 'For as the old proverb correctly states: To rule is to have the power of a god' (Artemidorus, *The Interpretation of Dreams* 2.36). The hatred expressed by Pliny reflected the disillusionment which men experienced when their expectations were betrayed by a bad ruler.

The importance of the emperor in the minds of men and the close association of the emperor with the gods can be seen in the Roman response to attacks upon their religious-political culture. The most systematic attacks were launched by Christians and by Jews. These attacks induced Romans in positions of power to identify the central elements in their own culture, which distinguished them from their attackers. Roman accusations against the Christians, according to the Christian apologist Tertullian, for example, were: 'You do not worship the gods; you do not offer sacrifice for the emperors' (*Apology* 10). Thus, emperor worship, in association with the worship of the other pagan gods, had become a defining characteristic of the Roman political system, a test by which one Roman recognised another as a full member of the society.[37] Indeed loyalty to the emperor, seen as divine or favoured by the gods, was probably the only universal symbol of belonging available to the Romans and valid for all social groups in all provinces of the empire.

Let me illustrate this point by quoting from the dramatic dialogues between Roman judges and Christian martyrs. The hagiographical literature is suspect in many ways, but I shall quote here from those Acts of the Martyrs, or those passages in the Acts which are considered genuine records of court cases. The first excerpt is from the Acts of the twelve Scillitan Martyrs, executed in Africa in AD 180; their leader was Speratus.

Saturninus the proconsul said: You can earn the pardon of our Lord the Emperor if you return to your senses.
Spearatus said: We have done no wrong, we have never turned our hands to wickedness, we have cursed no one, but return thanks when we are abused, and therefore we are loyal to our Emperor.
Saturninus the proconsul said: We too are religious, and our religion is simple, and we swear by the Genius of our Lord the Emperor, and we make offerings for his safety, which you ought to do too.
Speratus said: If you will listen, I shall tell you a mystery of simplicity.

[37] F. Millar, 'The Imperial Cult and the persecutions' in *Le culte des souverains* (see note 10) 145ff. has argued powerfully, and I think wrongly, for the unimportance of the imperial cult in the Christian persecutions before the mid third century. In his view, moderns have underestimated the pagan religious elements in the persecutions; in many or most of the persecutions of Christians, he claims, the critical test was sacrifice to the gods; the worship of the emperor, and sacrifice to the gods for the emperor's welfare, were in his view of modest importance, partly because emperor worship was integrated into the wider spectrum of pagan cults.

I agree that the imperial cult was less important in most circumstances than other major pagan cults, and that the motive for persecuting Christians was probably fear that neglect of pagan gods would damage humans, Romans, everybody. But I think that the evidence also shows that the emperor, and his close association with the gods, repeatedly appeared as a critical element in most accounts of the prosecution of Christians.

Saturninus said: I shall not listen if you speak evil of what we hold sacred;
please swear by the Genius of our Lord the Emperor.
Speratus said: I do not recognise the empire of this world; I serve instead the
God whom no man has ever seen or can see with mortal eyes. I have not
committed theft; but if I buy anything, I pay the tax on it; for I recognise
my Lord, The King of Kings and Emperor of all Mankind.
Saturninus the proconsul said to the rest: Stop being of this belief... Do not
be involved in this man's madness. (*Acts of the Scillitan Martyrs*).[38]

They refused, the proconsul offered them a period of thirty days in
which to think it over; they refused. So he ordered them to be
beheaded. They all said: 'Thanks be to God; and so they were all
crowned with martyrdom together and reign with the Father, the Son
and the Holy Spirit for ever and ever. Amen.'

The sequence is similar in other acts of the martyrs. If these reports
are accurate, they reflect surprisingly well on the Roman magistrates
who clearly preferred to reform rather than punish Christians. But
once the Christians had adamantly refused to recant, and had boldly
professed their faith, they often earned martyrdom only after the most
terrible tortures. Two further examples of official conversations
illustrate the centrality of the emperor's divinity: '...they tried to
persuade him, saying "Now what harm is there in saying Caesar is
Lord...Swear by the Genius of Caesar"' (*The Martyrdom of St Polycarp*
8–9). 'Change your mind, said the proconsul Perennis; take my advice,
Apollonius, and swear by the Genius of our Lord the Emperor Commodus', and then again '...sacrifice to the gods and to the image of
the Emperor Commodus' (*The Martyrdom of St Apollonius* 3 and 7). Of
course; (*a*) sacrifice to the image of the emperor or (*b*) swearing by
the emperor's genius or (*c*) sacrificing to the gods for the welfare of
the emperor are distinctly different acts, but they can all be understood
as blending into each other, as a fusion of religious and political
processes.

In yet other prosecutions of Christians, the emperor appeared first
as the political authority who had ordered the observation of pagan
rites. 'You surely know the emperors' decrees that you must honour
the gods' (*The Martyrdom of Saints Carpus, Papylus and Agathonice* 4 (cf.
11 Greek version).[39] But even this presentation of the emperor as

[38] I follow here the translation of T. D. Barnes, *Tertullian* (Oxford, 1971) 61; his
chapter on the persecutions is excellent, as is his article 'Legislation against the
Christians', *Journal of Roman Studies* 58 (1968) 32ff. See also W. H. C. Frend, *Martyrdom and Persecution in the Early Church* (Oxford, 1965) and G. E. M. de Ste Croix,
'Why were the early Christians persecuted?' in M. I. Finley ed.; *Studies in Ancient
Society* (London, 1974) 210ff. For the other martyr acts, I broadly follow the translations given by H. Musurillo, *The Acts of the Christian Martyrs* (Oxford, 1972).

[39] For similar passages, see also the martyrdoms of *St Justin* (B) 2 and *St Pionius* 3, cf.
5.2 and 8.4.

protector of the faith seems important, and his divine associations were only just in the background: 'By allowing you to babble on so much, said the proconsul, I have allowed you to blaspheme the gods and the August Emperors' (*ibid.* 21). From the pagan side, we get a similar story; the following excerpt comes from the famous letter written by the provincial governor Pliny to the emperor Trajan:

For the moment this is the line I have taken with all persons brought before me on the charge of being Christians. I have asked them in person if they are Christians, and if they admit it I repeat the question a second and third time, with a warning of the punishment awaiting them. If they persist, I order them to be led away for execution...

Now that I have begun to deal with this problem, as so often happens, the charges are becoming more widespread and increasing in variety. An anonymous pamphlet has been circulated which contains the names of a number of accused persons.

Among these I considered that I should dismiss any who denied that they were or ever had been Christians, when they had repeated after me a formula of invocation to the gods and had made offerings of wine and incense to your statue (which I had brought near for this purpose along with the images of the gods)...(Pliny, *Letters* 10.96 from the translation by B. Radice, Loeb Classical Library)

It seems quite clear from this considerable evidence that acknowledgement of the emperor's divinity or of his close association with the pagan gods played a critical part in the formal judgement that self-confessed Christians were not full members of Roman society.

Of course, it is difficult to know what most provincials felt about the emperor. I do not want to exaggerate or to romanticise their attachment. It seems obvious that some prayers to the emperor were recited without feeling, that some games were celebrated only nominally in the emperor's honour, and that some altars or statues were erected by magistrates to emperors primarily out of duty or to advertise the donor's generosity. Yet the several thousand surviving inscriptions honouring the emperor represent considerable solemn ceremony. Public bodies, local magistrates and private citizens voted honours, dedicated altars and public buildings to the emperor. They have been found all over the empire, from the east and from the west and from Italy, and from all periods including the reign of Augustus: triumphal arches, huge altars, porticoes, temples, colossal statues of stone, or small ones of silver or bronze; some, as we have seen, declaimed the full title of the emperor and asserted his legitimate succession stretching back over generations. Others associated the emperor more or less directly with a god or gods. Two examples from Roman Africa and Syria, and from the first and second century respectively will suffice:

Sacred to Ceres Augusta
C. Rebellius Blandus consul, state priest, Governor [of the Province]
Dedicated
Suphunibal Benefactress of her home town Annobal Ruso
Provided With her own Money for the Erection
(*The Inscriptions of Roman Tripolitania* 269; from Leptis Magna, an altar of ten limestone blocks altogether 12 m long; AD 35–6)

To Jupiter Best and Greatest, to Venus, Mercury and the Gods of Heliopolis
For the Safety and Victories of our Lord Antoninus Pius Felix Augustus
And of Julia Augusta, Mother of Our Lord, and for the Army, Senate and Fatherland
Aurelius Antoninus Longinus, military policeman (*speculator*) of the 3rd Legion – the Gallic Antonine
Has given the Capitals of Two Columns in Gilded Bronze at his own Expense Willingly in Accomplishment of his Vow
(*Inscriptions grecques et latines de la Syrie* vol. 6, 2711–12; Baalbek, early third century).

The synthesis of gods with Augustus in a single dedication (for example, to Apollo Augustus, Mars Augustus) is extremely interesting. Hundreds of similar inscriptions have been found from all over the empire and all periods. The emperor was associated with almost every god, for example with Aesculapius, Ceres, Hercules, Isis, Mercury, Neptune and Venus, and on monuments great and small: ranging from the huge temple of Jupiter Augustus in Cyrene set up in the reign of Augustus (*PBSR* 26 (1958) 38) to a humble undated stone slab set up in southern Spain to Apollo and Aesculapius Augustus (*CIL* 2.2004).

It is possible that men had in their minds only the god, to whom they gave the added title Augustus. But even that is revealing. The local gods of conquered peoples were slowly assimilated to the Graeco-Roman Pantheon of the conquerors. Sometimes, the Roman and native gods merged into one, as for example in Britain and Gaul, where several dedications to Mars Lenus have been found (*RIB* 309; *CIL* 13.3654). Sometimes a Roman god received the attributes of a native god and vice versa. For example, Jupiter was sometimes represented in Britain with a wheel (the attribute of the native god Taranis), or Celtic gods were depicted in traditional animal form, accompanied by the thunderbolt of Jupiter. In yet other cases, two gods, one Roman, one native were joined in a single cult, for example of Mercury and Rosmerta. Yet almost all of these numerous cults were only local. The Greek and Roman Pantheon served to integrate local gods into the religious frame of the conquerors. And beyond this, Augustus served as the integrating title of them all. Most people may have been hazy about what this meant; only sophisticated litterateurs would have thought about it, and even then perhaps not clearly.[40] It is enough that many people thought in a vague way that kings like gods had mystical powers, worth invoking in a public crisis and worth being grateful to for public well-being. Both the religious and the political world were under a single government – identified in one second-century inscription from near Cordoba in Spain as Jupiter Pantheus Augustus (*CIL* 2.2008).

OMENS AND PORTENTS

Mystical power and close association with the gods implied magical power. This attribute of kings is well attested in other cultures. In England, for example, in the mid-seventeenth century, Charles II touched about eight thousand people in one year to cure them of the King's Evil.[41] His legitimacy was confirmed, both to himself and his people, by the ritual touch. For our present purposes, it was not the cure that mattered, but the widespread reporting of such cures as took place and the widespread belief in the King's curative powers.

What of Roman emperors? Almost the only known miracles were performed by Vespasian just after his accession to the throne in AD 69 while he was at Alexandria waiting to sail to Rome. Tacitus wrote that at this time 'many miracles occurred'.

There seemed to be indications that Vespasian enjoyed heaven's blessing and that the gods showed a certain leaning towards him. Among the lower classes at Alexandria was a blind man whom everybody knew as such. One day this fellow threw himself at Vespasian's feet, imploring him with groans to heal his blindness. He had been told to make this request by Serapis, the favourite god of a nation much addicted to strange beliefs. He asked that it might please the emperor to anoint his cheeks and eyeballs with the water of his mouth. A second petitioner, who suffered from a withered hand, pleaded his case too, also on the advice of Serapis: would Caesar tread upon him with his imperial foot?

At first Vespasian laughed at them and refused. When the two insisted, he

---

[40] The sophistication of philosophers and litterateurs was beyond most people. On this see the interesting book on the religious beliefs of a single village and the different levels of knowledge about the Buddhist and Taoist pantheon by D. K. Jordan, *Gods, Ghosts and Ancestors* (Berkeley, Calif.; 1972). For Roman religlion, J. Toutain, *Les cultes paiens dans l'empire romain* (Paris, 1907–20) 3 vols. still seems best; cf. J. Ferguson, *The Religions of the Roman Empire* (London, 1970) for a brief account.

[41] In general, M. Bloch, *Les rois thaumaturges* (Strasbourg, 1924) and the brilliantly evocative book by K. Thomas, *Religion and the Decline of Magic* (London, 1973). On Vespasian's miracles, see A. D. Nock, *Essays on Religion and the Ancient World*, ed. Z. Stewart (Oxford, 1972) vol. 2, 838. Hadrian was also said to have cured a man and a woman of their blindness (*SHA, Hadrian* 25); but on the whole recorded magical cures by Roman emperors were rare.

hesitated. At one moment he was alarmed by the thought that he would be accused of vanity if he failed. At the next, the urgent appeals of the two victims and the flatteries of his entourage made him sanguine of success. Finally he asked the doctors for an opinion whether blindness and atrophy of this sort were curable by human means. The doctors were eloquent on the various possibilities...Perhaps this was the will of the gods, they added perhaps the emperor had been chosen to perform a miracle. Anyhow, if a cure were effected, the credit would go to the ruler, if it failed, the poor wretches would have to bear the ridicule. So Vespasian felt that his destiny gave him the key to every door and that nothing now defied belief.

With a smiling expression and surrounded by an expectant crowd of bystanders, he did what was asked. Instantly the cripple recovered the use of his hand and the light of day dawned against upon his blind companion. Both these incidents are still vouched for by eye-witnesses, though there is nothing now to be gained by lying. (Tacitus, *Histories* 4.81 translated by K. Wellesley, Penguin Books)

Several aspects of this dramatic account are interesting: the emperor's hesitation, his request for scientific information, the temporising doctors, the pressing flattery of the courtiers, the magical cure, the lasting belief. As with Christ, miraculous cures were part of the process of legitimation. Vespasian needed it, because 'he lacked authority and majesty, since he was unexpectedly and recently called to the throne' (Suetonius, *Vespasian* 7). Portents provided an answer. In Suetonius' biographies of the first nine emperors, by far the highest number of portents presaging an emperor's rule relate to Augustus and Vespasian, both founders of a dynasty. To quote but one example of many: an ox on Vespasian's country estate shook off its yoke when it was ploughing, burst into the dining-room where Vespasian was at table, scattered his servants and then, as if weary, knelt down and bowing its neck placed its head beneath Vespasian's feet (Suetonius, *Vespasian* 5). In Krauss' interpretation, the ox was the state; the overthrown symbolised Nero's tyranny.[42] The truth of such stories and of their interpretation matters less than the fact that they were told and believed, not only by common folk but also by elite historians and litterateurs.

Miracles, omens and portents, like ritual incantations, curses, astrological predictions, divinations, the interpretation of dreams, and belief in omnipresent maleficent and benevolent forces all contributed to the atmosphere in which Romans regarded their emperors as in

[42] K. Scott, *The Imperial Cult under the Flavians* (Stuttgart, 1936) 4; F. B. Krauss, *An Interpretation of Omens*...(Diss. Philadelphia, 1930) 173. On the number of portents, see R. Lattimore, *Classical Journal* 29 (1934) 443; Augustus had 17, Vespasian 12; the next highest was Galba 6, Tiberius 5 and Vitellius 3. The discrepancies are too marked to be meaningless.

some sense like gods. Because of our modern rationalistic prejudices, we tend to underestimate the pervasiveness of the unpredictable, the inexplicable and the magical in the daily life of Romans, rich and poor, educated and uneducated. Yet even a cursory inspection of Artemidorus' *Dream-book* (especially Book 5) or Firmicus Maternus' text book on astrology or Julius Obsequens' book of prodigies should convince us how persecuted Romans were by the unknown; they sought to control it by propitiating sacrifice, prayer and magical incantation, and to understand it by the interpretation of signs.[43] To be sure, the books I have mentioned are store-houses of what we and some disbelieving Romans might have called superstition, although it is worth recalling how seriously they were taken by most of their readers. Several emperors were devotees of astrology; magic men like Apollonius of Tyana were held in high social regard, and were consulted by both emperors and senators. Tricksters like Alexander from Abonoteichus held whole provinces to ransom, and induced even the emperor Marcus Aurelius in the hope of victory against border tribes to have two lions thrown into the Danube with a load of perfumes – the lions swam to the other bank, and the Romans suffered a tremendous defeat (Lucian, *Alexander* 48). Serious and scholarly historians and litterateurs, doctors and philosophers mingled careful observation and cynical detachment with credulous superstition. In our attempts to find out what 'really happened', we should be careful not to suppress what Romans thought was happening.

It seems impossible to find a satisfactory index of the pervasiveness of what we might today call the irrational elements in Roman public life. We shall have to be content with illustrations. For this purpose, I shall concentrate on astrology. Of course, people look up their fate

---

[43]   It is difficult to integrate what we know of Roman magic with Roman elite politics; usually the two have been considered separately. A. Bouché-Leclercq, *L'astrologie grecque* (Paris, 1899) 543–627 still serves as a useful introduction. R. Macmullen, *Enemies of the Roman Order* (Harvard, 1966) 95–162 has brought much recondite material together; his account is both tantalising and evocative, but the overall impression is confusing. W. and H. G. Gundel, *Astrologoumena* (Wiesbaden, 1966) give an excellent account of the astrological tradition, including Firmicus Maternus. A. Barb, 'The Survival of Magic Arts' in A. D. Momigliano ed.; *The Conflict between Paganism and Christianity* (Oxford, 1963) illustrates excellently what we know of magic and politics in the fourth century and P. Brown (*Religion and Society in the Age of St Augustine* (London, 1972) 119–46) subtly interprets accusations of sorcery as weapons between established and unestablished factions in the elite. But above all, I must stress the pervasiveness of what we would call superstitious practices. For example, Augustus is said to have carried an amulet of seal-skin as a protection against thunder and lightning which frightened him (Suetonius, *Augustus* 90) and Julius Caesar is said to have repeated a prayer three times whenever he entered a carriage, to ensure a safe journey, 'just as most people do nowadays' (Pliny, *Natural History* 28.21).

Divine emperors

in the stars nowadays, but among the Roman elite astrology was a major intellectual pursuit, a preoccupation which, like economics nowadays, coloured serious political behaviour.[44] Men were killed for it.

Domitian, for example, had a senator executed because it was generally known that he had an imperial horoscope (Suetonius, *Domitian* 10), and it was said that he would have killed his successor Nerva but for a friendly astrologer who assured the emperor that Nerva would die soon anyhow (Dio 67.15; cf. a similar story about Tiberius – Dio 58.27). Astrologers also predicted the manner, day and hour of Domitian's own death – and this may well have encouraged his assassins.[45]

On the day before he was murdered, some apples were brought to him. 'Serve them tomorrow', he said and added 'if it comes to pass.' Then turning to his companions, he remarked 'There will be blood on the moon as she enters Aquarius and a deed will be done, which men will talk about all over the world.' In the middle of the night Domitian was so terrified that he jumped out of bed; first thing in the morning, he tried a sooth sayer, who had been brought from Germany on a charge of predicting a change of government...and condemned him to death. While he was scratching vigorously at the festering wart on his forehead, he drew some blood; 'I hope this is all the blood required', he said. (Suetonius, *Domitian* 16)

He then asked the time; his attendants lied to him that it was the sixth hour, because they knew that he feared the fifth. 'Convinced that the

[44] For example, the story is told that Nero was worried by the appearance of a comet on successive nights, since it was commonly believed to be a portent of the death of kings. The court astrologer (Balbillus, the son of Thrasyllus who was astrologer to Tiberius, see below *ad* note 46) advised Nero that kings usually averted the danger by killing some nobles. Nero set about this, all the more willingly when he discovered two conspiracies against him (Suetonius, *Nero* 36). Other emperors killed men who had imperial horoscopes: Tiberius (Dio 57.19), Domitian (Dio 67.15), Hadrian (*SHA, Hadrian* 23; *CCAG* 8.2.85: the horoscope of an ill-advised young man). In general, see the readable and informative book by F. H. Cramer, *Astrology in Roman Law and Politics* (Philadelphia, 1954).

[45] For the prediction, see Suetonius, *Domitian* 14 and Cramer (1954) 144; it is unreasonable to suppose that all such predictions took place after the event, although some obviously did. For example, Apollonius of Tyana, according to Philostratus (8.26), was credited with supernatural vision; when he was at Ephesus, he saw what was happening at Rome, stopped in the middle of a philosophical discussion and shouted: 'Strike the tyrant; strike him', as though he saw the murder taking place; incidentally the time of day and other details are different from those recorded by Suetonius. Accuracy mattered less than the moral of the story: the confrontation of philosopher and tyrant (7.1ff.). The philosopher always won; for example, when he was brought to court before Domitian himself, he was accused of contempt; he is told to keep his eyes 'on the God of all Mankind'; 'at which he turned his eyes to the ceiling, to show that he had his eyes on Zeus' (8.4). This anti-establishment literature was careful to attack an emperor whose memory had been officially damned; even so, it still upheld the possibility of criticism.

danger had passed' Domitian happily went off to have a bath and was murdered.

In such accounts, and there are several similar, it is difficult to distinguish truth from fiction. Do we have to? Once told and repeated such stories became part of the myth of kingship; the actors were not only assassins but agents of Fate. What happened had to be. In fact Suetonius lived through the reign of Domitian and was well connected at court; the story probably has some truth in it. However that may be, we know from him and from other historians and litterateurs that successive emperors Tiberius, Caligula, Nero, Vespasian, Titus, Domitian and Hadrian (the list is not exhaustive) all took astrology seriously.

And so, in antiquity, did their historians. Tacitus, for example, related how Thrasyllus, scholar and astrologer, became the confidant of Tiberius. When he was in exile in Rhodes, and his succession to the throne was very much in doubt, Tiberius took Thrasyllus, as he had taken other astrologers, to a high cliff and questioned him about his chances of becoming emperor. Tiberius was impressed by Thrasyllus' answers. Finally, he asked Thrasyllus about his own horoscope for that day. Thrasyllus pondered, shuddered with fear and said he was threatened with a crisis. 'Then Tiberius embraced him and congratulated him on his fine prescience of danger and of his escape [from being thrown over the cliff], treated everything which Thrasyllus had told him as an oracle, and kept him among his closest friends' (Tacitus, *Annals* 6.21). The same story is told with minor variations by Suetonius and Dio and appears in an anonymous Byzantine astrological fragment (*CCAG* 8.4.99). But it is also told *mutatis mutandis* in the Greek, Armenian, Syriac and Ethiopic versions of the romantic and semi-fictional life of Alexander the Great.[46]

The recurrence of this myth in a different context casts some doubt on its credibility. That matters, but not as much as one might at first think. Political power and legitimacy rest not only in taxes and armies, but in the minds of men. The myths made up and told about emperors were part of the mystification which elevated the political sphere above everyday life. The stories circulated and were told whether they were true or not. Obviously emperors neither created nor controlled their currency (although they tried to), since emperors were often depicted

---

[46] The Greek story is conventionally attributed to Ps. Callisthenes, *Historia Alexandri Magni* ed. Kroll (Berlin, 1926) 1.14. In the oldest (fifth-century) Armenian version, *The Romance of Alexander the Great* tr. A. M. Wolohojian (New York, 1969) the story is slightly different, but the Syriac version is substantially the same with virtuoso variations (tr. E. A. W. Budge (Cambridge, 1889) 15–16) and so is the simpler Ethiopic version (tr. E. A. W. Budge (London, 1896) vol. 2, 32).

in a light which they would not have chosen for themselves. The stories were created by subjects and so served as the battleground and the catharsis of the conflicting emotions which power aroused.

A comparison may help clarify the point. In a modern university, myths and stereotypes of the pedantic and absent-minded professor in one sense elevate him above other more worldly professors and students and yet at the same time depreciate him as merely 'academic'. The stories of the absent-minded professor's antics help preserve respect for the institution's core values, while allowing students a pigeon-hole into which they can dismiss those values as being inapplicable to themselves. Similarly, the story about the emperor and the astrologer implicitly deprecated the emperor's cruelty, while admitting his power (to kill astrologers) and acknowledging his final mercy; it also contrasted the foolishness of most astrologers with the conquering wisdom of the astrologer royal (and perhaps by implication, of the story-teller). The royal astrologer survived to show that if properly done, astrology works.

Roman astrologists felt most comfortable with the prediction of events which had already occurred. We can see this in the hundred or so surviving retrospective horoscopes recorded by Vettius Valens in the second century and the horoscope of the emperor Hadrian, cast after his death by Antigonus of Nicaea:[47]

[At his birth, Hadrian had] the Sun in Aquarius 8 degrees, the Moon and Jupiter and the Horoscopos, the three together at the first degree of the same sign, namely Aquarius; Saturn in Capricorn 5 degrees and Mercury with it at 12 degrees... He was adopted by a certain emperor [Trajan] related to him They lived together for two years and then he became emperor. He was wise and educated so that he was honoured in shrines and temples. He married only once; she was a virgin; they had no children. He had one sister; he quarrelled violently with his relatives. At the age of 63, he died of dropsy and difficulty of breathing (?asthma). (*Catalogus codicum astrologorum graecorum* = *CCAG* vol. 6, ed. W. Kroll (Brussels, 1903) 67–8; partly translated by O. Neugebauer and H. B. von Hosen, *Greek Horoscopes* (Philadelphia, 1959) 90.)

The astrologer then took each of these scanty pieces of information and explained which conjunction of the stars was responsible, and sometimes added how slight changes in the stars would have effected a different outcome. For example:

[47] Vettius Valens, *Anthologiae* ed. W. Kroll (Berlin, 1908). O. Neugebauer and H. B. Van Hosen, *Greek Horoscopes* (Philadelphia, 1959; see especially 81 ff. and 176ff.) translate many of Valens' horoscopes and also date them by the conjunction of stars. Such retrospective horoscopes were used to instruct would-be astrologers. Valens expected his readers to swear to keep what they read 'mysterious and guarded' (7, pr.).

He was wise and educated and stern because Mercury with Saturn was in the morning phase in the twelfth locus with the Sun attendant... He was honoured and worshipped by all, because with the Sun attendant, the star of Jupiter occupied a cardinal point...and he gave benefits to many and was worshipped by many, as I have said, because of the cardinal position of the Sun and the Moon...(*CCAG* 6.69–70)

These interpretations were more contentious than is at first apparent. Was the emperor controlled by the stars? Was it proper for his subjects to know his fate? And, most important, who were the others fated to become kings? According to the lawyer Ulpian, nearly every emperor prohibited astrology; on ten occasions in the first century astrologers were expelled from Rome; meanwhile emperors retained their services, and senators continued surreptitiously to consult them even in exile (for one example, see Tacitus, *Annals* 16.14).[48] The proscriptions probably had the opposite effect from the one intended: they increased astrologers' prestige (Juvenal, *Satires* 6.557ff.). Besides, the sheer repetition of the laws illustrates their ineffectiveness, the demand for magic was too strong to be suppressed by law.

In recognising astrology, emperors acknowledged the existence of an authority higher than themselves. Of course, unlike Christianity, astrology was not based on a single sacred text, interpreted into an orthodox dogma by a hierarchy of priests with exclusive congregations of parishioners. Unlike Christianity, therefore, astrology and other pagan beliefs posed no substantial threat or limitation to imperial power. Nevertheless, emperors even if they could not gain a monopoly by exiling astrologers, wanted to control access to them.

Ideally, they succeeded. The following extract is taken from the book of astrological learning (*Mathesis*) written by the senator Firmicus Maternus in the fourth century; some of his formulations were contemporary, but much of his work was copied from earlier treatises which have been lost.

Never reply to anyone who asks about the condition of the State or the life of the Roman emperor. It is both morally wrong and illegal... An astrologer who replies when he is asked about the fate of the emperor is a disgrace and deserves all the punishment he gets, because he really can neither say nor discover anything...

---

[48] The recorded expulsions of astrologers are listed by Cramer (1954: 234). 'Prophets who pretend to be inspired by a god are by decree expelled from the state, lest public morals be seduced by human credulity into hoping for change, or lest they excite the minds of the people...Who ever consults astrologers, soothsayers, omen-interpreters or prophets about the health of the emperor or about high matters, shall be executed together with the person who gave an answer...And if slaves consult about the health of their masters, they are to be punished with crucifixion' (Paul, *Opinions* 5.21); cf. Ulpian, *Comparison of the Laws of Moses and the Romans* 15.2.

In fact no astrologer could find out anything true about the destiny of the emperor. The emperor alone is not subject to the course of the stars and in his fate alone the stars have no powers of determination. Since he is the master of the whole world, his destiny is governed by the judgement of the god most high; since the whole of the earth's surface is subject to the power of the emperor, he himself is also considered among those gods whom the supreme power has set up to create and conserve all things...

For all free-born men, all orders, all the rich, all the nobles, all the officials, all powers serve him; he is endowed with the power of divine authority and immortal freedom and is numbered among the first rank of the gods. (*Mathesis* 2.30; translation adapted from J. R. Bram, *Ancient Astrology* (Park Ridge, N.J.; 1975))

In practice, these prohibitions were ignored. Ptolemy, the great astronomer and geographer of the second century, also wrote an astrological treatise, in which *inter alia* he recorded the conjunction of the stars which would bring a new-born child to imperial power (*Tetrabiblos* 4.3). In spite of the risk, senators repeatedly sought out imperial horoscopes and emperors repeatedly executed those whom they considered potential even if improbable rivals. One rare exception was noted by Suetonius: the emperor Titus was so confident in the security of his own Fate that he spared two patricians who had been convicted of aspiring to the throne.

...his only reaction was to advise them to desist, since...the Principate was a gift of Fate...the next day, he deliberately seated them near him at a gladiatorial show and offered them the combatants' swords brought to him for inspection. It is also said that he consulted the horoscopes of both men and warned both of them that they would be in danger, but at some other time and from someone else – quite correctly as events proved. (Suetonius, *Titus* 9)

Fact or fiction, astrology the real reason or an embroidered pretext for well-considered ostentatious clemency? We do not now, nor do we have to choose. As we have seen, such stories circulated in court circles and among the population at large. They were the currency of the political system. They have been largely ignored or underestimated by rationalistic historians, partly because historians are looking for something more recognisably 'fact', and partly because such accounts fuse moral and metaphysical myth with what we might rashly and in an old-fashioned way call objective truth. However much we may regret this fusion, we can at least be glad that Suetonius, Tacitus and Pliny did not write modern scholarly histories.

I took astrology as an example because it provided the Roman upper-class with a theatre for the fusion of their moral, mystical and political views. Of course, it provided much else as well: predictions about length of life, character, wealth, happiness, the choice of a wife, the sex of children, the outcome of an illness and style of death (cf. Ptolemy, *Tetrabiblos* 4.1–9).

Instead of astrology, it would have been possible to use dreams, or omens or magic (each was prevalent at all levels of Roman society, from emperors to beggars), to illustrate not merely the nature of Roman 'superstititions', but also the force of the supernatural which rulers and subjects had to take into account. For example, Tacitus reported how Germanicus Caesar, the emperor Tiberius' adopted son died; he had a relapse aggravated by his belief that Piso, the governor of Asia, in whose house he was staying had poisoned him; he had his sick-room investigated. 'Examination of the floor and walls of his bedroom revealed the remains of human bodies, spells, curses, lead tablets inscribed with the patient's name, charred and bloody ashes and other malignant objects which were supposed to consign souls to the powers of the tomb' (*Annals* 2.69 transl. by M. Grant, Penguin books).

Of course, we know that Germanicus did not die from magic; but Germanicus as reported by Tacitus, clearly thought otherwise (*ibid.* 2.71). And the emperor Hadrian on a visit to Egypt was reportedly impressed by the magical skill of the priest of Isis:

Pachrates, the prophet of Heliopolis, demonstrated the spell to the emperor Hadrian, to reveal the power of his magic. For by his spell, he caused a man to come to him within one hour, caused him to take to his bed within two hours and caused his death within seven hours. He also caused a dream to be sent to the emperor himself which [acquainted] him with the complete truth about his magical powers. The emperor was amazed by the prophet and ordered that he be given a double salary. (*Papyri graecae magicae* ed. K. Preisendanz, vol. 1, 148)

In most cases, presumably, magic was used in the service of highly personal interests, as in lovers' spells, remedies for sickness, or in curses on the unfaithful.[49] For example, figurines have been found, with heads cut off, arms and legs tied tight behind the back with leaden cords; bronze nails transfix the heart and stomach. With these figures went curses inscribed on lead tablets invoking outlandish gods; the following example was found in north Africa; it was written in Latin transcribed into Greek letters, perhaps to make it more mysterious and effective:

[49] On figurines, see A. Audollent, *Defixionum Tabellae* (repr. Frankfurt, 1967) esp. LXXIX and Sophronius, *Miracles of St. Cyrus and St. John* (*PG* 87.3541–8); on magical spells, see K. Preisendanz, *Papyri graecae magicae* (Stuttgart², 1973–4) with a German translation; S. Eitrem, *Magical Papyri = Papyri Osloenses* 1 (Oslo, 1925); and recently a long example translated and explained by D. Wortmann, 'Neue magische Texte', *Bonner Jahrbücher* 168 (1968) 85ff.

I call to witness and entreat...by the great god and by Anterotas and by him who has a hawk above his head and by the seven stars, that from the moment I have written this, Sextilius son of Dionysia may not sleep, but will burn with fever; let him not sleep, sit nor speak, but let him have me Septima, daughter of Amoena on his mind; let him burn furiously with love and desire for me, let the mind and heart of Sextilius son of Dionysia burn with love and desire for me Septima, daughter of Amoena. And you Abar Barbarie Eloe Sabaoth Pachnouphy Pythipemi, ensure that sleep does not touch Sextilius son of Dionysia, but let him burn with love and desire for me, let the spirit, heart and all the limbs of the whole body of Sextilius son of Dionysia be on fire. If you do not achieve this, I shall go down to the shrine of Osiris and dismantle the tomb and send it to be torn away by the river, for I am the great deacon of the great god Achrammachalala...(A. Audollent, *Defixionum Tabellae* (repr. Frankfurt, 1967) 270)

Yet sometimes as in astrology, personal magic and the political sphere overlapped. The following curse, one of several against adversaries in court-cases, was uttered against Theodorus tentatively identified as a governor of Cyprus: 'Spirits below the earth, spirits everywhere...take away the danger of Theodorus against me...take away his power and strength, make him lifeless and speechless...' (T. B. Mitford, *The Inscriptions of Kourion* (Philadelphia, 1971) 130–1). And there followed a curse, which might have sounded impressive, but which seems unintelligible. Yet other spells were thought to be immensely powerful; 'brings victory, works even with kings'...'also brings men to women and women to men, and makes virgins run out from their homes' (*Papyri Osloenses* 1). These infernal forces could either help emperors or hinder them. Therefore they had to be dealt with, placated and sometimes their agents on earth had also to be indulged. Since kings and gods had many similar powers, it was important to make sure that they were all fighting on the same side.

I am Isis...I gave and ordained laws unto men, which no one is able to change...I divided the earth from the heaven...I ordered the course of the sun and the moon...I made strong the right. I brought together woman and man...I ordained that parents should be loved by their children...I taught men to honour images of the gods...I broke down the government of tyrants. (*IG* 12.5.14; an inscription from Ios, second or third century AD; transl. A. Deissmann (1910: 136–7))

Religion, as the Christians showed, was the one power-base within Roman society from which opposition against the regime could be effectively launched.

Conclusions

CONCLUSIONS

The prevalence of magical practices and of astrological beliefs among rich and poor, powerful and weak does not explain emperor-worship. Nor does the pervasiveness in daily life of unknown mystic powers. But they provided the necessary conditions in which emperor worship flourished. We started with the question: Why did the Romans, contrary to their dominant political and religious traditions, grow to accept the idea that their visibly human ruler was a god? To answer this, we invoked in the traditional way a whole array of factors concerning the origin, transmission, acceptance and institutionalisation of emperor cults, without being able to attach specific weight to any of them. They included: the reluctant acceptance of eastern 'flattery', popular belief in Julius Caesar's and Augustus' divine connections, the close association of Augustus and the succeeding emperors with a divine father and with other gods, the appeal to emperors in public and private oaths, and the widespread initiative of provincials in celebrating the emperor's divinity with sacrifices, statues and festivals.

Our initial question (why did Romans worship emperors?) had its origins not only in the earlier Roman sceptical dismissal of emperor-worship as alien, but also probably in our modern rationalistic antipathy to 'superstition' as unworthy of a 'fact-based' history. This antipathy has allowed modern scholars systematically to under-value repetitive and inflated honorary decrees and the myths whether true or fabricated, reported by serious Roman historians. Modern scholarly concentration on 'facts' and on the surviving epigraphic 'evidence' has diverted attention from the beliefs and feelings which prompted the creation of the evidence.

Investigation along these lines gradually changed the focus of our discussion. We already know that in Graeco-Roman culture the distinction between man and god was blurred, not only by the existence of semi-divine figures, such as Hercules, and by spirits (*manes, daimones*), but also by ambiguities in feelings and expression. Belief can be, and often is, at odds with action; indeed there would be little point in having ideals if they were always or even often realised. Nor is there any profit in accusing the inconsistent of hypocrisy or deceit; spoken scepticism and conformist superstition may simply belong to different pigeon-holes or different social contexts. It is dangerous therefore to deduce behaviour from statements about beliefs. As Pliny wrote: '. . . Do magic words and incantations have any power? . . . individually, one by one, our wisest minds have no faith in such things; but in mass, throughout their everyday lives, they act as though they believe, without being aware of it' (*Natural History* 28.3).[50] Sophisticated Romans may not have believed that the emperor was a god, nor did the courtiers who saw him, but they sacrificed to him, as though he was a god, and perhaps they covered the conflict of evidence with a metaphysical metaphor – god made manifest, son of god, the least of gods but highest of mortals, son of Apollo, Hercules on earth. Most people probably did not bother with the demarcation; the emperor was clearly both man and god.

In the last part of this chapter, we returned to our main theme. The unity of a political system rests not only in shared institutions, taxes and military defences, but in shared symbols, in the minds of men. Emperor cults, and all that they involved: oaths, sacrifices, sharing meat and wine, processions, games, statues, images, the reading and recording of pompous decrees which under the pretext of honouring the emperor recorded the reluctant generosity of some local burgher, the hopeful embassies to the distant capital, the distant memory of an emperor's visit, the stories of sudden success at court, of the emperor's cruelty – all these provided the context in which inhabitants of towns spread for hundreds of miles throughout the empire could celebrate their membership of a single political order and their own place within it. Small wonder, then, if for such important purposes the distant emperor was in the collective mind 'transformed into a god among men' (Stobaeus, *Anthologium* 7.61 – see p. 198 above).

[50] See V. Pareto, *Mind and Society* (London, 1935) vol. 1, 106ff. for surely the best sociological discussion of these aspects of Roman religion.

BIBLIOGRAPHY

MODERN WORKS CITED IN CHAPTER I

Afzelius A. (1944). *Die römische Kriegsmacht*, Copenhagen.
Andreski S. (1954) *Military Organization and Society*, London.
Ashby T. (1973) *The Aqueducts of Ancient Rome*, repr. Washington, D.C.
Astin A. E. (1967) *Scipio Aemilianus*, Oxford.
Badian E. (1962) 'From the Gracchi to Sulla', *Historia* 11, 203ff.
Badian E. (1968) *Roman Imperialism in the Late Republic*, Oxford.[2]
Badian E. (1972) *Publicans and Sinners*, Oxford.
Badian E. (1972 bis) 'Tiberius Gracchus and the beginning of the Roman Revolution' in H. Temporini, ed., *Aufstieg und Niedergang der römischen Welt*, Berlin, vol. 1.1, 668ff.
Baehrel R. (1961) *Une Croissance*, Paris.
Beloch K. J. (1886) *Die Bevölkerung der griechisch-römischen Welt*, Leipzig.
Beloch K. J. (1926) *Römische Geschichte*, Berlin.
Besnier R. (1955) 'L'Etat économique de Rome [500–264 BC], *Revue historique de droit français et étranger* 33, 195ff.
Bleicken J. (1968) *Das Volkstribunat der Klassischen Republik*, Munich[2].
Brunt P. A. (1950) 'Pay and superannuation in the Roman Army', *Papers of the British School at Rome* 18, 50ff.
Brunt P. A. (1961) 'Charges of provincial maladministration under the Early Principate', *Historia* 10, 189ff.
Brunt P. A. (1962) 'The army and the land in the Roman Revolution', *Journal of Roman Studies* 52, 69ff.
Brunt P. A. (1965) 'The Equites in the Late Republic', *Second International Conference of Economic History, 1962*, Paris, vol. 1.
Brunt P. A. (1971) *Italian Manpower 225 BC–AD 14*, Oxford.
Brunt P. A. (1971 bis) *Social Conflicts in the Roman Republic*, London.
The New Cambridge Modern History, vol. 7 ed. J. O. Lindsay, Cambridge, 1957; vol. 9 ed. C. W. Crawley, Cambridge, 1965.
Carcopino J. (1967) *Autour des Gracques*, Paris[2].
Chandler T. and Fox G. (1974) *3000 Years of Urban Growth*, New York.
Clarke M. L. (1953) *Rhetoric at Rome*, London.
Clarke M. L. (1971) *Higher Education in the Ancient World*, London.
Crawford M. H. (1974) *Roman Republican Coinage*, Cambridge.
Delbrück H. (1920) *Geschichte der Kriegskunst*, Berlin, vol. 4.

Modern works cited in Chapter 1

Domaszewski A. von (1967) *Die Rangordnung des römischen Heeres*, Cologne[2].

Dore R. P. (1959) *Land Reform in Japan*, London.

Duncan-Jones R. P. (1974). *The Economy of the Roman Empire*, Cambridge.

Earl D. C. (1963) *Tiberius Gracchus*, Brussels.

Eisenstadt S. N. (1963) *The Political Systems of Empires*, New York.

Eisenstadt S. N. (1971) *Social Differentiation and Stratification*, Glenview, Ill.

Finer S. E. (1962) *The Man on Horseback*, London.

Finley M. I. (1973) *The Ancient Economy*, London.

Finley M. I. (1977) 'The City from Fustel de Coulanges to Max Weber and Beyond', *Comparative Studies in Society and History* 19, 305ff.

Frederiksen M. W. (1966) 'Caesar, Cicero and the problem of debt', *Journal of Roman Studies* 56, 128ff.

Gabba E. (1976) *Republican Rome, The Army and the Allies*, Berkeley.

Gelzer M. (1969) *The Roman Nobility*, Oxford.

Greenidge A. H. J. (1901). *The Legal Procedure of Cicero's Time*, Oxford.

Gruen E. (1968) *Roman Politics and the Criminal Courts 149–78 BC*, Harvard.

Gruen E. (1974) *The Last Generation of the Roman Republic*, Berkeley, Calif.

Gwynn A. (1926) *Roman Education from Cicero to Quintilian*, Oxford.

Hamilton L. J. (1957) *War and Prices in Spain 1651–1800*, New York.

Hardy E. G. (1912) *Roman Laws and Charters*, Oxford.

Harmand J. (1957) *L'armée et le soldat à Rome*, Paris.

Harris W. V. (1978) *War and Imperialism in Republican Rome 327–70 BC*, Oxford.

Heer D. M. (1968) *Society and Populations*, Englewood Cliffs, N. J.

Heitland W. E. (1921) *Agricola*, Cambridge.

Helleiner K. F. (1967) in the *Cambridge Economic History*, Cambridge, vol. 4.

Hindess B. and Hirst P. Q. (1975) *Pre-Capitalist Modes of Production*, London.

Hopkins K. (1966) 'Civil–military relations in developing countries', *British Journal of Sociology* 17, 165ff.

Hopkins K. (1968) 'Structural differentiation in Rome' in I. M. Lewis, ed., *History and Social Anthropology*, London.

Hopkins K. (1978) 'Economic growth in towns in Classical Antiquity' in P. Abrams and E. A. Wrigley, ed., *Towns in Societies*, Cambridge.

Horowitz I. (1966) *Three Worlds of Development*, New York.

Jolliffe R. O. (1919) *Phases of Corruption in Roman Administration*, Diss. Menasha, Wisc.

Jolowicz H. F. (1972) *A Historical Introduction to Roman Law*, Cambridge[3].

Jones A. H. M. (1972) *The Criminal Courts of the Roman Republic and Principate*, Oxford.

Jones A. H. M. (1974) *The Roman Economy*, edited by P. A. Brunt, Oxford.

Kelly J. M. (1966) *Roman Litigation*, Oxford.

Kunkel W. (1967) *Herkunft und soziale Stellung der römischen Juristen*, Graz[2].

Kunkel W. (1973) *An Introduction to Roman Legal and Constitutional History*, Oxford.

Liebenam W. *sv Dilectus* in *RE*.

Macmullen R. (1974) *Roman Social Relations*, New Haven.

Marrou H. I. (1956) *A History of Education in Antiquity*, London.

Marsh F. B. (1927) *The Founding of the Roman Empire*, Oxford.

Modern works cited in Chapter 1

Meier C. (1966) *Res Publica Amissa*, Wiesbaden.
Mingay G. (1963) *English Landed Society in the Eighteenth Century*, London.
Morgan O. S. (1933) ed., *Agricultural Systems of Middle Europe*, New York.
Morris I. (1964) *The World of the Shining Prince*, Oxford.
Nicolet C. (1966) *L'ordre équestre à l'époque républicaine*, Paris.
Ogilvie R. M. (1965) *A Commentary on Livy*, Oxford.
Pais E. and Bayet J. (1926) *Histoire Romaine*, Paris.
Parsons T. (1966) *Societies: Evolutionary and Comparative Perspectives*, Englewood Cliffs, N.J.
Rawson E. (1976) 'The Ciceronian aristocracy and its properties', in M. I. Finley, ed., *Studies in Roman Property*, Cambridge.
Ringrose D. R. (1968) Transportation and economic stagnation in 18th-century Castille', *Journal of Economic History* 28, 51ff.
Rostovtzeff M. I. (1902) *Geschichte der Staatspacht*, Leipzig.
Rostovtzeff M. I. (1957) *Social and Economic History of the Roman Empire*, Oxford².
Rozman G. (1973) *Urban Networks in Ch'ing China and Tokugawa Japan*, Princeton.
Salmon E. T. (1969) *Roman Colonization under the Republic*, London.
Sauerwein I. (1970) *Die Leges Sumptuariae*, Diss. Hamburg.
Schtaerman E. M. (1969) *Die Blütezeit der Sklavenwirtschaft in der römischen Republik*, Wiesbaden.
Schulz F. (1946) *History of Roman Legal Science*, Oxford.
Schwahn W. *sv Tributum* in *RE*.
Shackleton Bailey D. R. (1965–70) *Letters to Atticus*, Cambridge.
Shatzman I. (1975) *Senatorial Wealth and Roman Politics*, Brussels.
Silverman S. F. (1970) 'Exploitation in rural central Italy', *Comparative Studies in Society and History* 12, 327ff.
Smelser N. J. (1963) in B. F. Hoselitz and W. E. Moore, *Industrialization and Social Change*, Paris.
Smith R. E. (1958) *Service in the Post-Marian Army*, Manchester.
Stone L. (1973) *Family and Fortune*, Oxford.
Taylor L. R. (1944) *Party Politics in the Age of Caesar*, Berkeley.
Tibiletti G. (1948) 'Il Possesso dell' Ager Publicus', *Athenaeum* 26, 173ff.
Toynbee A. J. (1965) *Hannibal's Legacy*, Oxford.
United Nations (1956) 'Methods for population projections by sex and age', *Population Studies*, New York.
Urögdi G. *sv Publicani* in *RE*.
Versnel H. S. (1970) *Triumphus*, Leiden.
Vittingoff F. (1951) *Römische Kolonisation und Bürgerrechtspolitik*, Wiesbaden.
Weber M. (1891) *Die römische Agrargeschichte*, Stuttgart.
Weber M. (1968) *Economy and Society*, New York, vol. 3.
White K. D. (1970) *Roman Farming*, London.
Yang C. K. (1959) *A Chinese Village*, MIT.
Yang C. K. (1959 *bis*) in D. S. Nivison and A. F. Wright, *Confucianism in Action*, Stanford.

MODERN WORKS CITED IN CHAPTER II

Alföldy G. (1972) 'Die Freilassung von Sklaven', *Rivista storica dell' antichità* 2, 97ff.

Amelotti M. (1966). *Il testamento romano*, Florence.

Anderson P. (1974) *Lineages of the Absolutist State*, London.

Bellen H. (1971) *Studien zur Sklavenflucht im römischen Kaiserreich*, Wiesbaden.

Beloch K. J. (1886) *Die Bevölkerung der griechisch-römischen Welt*, Leipzig.

Bömer F. (1958) *Untersuchungen über der Religion der Sklaven in Griechenland und Rom* part 1, Wiesbaden.

Boulvert G. (1970) *Esclaves et affranchis impériaux sous le haut-empire*, Naples.

Brunt P. A. (1971). *Italian Manpower 225 BC–AD 14*, Oxford.

Buckland W. W. (1908) *The Roman Law of Slavery*, Cambridge.

Davies O. (1935). *Roman Mines in Europe*, Oxford.

Davis D. B. (1966) *The Problem of Slavery in Western Culture*, Ithaca, N.Y.

Delumeau J. (1959) *La vie économique et sociale de Rome*, Paris, 2 vols.

Douglass F. (1855) *My Bondage and My Freedom*, New York.

Duckworth G. E. (1952) *The Nature of Roman Comedy*, Princeton.

Duff A. M. (1958) *Freedmen in the Early Roman Empire*, repr. Cambridge.

Duncan-Jones R. P. (1974) *The Economy of the Roman Empire*, Cambridge.

Duncan-Jones R. P. (1976) 'The size of the Modius Castrensis', *Zeitschrift für Papyrologie und Epigraphik* 21.

Eistenstadt S. N. (1963) *The Political Systems of Empires*, New York.

Elkins S. M. (1963) *Slavery*, New York.

Finley M. I. (1960) ed., *Slavery in Classical Antiquity*, Cambridge.

Finley M. I. (1964) 'Between slavery and freedom', *Comparative Studies in Society and History* 6, 233ff.

Finley M. I. (1968) *sv* Slavery in *The International Encyclopaedia of the Social Sciences*, New York.

Finley M. I. (1973) *The Ancient Economy*, London.

Finley M. I. (1976) ed., *Studies in Roman Property*, Cambridge.

Fisher A. G. B. and H. J. (1970) *Slavery and Muslim Society in Africa*, London.

Frank T. (1916) 'Race mixture in the Roman Empire', *American Historical Review* 21, 689ff.

Freyre G. (1946) *Masters and Slaves*, New York.

Friedländer L. (1921) *Sittengeschichte Roms*, Leipzig[10], vol. 4.

Gülzow H. (1969) *Christentum und Sklaverei*, Bonn.

Heer D. M. (1968) *Society and Population*, Englewood Cliffs, N.J.

Kaser M. (1938) 'Die Geschichte der Patronatsgewalt über Freigelassene', *Zeitschrift der Savigny Stiftung (rom. Abt.)* 58, 88ff.

Kaser M. (1971) *Das römische Privatrecht*, Munich[2].

Klein H. S. (1967) *Slavery in the Americas*, London.

Mandel E. (1968). *Marxist Economic Theory*, London.

Meillassoux C. (1975) *L'esclavage en Afrique précoloniale*, Paris.

The Minutes of the Evidence taken before a Committee of the Whole House 1789–91.

Morgan O. S. (1931) *Agricultural Systems of Middle Europe*, New York.

Morrison S. E. *et al.* (1969) *The Growth of the American Republic*, New York[6].

Modern works cited in Chapter II

Murdock G. P. (1967) 'Ethnographic Atlas: a summary', *Ethnology* 6, 109ff.

Nieboer H. J. (1910) *Slavery as an Industrial System*, The Hague[2].

Nörr D. (1965) 'Zur Bewertung der freien Arbeit in Rom', *Zeitschrift der Savigny Stiftung (rom. Abt)* 82, 90ff.

Osofsky G. (1969) *Puttin' on Ole Massa*, New York

Patterson O. (1967) *The Sociology of Slavery*, London.

Pflaum H. G. (1950). *Les procurateurs équestres sous le haut-empire romain*, Paris.

Prado C. (1963) *História econômica do Brasil*, São Paolo[8].

Robertis F. M. de (1963) *Lavoro e laboratori nel mondo romano*, Bari.

Salmon E. T. (1969) *Roman Colonization under the Republic*, London.

Sargent R. L. (1924) *The Size of the Slave Population at Athens*, Urbana, Ill.

Schtaerman E. M. (1969) *Die Blütezeit der Sklavenwirtschaft in der römischen Republik*, Wiesbaden.

Schtaerman E. M. and Trophimova M. K. (1971). *Slave-ownership in the Early Roman Empire*, Moscow (in Russian).

Sio A. (1964/5) 'Interpretations of slavery', *Comparative Studies in Society and History* 7, 289ff.

Stampp K. M. (1964) *The Peculiar Institution*, London.

Taylor L. R. (1961) 'Freedmen and freeborn in the epitaphs of imperial Rome', *American Journal of Philology* 82, 113ff.

Treggiari S. (1969) *Roman Freedmen during the Late Republic*, Oxford.

United Nations (1953) *Determinants and Consequences of Population Trends*, New York.

Varga E. 'Uber die asiatische Produktionsweise', *Jahrbuch für Wirtschaftsgeschichte* (1967, 4) 181ff.

Vittinghoff F. (1960) 'Die Theorie des historischen Materialismus über den antiken Sklavenhalterschaft', *Saecululm* 11, 89ff.

Vogt J. (1957) *Struktur der antiken Sklavenkriege*, Wiesbaden.

Vogt J. (1972). *Sklaverei und Humanität*, Historia Einzelschrift 8, Wiesbaden[2].

Vogt J. (1974) *Ancient Slavery and the Ideal of Man*, Oxford.

Wallon II. (1879) *Histoire de l'esclavage dans l'antiquité*, Paris, vol. 3.

Weaver P. R. C. (1972) *Familia Caesaris*, Cambridge.

Weber M. (1971) 'The social causes of the decline of ancient civilization', translated in J. E. T. Eldridge, *Max Weber*, London.

Weber, M. (1976) *Agrarverhältnisse im Altertum* = *The Agrarian Sociology of Ancient Civilizations*, trans. R. I. Frank, London.

Westermann W. L. (1955) *The Slave Systems of Greek and Roman Antiquity*, Philadelphia.

White A. N. Sherwin- (1973) *The Roman Citizenship*, Oxford[2].

White K. D. (1965) 'The productivity of labour in Roman agriculture', *Antiquity* 39, 102ff.

White K. D. (1970) *Roman Farming*, London.

Williams E. (1964) *Capitalism and Slavery*, London.

Wilson A. J. N. (1966) *Emigration from Italy in the Republican Age of Rome*, Manchester.

Yeo C. A. (1952) 'The Economics of Roman and American slavery', *Finanzarchiv* 13, 445ff.

Modern works cited in Chapter III

MODERN WORKS CITED IN CHAPTER III

Alföldy G. (1972) 'Die Freilassung von Sklaven in der römischen Kaiserzeit', *Rivista storica dell'antichità* 2, 97ff.

Bloch M. (1914) *Die Freilassungsbedingungen der Delphischen Freilassungsurkunden*, Diss. Strasburg.

Bömer F. (1960) 'Die sogenannte sakrale Freilassung', *Abhandlungen der Akad. Mainz, geistes- und sozialwiss. Kl.* (1960, 1).

Buckland W. W. (1908) *The Roman Law of Slavery*, Cambridge.

Calderini A. (1908) *La manomissione e la condizione dei liberti in Grecia*, Milan.

Cameron A. (1939) 'Sacral manumission and confession', *Harvard Theological Review* 32, 148ff.

Cameron A. (1939 *bis*) 'Threptos and related terms in the inscriptions of Asia Minor', *Studies Presented to W. H. Buckler*, Ed. W. M. Calder and J. Keil, Manchester, 27ff.

Collitz H. (1899) Baunack J. *et al. Sammlung der griechischen Dialekt-Inschriften*, Göttingen.

Daux G. (1936) *Delphes au IIe et Ier siècle*, Paris.

Daux G. (1943) *Chronologie Delphique*, Paris.

Flacelière R. (1965) *Greek Oracles*, London.

Finley M. I. (1960) 'The servile statuses of Ancient Greece', *Revue internationale des droits de l'antiquité* 7, 165ff.

Finley M. I. (1964) 'Between slavery and freedom', *Comparative Studies in Society and History* 6, 233ff.

Finley M. I. (1973) *The Ancient Economy*, London.

Foucart P. (1867) *Mémoire sur l'affranchissement des esclaves*, Paris.

Genovese E. (1975) *Roll Jordan Roll*, London.

Gouldner A. (1965) *Enter Plato*, New York.

Hopkins K. and Roscoe P. J. (forthcoming) *Manumissions in Thessaly*.

Kaser M. (1938) 'Die Geschichte des Patronatsgewalt über Freigelassene', *Zeitschrift der Savigny Stiftung* (*rom. Abt.*) 58, 88ff.

Klein H. S. (1967) *Slavery in the Americas*, Chicago.

Koschaker P. (1931) 'Über einige griechische Rechtsurkunden aus der östlichen Randgebieten des Hellenismus', *Abhandlungen Sächs. Akad. Wiss phil.-hist. Kl.* 42, 1ff.

Marinovich L. P. (1971) 'Paramone in Delphic manumissions of the Roman period', *Vestnik Drevnei Istorii* 118, 27ff. (in Russian)

Mendelsohn I. (1949) *Slavery in the Ancient Near East*, New York.

Nörr D. (1965) 'Zur Bewertung der freien Arbeit in Rom', *Zeitschrift der Savigny Stiftung* (*rom. Abt.*) 82, 90ff.

Parke H. W. and Wormell D. E. W. (1956) *The Dephic Oracle*, Oxford[2].

Rädle H. (1969) *Untersuchungen zum griechischen Freilassungswesen*, Diss. Munich.

Rawick G. P. (1972) *The American Slave, From Sundown to Sunup*, Westport, Conn.

Rawick G. P. (1972–) *The American Slave, A Composite Autobiography*, Westport, Conn., 19 vols.

Robertis F. M. de (1963) *Lavoro e lavoratori nel mondo romano*, Bari.

Modern works cited in Chapter III

Rostovtzeff M. I. (1941) *Social and Economic History of the Hellenistic World*, Oxford.

Samuel A. E. (1948) 'The role of paramone clauses in ancient documents', *Journal of Juristic Papyrology* 2, 221ff.

Schtaerman E. M. (1969) *Die Blütezeit der Sklavenwirtschaft in der römischen Republik*, Wiesbaden.

Segré M. (1944–5) ed., 'Tituli Calymnii', *Annuario della Scuola archaeologica di Atene* 22/3, 169ff.

Stampp K. (1964) *The Peculiar Institution*, London.

Treggiari S. (1969) *Roman Freedmen during the Late Republic*, Oxford.

Westermann W. L. (1945) 'Between slavery and freedom', *American Historical Review* 50, 213ff.

Westermann W. L. (1948) 'The paramone as a general service contract', *Journal of Juristic Papyrology* 2, 9ff.

Westermann W. L. (1955) *The Slave Systems of Greek and Roman Antiquity*, Philadelphia.

White A. N. (1966) Sherwin– *The Letters of Pliny*, Oxford.

United Nations (1956) 'Methods for population projections by sex and age', *Population Studies*, New York.

Zel'in K. K. (1969) *Forms of Dependency in the Eastern Mediterranean in the Hellenistic Period* by K. K. Zel'in and M. K. Trophimova, Moscow.

MODERN WORKS CITED IN CHAPTER IV

Alföldi A. (1934) 'Die Ausgestaltung des monarchischen Zeremoniells', *Mitteilungen des deutschen archäologischen Instituts* 49, 1ff., reprinted in *Die monarchische Repräsentation im römischen Kaiserreiche*, Darmstadt, 1970.

Barnes T. D. (1976) 'Imperial campaigns 285–311', *Phoenix* 30, 182ff.

Bremer J. J. (1958) *Asexualisation*, Oslo

Ch'ien T. S. (1950) *The Government and Politics of China*, Harvard.

Costa E. A. (1972) 'The Castrensis Sacri Palatii', *Byzantion* 42, 358ff.

Dorfman R. I. and Shipley R. A. (1936) *The Androgens*, New York.

Dozy R. P. A. (1913). *Spanish Islam*, London.

Dunlap J. E. (1924) *The Office of the Grand Chamberlain in the Later Roman and Byzantine Empires*, University of Michigan, Humanistic Series, 14, New York.

Elias N. (1939). *Uber den Prozess der Zivilisation*, Basel.

Elias N. (1969). *Die höfische Gesellschaft*, Berlin.

Ensslin W. *sv Praepositus Sacri Cubiculi* in *RE*, Supplementband 8.

Gaiffier B. de (1957) 'Palatins et eunuques dans quelques documents hagiographiques', *Analecta Bollandiana* 75, 17ff.

Gibbon E. (1896) *The History of the Decline and Fall of the Roman Empire*, ed. J. B. Bury, London, in seven volumes.

Guilland R. (1943) 'Les eunuques dans l'empire byzantin', *Etudes Byzantines* 1, 197ff.

Herter H. *sv Effeminatus* in *Reallexikon für Antike und Christentum*

Hopkins K. (1963) 'Eunuchs in politics in the Later Roman Empire', *Proceedings of the Cambridge Philological Society* 189, 62ff.

Hug *sv Eunuchen* in *RE*, Supplementband 3.

Modern works cited in Chapter IV

Jones A. H. M. (1964) *The Later Roman Empire*, Oxford.

Kasanin J. and Biskind G. R. (1943) 'Personality changes following substitution therapy in pre-adolescent eunuchoidism', *Journal of the American Medical Association*, 1317ff.

Levy H. S. (1958). *Harem Favourites of an Illustrious Celestial*, Taiwan.

Matignon J. J. (1896) 'Les eunuques du palais impérial à Pékin', *Bulletin de la société d'anthropologie de Paris*, 4ᵉ série 7, 334ff.

Matthews J. F. (1975) *Western Aristocracies and Imperial Court*, Oxford.

Mez A. (1922) *Die Renaissance des Islams*, Heidelberg.

Millar F. (1977) *The Emperor in the Roman World*, London.

Runciman S. (1933) *Byzantine Civilisation*, London.

Schnee H. (1953–5) *Die Hoffinanz und die moderne Staat. Geschichte und System der Hoffaktoren an deutschen Fürstenhofen im Zeitalter des Absolutismus*, Berlin.

Setton K. M. (1941) *Christian Attitudes towards the Emperor in the Fourth Century*, New York.

Simpson S. L. (1957) 'Hormones and behaviour patterns', *British Medical Journal*, 839.

Stern S. (1950) *The Court Jew, A Contribution to the History of Absolutism in Central Europe*, Philadelphia.

Tschepe P. A. (1909) *Histoire du royaume de Ts'in (777–207 av. J.-C.)*, Shanghai.

Thompson E. A. (1947) *The Historical Works of Ammianus Marcellinus*, Cambridge.

Weber M. (1968) *Economy and Society*, New York.

Williams S. W. (1904) *The Middle Kingdom*, New York.

Wittfogel K. A. (1957) *Oriental Despotism*, New Haven.

Yang L.-S. (1958) 'Great families of Eastern Han' translated in *Chinese Social History*, Washington.

MODERN WORKS CITED IN CHAPTER V

Anderson P. (1974) *Lineages of the Absolutist State*, London.

Barb A. (1963) 'The survival of magic arts' in A. D. Momigliano, ed., *The Conflict between Paganism and Christianity*, Oxford.

Barnes T. D. (1971) *Tertullian*, Oxford.

Barnes T. D. (1968) 'Legislation against the Christians', *Journal of Roman Studies* 58, 32ff.

Beaujeu J. (1955) *La religion romaine à l'apogée de l'empire*, Paris.

Bellen H. (1971) *Studien zur Sklavenflucht im römischen Kaiserreich*, Wiesbaden.

Bickerman E. (1972) in *Le culte des souverains dans l'empire romain, Fondation Hardt, Entretiens* 19, Geneva.

Bloch M. (1924) *Les rois thaumaturges*, Strasbourg.

Bouché-Leclercq A. (1899) *L'astrologie grecque*, Paris.

Bowersock G. (1972) in *Le culte des souverains dans l'empire romain, Fondation Hardt, Entretiens* 19, Geneva.

Boyce G. K. (1937) 'Corpus of the Lararia of Pompeii', *Memoirs of the American Academy at Rome* 14.

Modern works cited in Chapter v

Brown P. (1972) *Religion and Society in the Age of St Augustus*, London.

Cramer F. H. (1954) *Astrology in Roman Law and Politics*, Philadelphia.

Croix G. M. de Ste (1974) 'Why were the early Christian Persecuted?' in M. I. Finley, ed., *Studies in Ancient Society*, London.

Deissman A. (1910) *Light from the Ancient East*, London.

Delatte L. (1942) *Les traités de la royauté*, Liège.

Duthey R. (1972) 'La fonction sociale de l'Augustalité', *Epigraphica* 36, 134ff.

Eisenstadt S. N. (1963) *The Political Systems of Empires*, New York.

Etienne R. (1958) *Le culte impérial dans la péninsule ibérique*, Paris.

Fears J. R. (1977) *Princeps a Diis Electus*, Papers and Monographs of the American Academy in Rome 26, Rome.

Ferguson J. (1970) *The Religions of the Roman Empire*, London.

Fink R. O., Hoey A. S. and Snyder W. F. (1940) 'The Feriale Duranum', *Yale Classical Studies* 7, 1ff.

Frend W. H. C. (1965) *Martyrdom and Persecution in the Early Church*, Oxford.

Geertz C. (1977) 'Centers, Kings and Charisma' in Ben-David J. and Clark T., eds., *Culture and Its Creations*, New York.

Goodenough E. R. (1928) 'The political philosophy of Hellenistic kingship', *Yale Classical Studies* 1, 55ff.

Gundel W. and H. G. (1966) *Astrologoumena*, Wiesbaden.

Jones A. H. M. (1960) *Studies in Roman Government and Law*, Oxford.

Jordan D. K. (1972) *Gods, Ghosts and Ancestors*, Berkeley.

Kramolisch H. (1975) 'Zur Ära des Kaisers Claudius in Thessalien', *Chiron* 5, 337ff.

Krauss F. B. (1930) *An Interpretation of Omens...*, Diss. Philadelphia.

Kruse H. (1934) *Studien zur offiziellen Geltung des Kaiserbildes im römischen Reiche*, Paderborn.

MacCormack S. (1972) 'Change and continuity in late antiquity: the ceremony of *adventus*', *Historia* 21, 721ff.

McIlwain C. W. (1965) *The Political Works of James I*, New York.

Macmullen R. (1966) *Enemies of the Roman Order*, Harvard.

Marquardt J. (1957) *Römische Staatsverwaltung*, repr. Darmstadt, vol. 3.

Mau A. (1908) *Pompeii in Leben und Kunst*, Leipzig.

Millar F. (1972) 'The imperial cult and the persecutions' in *Le Culte des souverains dans l'empire romain*, Fondation Hardt, Entretiens 19, Geneva.

Musurillo H. (1972) *The Acts of the Christian Martyrs*, Oxford.

Neugebauer O. and Van Hosen H. B. (1959) *Greek Horoscopes*, Philadelphia.

Nock A. D. *Essays on Religion and the Ancient World*, ed. Z. Stewart, Oxford.

Pareto V. (1935) *Mind and Society*, London.

Pearce T. E. V. (1970) 'Notes on Cicero, In Pisonem', *Classical Quarterly* 20, 313ff.

Premerstein A. von *sv Augustales* in *DE*.

Ryberg I. S. (1955) 'Rites of the state religion in Roman art', *Memoirs of the American Academy in Rome* 22.

Samuel A. E. (1972) *Greek and Roman Chronology*, Munich.

Scott K. (1924) *The Imperial Cult under the Flavians*, Strasbourg.

Scott K. (1931) 'Honorific months', *Yale Classical Studies* 2, 243ff.

Modern works cited in Chapter v

Setton K. M. (1941) *Christian Attitudes Towards the Emperor in the Fourth Century*, New York.

Taeger F. (1957–60) *Charisma*, Stuttgart, 2 vols.

Taylor L. R. (1931) *The Divinity of the Roman Emperor*, Middletown, Conn.

Thomas K. (1973) *Religion and the Decline of Magic*, London.

Toutain J. (1907–20) *Les cultes paiens dans l'empire romain*, Paris, 3 vols.

Vogel L. (1973) *The Column of Antoninus Pius*, Cambridge, Mass., 32ff.

Weber M. (1968) *Economy and Society*, New York.

Weinstock S. (1971) *Divus Julius*, Oxford.

Wortmann D. (1968) 'Neue magische Texte', *Bonner Jahrbücher* 168, 85ff.

SUPPLEMENTARY BIBLIOGRAPHY

ROMAN HISTORY FOR SOCIOLOGISTS AND SOCIOLOGY FOR

ROMAN HISTORIANS

Several sociologists have written about the ancient world. At first sight, their works may seem an obvious starting point for students of sociology and ancient history who wish to explore the overlap between the two disciplines. But none is designed as introductory reading. For example, it is I think preferable to begin with M. Weber, *Economy and Society* (New York, 1968) especially volume 3, rather than with the same author's more obviously relevant *The Agrarian Sociology of Ancient Civilizations* (London, 1976). K. Marx, *Pre-capitalist Economic Formations* (London, 1964) is shorter and more readable than his *Grundrisse* (London, 1973); like V. Pareto, *The Mind and Society* (London, 1935), it contains illuminating comments on Roman society, but no extended discussion of Roman society alone. Perhaps the best recent sociological book on the ancient world is A. W. Gouldner's, *Enter Plato* (London, 1967), especially the first part, but that is about Greece not Rome. B. Hindess and P. Q. Hirst, *Pre-Capitalist Modes of Production* (London, 1975) is 'a work of Marxist theory' with chapters on the ancient mode of production and on slavery; I admire their intellectual gymnastics while being oppressed by their ignorance. I should like to mention two more works, an essay in a collection which might interest historians, and a book: R. A. Nisbet, 'Kinship and political power in first-century Rome' in W. J. Cahnman and A. Boskoff, *Sociology and History* (New York, 1964) and G. E. Lenski, *Power and Privilege* (New York, 1966) which is in effect a sociological history of the social evolution of inequality, with a long section on agrarian societies.

Some sociologists may like their history straight. The following are all, in my opinion, excellent and unlike many Roman history books are written so as to be intelligible to those who know little Roman history: E. Badian, *Roman Imperialism in the Late Republic* (Oxford[2], 1968); P. A. Brunt, *Social conflicts in the Roman Republic* (London, 1971); M. I. Finley, *The Ancient Economy* (London, 1973); W. Kunkel, *An Introduction to Roman Legal and Constitutional History* (Oxford, 1973); M. I. Rostovtzeff, *Social and Economic History of the Roman Empire* (Oxford[2], 1957); C. G. Starr, *Civilization and the Caesars* (New York, 1965); and a source book: N. Lewis and M. Reinhold, *Roman Civilization* (New York, 1966).

Bibliography: sociology

For Roman historians who want to read sociology without being crushed by jargon or by text-books, I tentatively suggest the following, some of which are comparative history or good social history rather than straight sociology: P. Anderson, *Lineages of the Absolutist State* (London, 1974) – it is, I think, much better than his *Passages from Antiquity to Feudalism* (London, 1974); C. M. Arensberg and S. T. Kimball, *Family and Community in Ireland* (Cambridge, Mass., 1948); F. Braudel, *Capitalism and Material Life 1400–1800* (London, 1967); M. Elvin, *The Pattern of the Chinese Past* (London, 1973); M. Freedman, *Lineage Organization in Southeastern China* (London, 1958); B. Moore, *Social Origins of Dictatorship and Democracy* (London, 1967); R. A. Nisbet, *Social Change and History* (New York, 1969); J. D. Spence, *Emperor of China* (London, 1974); K. Thomas, *Religion and the Decline of Magic* (London, 1971); I. Wallerstein, *The Modern World-System* (New York, 1974).

INDEX OF SUBJECTS

eunuchs: (cont.)
  sonal characteristics, 173, 180, 193–5; power at court, 173, 177, 179–81, 190–1, 196; ranks, 174–6; sudden demise, 174, 180–1, 190; wealth, 174, 178, 190
ex-slaves, see slaves
expectation of life, 21, 34, 50
exploitation: forms, 114, 125–6; limited by political structure, 24, 112, 114; of citizens, 14; of provinces, 41; of slaves, 114

family, life cycle, 22
family, as unit of labour, 109, 111, 125–6
farms: single family, 4; increase in size, 105
folk-heroes, 21, 25
food: distribution to poor, 13; see also wheat
fortunes, size of, 39
foundlings ((threptoi), 158
free labourers, 9–10
free peasants, 5, 7
freedman, see slaves, ex-slaves

games, public, 38, 95, 119, 206–8
genius, 201–2, 214; of emperor, 204, 212, 224, 228
grammarians, see Greek and Latin culture
Greece, conquered by Romans, 135
Greek: culture, 76–9, 83; economy, 134; manumission, 130, 133, 153; slaves, 124; slave society, 99

hereditary status, 184–5

ideals: of aristocracy, 45, 52; Christian, 122; of clientship, 23; legal, 88; of philosophers, 121–2; of Principate, 182, 199–200, 203, 226; rhetorical, 28, 198–200; of slave-owners, 15, 121–3, 129–30
inflation of titles, 174
inheritance, as channel of wealth, 48
innovation, resisted, 78, 91
inscriptions: honorary, 198, 211; recording manumissions, 133

Jews, Court, 173–4, 190
juries, 84
justice, 43, 81ff., 222

king, English, French, 197, 231
kinship, 88
knights (equites): against senators, 46–7, 90–1; army officers, 184; imperial administrators, 125, 182, 184; killed, 71; land-owners, 49–51, 66; lawyers, 86; tax-farmers, 45–7, 51

labour: cost subsidised, 39; input of peasants, 110; productivity increased, 36; of slaves, 10, 110; see also wage-labour
land: arable to pasture, 3; the basis of wealth, a safe investment, 6, 11, 13, 48–51, 65, 104–5, 107, 113; outside Italy, 95, 105; in politics, 6, 50, 59, 63, 66; as security for contracts, 51; small-holdings, 21; to soldiers, 30, 36, 39, 50, 70, 105
land-commission, 5, 63–4
land-laws, 5, 50, 58–64, 66
lar, see genius
large landholdings: formation of, 4, 11, 35, 48–9, 54, 56, 60, 105, 111; slaves on, 55, 109; see also slaves
Latin culture, 76–8
law: codification, 86; see also Twelve Tables; criminal, 84–5, 93; ineffectiveness, 115, 122–3, 237; praetorian, 84; protecting property, 85; rule of, 93–5; substantive, 83, 85
laws (specific): on astrology, 237; debt, 50; employment of free men, 109; ship-owning by senators, 52; slaves, 115, l 120, f 122, 128–9, 222; sumptuary, 49
law courts: criminal, 81, 84; emperor's portrait in, 223–4; extortion, 41–2, 46–7; magic in, 240; specialised, 81, 89
lawyers, 37, 80, 83–7
legal: consultants, 86; fictions, 82, 125; formulae, 82, 86; judgements, execution of, 81; language, 80–1; rubrics – terms of reference, 83, 86; system, 81–3

INDEX OF PROPER NAMES

Index of Proper Names